Margaret E. Bentley
Division of Human Nutrition
School of Hygiene and Public Health
The Johns Hopkins University
615 North Wolfe Street
Baltimore, Maryland 21205-2179

HUNGER IN HISTORY

B

HUNGER IN HISTORY

Food Shortage, Poverty, and Deprivation

General Editor
Lucile F. Newman

Associate Editors
William Crossgrove
Robert W. Kates
Robley Matthews
Sara Millman

BLACKWELL
Oxford UK & Cambridge USA

Copyright © World Hunger Program, Brown University 1990

First published 1990
Reprinted 1992

Blackwell Publishers
238 Main Street, Suite 501
Cambridge, Massachusetts 02142, USA

108 Cowley Road, Oxford OX4 1JF, UK

Library of Congress Cataloguing in Publication Data

Hunger in history : food shortage, poverty, and deprivation/Lucile F. Newman, general editor : William Crossgrove . . . [et al.] associate editors.
p. cm.
Includes bibliographies and index.
ISBN 1–55786–044–0
1. Famines — History. 2. Food supply — History. 3. Poverty — History. I. Newman, Lucile F.
HC79.F3H86 1990
363.8′09—dc 20

British Library Cataloguing in Publication Data
A CIP catalogue record for this book is available from the British Library.

Designed by Chase Production Services, Oxford

Typeset in 10 on 12pt Linotron Ehrhardt
by Setrite Typesetters Limited, Hong Kong

Printed in Great Britain by
Antony Rowe Ltd, Chippenham, Wiltshire

This book is printed on acid-free paper

Contents

Preface

Hunger has haunted humankind throughout the known history of the world. What have been the causes and consequences of hunger events? How have the peoples of the world faced fear of hunger, the prospect of starvation, devastation by famine in their lands? How have they adapted to these conditions? What strategies have they used toward survival? Can the past teach us anything about the present?

As one of the first activities of the Alan Shawn Feinstein World Hunger Program at Brown University, a year-long interdisciplinary seminar was convened to discuss what could be learned about the current problem of hunger from the history of hunger. An interdisciplinary group of faculty gathered regularly to discuss the issues, and distinguished speakers were invited to present their views for discussion. An extensive bibliography and reference library assisted the process of assimilation of this very diversified material.

A logarithmic format was designed, considering hunger in four time periods – the ages of early humans, distant millennia, past centuries, and recent time. The earliest level is the age of the transition from hunting and gathering to the origins of agriculture. The development of urban centers characterizes the millennial level, from Mesopotamian temple cities to Rome and medieval Europe. The centuries level saw the development of a world-wide economic system, and the recent past has witnessed a global food system. Through this design we hoped to determine what could be learned from the methods and models of the various fields engaged in study in these different time dimensions.

Working groups addressed questions of health implications of starvation, development of food production, trade and international economic structures of food distribution, and the culture of survival in difficult times in each period. We learned, for example, that it is not possible to assume present-day climatic conditions in studying the origins of agriculture ten thousand years ago, and that it is necessary to recognize the co-evolution of humans, other animals, and plants over time as all became to some extent "domesticated." In certain times and places we have seen the exponential growth that Malthus envisioned, while sometimes population has remained constant for centuries, or declined unaccountably.

The nature of the evidence and inferences drawn from it vary widely. Archeological remains of foraging paleolithic peoples indicate the mix of foods consumed, and by inference the natural resources used, as well as some of the tools and weapons used in procurement and processing, and the sizes of families and multifamily groups. But it is only with ethnographic observation of remaining small foraging groups over the last century that some common social features seem to emerge from which one can imagine livelihood systems of 20,000 years ago. Finally, during this time, the large changes in climate that occurred over the ages led to basic changes in vegetative and animal resources. In the prehistoric period during which settled agriculture emerged, it is necessary to rely on inference from evidence more related to the causes of hunger, such as climatic changes, or to the consequences of hunger, such as inferences drawn from evidence of human migration or from human remains (chapter 2). Paleopathology uses characteristics of bone and teeth as clues to age at death, height, periods of growth and interrupted growth, gender differences, illnesses, and diet (chapter 3). The one measure of nutritional adequacy used for all four periods, human stature (chapter 15), can be derived from human remains by using the close correlation observed in modern humans between the long bones, femurs and tibias, and height. Drawing inferences from these burial remains, however, is complicated by a variety of problems that include the small size of many of the samples, the dating of the burial sites, and, most important, the selectivity of burial and excavation for various social groups within a society.

The emergence of literate societies in China, Egypt, and Mesopotamia, and later in Greece and Rome, left a large corpus of tablets, papyri, epigraphs, and documents as well as archeological materials relevant to hunger (chapter 4). For the most part, what is written is writ large: famines, sieges, epidemics, and the responses to cope with them. There are scattered reports of breakdowns in food systems; production and destruction of crops, transport and piracy against grain shipments, hoarding of grain shipped, or attempts to control or corner the grain market. There are some references to seasonal or chronic hunger, and to a few recognizable nutritional diseases. There are consumption data for some enslaved, enrolled, or dependent populations that indicate perceived need and differences in food allocation by work status, gender, and age. Despite the bias to the rich and powerful (for whom the written word was produced) and the mundane (in the fragmented records of empire and commerce), the struggle to cope with the larger manifestations of hunger emerges as a major facet of organized social life. The problems of production and distribution of food and the causes and consequences of hunger events vary widely in geographic area: chapter 5 is concerned with the Graeco-Roman world, chapter 6 with ancient China, and chapter 7 with the rise and fall of the Mayan civilization in this period.

Written records are more abundant for the more recent centuries (chapter 8). Time series started to emerge for individual farms, estates, and monasteries, for city-states and principalities, and finally for nation-states. The organized church undertook population registration; it is possible to infer major demographic changes from these records. Taxes and tithes were taken in produce, so that their records provide evidence on production, land use, yields, and their fluctuations. Exploration and colonial plantation economies characterize the later centuries' perspective, including evidence of archives, eyewitness accounts of travels, and the reports of district officers. Height, as an indicator of nutritional adequacy, was recorded directly rather than having to be estimated from skeletal remains, although these measures are mainly from special populations such as soldiers, slaves, orphans, and school children, with the implied biases of selection. Inferences relating undernutrition with disease, derived from time series of food prices correlated with mortality and concomitant social dislocation, provide evidence for chapter 9, and chapter 10 reports on a unique databank of direct enumeration of food resources in Bern, Switzerland, in the nineteenth century.

The prevalence of hunger and its causes and consequences is most thoroughly known for the most recent past, when systematic attempts to study hunger for entire populations were made by national governments and international organizations (for the example of China, see chapter 12). Large-scale measurement efforts focus either on calculation of dietary intake or on hunger outcomes or symptoms. In the first approach, average dietary intakes are calculated for entire populations, based on national food balance calculations. These may be combined with some assumption (usually derived from studies of household food consumption, budgets, or income) regarding the distribution of food within the population, to estimate numbers with intake below some cutoff of a minimally adequate diet. In the second approach, such hunger outcomes as growth impairment or specific deficiency diseases (chapter 13) are measured individually for representative samples of the population. This kind of evidence is now available for many countries and forms a basis for estimates of the magnitude and geographic distribution of hunger worldwide (chapter 11). Added to these are data series, also available for most countries, of causal factors such as weather, crop production, and consumer food prices, as well as more general population and economic data. Extensive news gathering services, government reports, and academic analyses record most public reports of famine and scarcity, food-destructive conflicts, and hunger-related disasters.

Certain themes have recurred. Knowledge of the possibility of hunger, the necessity of balancing numbers of people and the resources required for their survival, strategies for maintaining this balance, and food enough for the people through increased production, import, and entitlement, all have characterized humankind at every level of history. So, too, have themes of expansion, warfare and siege, of destruction or withholding of resources for food production, of oppression through tribute and slavery. In addition, using the evidence of paleopathology and archeology, it became clear from variations in size and stature that humankind has not simply progressed from smaller to larger, but that there have been periods of smaller and larger stature in every era.

This book was conceived as the first in a series of studies from the World Hunger Program. Because it has been an extended group effort, many people have been involved in it. The faculty participants and their departmental affiliations are listed below. The interdisciplinary hunger history bibliography was developed by Suzie Ewing Nacar. Joy Csanadi coordinated our complex coming together. Jeanne X. Kasperson has built and shaped the World Hunger Program Library. Barbara DeMaio has supervised an elegant formatting and timely production of the book. Assistants and student participants have included Lisa Alschuler, Facika Tavara, Shreedevi Thacker, and Sarah Zaidi. We are grateful to Alice Goldstein, Jeanne X. Kasperson, Ellen Messer, Ken Newman, and Baxter Venable for critical reading of and commentary on the manuscript.

The Wayland Collegium at Brown University is composed of faculty committed to interdisciplinary exchanges of various kinds. One of its activities is to support faculty seminars, of which the Hunger History Seminar was one in the year 1986–7. Acknowledgement of this support is made to the Wayland Collegium and its senior fellow, Lina Fruzzetti.

The World Hunger Program was established at Brown in 1985 through the generous gift of Alan Shawn Feinstein. Its objectives are to promote research and study on a global basis, to teach and educate, and to present awards for outstanding efforts to reduce hunger. The focus of the program is on the causes and consequences of hunger and the effort required for reduction of hunger in a world of plenty.

Faculty Participants

Douglas Anderson	Department of Anthropology
Stanley M. Aronson	Program in Medicine
Alan Boegehold	Department of Classics
Robert S. Chen	Alan Shawn Feinstein World Hunger Program
William Crossgrove	Department of German and Medieval Studies

David Egilman	Program in Medicine
Lina M. Fruzzetti	Department of Anthropology
David Herlihy	Department of History
Peter Heywood	Division of Biology and Medicine
Marida Hollos	Department of Anthropology
Jeanne X. Kasperson	Alan Shawn Feinstein World Hunger Program
Robert W. Kates	Alan Shawn Feinstein World Hunger Progam
Robley Matthews	Department of Geology
Ellen Messer	Alan Shawn Feinstein World Hunger Program
Sara Millman	Department of Sociology and Population Studies and Training Center
Morris David Morris	Development Studies, Department of Sociology
Lucile F. Newman	Departments of Community Health and Anthropology
Rose Okello	The International Health Institute and Continuing Medical Education
Kurt Raaflaub	Department of Classics
Johanna Schmitt	Division of Biology and Medicine
Thompson Webb	Department of Geology
Albert Wessen	Departments of Community Health and Sociology
Van Whiting, Jr	Department of Political Science

Acknowledgments

The editors and publisher would like to thank the following for permission to reproduce material in this volume:

Kluwer Academic Publisher, for figure 4 from *Handbook of Vegetation Science*, vol. 7 (our figure 2.4); the World Bank for data from *China: The Health Sector* (our table 12.2); Oxford University Press for Table II from *China's Political Economy* (our table 12.4).

Part I
Introduction

The description and analysis of hunger throughout history begins in chapter 1, by Millman and Kates, in which the major theoretical formulations of the book are set out. Classic economic analyses of the origins of hunger include the theories of Thomas Malthus on the relations of resources and population, Karl Marx on exploitation and the excess appropriations of capitalism, Ester Boserup on the role of population increase in stimulating technological innovation, and Amartya Sen on the concept of entitlement as a right founded in law and tradition to provide access to food. A model of a causal structure of hunger, whose definitions appear throughout the book, differentiates among food shortage at the regional level, food poverty at the household or group level, and food deprivation at the individual level. The causes of hunger are seen as food system breakdown, entitlement failure, and environmental hazard. These formulations provide a basis for the studies of the various time dimensions from the origins of agriculture to the recent past, and raise the question as to whether failure to produce enough food is indeed the central cause of hunger.

1

Toward Understanding Hunger

SARA MILLMAN AND ROBERT W. KATES

Introduction

Why does hunger persist in a world of plenty? One of the great questions of our time, this is also a question of earlier times. It is a central finding of this enquiry that plenty as well as scarcity characterized times past, and that the history of hunger is embedded in the history of plenty. We learn from our perusal of history that the causes of hunger are multiple, the conditions of hunger are several, the consequences of hunger are varied, and the effort to prevent or alleviate hunger constitutes a major, continuing strand of human history. In this chapter, we draw upon several different intellectual perspectives to develop a model of hunger, focusing on the causes, conditions, and consequences of hunger and on human responses to it.

Food is among the most basic of human needs. We define hunger simply as an inadequacy in individual dietary intake relative to the kind and quantity of food required for growth, for activity, and for the maintenance of good health. While this definition is broad enough to include voluntary forms of self-denial, our concern is with involuntary hunger.

Although the experience of hunger and its most immediate consequences are individual in nature, this experience affects the functioning of the social aggregations within which hunger occurs as well as of hungry individuals themselves. Its root causes lie in the natural environment, the growth of human populations, their social organization and technologies, and the interrelations between populations and their environments. Human responses to hunger or to the fear of hunger can serve to prevent or reduce it or its consequences. Indeed, much of what we have learned pertains to change and continuity in how people organize themselves in relation to hunger.

Perspectives

We draw on several main bodies of thought in formulating a causal structure of hunger within which to fit what we have learned. Prominent among these are the effort to view hunger in the context of food systems, Sen's identification of the crucial role played in famine by entitlement mechanisms, and the approach to modeling represented in recent work on the causal structure of hazards.

Hunger as Food System Breakdown   A diverse literature, drawing on several disciplines, attempts to place hunger and people's need for food within a larger context or food system. The essential attribute that the various approaches to food systems research share is that they focus on the complex linkages among the production, distribution, and consumption of food. To look at hunger in the context of a food system requires that one transcend the disciplinary boundaries within which hunger is often viewed as simply an agricultural problem, or a nutrition problem, or an exchange problem.

Classic studies of local food systems influenced by European colonial economies, such as Audrey Richards's (1939) study of seasonal and more chronic hunger among the Bemba, provide ethnographic examples that examine locally the ecology of food production, social rules for distribution and cultural rules for consumption, and nutritional consequences of the resulting dietary patterns. For the Bemba, the local food system is set in the larger national and international context of colonial policies that draw men off to the mines, leaving a shortage of labor for food production and enmeshing those remaining at home in a cycle of undernutrition. Thus, the sources of hunger are seen to lie in inadequate local food production, due to insufficient labor and food energy at times of peak demand for agricultural labor. Responses to hunger in this context are seen in food sharing and rationing rules, in dietary practices that confront daily hunger with coarse, bulky foods that extend the period of satiety, and in food cultivation and gathering practices that use the whole ecosystem. But the overwhelming food shortages are seen as embedded in turn in the political and economic structures that created the dearth of male labor and foreclosed other local opportunities to earn income and attract food from other areas.

UNRISD (United Nations Research Institute for Social Development) evaluations of the impact of the Green Revolution on developing countries provide a second set of examples of food systems research (see, for example, Oteiza 1987). These studies inquired into the ecological, market, socio-economic, sociocultural, and nutritional/health consequences of the Green Revolution in Indonesia, India, Malaysia, Mexico, Bolivia, Sri Lanka, and the Philippines. The unit of inquiry, "food systems", was a departure from other evaluative studies of the Green Revolution that looked only at pro-duction, consumption, or both, but that did not look simultaneously at impacts on the distribution of resources, on the natural environment, or on the resulting vulnerability of local economies and local farmers in different social strata to international market fluctuations and/or political manipulations. Such studies as the UNRISD evaluations trace linkages through the system of interacting ecological, political, sociocultural, and nutritional health elements, and identify points of origin and response to hunger along multiple dimensions.

Hunger as Entitlement Failure   A crucial concept from a different source is a useful complement to the tradition of food systems research, helping to elucidate some of the implications of production and distribution systems for consumption possibilities, and thus for hunger. In the context of hunger, "entitlement" refers simply to the access to food enjoyed by a household by virtue of its socially recognized right to control certain resources (Sen, 1981). The resources on which entitlement is based may vary. Where all food is purchased, an adequate supply of cash ensures an adequate supply of food, if it is generally available. However, legitimate access to food need not always operate through purchasing power. Subsistence farmers' entitlement may be rooted in their ownership of land and of their own labor, and thus in a conventionally accepted right to dispose of what they grow. Sharecroppers earn a share of their crop while the rest goes to their landlords. In such cases the household may be able to command adequate food supplies in the absence of any cash income. In some other settings, social security arrangements guarantee a minimal level of access to food (in the form of food stamps, for example) to those for whom other resources are lacking.

Fluctuating terms of trade governing the exchange of one resource for another alter the relative access of different groups to food supplies, so that even if the sets of resources they control are unchanging, the food supplies to which these sets give them access may not be. In this view, food shortages operating through higher prices are certainly one cause of entitlement failure and thus of hunger. If available supplies decline, then for at least some households, the amount that can be commanded must fall. However, the loss of access to food may affect different people, depending on the particular causes of shortage. Furthermore, certain groups may lose their access even in the presence of abundant food: Sen (1981) documents several famines in which overall shortage either was absent or at least played a relatively minor role, while the failure of specific entitlement mechanisms created widespread and severe hunger for the particular households that had depended on them. Careful consideration of the various bases of entitlement is essential in understanding who is likely to be hungry under what conditions.

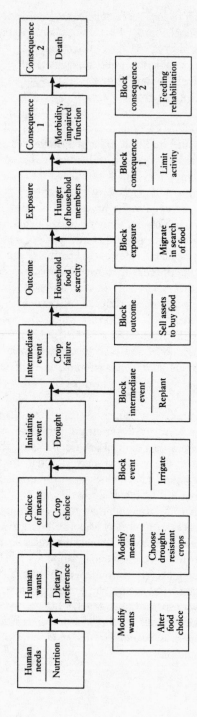

Figure 1.1 Hazard sequence representing the situation of a subsistence farm household faced with drought. Note the range of possible control interventions.

Hunger as a Hazard   Our third major theoretical source is recent thinking on modeling and managing hazards. If hazards are broadly defined as "threats to humans and what they value" (Kates et al., 1985:21), hunger surely qualifies. A threat is distinct from its realization, and current approaches to risk assessment distinguish between them. Further, the process by which threat is actualized is separated into a logical sequence of causally related occurrences. These causal chains link an activity, exposure, or accidental failure to harmful consequences, and can be expanded to include the context of the activity and several orders of consequences.

Several aspects of these recent efforts to model hazards seem particularly applicable to the problem of hunger. First, as a tool for management, the emphasis is on how a potentially dangerous situation develops. A simplified presentation trades off the attempt to capture the full complexity of causation against the value of clarity. Identification of the logical sequence of causally related occurrences facilitates thinking about options available to prevent or reduce the hazard at each stage, even if no method is currently available. Strategies for hazard management may include attempts to avoid hazardous events by interference in the stream of occurrences leading to them, to limit their impact, and to repair the damage when they occur. Such strategies often involve a sort of anticipatory reaction to some threat of effects that have not yet occurred.

In figure 1.1, we show an example in which this approach is applied to the situation faced by a subsistence farmer when drought occurs. It is important to understand that this diagram represents only one in a wide range of sequences which could lead to hunger; clearly there are many other possibilities. Households may find themselves with insufficient food for reasons other than crop failures, and hunger often occurs even in families that do have enough food. The specific scenario shown could be extended, for instance, to consider consequences for households and for larger aggregations as well as for individuals, or to add feedback loops (such as death of a household member, and thus loss of earnings, reinforcing the household's difficulty in obtaining enough food). The power of this analytic approach, however, lies largely in the simplification that focuses on a single sequence of events rather than modeling causation so thoroughly that every possibility is covered. In particular, note the series of intervention possibilities that emerge as a result of asking oneself what it would take to prevent each step in the sequence from leading to the next.

Population and Production   Three additional theoretical perspectives bearing on the relationship between population growth and the growth of production in general are highly relevant to any long-term analysis of hunger. These are the work of Thomas Malthus and Ester Boserup, and of Karl Marx, whose view of the causes of human misery sharply rejected the Malthusian analysis.

Malthus, writing late in the eighteenth century, was the first to focus on limits to population growth imposed by the natural environment. Starting from the basic assumptions that population is capable of growing geometrically (exponentially) and the means of subsistence only arithmetically (linearly), he concluded that the superior power of population to expand must in general tend to be kept in check by requirements of food and other necessities whose production cannot be increased so rapidly. The necessary balance between population and the means of subsistence could be maintained either by the "preventive checks" of fertility limitation (which, with the exception of delayed marriage and lifelong celibacy, he found morally abhorrent) or by the "positive checks' of mortality, including famine, pestilence, warfare, and so forth. In this view, hunger and other forms of human poverty and misery are an inevitable consequence of the pressure of population growth on limits of productive capacity.

Although population plays no central role in the Marxist analysis, the reaction to the Malthusian view is noteworthy. Marx disagreed vehemently with Malthus, finding the roots of hunger and other forms of human misery in relations of oppression and exploitation tied to the organization of production. Marx's theory of population is specific to the capitalist mode of production. Within such productive systems, the rapid accumulation of capital reduces the need for labor, creating a relative surplus of labor, an "industrial reserve army," condemned to unemployment or underemployment, low wages, miserable living conditions, and persistent hunger. It is the fact that the organization of production excludes some from full participation that generates this hunger-prone group, rather than any inadequacy of production possibilities relative to consumption requirements for the population as a whole.

Boserup, in contrast, sees population growth as a force favoring the adoption and diffusion of technological innovation. While in the short run this technological "progress" may only permit maintaining a larger population at a similar standard of living by virtue of harder work, in the long run it generates a momentum which, together with achievement of sufficient population density to support the infrastructure of transportation and communication essential for trade, yields real increases in per capita production. Although the Boserupian analysis makes no claim to universal applicability, it does identify a means by which population growth, instead of perpetuating poverty, may contribute to rising living standards.

A Conceptual Framework for Hunger

We draw upon these perspectives in describing a model of hunger that serves to organize the many themes of this volume. Like others using a food systems approach, we try to link hunger to its broader context in nature and society. Specifically, we adopt three levels of interacting hunger situations: regional or societal, household, and individual. We examine how the locus of causation and human response changes between levels over time and how the context widens.

Seeing the proximate causes of hunger in terms of entitlement loss or failure is central to our understanding of the causes and persistence of hunger. It provides a common language to connect the insights of those who view hunger as a product of food shortage and those who see hunger as caused by broader socioeconomic forces.

Finally, we draw on the tradition of hazard modeling. The importance of distinguishing between hunger itself and its causes and consequences is manifold. First, the distinction introduces a helpful level of analytic precision to the difficult questions we are addressing. It is necessary to identify and document plausible chains of causation to explain the persistence of hunger. Second, the distinction introduces a probabilistic element that mirrors the complexity and uncertainty of the real world. Not all food shortages lead to hunger; not all hunger results in starvation; not all starvation causes death. Third, by identifying a chain of causation with multiple links, we can see more clearly the opportunity each link offers to break or to interrupt the chain by taking deliberate action to prevent or limit hunger or to reduce its consequences. Fourth, for many periods in our study, direct evidence of hunger is missing or sparse. Understanding the forward and backward linkages between hunger itself and its causes and consequences permits us to draw inferences regarding the extent of hunger from evidence of its causes or consequences even when direct measures of hunger itself are lacking.

Causes

We begin with the causes of hunger. If the ultimate causes lie in human nature and the laws of physics or even metaphysics, our explanatory framework starts at a later step: the causes we focus on are the underlying and the immediate, and their story is inseparable from the history of plenty.

Underlying Processes   The history of hunger is interwoven with the history of plenty. The central long-term thread is the growth of food productivity and a system of food security. This begins with the origins and diffusion of agriculture, intensifies with technological development and social organization, expands with greater storage and transport of food products, and extends ties of responsibility and interdependence to connect increasingly diverse and distant groups.

Over time, this growing capability to create a surplus above that needed to reproduce crops and their producers supports population growth and permits massive change in social organization. Since proportionately fewer people are required in agriculture, increasing numbers are freed to engage in other activities. Urban concentrations become possible, and the sheer existence of surplus which can be appropriated permits the development of hierarchically stratified societies.

Hunger arises in the interstices of these strands of greater productivity, growing population, economic specialization, and surplus appropriation, and their uneven unfolding and interaction over time, against a background of natural variation in the resources and hazards affecting food production. Thus in particular places and in particular times, productivity falters, numbers increase too rapidly, exchange mechanisms necessitated by an increasingly complex division of labor fail, and the extractions of the powerful exceed the capabilities of the producers.

Immediate causes Within this framework of long-term structural change in productivity, in numbers, in division of labor, and in appropriation, specific occurrences of natural variation and disease, intentional deprivation by war or appropriation, and incidents of mismanagement and failed adjustment serve as the immediate causes of hunger. Environmental variations of climate and diseases of plants, animals, and people stress the productivity system or people's ability to absorb food. Sieges and blockades employ hunger as a weapon. Social systems as varied as slavery, feudalism, capitalism, and socialism maintain significant populations at the margins of survival. Greed, corruption, ignorance, and ineptitude lead to mismanagement of the food production and security system. And adjustment systems, intended to buffer natural variation in production and distribution, prove inadequate.

These immediate causes of hunger can be generalized by function and linked to scarcity of food at various levels. They limit food availability, appropriate an excessive share of production, reduce individual food absorption, and are compounded by failed adjustments. Thus the deaths, food crises and shortages, famines, and widespread hunger and starvation that so mark the history of hunger are in the main linked to production losses brought about by natural hazards and acts of war exceeding the capability of the society to buffer such losses. These bear most heavily on those close to the margin of existence even in the best of times. Chronic hunger, malnutrition, and undernutrition, affecting certain households even at times of plenty, are due primarily to inadequate access to resources for food production or food exchange or to direct excessive appropriation of food supplies. Disease limits intake and restricts food absorption, creating hunger and under-nutrition. Customs of fasting and other forms of self-denial, or selective deprivation of particular categories of individuals, keep some hungry even within households with adequate access to food.

Food Scarcity and Levels of Aggregation

We find it useful, in considering the causes of hunger, to distinguish three levels at which a scarcity of food may manifest itself. These are the bounded region, the household, and the individual. First, we define *food shortage* as the insufficient availability of food within a bounded region. Here sufficiency or insufficiency is defined relative to the usual or expected supplies to the area. Second, we define *food poverty* as the situation in which a particular household cannot obtain supplies of food that are adequate to meet the needs of all members given the customary pattern of allocation within the household. Researchers in different disciplines employ a wide variety of definitions for the term "household." For present purposes, the defining characteristic of a household is that it is the smallest organizational unit within which individuals routinely share food. While households defined by this criterion are likely to overlap considerably with those alternatively identified in terms of coresidence or kinship, the correspondence need not be perfect. Third, *food deprivation* refers to the inadequacy of individual intake relative to individual need. In the final analysis, if there is no food deprivation there is no hunger. Food poverty generates hunger only to the extent to which it translates into the individual deprivation of some or all household members. Similarly, food shortage leads to hunger only if it first pushes certain households into food poverty and thus some individuals within these households into food deprivation.

At each level of aggregation, factors other than actual scarcity may also operate. Thus, changes in the inequality of access to food may increase or decrease the number of households that cannot obtain adequate supplies even while availability within the region as a whole remains unchanged. Conflict and competition between groups, and intergroup differences in relations to the means of production, are central to the questions of how many and which households cannot command enough food for their members' needs. Factors affecting the relative viability of different forms of entitlement to food may lead to shifts in both the number and the identity of households in food poverty. Indeed, shifts in the distribution of entitlement across households may either dampen or amplify the translation of food shortage into actual hunger, and shifts in the allocation of food within households may reinforce or partially counter the tendency of food poverty to generate food deprivation.

Food Shortage In general, food shortages occur when the mechanisms by which a region is normally provisioned fail. Over time, the size and scale of such regions change. In an increasingly interconnected world, boundaries are increasingly permeable. At a global scale, in a world of overflowing granaries and mountains of butter, there is never any shortage.[1] Indeed, for the world as a whole, food supplies have been sufficient since the early 1960s to provide an ample although near-vegetarian diet to all if distributed according to need (Kates et al., 1988).

Historically, harvest failures are perhaps the most obvious causes of food shortages. These may entail reduced production either of food itself, or of cash crops traded for food. For areas importing any substantial portion of their food supplies, disruption of the flow of imports may cause shortages. We see such disruption as a function of war and other hostile actions and of shifts in the terms of trade that make foreign exchange needed to purchase food imports (or imports of goods used as inputs to agricultural production) less available. Shortage also occurs, in previously dominant centers, through loss of control over areas from which surplus food production has been extracted, or in areas dominated, through appropriation of too high a proportion of the food produced or goods exchanged for food.

Food Poverty When food shortage does occur, it is not likely to have the same impact on all households in the affected area. In general, we may expect that those households whose access to food is barely adequate in normal times will no longer be able to obtain needed supplies, while the relatively well-off will be less likely to suffer. Exactly who is most affected, however, is likely to be a function of the specific cause of the shortage as it relates to the various bases of household entitlement to food. Thus, those who grow their own food will be relatively mildly affected by a shortage rooted in import problems which reduces the amount of food available for sale and drives food prices sharply upwards; in this form of shortage, those who must buy their own food, and who barely have enough income to do so in normal times, will be more severely affected. In contrast, if drought or flood causes harvest failure, those whose only form of entitlement is subsistence agriculture are likely to bear the brunt of the shortage. They will have no alternative but to buy food. Their entry into the market may drive up prices for all, but at least others have some income to trade for food on the market. For the subsistence agriculturalist, buying food may require sale of productive assets such as land or livestock, or of future crops or labor. Thus a household's bases of future entitlement may be traded off for food supplies during a crisis in which these bases are temporarily devalued. If this occurs, food poverty for the household may persist long after the shortage which precipitated it is over.

Food poverty may be seen at levels beyond the household, such as ethnic, caste, or social class groups, or in marginalized aggregations of households within an area. It is, however, experienced in the household. Unfortunately, for many households, food poverty is an everyday condition despite the absence of shortage. Those households are unable to command adequate supplies of food even when it is locally available. Whether causes for such marginality are viewed as idiosyncratic or deeply rooted in social structure, it is a secure basis of entitlement that is lacking.

Food Deprivation   Within households, some individuals may experience food deprivation despite adequate household food supplies. Diseases that reduce absorption of nutrients can cause malnutrition even if intake is normal, while disease-associated loss of appetite can cause inadequate intake even if plenty of nourishing food is available to the individual. Differential access of individuals to food may also be a factor. Where certain foods are traditionally viewed as inappropriate for certain categories of individuals (for example, high-protein foods for pregnant women), the quality of the diet may vary sharply among household members.

Since individual needs do vary, meeting the needs of all household members may require some differentiation in access to food. For example, caloric requirements are less in old age than for those in the prime of life, while the constraint a child's small stomach places on the volume of food it can consume calls for a higher concentration of calories and protein than an adult would need. If we think of an equitable allocation of food within the household as one in which the ratio of nutrients consumed to those needed is the same for all members, departures from equity may result either from incomplete understanding of this variable need or from deliberate decisions to favor some members over others. Incomplete understanding of need may well lead to malnutrition in individuals with special needs (such as small children or reproductive-aged women) even when the household is experiencing no scarcity. In contrast, we speculate that deliberate decisions to give some members less than they are perceived as needing may be precipitated by the great stress of food poverty.

In sum, there is a chain of causation that begins with the long-term trends in productivity, numbers of people, economic specialization, and surplus appropriation. The chain leads via specific instances of interference with food supply or failure of access to supplies (the immediate causes) to hunger for individuals, groups, or entire populations. In figure 1.2 we illustrate the relations among these underlying processes and immediate causes, the situations of food shortage, poverty, and deprivation, and the consequences of hunger for individuals, households, and regions. We turn next to a discussion of these consequences. These include, at the individual

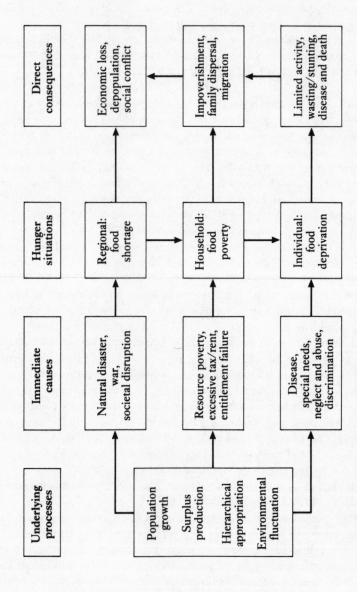

Figure 1.2 A causal structure of hunger

level, limits on development and activity, illness, and death; and for households and other groupings, a range of impacts that include but are not
limited to the sum of the direct impacts of each individual member's own
hunger on himself or herself. To cope with these consequences, societies
develop adaptations that affect the long-term trends, and short-term adjustments that include use of alternative foods, stocks, other sources,
exchanges, and gifts.

Consequences

In our discussion of the consequences of hunger, we focus first on the
effects of undernutrition and malnutrition on individuals in general, and
then on those with special needs. The direct physiological effects have
implications for morbidity and for the demographic processes of mortality
and fertility, as well as for behavioral and cognitive functioning, which in
turn may condition social, economic, and political processes for groups.
Some of the links in this chain are relatively well established; others remain
somewhat speculative at this time.

Common Individual Consequences   The specific experience of hunger depends
on which essential nutrients are deficient and on the duration and extremity of
this deficiency. Inadequate intake of some vitamins, such as A, B_1, or C, or
trace minerals, such as iodine or zinc, can bring about very specific disease
states, as discussed in chapter 13. The most common form of hunger,
however, is an insufficient intake of dietary energy (calories), sometimes
compounded by protein deficiency.

When less energy is consumed than is usually expended, energy is
conserved by reducing expenditure. In part this occurs through a behavioral
mechanism, the curtailment of physical activity. This behavioral shift has
an emotional analog in apathy and sometimes irritability. Some physiological adaptation to scarcity also occurs: the basal metabolic rate, or use of
energy to power such basic and essential life processes as respiration and
circulation, is reduced.

Energy expenditure may also be maintained by metabolizing reserves in
the form of stored fat, the outcome we seek when we diet. Lean body mass
in the form of muscle and eventually even organ tissue will also be
consumed if inadequate intake persists long enough. The term "starvation"
refers to this combined reduction of energy expenditure and self-
consumption. If the process continues long enough, it will eventually lead
to death, with intractable diarrhea often the immediate cause.

Most hunger-related deaths, however, are probably from disease rather
than from starvation per se. With severe malnutrition, resistance to certain

infectious diseases (such as polio and tuberculosis) deteriorates sharply, while the social disorganization associated with widespread hunger may create conditions favoring the spread of other diseases even if individual vulnerability is not increased by malnutrition (see chapter 9). The relationship between malnutrition and disease is a reciprocal one. Disease may be a cause as well as a result of malnutrition. Effects of disease on malnutrition operate through shifts in food consumed, whether due to custom or loss of appetite; through decreased absorption, as in diarrhea; through infestation with parasites which may interfere with the processing of nutrients, as in schistosomiasis; and through increased nutritional requirements to fight off infection.

Functionally, we see the effect of sustained hunger largely as lethargy. Ability to carry out heavy manual labor is impaired; the periods over which substantial physical effort can be maintained are reduced. An undernourished manual worker is likely to be less productive than a well-nourished one, to need longer breaks between periods of effort, to be able to work fewer hours a day, and to need to spend more non-working time resting (Spurr, 1983). The effects of hunger on work capacity have led some to view it as a major obstacle to economic development as well as a problem in its own right. It is an unfortunate irony that those who earn their living through hard physical labor are probably on average less able to afford a given diet than those whose occupations are physically less demanding.

Even aside from performance on the job, the restriction of physical activity clearly implies a reduced quality of life. The poor quality of life associated with hunger manifests itself in subtler ways as well. In the Gambia, one unanticipated effect of an experimental program to supplement women's diets was that for the first time they sang as they worked (Whitehead, personal communication, as cited in Beaton, 1983:338). Depression and anxiety were experienced by a group of volunteers for a study of the effects of starvation, despite the fact that they were under close medical supervision and thus protected from some of the adverse consequences hunger has under less favorable conditions (Guetzkow and Bowman, 1946).

Pregnant and lactating women, and children under five years, are often identified as groups especially vulnerable to hunger. Such assertions seem to rest on one or both of two distinct kinds of arguments: that the likelihood of hunger is particularly high for these groups, and that if hunger does occur, the likely consequences for them are particularly serious. Thus, if intake is not adjusted to meet the special requirements imposed by gestation and lactation in a mother or growth and development in a small child, hunger will be more frequent for mothers and small children than for others. We focus here, however, on the second set of arguments, the more serious consequences likely to follow from hunger in these groups.

At least at the extremes of malnutrition, the physical ability to become pregnant or to carry a pregnancy to term may be reduced (see, for example, Bongaarts, 1980, and Frisch, 1978, for two perspectives on this issue). Even with less extreme deprivation, inadequate intake during pregnancy may impair fetal development — and damage may be permanent. Maternal nutrition during pregnancy is an important correlate of low birth weight; in turn, babies who are very small at birth are much likelier than others to die during infancy, while those who survive are likelier than normal-weight babies to suffer from problems ranging from respiratory disorders to mental retardation. Further, an infant who is relatively weak at birth may be unable to breastfeed, and this inability may compound the disadvantage of the child's initial weakness. The mother's ability to produce adequate amounts of high-quality milk is surprisingly robust despite shortcomings in her own diet, but at the extremes of maternal malnutrition the availability of breast milk to the infant is jeopardized. To some extent the demands of fetal development and lactation seem to take precedence over the mother's own needs, so that a woman may be able to carry a pregnancy to term, deliver a reasonably healthy baby, and breastfeed it successfully in the face of inadequate intake. But to do so, she draws down supplies of essential nutrients in her own body, and if these reserves are not built up again between pregnancies, the effect may be cumulative. One manifestation of this phenomenon, termed the "maternal depletion syndrome," is the higher prevalence of anemia among reproductive-age women than among others (ACC/SCN, 1987:38).

In childhood, hunger may interfere with various aspects of growth and development, sometimes causing permanent damage. For children as for adults, adjustments to scarcity may entail reduced energy expenditure as well as metabolism of body tissues. In children, an additional means of reducing energy expenditure is the slowing or cessation of physical growth. This will be particularly damaging if its timing coincides with crucial growth processes which simply do not occur at all if they do not occur within a narrowly delimited period. Brain development may be one such process: brain cells normally proliferate rapidly during the last part of gestation and the first months after birth, and if we can generalize from studies of rats, any failure of growth during this period results in a permanent deficit. In other instances, growth shortfalls associated with hunger episodes can be made up if subsequent nutrition is sufficient to sustain catch-up growth as well as normal requirements.

The small average stature of adults in many Third-World populations can undoubtedly be traced in large part to their limited food intake and their experience of nutritionally damaging childhood diseases during their growing years. Similarly, in this volume, secular trends in adult stature are interpreted as evidence of change in health and nutrition.

The limitation of physical activity because of hunger translates in children into a reduction in play, exploratory behavior, and interactions with others, all of vital importance for intellectual and social development (Latham, 1974). Evidence is fairly clear that prolonged and severe childhood malnutrition is associated with impairment of social and intellectual functioning as well as with more tangible physical effects, at least during the period shortly following episodes of malnutrition. Important questions as to the permanence or reversibility of such damage, how severe or long-lasting hunger must be for it to occur, and even whether the damage is actually a result of malnutrition or of some set of factors (disease, an impoverished environment, etc.) leading both to hunger and to impaired development, remain unresolved.

Consequences for Households   The consequences of hunger at the household level exceed the sum of effects of each individual member's own hunger on that individual. The hunger of breadwinners is likely to reduce the amount of bread they can win; the hunger of mothers may lead to permanent damage to unborn or breastfed children, as well as to poorer child care and household maintenance in general; the hunger of children may lead to reduced potential in adulthood in terms of physical size and strength as well as social and intellectual skills. When a household member starves to death, or dies of an infectious disease to which hunger increased vulnerability, the roles he or she played are left vacant rather than just performed less effectively. If no one else is available to step into a particularly crucial vacated role, death of a member may devastate a household in very tangible ways.

Death can seriously disrupt the household as a functioning unit or institution, but so can the migration of members in search of employment or relief, or the sale or pledging of the household's assets to buy food. Much of the marginalization of households that lose their control over productive resources, such as land, water, trees, and herds, occurs at times of hunger stress.

Within households, hunger strains culturally defined relationships of leadership, responsibility, gender, and age. For example, when they cannot feed their families, heads of households can no longer fulfill their traditional responsibilities; their self-respect and the esteem of others may be rapidly eroded. Between households, the effect of hunger is spread as social and extended-family ties are called into play to buffer the household impact. And household formation itself is slowed as resources earmarked for dowry, bridewealth, or wedding celebrations are spent to feed the household.

Consequences for Regions and Societies   Similarly, social impacts extend well beyond the sum of household effects. Kingdoms and republics alike have found themselves shaken by food crises and have evidenced a growing willingness to employ resources to prevent or alleviate them. Over time, societies show an increasing propensity to seek to prevent or mitigate famine and widespread food shortage. Public concern with food poverty has been and continues to be more of a rarity.

Preventing and Reducing Hunger

Actions may be taken at each of the levels of aggregation considered above to try to keep potential hunger events from occurring or to limit their impact. In generic terms, such actions may be described under various rubrics, such as human responses, coping actions, adaptations, and adjustments. Following the terminology conventional in hazard assessment, we distinguish between short-term adjustments and long-term adaptations to specify the duration over which a response emerges. "Adjustment" refers to short-term measures for coping with a particular actual or potential hunger event, while "adaptation" signifies a longer-term shift which might result from the experience of repeated hunger events over time. Not all such actions are successful, and actions which are successful in averting hunger or minimizing its consequences for some groups may leave others worse off.

Long-Term Adaptations Over the long term, humans have developed a complex repertoire of technological and social practices to supply their basic food needs, to prevent hunger, and to cope with hunger when it occurs. These practices become deeply embedded in culture and reflect its almost infinite variety in human history and prehistory. Thinking in terms of a simple food system of production, distribution, and consumption sectors, and distinguishing between technological innovations and the social relationships that govern them, we can describe a limited repertoire of fundamental long-term adaptations to hunger. Over time, as human numbers rise, more and different foods are demanded, and dependent populations increase; food producers intensify their collection and production of food, creating a surplus over their immediate needs. This surplus is distributed across time and space, to feed the producers when needed during hungry seasons and years, and to feed at all times non-producers. In the consumption sector of the food system, we adapt biologically and socially to a variable supply.

Four major adaptations stand out in history and prehistory for producing sufficient food to prevent hunger among producers and non-producers alike. The earliest long-term adaptation was movement to locations of natural surplus with access to multiple ecological zones and seasons of natural productivity. Most important in the long run were the domestication of plants and animals, and the natural provision of plant and animal nutrition. This was done by locating and settling in areas of high natural productivity (flood plains, volcanic soils, etc.) and by increasing production through cultivation, irrigation, and protection from competitors. A third major adaptation in production was the induced creation of new plant and animal varieties, the artificial creation and provision of nutrients and pest protection, and the utilization of mechanical energy. A fourth is currently underway, manipulating genetic material and transforming the microenvironment of plants and animals through biotechnologies in agriculture and food science.

Equally important in the creation of surplus are those social inventions which compel or encourage surplus production. For household and self-provisioners, there is what Allan (1965) aptly called the "normal surplus," the extra production in good or average years that allows for a bare minimum in lean years. In order to encourage the additional hard work required for what is usually nonessential production in good or average years, societies evolve culturally defined flexible consumption needs – feasts, dowries, offerings – to absorb the surplus in good years and by their postponement in bad years to allow a buffer for harvest failure. As societies stratify hierarchically, the normal surplus becomes subject to appropriation, by tithe, tax, share, rent, and interest; and such extraction becomes codified by law and custom, and enforced through power. And with the evolution of markets, the creation of opportunities to exchange or sell a surplus further encourages its production.

For storage, human beings evolved a physiological energy storage capacity equivalent in the healthy adult to 30–50 days of basal metabolism. Lactating mothers provide a reserve for their infant children. Household techniques developed to store seed or other dry matter or living materials as root, tree, animal, or fish stocks, as well as processed materials such as olive oil, wine, or cheese, which ultimately became trade goods. Cities became the great storage reservoirs and redistributors for food. The birth of urban life in Mesopotamia is linked to surplus production, its storage, and the evolution of temple and palace, appropriating the surplus, storing, and redistributing it.

Long-distance food movement, as opposed to trade in precious minerals and luxury goods, awaited major innovations in transport, primarily by water, along canals, rivers, and across seas, and the social inventions of empire, mercantilist guild, and capitalist enterprise. Intricate systems of redistribution emerge through social organization: entitlement of food flows within kin-based households, stratified societies, and exchange-based systems.

We also adapt our needs to variable food supplies in more subtle ways.

Within the individual life cycle, those who experience limited nutrition early adapt by limiting growth, thus keeping requirements lower in later life. Populations in which food supplies remain scant over extended periods develop lifestyles in which discretionary physical activity is kept to a minimum, further reducing requirements. Some may also limit reproduction, although specific practices employed (such as extremely prolonged lactation) may be seen as responses to a very different set of imperatives than any concern over excessive childbearing. The latter two adaptations, restricted activity and limited reproduction, involve social and ideological adaptations as well as physiological ones, with metaphors of feast and famine in religion, folk tales, and literature reflecting needs for differential consumption.

Short-Term Adjustments In contrast to these sustained long-term adaptations, deeply embedded in biology and culture, short-term responses are for the most part intentional actions undertaken to anticipate, prevent, and reduce hunger or mitigate its consequences. In a sense, the repertoire of short-term adjustment, taken as a whole, is a long-term adaptation. Indeed, many of these practices are quite old. Adjustments primarily provide for use of alternative foods or alternative sources of foods, both from storage and other places; for exchange of labor or property for food; and for the provision of loans, gifts, charity, and relief in the form of food or exchangeable goods.

Faced with the prospect of harvest failure, a producing household may replant, sometimes in more appropriate locations, plant alternative failure-resistant crops, draw down supplies of stored roots, trees, and livestock, use foods which are not normally consumed, or collect non-domesticated foods. Non-producing households use stored supplies, use foods which are not normally consumed, or draw down stocks of wealth to maintain consumption. All households redefine their needs, limiting activity and postponing celebrations, feasts, and offerings. As hunger deepens, movement ensues, in search of work, food, kin, or relief, and reproduction may cease.

Actions may be taken at the regional level to safeguard food supplies, as by emergency increases of food imports (either purchased or donated), or to protect certain groups from bearing too much of the impact of shortage. Governments which set up rationing systems or soup kitchens under such circumstances are attempting to insure some minimal level of entitlement for those who might otherwise be pushed into food poverty; these actions are sometimes taken in the absence of shortage if traditional entitlement mechanisms fail so that some specific group loses access to food despite its abundant availability.

Possible responses to shortage, or to the perceived threat of shortage, may either increase or decrease the equality of access to food. The former occurs as a deliberate policy response of governments to prevent the shortage from pushing disadvantaged groups into food poverty, and may take the form of various kinds of rationing. Unless the shortage is so severe that there is too little to go around even with more equitable distribution, this response may keep it from causing any increase in food poverty. In contrast, individuals who foresee a food shortage may attempt to gain control over as much food as possible before the shortage materializes, whether for their own consumption or to sell at inflated prices once the shortage hits. Since only those who are already relatively well-off are in a position to stockpile, the net result of this behavior is to widen the gulf between the haves and the have-nots. Panic buying and hoarding, in fact, can push those not in a position to participate into food poverty even if the anticipated shortage fails to materialize.

Maladjustment and maladaptation Strategies to avoid hunger sometimes operate to perpetuate it, while attempts of one group to minimize hunger for itself may make the situation of others more precarious. For example, long-term productive opportunities may be jeopardized to maintain consumption during a crisis, as when starving farmers eat grain reserved for seed or are forced to sell land or livestock. These strategies may indeed stave off starvation in the present, but at the cost of increased risk of hunger in the future. Similarly, those who stockpile food at the first sign of shortage may succeed in averting hunger for themselves, but increase risk for others. Maladaptation is also possible. Thus intensification of agriculture may increase production in the short run but decrease it in the long run if methods used are environmentally damaging; subsidized imports of food to meet the needs of urban populations may reduce incentives and hence production in rural areas, while a parallel argument claims that food aid often undermines a society's capacity to provision itself in the future even as it responds to crisis in the present.

Conclusions

The history of hunger is for the most part unwritten. The hungry rarely write history, and historians are rarely hungry. There have been a few attempts to bring together what is known for some periods or from some disciplinary perspectives. Of these, the most recent (Rotberg and Rabb, 1985) assembles papers from an inter-disciplinary conference focusing mainly on the European experience of the last several centuries.

Overall, considerable ingenuity has been expended to extract from diverse materials the evidence of hunger. In a world where current estimates of the number of hungry vary by a factor of three, the evidence from the past must be carefully weighed. Indeed, there is clearly a double standard in our willingness to accept indirect evidence, small, unrepresentative samples, and large assumptions in our attempt to assemble a picture of the distant past of hunger and to apply stricter standards of evidence for the more recent past. This double standard is not unique to the history of hunger, but occurs whenever questions are addressed for which available evidence is less than ideal.

In the chapters that follow, the conceptual framework and the concepts introduced above are used to organize and interpret the evidence available at various time scales, and to fit together the insights of specialists writing on particular instances or aspects of hunger. In succeeding sections, we address the history and prehistory of hunger by periods: ages, millennia, centuries, and decades. Where possible, the editors have sought cause, disaggregated condition, elaborated consequence, and specified adjustment and adaptation. In the final chapter, we distill the changes and continuities in the history and prehistory of hunger, employing these central concepts. Our contribution to the history of hunger lies not only in the information we have assembled, but also in the development and application of an integrative model of the causes, conditions, and consequences of hunger.

NOTES

1 Our three levels of aggregation may be extended, in principle without limit, to consider multiple nested units between the household and the world, such as local community, market area, country, subcontinent, or cross-cutting units, such as ethnic groups or social class categories, representing aggregations of households within an area. Such an elaboration can usefully treat scarcities at each level as a function of entitlement failures at the same level of aggregation. Thus, for instance, shifts in the terms of trade which make food imports more expensive can be viewed as a loss of entitlement at the national level.

REFERENCES

ACC/SCN 1987: *First Report on the World Nutrition Situation.* Rome: United Nations, Administrative Committee on Coordination, Subcommittee on Nutrition.

Allan, W. 1965: *The African Husbandman.* Edinburgh: Oliver and Boyd.

Beaton, George H. 1983: Energy in human nutrition: Perspectives and problems. *Nutrition Reviews*, 41(11), 325–40.

Bongaarts, John 1980: "Does malnutrition affect fecundity? A summary of evidence." *Science*, 208, 564–9.

Boserup, Ester 1965: *The Conditions of Agricultural Growth*. Chicago: Aldine.

Frisch, Rose 1978: Nutrition, fatness, and fertility. In W. Henry Mosley (ed.), *Nutrition and Human Reproduction*, New York and London: Plenum, 91–122.

Guetzkow, Harold Steere and Bowman, Paul Hoover 1946: *Men and Hunger*. Elgin, Ill.: Brethren Publishing House.

Kates, Robert W., Hohenemser, Christoph, and Kasperson, Jeanne X. 1985: *Perilous Progress: Managing the Hazards of Technology*. Boulder, Col., and London: Westview Press.

Kates, Robert W., Chen, Robert S., Downing, Thomas E., Kasperson, Jeanne X., Messer, Ellen, and Millman, Sara 1988: *The Hunger Report 1988*. Brown University, Providence: The Alan Shawn Feinstein World Hunger Program.

Latham, Michael 1974: Protein-calorie malnutrition in children and its relation to psychological development and behavior. *Physiological Reviews*, 34(3), 541–65.

Malthus, Thomas 1970: An Essay on The Principle of Population. Edited by Anthony Flew. Harmondsworth: Pelican Books.

Marx, Karl 1889: *Capital*. Translated from the third German edition by Samuel Moore and Edward Aveling. New York: International Publishers.

Oteiza, Enrique 1987: Preface, in *Food Systems and Society in Eastern India: Selected Readings*. Geneva: United Nations Research Institute for Social Development, Report No. 87.3.

Richards, Audrey 1939: *Land, Labour, and Diet in Northern Rhodesia: An Economic Study of the Bemba Tribe*. London and New York: Oxford University Press.

Rotberg, Robert I. and Rabb, Theodore K. (eds) 1985: *Hunger and History*. New York: Cambridge University Press.

Sen, Amartya 1981: *Poverty and Famines: An Essay on Entitlement and Deprivation*. New York: Oxford University Press.

Spurr, G. B. 1983: Nutritional status and physical work capacity. *Yearbook of Physical Anthropology*, 26, 1–35.

Part II
Hunger in Prehistoric Societies

The prehistoric period was the period of the Neolithic Revolution, in which domestication of plants and animals and the development of agriculture occurred. The Working Group reviews the forms of evidence available over the past 20,000 years, including climatological evidence, pollen studies, the archeological excavations of ancient cities in the Near East and south Asia, and various theories of the origins of agriculture. Major changes in the environments of human food supplies are recorded in the paleoclimatic record. Mark Nathan Cohen extends the discussion specifically on the history of hunger as recorded in the bones and teeth of humans and the archeology of human habitation and irrigation. While the evidence is fragmentary, imaginative efforts at synthesis have provided a picture of major changes having taken place in modes of food production and ways of life, as agriculture replaced hunting and gathering, and previously mobile peoples settled down.

2

Global Climate and the Origins of Agriculture

ROBLEY MATTHEWS, DOUGLAS
ANDERSON, ROBERT S. CHEN, AND
THOMPSON WEBB

Introduction

During the last two million years of their existence, humans have faced hunger and developed technologies to decrease it. Improvements in tool-making represent one development, and the relatively recent introduction of agriculture some 8–10,000 years ago is another. Both before and after the development of agriculture, human populations have had to move and adapt in the face of large and continuous environmental changes including the advance and retreat of glaciers as well as the intensification and weakening of the monsoons. The consequent movements and population growth and decline have led to and been affected by various social conflicts, inequities, and cultural change. All of these factors have contributed to food shortage for many human populations, food poverty within communities, and food deprivation within households.

This chapter focuses first on the evidence for global climatic change and associated ecological changes throughout the period during which agricultural techniques spread. Paleoenvironmental research has revealed large and often rapid climatic shifts even within the relatively warm "interglacial" period of the past 14,000 years. For example, some 11,000 years ago during a short-term climate oscillation called the "Younger Dryas," an ice sheet spread across much of Scotland in 100 years or less and lasted for at least 300 years (National Academy of Sciences, 1975). During the past 10,000 years, many climatic indicators such as water levels in lakes, the distribution of vegetation, and ice-sheet boundaries have all varied and shown continent-wide patterns of change. Recent climate modeling studies have shown how the known long-term (10,000-year) variations in the seasonal intensity of insolation have influenced monsoonal circulation, first by intensifying the summer monsoonal precipitation, which filled lakes in the Sahara and India, and later by decreasing the monsoon, which led to the lakes drying out (Kutzbach and Street-Perrott, 1985; Swain et al., 1983). It is against this backdrop of widespread climatic and ecological variations that human populations expanded, migrated, replaced hunting and gathering with agriculture, moved on to the floodplains, and experienced hunger. Within our chapter, we provide an introduction to these environmental changes.

The second focus of this chapter is on the origins of agriculture and the beginning of urban civilization. By 30,000 years ago, the progenitors of modern humans had already evolved into *Homo sapiens*, and occupied most of the Old World, including Australia. They had occupied the islands of Japan and Indonesia, but had not yet ventured out into the Pacific Islands. They had occupied all of ice-free Europe and western Siberia, but probably had not yet moved into eastern Siberia. Since they were not in the north-easternmost part of Asia, they had not begun their migrations into the New World. *Homo sapiens* achieved their full modern distribution only after the last glacial maximum; perhaps as recently as 12,000 years ago on the continents and 2,500 years ago on the major islands of the Pacific.

In the lower latitudes, *Homo sapiens* also experienced a population explosion shortly after 10,000 years ago. There is still considerable controversy whether this increase was due to the emergence of agriculture or whether agriculture was a response to the increase in population. If the latter is the case, then one could rightly argue that hunger has played a significant role in the development of the world's agricultural systems. Between 5,000 and 7,000 years ago, agriculture-based civilizations were flourishing in such diverse areas of the Old World as China, the Indus Valley, Egypt, and parts of southwestern Asia and southeast Europe.

Direct evidence of hunger-related stress can be found in human skeletal remains. Bones and teeth provide unique records of nutritional deficiencies, disease, and other conditions that reflect the hunger and malnutrition experienced by an individual. Estimates of stature for both adults and children can be derived from measurements of the length and width of long bones. Deficiencies in enamel thickness (hypoplasia) and microdefects in enamel and bones (such as Harris lines) have been extensively investigated for their relationship to both general and episodic stress. "Spongy" lesions in the skull have been associated with anemia and infectious diseases. Traumatic lesions may be indicative of such social behavior as involvement in accident-prone activities, inter-personal violence, and use of surgical techniques (for example, amputation). Variations in the frequency of such indicators suggest significant differences across age, class, and sex lines

(Goodman et al., 1984). As Cohen discusses in the next chapter, paleo-pathological evidence demonstrates the existence and to some extent the prevalence of hunger and malnutrition in many different human populations throughout at least the past 10,000 years.

How and to what degree natural variations induced hunger in early human populations are, of course, controversial questions. In historical periods, we know of many instances when drought, floods, or other environmental hazards had a severe impact on food supply and distribution. Unfortunately, interdisciplinary research on how long-term environmental change affected prehistoric human populations has been rare. In part, this dearth stems from incompatibilities in resolution and coverage between paleoenvironmental data sets and data on human populations. It also reflects the many obstacles to interdisciplinary research that involves both natural and social scientists, including different terminologies, disparate analytic capabilities and paradigms, and the prevalence of discipline-oriented scientific institutions (see, for example, Chen, 1983). Our primary objective therefore is to help expand discussion between the various disciplines. As an initial step, this chapter reviews recent developments in paleoclimatology and in anthropology that are likely to be of mutual, interdisciplinary concern.

Twenty Thousand Years of Climate History: Models, Methods, and Data

The observed record of climate change shows that climate varies on all time scales from years to hundreds of thousands of years (figure 2.1). Over the past million years, humans have faced climate changes as short as two- to ten-year droughts and as long as the 10,000-year or longer expansion and contraction of ice sheets. Climate records derived from instruments are too short to register most of the century-or-longer changes in climate, and a variety of natural "sensors" of climate have had to be used. These range from tree rings to fossils preserved in sediments or rocks (figure 2.2). Long time series of these data from diverse locations help in testing the various hypotheses about the causes of past climatic changes (National Academy of Sciences, 1975). For variations on time scales of 1,000 to 1 million years, key studies have revealed the controlling influence of the variations in solar radiation determined by identifiable variations in the earth's orbital elements (Berger et al., 1984). These variations not only pace the growth and retreat of ice sheets, but also influence the intensity of monsoons in the tropics and elsewhere (Kutzbach and Street-Perrott,

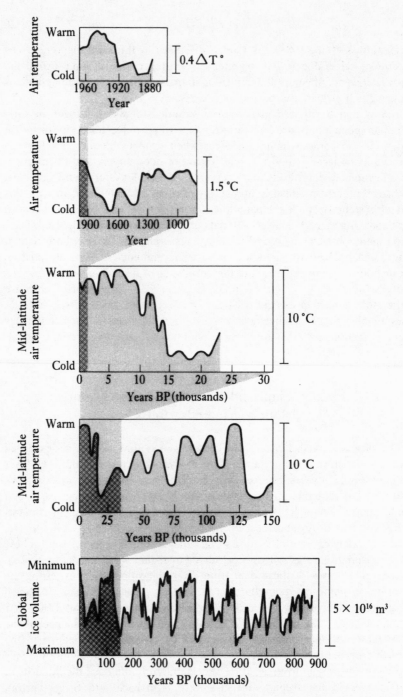

Figure 2.1 General trends in global mean temperature for time scales ranging from decades to hundreds of millennia

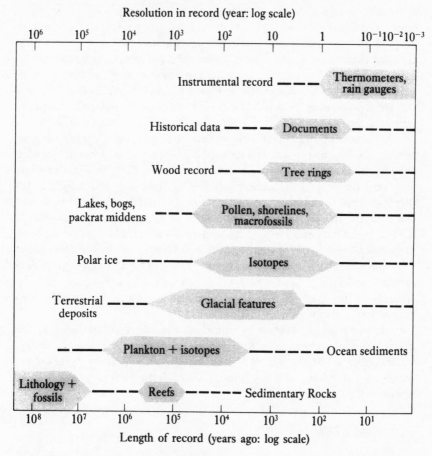

Figure 2.2   The time span and resolution of various climatic records from decades to hundreds of millennia

1985). Paleoclimatologists have also studied and modeled the climatic impacts of meteorites and of volcanism and have revealed interactions between the biosphere, hydrosphere, and geosphere that are critical to understanding the various geochemical cycles, including variations in atmospheric concentrations of carbon dioxide (Pisias and Shackleton, 1984). Such research is critical for understanding future climate changes including those being expected to result from human-induced increases in carbon dioxide and other greenhouse gases, such as methane.

Analyses of climatic variations at the time scale of 1,000 to 1 million years generally follow one of two interrelated approaches. In a *data-oriented* approach, geological evidence is mapped and interpreted in paleoclimatic terms (Bradley, 1985; Hecht, 1985). In a *modeling* approach, climate models, adapted to past conditions, are used to simulate the patterns of past climates (Kutzbach, 1985). The data-oriented approach can be thought of as a "bottom-up" or inductive analysis of past climates, because many paleoclimatic data are assembled and used to infer the general state of the climate system at a particular time. The inferences are often aided by statistical analysis of the diverse data. The modeling approach, in contrast, can be thought of as a "top-down" or deductive analysis of climate because climate models incorporate meteorological theory and generate testable hypotheses about the patterns and causes of past climates. The two approaches are related because paleoclimatic data are necessary (a) for specifying the "boundary conditions" for the model simulations of past climates and (b) for validating the results of the simulation experiments (COHMAP Members, 1988). The models in turn may be used to evaluate the physical consistency of sometimes disparate compilations of paleoclimatic evidence (Kutzbach and Street-Perrott, 1985). The testing of numerical climate models is a key focus for paleoclimatic research today, and the climates of the past 20,000 years serve as a critical database for this research (Webb and Wigley, 1985).

In the rest of this section, we describe the major components of the climatic system and the climatic variations on different time scales. Finally, we speculate about the role of climate change as a backdrop both for the origin of agriculture and for the onset of hunger as a major human problem.

Climate and Climatic Variability

Components of the Climate System   The components of the climate system are the atmosphere, oceans, ice sheets, earth surface, and biosphere. Individual components, such as ice sheets and the ocean surface, have different thermal characteristics and response times. The atmosphere responds relatively rapidly to changes in solar insolation and other external controls, but the ocean surface and upper layers of the ocean vary more slowly, and the deep ocean and continental ice sheets respond extremely slowly (Saltzman, 1985). Individual climate variables may be categorized into: (a) those that describe the *boundary conditions* or the external controls of the climate system (such as solar radiation and, on certain time scales, ice sheets); (b) those that describe *slowly varying* components (such as atmospheric composition); and (c) those that describe *fast-response* components (such as surface temperature, winds, and precipitation).

Controls of Climate Variations The components of the climate system are related to one another through transfers of mass and energy. These transfers occur along many pathways and involve many feedback mechanisms. Such interconnectedness may allow certain variations in a particular component to result from purely internal, "free" variations, as opposed to externally "forced" variations (Saltzman, 1983: 203). Because the free variations occur in the absence of external changes in the system, they are inherently unpredictable in detail, although their statistical properties can be described. The exact record of a particular component of the system as it participates in such free variations, therefore, may not be describable, but the general characteristics of the record (its variability or persistence, for example) may be. The potential existence of such internally driven variations places an upper limit on the success of explicit long-term climatic predictions.

The concept of "free" variation notwithstanding, the climate system has several external controls that cause "forced" variations. These include the incoming solar radiation, the composition of the atmosphere, and the arrangement and size of the continents, oceans, and ice sheets. The importance of these factors varies with time scale, and for short enough time periods certain of these factors may be considered fixed boundary conditions. Of particular interest for studying the past 20,000 years are the orbitally induced variations in the seasonal intensity of solar radiation and the retreat of the northern hemisphere's ice sheets.

The explicit definition of what factors control climatic variations is further complicated because the role of some components in the climate system is imperfectly understood, or their future variations are inherently unpredictable. The concentration of carbon dioxide in the atmosphere is typical of such a component. During Quaternary time, the concentration of carbon dioxide in the atmosphere has varied in a fashion consistent with global climatic variations and seems to be part of the climate-system response to external forcing (Pisias and Shackleton, 1984). During the past century, however, the concentration of carbon dioxide in the atmosphere has increased as a result of industrialization, a process clearly outside of the climate system and whose future course is inherently unpredictable (Kellogg and Schware, 1981). In similar fashion, the dust loading of the atmosphere can be considered as an externally determined variable, as in the case of volcanic eruptions (Bryson and Goodman, 1980) or nuclear wars (Pittock et al., 1986). Both dust and carbon dioxide concentration are usually considered as "prescribed" or arbitrarily set boundary conditions in the experiments performed by climate models, because the nature of their variations is imperfectly known.

Temporal Variations A "powers-of-ten" approach effectively illustrates the magnitude of climatic variations at different time scales (figure 2.1). The global mean temperature has differed by about $6° ± 1°C$ between glacial and interglacial periods (Manabe and Hahn, 1977), but varied by only $0.5°C$ between the middle of the last century (the end of the "Little Ice Age") and the present (Wigley et al., 1985). These variations in the global mean temperature help to characterize the main changes in climate over the past million years; but because the global mean temperature, by definition, is the average of positive and negative temperatures at the regional scale, the relatively small variations in global mean temperatures underestimate the large temporal variations in temperature, moisture, and seasonality in regions the size of New England (20,000 sq. km) (figure 2.3). These regional climatic variations are what affect ecosystems, agricultural crops, and human activity, however, and an understanding of climate change requires maps of temporal changes in climate. The time series of global mean values can therefore serve only as a rough proxy for the climate changes that affect humans.

Spatial Variations Climatic variations at a particular location are embedded in a hierarchy of large-scale variations. In northern mid-latitudes, for example, precipitation at a point is generated by clouds, fronts, and low-pressure systems with life spans of the order of hours to days. These weather systems are in turn embedded in hemispheric-scale atmospheric circulation anomalies with life spans of the order of months or seasons (Namias, 1975). Finally, large-scale circulation features are related to hemispheric or global scale variations in the energy balance of the earth-atmosphere system. A climatic change in a given region may therefore have a *proximate* cause, such as a change in the duration of different air masses or the relocation of a storm track, that in turn is related to an *ultimate* cause of hemispheric or global extent. The hierarchical nature of climate variation implies that the climatic record of a particular region cannot be explained (and, hence, predicted) in isolation. Local climatic variations are indeterminate with respect to larger-scale variations: the same local record could be generated by a range of larger-scale variations. Climate explanation *must* therefore proceed in a "top-down" or deductive fashion from large-scale, external *controls* to the smaller-scale, dependent *responses* that may or may not be predictable in detail.

The Past 18,000 Years: Glacial Maximum to Interglacial Conditions The past 18,000 years include the extremes of the glacial-interglacial climates in which the global volume of ice varied from a maximum amount about 18,000 years ago to a minimum between 8,000 and 4,000 years ago (figure

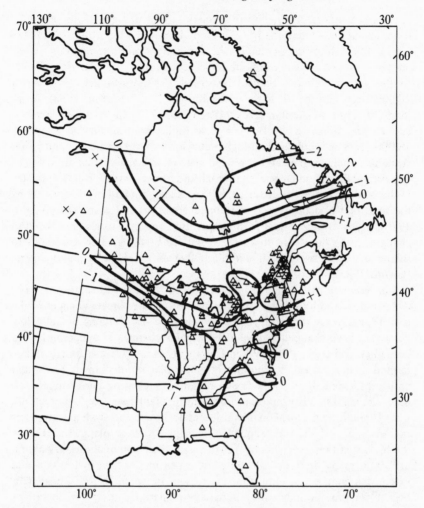

Figure 2.3   Mean July temperature differences between 6,000 BP and today

2.1). The global mean temperature varied by about 6 ± 1°C between these extremes and is about 1 ± 1°C lower today than it was 4,000 to 8,000 years ago. Between 18,000 years ago and today, the regional changes have varied from small (<2°C) in certain tropical to subtropical parts of the oceans to as large as 10 to 15°C in the northern North Atlantic Ocean and in regions near the ice sheets. Both at 18,000 years before the present (BP) and at 6,000 years BP, the available maps of temperature show patterns with regions of temperatures higher than today as well as regions with temperatures lower than today (figure 2.3; Bartlein and Webb, 1985; CLIMAP, 1981). The pattern in regional climates is evident on these maps as well as on maps of past moisture conditions (Street-Perrott and Harrison, 1985). In the western United States, the Great Basin was much more moist 20,000 years ago than it is today (Smith and Street-Perrott, 1983). More than 30 large freshwater lakes existed within it. In contrast, lakes in eastern and northern Africa as well as India were smaller or even dry 18,000 years ago, but reached high-water levels between 12,000 and 5,000 years ago when swamps and grassland vegetation grew in what are now the Sahara and Rajasthan Deserts (Kutzbach and Street-Perrott, 1985). Climates in the Middle East were dry at 18,000 years ago, but had become wetter by the time that agriculture was developed about 10,000 years ago (Wright, 1976). Many of these changes in temperature and moisture were related to changes in the monsoons that were enhanced by the greater seasonality in solar radiation between 12,000 and 5,000 years BP (Kutzbach and Street-Perrott, 1985).

The vegetational changes in eastern North America illustrate the types of ecosystem and biospheric changes induced by the climate changes of the past 18,000 years (figure 2.4). The geographic distributions of individual plant taxa have changed in response to major changes in temperature and rainfall (Webb et al., 1987). When Europeans came to North America, they farmed in many areas but ultimately found that the deciduous forest and prairie provided the most favorable regions for growing corn, wheat, and other grains. The distribution of forb (prairie plants) and oak pollen at 500 years BP indicate the location of prairie and deciduous forest when Europeans first arrived, and the time sequence of maps for these plant groups show the history of these vegetational regions with their potential for agricultural use. The maps therefore illustrate the types of changes in location and extent that climate can induce for the regions in which corn or wheat grow best. Over time periods with comparable climate changes, human groups dependent upon such crops would either be forced to move as the "cornbelt" (that is, the Iowa prairie) moved or, if they did not move, to change the crops that they planted. Since the advent of agriculture 12,000 years ago, human groups have faced such decisions many times, on time scales from centuries to millennia.

Short-term Changes: Neoglacial Events and Droughts Embedded within the global climate changes of the past 20,000 years (figure 2.1) are several 300- to 500-year-long neoglacial episodes when regional ice sheets and alpine glaciers expanded (Porter, 1981). These include the Younger Dryas climatic oscillation in northwest Europe about 11,000 years ago and the Little Ice Age that was recorded globally between 1450 and 1850 AD. Street-Perrott and Roberts (1983) describe evidence that lake levels dropped drastically two or three times within the wet period from 12,000 to 5,000 years BP in Africa. These brief dry episodes, in which precipitation decreased by as much as 25 per cent for 200 to 500 years, may be linked to neoglacial events in mid- to high-latitudes. Records from Europe show that the Little Ice Age was a much wetter and colder period there (Lamb, 1982). In North America, the east was colder than today but the west may have been warmer (Wahl and Lawson, 1970). The impact of this climatic episode on human affairs is well recorded in the harvest records of wind grapes and in North Atlantic fisheries (Rotberg and Rabb, 1981; Wigley et al., 1981). The human populations in Iceland and Greenland were also adversely affected.

On interannual and decadal scales, droughts and variations in atmospheric circulation alter local and regional climates (Hecht, 1981). Several droughts have had widespread economic impacts, such as the drought in the 1930s in the Great Plains of the United States (Borchert, 1971) and the Sahel drought of the 1970s and 1980s (Butzer, 1983). Droughts are related to changes in atmospheric circulation, but the relationship between these circulation changes and the variations in the global mean temperature is not fully established. Much recent attention has focused on the El-Nino-Southern-Oscillation system (ENSO) that involves quasi-biennial changes in the ocean and atmospheric circulation in the tropical Pacific Ocean. Oscillations in wind speeds and ocean current connect climate variations in South America and southern Asia and even influence the Asian and African monsoonal circulation.

Thus, within the time scale of ages, human efforts to gain subsistence had to cope with a great post-glacial warming, periods of little ice ages and warm spells, extreme events whose frequency was measured in decades, and oscillations in weather measured in years. Within this background of environmental fluctuation, agriculture developed.

World Hunger and the Origins of Agriculture

The Why of Agriculture

We do not know why people began to produce their own food after having been successful for so long in procuring it through hunting, fishing, and gathering wild plants. Agriculture did not originate simply from the "discovery" that seeds dropped into the ground would grow into food plants. The major issue involves the questions of the extent to which people were "forced" into producing food because of increasing scarcity of wild resources and/or the extent to which they were spurred on by their own recognition that growing their own plants was productive and useful.

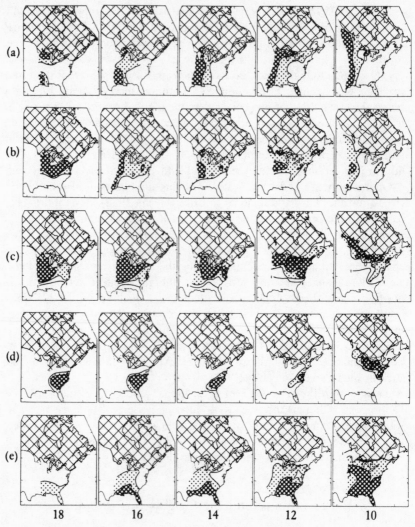

(a) Prairie forbs (ragweed, pigweed, sage, and daisy family)
(b) Sedge
(c) Spruce
(d) Pine
(e) Oak

Figure 2.4 Contour maps showing distribution of the abundance of forb, sedge, spruce, pine, and oak pollen from 18,000 BP to 500 BP for eastern North America.

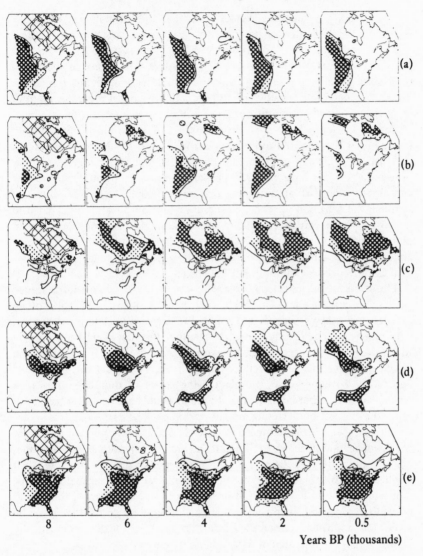

Years BP (thousands)

The darker the shading the higher the abundance for each pollen type. Cross-hatched area indicates the changing position of the Laurentide ice sheet from 18,000 to 6,000 yrs BP.

The Stress Model The stress model of cultural and technological change is based on the idea that change occurs only under some form of stress (Binford and Binford, 1968; Childe, 1952).[1] The stress model attempts to answer the question of why people would change from a proven successful food-getting strategy (hunting and gathering) without being forced to, especially since the alternative (food production) requires a greater input of labor relative to the amount per food output — at least during its initial stages of development — than does hunting.[2] Why would people want to change their lifestyle to a more labor intensive, less productive one, unless they had to? This approach emphasizes the dynamic role hunger — or fear of hunger — might have played in propelling humankind into farming. The continuation of this argument is that once people were committed to farming, the selection of seeds, both natural and purposeful, quickly led to improved yields, which eventually reversed the labor input/food output ratio in favor of output. As an added benefit, labor input could be increased almost without limit with a commensurate increase in yield, whereas this could not be said of hunting and gathering.

The stress model starts from the assumption that food production emerged among hunting, fishing, and gathering peoples who — because of an imbalance between resources and population — began to experience hunger. The imbalance could have come about either through population growth, where the resource potential remained unchanged; or through a deterioration of the environment, which reduced the resource potential within a stable population. In either case, the plant-using sector of the economy, which tends to be more labor intensive than hunting, would have been emphasized to fill in the gap left by declining animal resources. The plant gathering areas would have been exploited more intensively and intentionally improved for seed propagation of the desired plants. In regions experiencing desiccation, labor would have even been invested in water management projects (such as check dams). Finally, areas formerly peripheral to the normal range for food-getting would have received increasing attention as part of the overall effort to expand and intensify the one part of the food sector that could be somewhat controlled. (Increased labor in hunting quickly exhausts the animal supply and no amount more labor can improve the situation, whereas increased labor in plant-gathering can.) Then, as human interactions with the plants intensified and spread, the plants began to evolve though natural selection, and later through intentional selection.

The Co-evolution Model The second view of the beginnings of agriculture focuses on food production as the result of a co-evolutionary process (Rindos, 1984). Rindos suggests that previous theoretical propositions tend to separate humankind from the natural order. "We view civilization as . . . based on control both of nature and of human beings, and having properly identified agriculture as the foundation of civilization, we proceed to read this 'paradigm of consciousness' back in time to account for the very origin of agriculture, and thus of civilization itself" (1984:4). The co-evolution model, then, suggests that humans, animals, and plants underwent a mutual process of domestication. In this model, the increased utilization of wild plants by an increasingly large human population led *naturally* to an increased yield of food plants. This increased yield stemmed from evolutionary changes, through biological selective pressures, as a result of areal expansions of disturbed ground within a region, increased numbers of human beings, and increased human sedentism, operating in concert. In this scenario, the critical variables are the frequency of use of specific plant species, human population density and settlement patterns, and the nature of the specific plant–human interactions (which would determine the precise selective pressures on the plants). Where human populations were increasing in size and density and were settling down on the landscape, the plants would have undergone an ever-increasing degree of selective pressure. Plants that thrived on disturbed or open ground would have been selected over others, as would plants that had evolved seed dispersal methods compatible with human use (such as the ability to survive and propagate after having been harvested, stored, and possibly carried around for long periods of time).

The emphasis in the co-evolutionary model is on the *use* of plants. The use (that is, plant–human interaction) determines the selective pressures, and these chart the course of plants' evolution. Within this framework, the frequency of plant use and the nature and degree of landscape alteration by people are highly significant variables. Both are largely functions of the size, density, and sedentism of the human populations. These variables would have resulted in the unintentional improvement of soil conditions – through the disposal of organic nutrients in the soil as human waste or garbage and through the elimination of forest cover – for many of the plants that later became cultigens. Even the intentional clearing away of unwanted vegetation from around wild plant foods would have created selective pressures on the cultigens. The point to the argument is that the plants that later became cultigens had likely already evolved genetically through the natural selection of traits desired by human beings long before people began to plant seeds or prepare farmlands intentionally.

Archeological Evidence With respect to archeological evidence, the difference between the stress and co-evolutionary models is subtle. The most reasonable explanation for the beginnings of food production is a combination of the two models. Even though human populations were increasing and becoming sedentary, the initial evolution of cultigens through intensified plant use undoubtedly occurred long before humans actually thought about producing food. Use of plants by humans probably did constitute an environmental stress on the plants. However, it is near-impossible to separate this stress from stress induced by seasonal fluctuations in weather and/or longer-term climatic change. Every perturbation of weather or climate that decreases the number and availability of animals or wild plants places a human group in a stress situation. This alone is sufficient cause, as it is now, for people to invest in labor-intensive, risk-minimizing strategies, which from the standpoint of optimal conditions seem excessive. For pre-agricultural peoples, these are frequently accomplished by patterns of seasonal migration (transhumance) which allow an easy redistribution of the populations over the landscape.[3]

The same emphasis on risk-minimizing strategies must have been in effect among the more sedentary pre-agricultural populations. Patterns of mobility differed; but with a greater investment in their settlements, labor intensification must have been especially important. All of the factors of stress identified by the proponents of the stress model were probably operating in these communities as a matter of course. There is no need, therefore, to invoke long-term climatic change as the cause of the stress.[4]

Once food production reached the stage in which people were settled, and began to modify the landscape for water management and soil improvement, all of the mechanisms were in place to insure the continued development of plant production following the scenarios familiar to all (clearing larger areas, developing customs that had the effect of insuring the best seeds were selected for replanting, taking advantage of favorable plant mutation, etc.)

The Timing of Agriculture

As with all evolutionary sequences, the beginnings of food production are difficult to identify. Even the criteria for identifying initial food production are difficult to define. The earliest accepted evidence of agriculture — defined as the intentional planting of plants for food and subsistence/ settlement pattern modified to implement the planting and harvesting of the plants — dates to the eighth millennium BP (Reed, 1977). The global pattern for the origin and spread of agriculture is summarized in figure 2.5a–h.

Around 9,000 years ago, wheat and barley were apparently grown in the Near East from Anatolia to present-day Iran (Harlan, 1977). At the same time, yams, a root crop, were grown in prepared ground in New Guinea (Golson, 1985). By 8,500 years ago, agricultural communities growing wheat and barley had spread through the eastern Mediterranean to as far as northern Greece and to Iraq. Root crops continued in their original area of domestication, but did not spread outside there for millennia.

By 8,000 years ago, millet was grown in northern China (K. C. Chang, 1986) and wheat was continuing to spread to the rest of Greece (Phillips, 1981). Between 8,000 and 7,000 years ago, wheat and barley witnessed perhaps their greatest spread, reaching their maximum prehistoric distributions to the south and east. By the end of the seventh millennium, for example, the two crops were being grown from as far north and west as the Danubian region of Europe (Bogucki and Grygiel, 1983), as far south as Egypt, southern Ethiopia and the northern horn of East Africa, and as far east as the western flanks of the Indus Valley (Allchin and Allchin, 1969). During this same millennium, rice was domesticated in its core area of the Far East between 10° and 15°N latitude (T. T. Chang, 1976). Also, for the first time plants (namely squash) were being grown in the New World, in south-central Mexico (MacNeish, 1967).

By 6,500 years ago, wheat had spread as far north as Poland and as far west as Germany. Also, a major step in food production in the New World was accomplished with the domestication of maize in south-central Mexico (Mangelsdorf et al., 1964). By the end of the sixth millennium BP, wheat and barley neared their prehistoric northern limit of distribution, being grown in the Baltic and southern Scandinavia (Ammerman and Cavalli-Sforza, 1971). Rice spread throughout most of mainland southeast Asia and to northeastern India (Glover, 1985).

By 5,000 years ago, sorghum and millet were being grown from the eastern Sudan to northern Nigeria (Clark and Brant, 1984), and wheat had spread northward to the British Isles (Phillips, 1981). In the New World, squash spread to South America and maize to northern Mexico. Shortly after 4,500 BP wheat spread eastward from southwest Asia into the Indus Valley (Allchin and Allchin, 1982). Around 4,000 years ago, sorghum and millet spread southward in Africa to Kenya and Tanzania (Clark and Brant, 1984), wheat to Sweden (Phillips, 1981), and maize to the southwestern part of the United States and to Peru (Cohen, 1977; Fish et al., 1986; Simmons, 1986).

During the third millennium BP, numerous other crops were developed throughout the world. Chenopodium was grown in eastern Kentucky, USA (Ford, 1985), oil palm was grown in Ghana (Clark and Brant, 1984), and manioc was grown in Peru and Columbia (Cohen, 1977). Rice spread westward to the Indus Valley as did sorghum, and late in the millienium rice found its way throughout most of Pakistan (Misra and Bellwood, 1985). In the New World, squash spread as far northeast as Pennsylvania, USA (Ford, 1985).

During the second millennium BP, maize spread to the upper Mississippi— Ohio River Valley, USA (Ford, 1985), and rice spread to the northern shores of Indonesia (Sumatra and also southern Sulawesi) (Bellwood, 1985). By the end of the second millennium BP, most crops had achieved their maximum distributions prior to the modern geographic extensions by European and other explorers and settlers.

At the scale of tens of millennia, the outstanding events in the history of hunger are the great climatic changes and the origins of agriculture. The

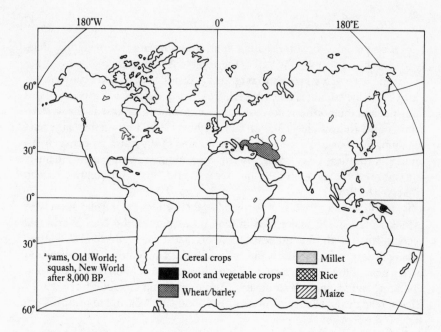

(a) Before 9,000 BP−8,500 BP

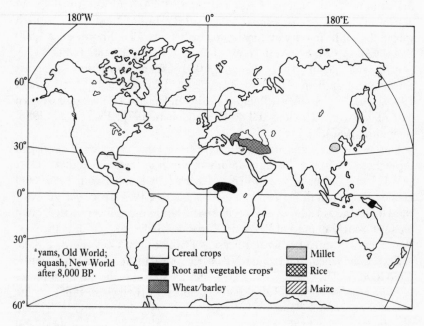

(b) To 8,000 BP

Figure 2.5 Introduction and early development of food production by millennium, 9,000 BP to 2,000 BP, representing initiation of plant domestication in different areas of the world

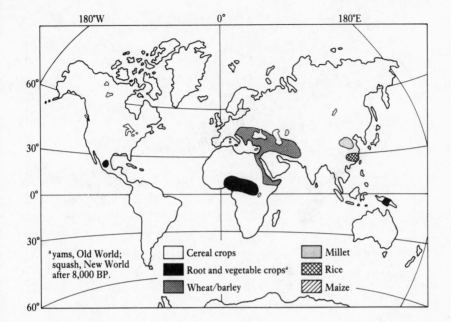

Cereal crops

Root and vegetable cropsᵃ

Wheat/barley

Millet

Rice

Maize

(c) To 7,000 BP

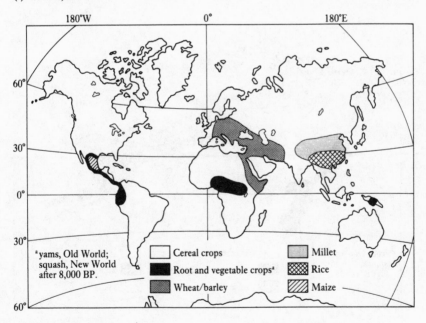

Cereal crops

Root and vegetable cropsᵃ

Wheat/barley

Millet

Rice

Maize

(d) To 6,000 BP

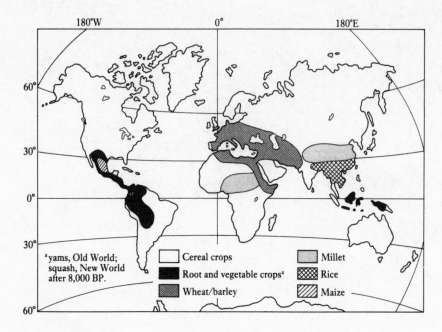

(e) To 5,000 BP

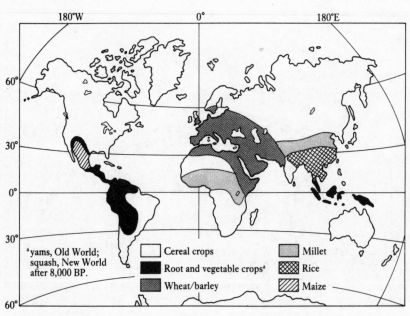

(f) To, 4,000 BP

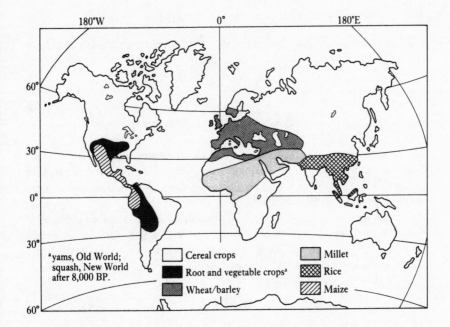

(g) To 3,000 BP

Legend:
- Cereal crops
- Root and vegetable crops[a]
- Wheat/barley
- Millet
- Rice
- Maize

[a] yams, Old World; squash, New World after 8,000 BP.

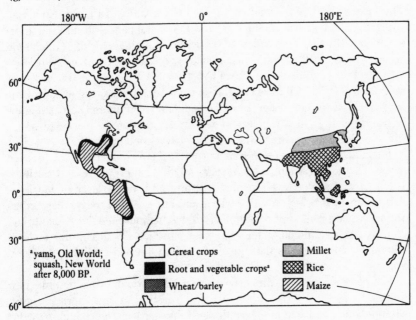

(h) To 2,000 BP

Legend:
- Cereal crops
- Root and vegetable crops[a]
- Wheat/barley
- Millet
- Rice
- Maize

[a] yams, Old World; squash, New World after 8,000 BP.

links between the two are uncertain, but one setting in which they may have converged is on the great alluvial flood plains.

The Rise of Urban Civilization

From time to time, humans and their domesticated plants and animals found geographic situations that were uniquely well suited for permanent occupation. With this sense of permanency came the construction of permanent buildings, the aggregation of relatively large groups of people, attendant specialization of labor, and the manufacture of an abundance of useful wares, tools, and/or objects of art; in a word, the rise of urban civilization. What can we learn regarding the history of hunger from the study of these first attempts at living together in large numbers in highly organized societies?

The Role of Alluvial Flood Plains

The rise of the Old Kingdom of Egypt (ca. 5,000 BP), the Sumerian civilization of Iraq (ca. 5,000 BP), and the Harappan civilization in India (ca. 4,500 BP) all placed sedentary agricultural humans for the exploitation of the naturally fertile floodplains of major rivers. These dates are coincident with the Holocene rise of sea level (Matthews, 1988). Deeply incised river valleys became flooded as sea level rose from 18,000 years ago to approximately 6,000 years ago. Many alluvial floodplains were literally created anew in this process. Thus, humans of five or six thousands years ago had a whole new environment in which to practice agriculture.

The alluvial floodplain is indeed a near-ideal environment for the practice of early settled agriculture (Fairservis, 1975; Vishnu-Mittre and Savithri, 1982). Seasonal flooding provides moisture and a new layer of nutrient-rich sediment in which to plant wheat and barley. Even today, these crops are cultivated on the floodplain of the Indus without ploughing, manuring, or providing additional water. The total absence of agricultural tools in Harappan sites suggests that this early civilization had similar agricultural practices (Vishnu-Mittre and Savithri, 1982:217).

The very success of the new environment would bring in time new problems. By and large, we know most of the success stories: Egypt, Mesopotamia, and China. More difficult, but perhaps more important for hunger history, are the suggestive remains of a great Indus Valley urban civilization.

The Indus Floodplain Scenario

Agriculture was developed more than 7,000 years ago by people already living a settled life in permanent villages along the upland tributary streams to the west of the Indus floodplain. These villages may have evolved from nomadic pastoralists who had settled in the area with domestic goats, sheep, and cattle more than 500 years earlier. Even prior to 7,000 BP, the early agricultural villages had granaries, which suggests some form of community- or hierarchy-organized handling of the food supply. Wheat, barley, and dates comprised the earlier of the agricultural products in the region. In the floodplain of the Indus River itself, the earliest agriculturalists were probably nutritionally better off than their more urbanized descendents, since hunting and especially fishing were surely more important earlier than later.

By 5,000 BP, the Indus Valley settlements had grown into towns, some with palaces, temples, and massive brick fortifications. During the fourth millennium BP, several of these towns emerged as full-fledged cities with planned government and religious districts and large public granaries.

Harappan civilization reached its maximum population, size of cities, and extent of foreign influence between 4,5000 and 4,000 years ago, and at its peak it covered nearly half a million square miles in extent (Allchin and Allchin, 1969). It declined rapidly, if not precipitously, just after the close of the millennium; and by 3,700 years ago, nearly all traces of the urban centers had disappeared, being replaced by small, pastoral villages.

From an archeological standpoint, the Harappan city of Mohenjodaro is especially well known. Kennedy (1982) has investigated the available skeletons and provides a particularly interesting view of life and death in Mohenjodaro. Bones and teeth generally indicate absence of nutritional stress. Likewise, the skeletal data do not indicate two classes of occupants (such as the well-off and the not-so-well-off). Osteological evidence for anemia is attributed to genetics. Indeed, it is argued that these are the genes which, when recessive, provide resistance against malaria and thalassemia. Although there are several extensive destructive levels at the site, the skeletal evidence does not indicate armed invasion by anatomically different people. Further, no weapons or armor are associated with any of the skeletons. Thus one might infer from these observations that the destructive levels at Mohenjodaro and (seemingly) related incomplete and distorted burials record natural catastrophe or perhaps rioting by locals.

The decline of Harappan civilization is unmistakably coincident with the decline in intensity of the southwest monsoon (Agrawal and Sood, 1982; Prell and Kutzbach, 1987; Swain et al., 1983). While much of the region surely remained inhabitable, old patterns of seasonal flooding must have

changed. Indeed, the sites of the Painted Grey Ware culture, which followed
the Harappan culture, are commonly located on the banks of the river;
suggesting that the river no longer came out of its banks and on to the
floodplain on a regular basis (Bryson and Baerreis, 1967). Thus, we see in
the Harappans of the Indus floodplain a people who made agriculture
thrive for a few hundred years, and then faded away into a pastoral
existence.

Conclusions

A well-known truism in historical geology states that near-recent events are
well known but of small magnitude, whereas events in the more distant past
are less well known but of larger magnitude. This truism may also apply to
the history of hunger. On the time scale of tens of thousands of years, we
are dealing with some truly spectacular climatic and human events; but the
relation of these events to hunger remains largely in the realm of speculation.

Climatic History

We understand how the climate system and climate change operate on the
global space scale and on the 10,000-year time scale. For example, drought
and famine in sub-Saharan Africa should not be viewed as a recent event
in the struggle of humans against nature. Rather, paleoclimatologists see
the modern problems of this region against the backdrop of a transition
from Saharan grasslands of 5,000 years ago to continuing advance of the
desert today. Likewise, annual variation in the strength of the southwest
monsoon in India should be viewed in the paleoclimatological context of a
steady decrease in strength of the southwest monsoon from 9,000 years
BP.

Paleoclimatic research involving comparisons between model results and
data should lead to useful scenarios for future climate. Such insight should
point the way to optimal land use as opposed to inappropriate stop-gap
solutions to immediate problems. The lesson of climatic history is that the
earth system changes dramatically on time scales that seem large from a
human perspective. The contribution of paleoclimatic studies to the alleviation of hunger will be to help planners better appreciate the variety of
climate changes on many time and space scales.

The Origins of Agriculture

The origin and spread of agriculture appears to have occurred independently
in at least three widely-separated areas of the world. Between 9,000 and
8,000 years ago, wheat and barley cultivation began in the Near East; from

7,000 or 8,000 years ago, millet and rice in China; and from 6,500 to 8,000 years ago, squash and maize in the new world. Each case almost certainly involves co-evolution of humans and their cultigens and an element of stress on the human population, whether brought on by climate change or by human culture itself.

We do not know whether agriculture was encouraged by rising population or whether it made population growth possible. We suspect that through an interactive process it did both, in different times and places. With the advent of agriculture, with the production of a surplus, there came new social stratification within groups, and resource differential introduced competition among groups. With competition among groups came the roots of *among-groups* entitlement issues.

The Rise of Urban Civilization

With the rise of permanent cities, the phrase "settled agriculture" takes on a new meaning. The cities were the center of culture, the site of centralized authority, the source of wares, and the location of granaries. As these enterprises reached the carrying capacity of the region, *within-group* entitlement issues must surely have arisen.

In summary, then, viewing the history of hunger from the perspective of tens of thousands of years affords recognition of the origins of root causes for hunger that persist right through the millennial, century, and modern perspectives. Hunger avoidance has been a focus for among-groups and within-group human interaction for at least 5,000 years. The history of hunger is intimately interwoven into the entire fabric of the last 5,000 years of human history. The problem is more complex than that of minimum dietary requirements; after all, these were known throughout antiquity. (See chapter 4.) The solution requires a historical perspective, regarding humans, the environment, and human interaction with the environment, that extends back at least 5,000 to 20,000 years.

NOTES

1   Childe (1952) suggested, for example, the "oasis theory," that as climate dried and the sources of water diminished, animals and plants would be forced to live in closer contiguity with humans, and domestication would then occur.

2   Another view, no longer widely held, is that plant domestication and social and cultural innovations such as sedentism did *not* begin among those subject to stress, but rather among those hunters and gatherers who had the resources and energy to experiment. Environmental and other stresses leading to hunger would therefore have been an *impediment* to the spread of agriculture. As in the "stress" model, hunger and malnutrition would have decreased with increasing success in agriculture.

3   See Rindos, 1984, for a more detailed treatment of this general topic.
4   Population growth under optimal conditions would approach the carrying capacity
    of the environment more rapidly than climate change might render the environ-
    ment less than optimal.

REFERENCES

Agrawal, D. P. and Sood, R. K. 1982: Ecological factors and the Harappan
    civilization. In G. L. Possehl (ed.), *Harappan Civilization: A contemporary
    perspective*, New Delhi: American Institute of Indian Studies, 223–31.
Allchin, Bridget and Allchin, Raymond 1969: *The Birth of Indian Civilization*.
    Baltimore: Penguin Books.
Ammerman, A. J. and Cavalli-Sforza, L. L. 1971: Measuring the rate of spread of
    early farming in Europe. *Man*, 6, 674–88.
Bartlein, P. and Webb III, T. 1985: Mean July temperature at 6,000 yr BP in
    eastern North America: Regression equations for estimates from fossil pollen
    data. *Syllogeus*, 55, 301–42.
Bellwood, Peter 1985: *Prehistory of the Indo-Malaysian Archipelago*. Sydney Academic
    Press.
Berger, A., Imbrie, J., Hays, J., Kukla, G., and Salzman, B. 1984: *Milankovitch and
    Climate*. Dordrecht: D. Reidel Publishing Co.
Bernabo, C. J. 1978: Proxy Data: *Nature's Records of Past Climates*. EDS Reprint,
    March 1978, US Department of Commerce, NOAA, Environmental Data
    Service, 2–7.
Binford, S. R. and Binford, L. R. 1968: *New Perspectives in Archeology*. Aldine:
    Chicago.
Bogucki, P. and Grygiel, R. 1983: Early farmers of the North European plain.
    Scientific American, 284, 104–13.
Borchert, J. R. 1971: The dust bowl in the 1970s. *Annuals of the Association of
    American Geographers*, 61, 1–22.
Bradley, R. S. 1985: *Quaternary Paleoclimatology*. Boston: Allen and Unwin.
Bryson, R. A. and Baerreis, D. A. 1967: Possibilities of major climatic modification and
    their implications: Northwest India, a case for study. *American Meteorological
    Society Bulletin*, 48, 136–42.
Bryson, R. A. and Goodman, B. 1980: Volcanic activity and climatic changes.
    Science, 207, 1041–4.
Butzer, K. 1983: Paleo-environmental perspectives on the Sahel drought of 1968–
    73. *GeoJournal*, 7, 369–74.
Chang, K. C. 1986: *The Archaeology of Ancient China*. New Haven: Yale University
    Press, fourth edition.
Chang, T. T. 1976: The rice cultures. In J. Hutchinson, G. Clarke, E. M. Jope,
    and R. Riley (eds), *The Early History of Agriculture, a joint symposium of the
    Royal Society and the British Academy*, Oxford: Oxford University Press, 143–57.
Chen, Robert S. 1983: Interdisciplinary research and integration: The case of

carbon dioxide and climate. In Robert S. Chen, Elise Bolding, and Stephen H. Schneider (eds), *Social Science Research and Climate Change*, Dordrecht: D. Reidel, 230–48.

Childe, V. G. 1952: *New Light on the Most Ancient East*. London: Routledge and Kegan Paul, fourth edition.

Clark, J. D. and Brant, S. A. 1984: *From Hunters to Farmers: The causes and consequences of food production in Africa*. Berkeley: University of California Press.

CLIMAP Project Members 1976: The surface of the ice-age earth. *Science*, 191, 1131–7.

CLIMAP Project Members 1981: Seasonal reconstructions of the earth's surface at the last glacial maximum. *Geological Society of America Map and Chart Series*, MC-36, 1–18.

Cohen, M. C. 1977: Population pressure and the origins of agriculture: An archaeological example from the Coast of Peru. In C. A. Reed (ed.), *Origins of Agriculture*, The Hague: Mouton Publishers, 135–77.

COHMAP Members 1988: Major climatic changes of the last 18,000 years: Observations and model simulations. *Science*, 241, 1043–52.

Fairservis, W. A. Jr. 1975: *The Roots of Ancient India*. Chicago: University of Chicago Press, second edition, revised.

Fish, P. R., Fish, S. K., Long, A., and Miksicek, C. 1986: Early corn remains from Tumamoc Hill, Southern Arizona. *American Antiquity*, 51, 563–72.

Ford, R. I. (ed.) 1985: *Prehistoric Food Production in North America*. Anthropological Papers 75, Michigan: Museum of Anthropology, University of Michigan.

Glover, Ian C. 1985: Some problems relating to the domestication of rice in Asia. In V. N. Misra and P. Bellwood (eds), *Recent Advances in Indo-Pacific Prehistory*, New Delhi: Oxford and IBH Publishing Co., 265–74.

Golson, Jack 1985: Agricultural origins in Southeast Asia: A view from the East. In V. N. Misra and P. Bellwood (eds), *Recent Advances in Indo-Pacific Prehistory*, Leiden: E. J. Brill, 307–14.

Goodman, Alan H., Martin, Debra L., Armelagos, George J., and Clark, George 1984: Indications of stress from bone and teeth. In Mark N. Cohen and George J. Armelagos (eds), *Paleopathology at the Origins of Agriculture*, New York: Academic Press, 13–49.

Gould, H. R. 1970: The Mississippi delta complex. In J. P. Morgan (ed.), *Deltaic Sedimentation, Modern and Ancient*, Tulsa: Society of Economic Paleontologists and Mineralogists, spec. pub. 15, 3–30.

Hansen, J., Lancis, A., Rind, D., Russell, G., Stone, P., Fung, I., Ruedy, R., and Lerner, J. 1983: Climate sensitivity: Analysis of feedback mechanisms. In J. E. Hansen and T. Takahashi (eds), *Climate processes and climate sensitivity*, Geophysical Monograph 29, Washington, DC: American Geophysical Union.

Harlan, J. R. 1977: The origins of cereal agriculture in the old world. In C. A. Reed (ed.), *Origins of Agriculture*, The Hague: Mouton Publishers, 357–84.

Hecht, A. D. 1981: The challenge of climate to man. *EOS*, 62, 1193–8.

Hecht, A. D. (ed.) 1985: *Paleoclimate Analysis and Modeling*. New York: J. Wiley and Sons.

Huntley, B. and Birks, H. J. B. 1983: *An Atlas of Past and Present Pollen Maps for Europe: 0–13,000 Years Ago*. Cambridge: Cambridge University Press.

Kellogg, W. W. and Schware, R. 1981: Climate Change and Society. Boulder, Colo: Westview Press.

Kennedy, K. A. R. 1982: Skulls, aryans and flowing drains: The interface of archaeology and skeletal biology in the study of Harappan civilization. In G. L. Possehl (ed.) *Harappan Civilization: A contemporary perspective*, New Delhi: American Institute of Indian Studies, 289–95.

Kutzbach, J. E. 1985: Modeling of paleoclimates. *Advances in Geophysics*, 28A, 159–96.

Kutzbach, J. E. and Street-Perrott, F. A. 1985: Milankovitch forcing of fluctuations in the level of tropical lakes from 18 to 0 kyr BP. *Nature*, 317, 130–4.

Lamb, H. H. 1982: *Climate, History and the Modern World*. London: Methuen and Co., Ltd.

MacNeish, R. S. 1967: A summary of the subsistence. In D. S. Byers (ed.), *The Prehistory of the Tehuacan Valley. Volume 1: Environment and Subsistence*. (Published for the Robert S. Peabody Foundation, Phillips Academy, Andover, Mass.) Austin, Tex.: University of Texas Press, 290–309.

Manabe, S. and Hahn, D. G. 1977: Simulation of an ice age. *Journal of Geophysical Research*, 82, 3889–911.

Mangelsdorf, P. C., MacNeish, R. S., and Galinat, W. 1964: Domestication of corn. *Science*, 143, 538–45.

Matthews, R. K. 1989: Quaternary sea level change. In Roger Revelle (ed.), *Sea Level Change*, NRC Studies in Geophysics, Washington, DC: National Academy of Science, in press.

Misra, V. N. and Bellwood, P. (eds) 1985: *Recent Advances in Indo-Pacific Prehistory*. Leiden: E. J. Brill.

Namias, J. 1975: Short period climate variations. In *Collected works of J. Namias, 1934–1974*, San Diego, Cal.: Graphics and Reproduction Services, University of California, 905.

National Academy of Sciences 1975: *Understanding Climatic Change: A Program for Action*. Washington, DC: National Academy of Sciences.

Phillips, P. 1981: *The Prehistory of Europe*. Harmondsworth: Penguin Books.

Pisias, N. G. and Shackleton, N. J. 1984: Modeling the global climate response to orbital forcing and atmospheric carbon dioxide changes. *Nature*, 310, 757–9.

Pittock, A. B., Ackerman, T. P., Crutzen, P. J., MacCracken, M. C., Shapiro, C. S., and Turco, R. P. 1986: *Environmental Consequences of Nuclear War, Vol. 1: Physical and Atmospheric Effects*. New York: John Wiley and Sons.

Porter, S. C. 1981: Glaciological evidence of Holocene climatic change. In T. M. L. Wigley, M. J. Ingram, and G. Farmer (eds), *Climate and History*, Cambridge: Cambridge University Press, 82–110.

Prell, W. L. and Kutzbach, J. E. 1987: Monsoon variability over the past 150,000 years. *Journal of Geophysical Research*, 92, 8411–25.

Reed, C. A. (ed.) 1977: *Origins of Agriculture*. The Hague: Mouton Publishers.

Rindos, D. 1984: *The Origins of Agriculture: An Evolutionary Perspective*. New York: Academic Press.

Rotberg, R. I. and Rabb, T. K. (eds) 1981: *Climate and History.* Princeton: Princeton University Press.

Saltzman, B. 1983: Climatic systems analysis. *Advances in Geophysics,* 25, 173–233.

Saltzman, B. 1985: Paleoclimatic modeling. In A. D. Hecht (ed.), *Paleoclimate Data and Modeling,* New York: J. Wiley and Sons, Inc., 341–96.

Simmons, A. H. 1986: New evidence for the early use of cultigens in the American southwest. *American Antiquity,* 51, 73–89.

Smith, G. I. and Street-Perrott, F. A. 1983: Pluvial lakes of the western United States. In S. C. Porter (ed.), *Late-Quaternary Environments of the United States. Vol. 1: The Late Pleistocene,* Minneapolis: University of Minnesota Press, 190–212.

Street-Perrott, F. A. and Harrison, S. P. 1985: Lake-level fluctuations. In A. D. Hecht (ed.), *Paleoclimate Data and Modeling,* New York, J.Wiley and Sons, Inc.

Street-Perrott, F. A. and Roberts, N. 1983: Fluctuations in closed-basin lakes as an indicator of past atmospheric circulation patterns. In F. A. Street-Perrot, M. A. Beran, and R. A. S. Ratcliffe (eds.), *Variations in the Global Water Budget,* Dordrecht: D. Reidel Publishing Co., 331–45.

Swain, A. M., Kutzbach, J. E., and Hastenwath, S. 1983: Estimates of Holocene precipitation for Rajasthan, India, based on pollen and lake-level data. *Quaternary Research,* 19, 1–17.

Vishnu-Mittre and Savithri, R. 1982: Food economy of the Harappans. In G. L. Possehl (ed.), *Harappan Civilization: A contemporary perspective,* New Delhi: American Institute of Indian Studies, 205–21.

Wahl, E. W. and Lawson, T. L. 1970: The climate of the mid-nineteenth century United States compared to the current normals. *Monthly Weather Review,* 98, 259–65.

Webb III, T. and Wigley, T. M. L. 1985: What past climates can indicate about a warmer world. In M. C. MacCracken and F. Luther (eds), *Projecting the Climatic Effects of Increasing Carbon Dioxide,* Washington, DC: DOE/ER-0237, Department of Energy, 235–57.

Webb III, T., Bartlein, P. J., and Kutzbach, J. E. 1987: Climatic change in eastern North America during the past 18,000 years: Comparison of pollen data with model results. In W. F. Ruddiman and H. E. Wright, Jr (eds), *North America and Adjacent Oceans During the Last Deglaciation,* Boulder, Colo.: The Geology of North America, v. K-3, Geological Society of America, 447–62.

Wigley, T. M. L., Angell, J. K., and Jones, P. D. 1985: Analysis of the temperature record. In M. C. MacCracken and F. M. Luther (eds), *Detecting the Climatic Effects of Increasing Carbon Dioxide,* Washington, DC: DOE/ER-0235, Department of Energy, 55–90.

Wigley, T. M. L., Ingram, M. J., and Farmer, G. 1981: *Climate and History.* Cambridge: Cambridge University Press.

Williams, J. R., Barry, R. G., and Washington, W. M. 1974: Simulation of the atmospheric circulation using the NCAR global circulation model with ice age boundary conditions. *Journal of Applied Meteorology,* 13, 305–17.

Wright, H. E. 1976: The environmental setting for plant domestication in the Near East. *Science,* 194, 385–9.

3

Prehistoric Patterns of Hunger

MARK NATHAN COHEN

The time span of 30,000 years encompasses the end of an ice age and a major part of the expansion of the human species into northern latitudes and through the Bering Strait to the New World. It also encompasses a series of social and economic revolutions which archeologists refer to as the Broad Spectrum (or intensive gathering) Revolution, the Neolithic (or farming) Revolution, and the Urban Revolution (or rise of civilization). Each of these transitions rivals or surpasses the recent Industrial Revolution in its impact on human economy and social organization. Through these revolutions, small, mobile, autonomous bands of hunter-gatherers first broadened the range of their foraging activities; they centralized their foraging and settled into sedentary communities; they began to grow their own food; their communities grew in size; and communities became incorporated into larger networks of trade, alliance, and power that we refer to as "civilization."

These transitions can be observed in many different parts of the world with some variations in the order of events.[1] In much of the Old World the sequence occupies nearly 30,000 years. In much of the New World (which human beings may have reached no more than 15,000 to 20,000 years ago), the same events are played out over the course of only a few thousand years (Childe, 1950; Cohen, 1977; Fagan, 1986; Fried, 1967; Harris, 1977; Price and Brown, 1985).

Analyzing changes in patterns of hunger across these transitions is complicated by the fact that in almost all parts of the world the transitions were accomplished without written record. Even the last transformation – the rise of urban states – was accompanied by written records only in its later stages and then only in a few parts of the world.

Analyzing patterns of hunger across this time span is also complicated by strong biases inherent in our sense of history. We assume that the record is one of improving economic homeostasis marked by decreasing frequency of "crop" failure and starvation. We tend to assume that the economic transformations which have occurred represent improvements in the capacity of the species to feed itself and to protect itself against famine.

Our sense of progress is based on several things. With the chauvinism characteristic of all societies, we tend to assume that our ways of doing things are better than observed alternatives. Moreover, we can measure the improvements in human nutrition and life span which have occurred in Europe since the eighteenth century and assume that we can project the pattern of improvement into the unknown past: that is, we tend to assume that measurable improvements in nutrition and health since the eighteenth century are only the most recent and visible parts of human progress. (In fact Europe of the fifteenth to eighteenth centuries – and particularly urban Europe of that time – may represent a real nadir in the history of human health.) In addition, we see the peculiar eating habits and poor health of the "primitive" groups most often observed under conditions of colonial restraint. Finally, it is often assumed that stringent Malthusian checks, including starvation, played a major part in slowing the growth of the human population until the very recent past. It is clear that recently observable population growth rates of 1 percent or more per year cannot long have characterized the human species or there would be far more of us than the earth's resources can handle.

However, even a cursory review of the nature of the economic transitions involved suggests that, although they undoubtedly increased the total supply of food and supported larger human populations, these transitions need not always have represented improvements in the quality or reliability of the food supply. For example, the Broad Spectrum Revolution involved the development of a number of new technologies such as grindstones, small projectiles, fishing equipment, and perhaps nets and snares which permitted groups to exploit – obtain and process – a wider variety of wild foods. Typically broad-spectrum foragers (Mesolithic groups in the Old World, Archaic or Woodland Period groups in the New World) exploited less large game but more small, trapped game, more birds, more aquatic foods (fish and shellfish), and more small seeds, such as the wild ancestors of the cereals, than did their Paleolithic or PaleoIndian forebears. These improvements in technology which expanded the range and total quantity of food available may have improved the quality of the diet and the reliability of the food supply (Hayden, 1981a). But the new technologies typically appear to have followed declines in the availability of large game and to have accompanied increasingly dense human population and tighter packing of human groups, so that they may only have offset a decline in the availability of preferred resources. In short, the evolution of foraging strategy in prehistory may have followed a "Boserupian" trajectory, in which an increase in total food was achieved only by a disproportionate increase in labor investment (see Boserup, 1965; Cohen, 1977; chapter 1, this volume). Several tests of hunting and gathering efficiency prompted by the recent development of optimal foraging theory (Winterhalder and Smith, 1981) in fact suggest that small game, shellfish, and small seeds are relatively inefficient resources to exploit compared to larger game, and some choice vegetable foods, even when Mesolithic technology is available (Cohen, 1987). The new technologies appear to represent a necessary adjustment to declining resources and/or increasing human population density, which was accompanied by diminishing returns for human labor, in keeping with the Boserupian model.[2] And, if the range of resources exploited expanded only in proportion to declining game, decreasing available territory, and reduced mobility, these changes may not have implied any improvement in the reliability of the resource base, especially because small animals are often "r-selected" species – that is, plentiful and rapidly reproducing organisms but ones prone to pronounced fluctuations in their own numbers (see E. O. Wilson, 1975).

Settling down and storing food have the obvious advantage that food need not be found on a daily basis and can be saved to provide for days when hunting is poor or people are sick. Moreover, food can be saved from seasons of plenty to provide for lean seasons. But stored food loses nutritional value and reliance on stored foods reduces dietary variety. Stored foods often cannot be kept sufficiently well from one season to the next to supply the needs of a group: they rot or are stolen by animal competitors (see, for example, Nurse, 1975; Ogbu, 1973). Perhaps most important, stored food can be, and often is, expropriated by other groups of people: sedentary populations with stored resources face a new, politically induced risk of hunger not faced by their more mobile forebears.

Settling down has one other important consequence: it is likely to be associated with an increase in infection and parasitization. Greater numbers of people facilitate disease transmission as does continued contact with garbage and garbage-eating animals, feces, and soil contaminated by feces (Black, 1975; Black et al., 1974; Cockburn, 1971; Fenner, 1970; Polgar, 1964). Even insect-borne diseases such as malaria may be affected (Livingstone, 1984). If domestic animals are kept, the risk of disease is even greater. Domestic animals are not only the immediate source of parasites such as salmonella or tapeworms, they are the ultimate source of many epidemic diseases including measles, smallpox, mumps, and influenza (see Cohen, 1989, for a review).

This increase in infection means, in turn, that individual human beings will lose more of their nutrients after ingestion (Beisel, 1982; Rosenberg et al., 1976). A particularly important risk exacerbated by sedentism may be weanling diarrhea, a major health hazard in much of the Third World even today, which affects toddlers' ability to absorb the nutrients in their food.

Domestication of plants and animals can help increase the growing range of selected crops and may enable more of the crop to be grown, but domestic crops often lack the nutritional quality of their wild counterparts or of other wild foods which prove less susceptible to human manipulation (Eder, 1978; Harlan, 1967; Lee, 1980; Wehmeyer et al., 1969). Domesticated crops also often lack the viability of their wild counterparts in the face of environmental fluctuation – particularly if, as is often the case, the domesticates are spread by human transport beyond their original native environments. Moreover, domestic crops are often grown in artificially dense fields or gardens which increase the risk of blight and soil exhaustion. Intensification of agriculture by irrigation may expand the food supply and may buffer agriculture against natural hazards such as fluctuations in rainfall; but such systems often have their own risks as, for example, the salting and silting of irrigation systems (Jacobsen and Adams, 1958).

Trade networks can provide a means of increasing dietary variety and smoothing out seasonal fluctuations in food supply as well as mitigating outright local famine (see, for instance, McAlpin, 1983). But the experience of contemporary trade networks suggests a number of problems which are likely to have plagued those of the past, even though such problems may be hard to diagnose archeologically. Trade networks may siphon off both variety and quantity of foods (Pelto and Pelto, 1985 – compare the discussion of nutrition in prehistoric Nubia by Martin et al., 1984, or of prehistoric Dickson Mounds, Illinois, by A. Goodman et al., 1984a). Both the technology and the political organization of trade may fail and cause difficulties, in much the manner that hunger in contemporary Africa is a result in part of failure to maintain road systems (Rotberg, 1983; Rotberg and Rabb, 1985). Large-scale civilized storage and trade, although potentially powerful in alleviating famine, also imply control by a political elite and the existence of classes of people who exert little economic or political demand in the system. Moreover, since civilization is a system of specialists, most people, particularly those in urban areas, lose control over their own food supplies and rely on economic or political leverage (entitlements) to obtain food. Starvation may become more a function of political and economic forces than of actual crop failure, as has been the case in many historic and modern contexts (Chafkin and Berg, 1975; Dando, 1976; Hufton, 1985; Sen, 1981; Tilley, 1985).

In short, there is no reason to assume that any or all of these transitions regularly improved the quality of diet or reduced the frequency of famine. The question of the relative frequency of hunger before and after each of these transitions is an empirical one. In order to get evidence about the real impact of these changes, in the absence of written records, archeologists have been forced to rely on a kind of triangulation between two imperfect but complementary sources of data: the health records of contemporary populations whose lifestyles still, at least roughly, approximate ancient lifestyles; and archeological evidence of health in ancient skeletons, which speaks directly to the past but only in limited and often oblique ways. Neither source can be considered wholly reliable, but at least they are prone to different kinds of error, so that each provides something of a check on the other. Whatever their drawbacks they represent the only windows that we have on the distant past.

The Ethnographic Record of Hunting and Gathering Societies

Contemporary hunter-gatherers are imperfect models for the past because all live in a world in which much former prey − particularly efficiently exploited large game − has disappeared as a result either of climate change or of prior human hunting. Most now live in "marginal" environments, such as deserts or the arctic, because they have been displaced from favored environments by more powerful groups. Moreover, many such groups compete for food with larger and better-armed groups of farmers and sportsmen; and many hunt and forage in areas where populations of game and their own movements are restricted by fences or where their hunting is restricted by law (Bleek, 1928; Morris, 1982). For these reasons contemporary groups may have a harder time of it than their prehistoric forebears.

On the other hand, most modern hunting and gathering groups have access to new tools such as iron-tipped spears, arrows, or even primitive (but rarely modern) guns, which may assist them; although efficiency tests of the type referred to above suggest that these improvements in weapons usually do not offset the loss of efficiency associated with the decline of larger game. In addition, most groups are in contact with civilization to various degrees. Food may now be available by trade in times of famine, which was not so in the past, and people may be able to give up hunting and gathering for other economic systems when times are hard. No group that has been observed lacks these contacts entirely (Schrire, 1984).

Qualitative Nutrition of Contemporary Hunter-Gatherers

Reports on the qualitative nutrition of contemporary foragers (that is, their access to protein and the various vitamins and minerals) suggests that in fact it is commonly quite good, for reasons quite independent of any trade. Contemporary foragers are commonly reported to eat a wide range of fresh foods providing good vitamin and mineral balance and to obtain a fairly high proportion of animal products in their diets.[3] Recorded meat and protein intakes, for example, are conspicuously good by world standards. Most reports suggest that hunter gatherers commonly obtain 100 g or more meat per person per day, although some report seasonal fluctuations. Only one or two groups approach the low Third-World average for meat or meat protein intake (Cohen, 1989).

Medical reports and informal medical observations on a number of such groups suggest that qualitative nutritional health is generally good by world – particularly Third-World – standards. Marginal iron or protein deficiency is occasionally reported but frank anemia is rare and frank kwashiorkor almost unknown. Most serum protein levels are considered healthy and serum albumin levels are healthy or marginally low, averaging 3.5 to 4 g per 100 ml in several groups reported. Marginal vitamin deficiencies (vitamins A and C) are occasionally reported but cases are generally mild and/or infrequent by the standard of neighboring groups.[4] Among observers in Australia there seems to be a consensus that in qualitative terms at least the poorest aboriginal diets are those found in groups resettled by the national government. In India, the nutrition of most hunter-gatherers appears to be conspicuously good in comparison to the rest of the population and to be best in those groups least integrated into regional trade networks (ARNIN, 1969; Malhotra, 1966; Morris, 1982; cf. B. J. Williams, 1974).

Pygmy populations from the central African rainforest provide something of an exception to the picture of good qualitative nutrition among hunter-gatherers. They live in an environment particularly permissive of parasite transmission and commonly live in association with larger groups of farmers. As a consequence they suffer heavily from parasitization despite their own small numbers and relative mobility. Most observers conclude that high parasite rates rather than poor dietary intake causes the marginal malnutrition that is observed (Cavalli-Sforza, 1986; Mann et al., 1962; Paolucci et al., 1969; Price et al., 1963). Similar arguments apply to marginally malnourished groups (of hunter-gatherers and farmers alike) in southeast Asian rainforests evaluated by Polunin (1953) and to (primarily agricultural) populations in the Amazon rainforest (see, for example, Colchester, 1982) who appear to suffer increased parasite loads as a result of recent increases in sedentism and group size. The most striking exception to the pattern of reasonable to good qualitative nutrition among small, isolated groups occurs among populations in highland New Guinea, where dense, sedentary populations (of foragers and horticulturalists alike) in animal-poor environments are forced to rely very heavily on wild sago palm starch or domestic sweet potatoes for their subsistence (Dennett and Connell, 1988; Townsend, 1971).

Table 3.1 Caloric intake by contemporary hunter-gatherers[6]

Group	Source	Measured intake (kcal/person/day)
Africa		
San	Lee, 1969	2,140
San	Tanaka, 1980	2,000
San	Wilmsen, 1978	2,200 (in good season)
Pygmy	Ichikawa, 1981, 1983	1,800–3,000 (with trade)
Efe	Bailey and Peacock, in press	126% RDA in lean season[a]
Hadza	Hawkes (personal communication)	3,497
India		
Onge	Sen Gupta, 1980	2,620
Birhor	B. J. Williams, 1974	1,518 (in trade)
Southeast Asia		
Batek	Eder, 1978	1,825–2,075 (after net loss in trade)
Australia		
Anbarra	R. Jones, 1980; Meehan, 1977a, 1977b	1,600–2500 (above RDA 11 of 12 months with or without trade)[a]
Alyawara	O'Connell and Hawkes, 1981	(obtain 3,000 kcal per hour of work)
Arnhemland	McCarthy and McArthur, 1960	1,170–2,160 (with disclaimer that observed individuals could have collected more food any day)
South America		
Cuiva	Hurtado and Hill, 1987	2,018
Ache	Hill et al., 1984	3,800

[a] RDA = recommended daily allowance.

Caloric Adequacy of Contemporary Hunter-Gatherer Diets

The caloric adequacy of hunter-gatherer diets is somewhat more questionable, and more often linked to trade in modern contexts. Modern hunter-gatherers are often small people and there is some suggestion that this represents caloric deprivation, which can be remedied by access to richer diets (Hausman and Wilmsen, 1985).[5] Caloric intake can indeed be low in an otherwise well-balanced foraging diet because of the low fat content of wild animals, the high fiber and low sugar content of most wild vegetable foods, and the scarcity of concentrated sources of calories (other than occasional honey). However, recorded caloric intakes are usually in the range of 2,000 kcal per person per day or more.

In most reports where specific figures are not provided caloric intake is considered adequate if not rich, at least in normal times[6] and reports of low caloric intake are sometimes accompanied by disclaimers suggesting that the individuals tested could have obtained more food had they wished (McArthur, 1960). The poorest populations appear to be those inhabiting extremely dry and/or cold climates (Gould, 1969a; Hayden, 1981b; Silberbauer, 1981); or they are those participating in particularly tightly controlled market economies. The poorest measured dietary intake I have seen for a hunting and gathering population is that of the Birhor of India, hunting in a game-depleted area where hunting is legally restricted and trading their game for domestic rice in village markets. They obtained only about 1,500 kcal per person per day (B. J. Williams, 1974). In contrast, many major modern nations including India and Bangladesh are estimated to average 2,100 kcal per person per day or less; and estimates for the contemporary urban poor are often substantially less, ranging well below 1,500 kcal (Basta, 1977; Bunting, 1970; Clark and Haswell, 1970; N. Hassan and Ahmad, 1984; Wenlock, 1979).

Reliability of Hunter-Gatherer Food Supplies

Hunter-gatherers, particularly in desert or arctic environments, commonly face lean seasons and can, more occasionally, face starvation when resources fail over too wide an area to traverse on foot Allen, 1974; Basedow, 1925; Grey, 1841; Holmberg, 1969; Moore, 1979; W. Peterson, 1981; Silberbauer, 1981; Sinha, 1972; Sweeny, 1947; Warner, 1937; Wilmsen, 1974). But by far the greatest frequency of severe hunger and starvation occurs to populations in extremely dry and/or cold environments in which no other human populations (except specialized, heavily capitalized, modern outposts of civilization) even attempt to live. (See, for example, tables in Hayden, 1981b.) It is not at all clear that hunger or starvation episodes are more frequent or more severe for contemporary hunter-gatherers than for subsistence farmers in similar environments, or for other participants in many less wealthy modern states (Annegers, 1973; Nurse, 1975; Nurse and Jenkins, 1977). One attempt to make cross-cultural comparison of the frequency of hunger and starvation among current hunter-gatherers and farmers (Gaulin and Konner, 1977) found a slight advantage to the hunter-gatherer groups. Perhaps most interesting, Hadza hunter-gatherers of east Africa — one of the few remaining hunting and gathering groups who occupy the kind of savanna environment preferred by their and our paleolithic forebears, rather than the marginal locations in which most modern hunters find themselves — appear to be essentially immune to real hunger. James Woodburn (1968, personal communication) reports that he has never observed them hungry except when they go to government settlements. He reports that they use the term "hunger" to refer to days when they must eat more vegetables and less meat than they would like. Kristen Hawkes and James O'Connell, who have recently undertaken a more detailed analysis of Hadza foraging (personal communication), also report that it is hard to imagine all of their resources disappearing at once.

In sum, stereotypes aside, there is little in contemporary ethnographic evidence to lead us to expect prehistoric hunter-gatherers, who lived in more select regions of a less populated world, to have been poorly nourished or to have suffered inordinately high rates of hunger or starvation — except to the degree that during glacial episodes a higher proportion of people were forced to live in arctic or subarctic conditions than is now the case.

Paleopathology: The Evidence of Prehistoric Human Remains

We can obtain direct, although often fragmentary, information about changes in human health and nutrition by comparing populations of human skeletons from prehistoric sites of various periods. The human skeleton records chronic quantitative and qualitative malnutrition in several ways. Protein calorie malnutrition is recorded in retarded growth of children (whose bones therefore appear short or thin relative to their dental age) and in reduced adult stature or other skeletal dimensions, including reduced bone cortical (cross-sectional) area. Anemia is recorded as thickening of the skull vault and surface porosity of the skull (porotic hyperostosis) or porosity of the eye orbits (cribra orbitalia). Vitamin D deficiency appears as rickets (soft bone distorted by the pull of gravity). Scurvy (controversially) appears as subperiosteal hemorrhaging and tooth loss. (For basic references in paleopathological diagnosis see: Cohen and Armelagos, 1984; Gilbert and

Mielke, 1985; Huss Ashmore et al., 1982; Ortner and Putschar, 1981; Steinbock, 1976.)

The skeleton does not record episodes of hunger or starvation in any definitive way. It does, however, record episodes of biological stress, including starvation but also infectious or functional disease, which produce growth disturbances in bones and teeth. The shafts of long bones grow and ossify outward from a central point. If growth is retarded and then rebounds, a scar or Harris line is formed marking the position at which rebound growth occurred. In an analogous manner, teeth develop along an axis from occlusal tip to root. Stress during the period of tooth formation may result in formation of an imperfect band of enamel, called a Wilson band if microscopic, and referred to as enamel hypoplasia when visible to the naked eye.

The two types of marker, Harris lines and enamel defects, each permit the age of stress to be identified based on the position of the scar on the bone or tooth. Each permits frequency and pattern of stresses to be assessed, and whether stresses are irregular, annual, or semi-annual. Recent work on microscopic structure of teeth suggests that much finer discrimination of patterns may be possible (Rose et al., 1985).

A number of paleopathological descriptions of individual prehistoric populations now exist which utilize these signs and symptoms. Direct comparison between populations often involves large differences in time, geography, and climate – and perhaps in genetics – as well as in human activities. If we are to evaluate the impact of changing human technology and society on health and nutrition, we need to compare sequential populations in the same environment, and ideally we should compare populations that follow one another in relatively rapid succession and which can be shown to be culturally and genetically similar to one another. Moreover, paleopathological indicators have proved hard to quantify and standardize with sufficient precision to permit direct comparison of the published work of different scholars or teams. The most valuable comparative statements, therefore, are those which result when a single individual or team has evaluated a series of sequential archeological populations from the same location. Most of the patterns described below were generated in this manner. However, given the imperfection of the archeological record, direct genetic and cultural continuity between groups can only rarely be demonstrated.

The size of samples and the degree to which they accurately represent the once living populations from which they are collected are obvious problems. This is particularly the case in the earliest archeological samples and those from the smallest and most mobile groups, in which the total available number may be no more than a few or a few dozen individuals.

Some patterns, such as age distribution at death, will be heavily influenced by sampling error; other variables, such as average adult stature or frequency of chronic malnutrition, should be less affected. In later, more sedentary groups, in which each sample compared usually numbers 100 to 200 individuals or more, the sampling problem is reduced. Moreover, comparison of the mortality profile to contemporary life tables (for instance, Buikstra and Mielke, 1985; A. Goodman et al., 1984a; Mensforth, ms.) may enable us to identify the missing segments of the population. The best control on sampling error, however, is probably replication — looking for patterns of change which occur in many different archeological sequences — which should eliminate random (though not systematic) sampling bias.

Paleopathology and the Broad Spectrum Revolution

Not surprisingly, evaluation of the Broad Spectrum Revolution, the earliest of the transitions in most parts of the world, is based on the most fragmentary evidence. In the Old World, where this transition occurred 10,000 or more years ago, most comparisons are based on collections of all known specimens from a particular period rather than from natural populations; and the conclusions are necessarily limited. However, several different studies in different parts of the Old World — the Mediterranean (Angel, 1984), the Levant (Smith et al., 1984), India (Kennedy, 1984), western and northern Europe (Frayer, 1981; Meiklejohn et al., 1984) — report that human stature declined at the time of the Broad Spectrum Revolution from the Paleolithic to the Mesolithic Period.

The significance of the decline is in dispute. Angel and Kennedy associate it with declining nutrition; Frayer attributes it to changing patterns of work; and changing climate may also be implicated since the decline in size is coeval with the end of the Pleistocene period. Angel notes that in the Mediterranean area the decline in stature is also accompanied by reduction in two other skeletal dimensions — the height of the base of the skull and the diameter of the pelvic inlet — which he has found to be correlated with nutrition in modern populations.

Two studies have compared rates of enamel hypoplasia between Paleolithic and Mesolithic groups. Smith et al. (1984) found no change in hypoplasia rates during these periods in the Levant. Brothwell (1963) found an increase in rates of hypoplasia during the Mesolithic Period in western Europe.

The Mesolithic Period in the Old World may also have been accompanied by a slowing in the growth of the human species compared even to slow Paleolithic rates of growth, if F. Hassan (1981: discussed below) is correct.

In the New World, where the Broad Spectrum Revolution occurred

Table 3.2 Changes in adult stature (cm)

Area	Source	Sex	Paleolithic	Mesolithic	Neolithic
Europe	Meiklejohn	M	170−4	165−8	164−7
		F	156−7	154−6	153−4
India	Kennedy	M	168−92	declining	....
		F	162−76	declining	....
Mediterranean	Angel	M	177	172	169
		F	166	160	156

relatively recently and relatively quickly, samples are more complete and comparisons more easily made. In California, where American Indians ultimately developed large and complex societies based on intense exploitation of fish and nuts without ever farming, the data on changing health and nutrition through time are mixed. McHenry (1968) reported some years ago that the frequency of Harris lines declined through time in central California Indian populations, suggesting an improvement in the reliability of their diets in accord with the then widely accepted assumption that progress meant improved nutrition. However, more recent study of enamel hypoplasia in these same populations suggests the opposite trend (Dickel et al., 1984). This apparent contradiction is discussed below. Moreover, Dickel (1985) using one of the nutritional indicators developed by Angel (height of the base of the skull) found a gradual decline in nutritional quality through time, although Dickel et al. (1984) report no significant change in adult stature through this time. In southern California, Walker (ms., 1985, 1986; Walker and de Niro, 1986) reports that the frequency of enamel hypoplasia increases through time, although he argues that background nutrition appears to be improving.

In Ohio, Robert Mensforth (1985, 1986), reporting on two large skeletal populations of relatively sedentary hunter-gatherers whose death profiles he has carefully checked for completeness against model life tables, finds that the later population displayed more frequent growth retardation and shorter diaphyseal (bone-shaft) lengths in children as well as higher rates of porotic hyperostosis. He argues that the differences primarily reflect the greater burden of infectious disease in the later population.

In Peru, Robert Benfer (1984, 1986) has described a sequence of preagricultural populations from the Paloma site and found that stature increased through time and the frequency of Harris lines decreased, although the frequency of enamel hypoplasia increased. Studies of tooth wear as well as coprolites suggested that later populations were consuming an expanding array of plant foods including an increasing proportion of coarse and fibrous foods. In later coastal sites Benfer found Harris lines to be less frequent but more massive, suggesting fewer but greater bouts of stress.

Finally, recent reinterpretation of the archeological sequence of hunting and gathering populations in Australia enables us to begin to trace changing patterns of diet and health. Webb (1984) has compared rates of pathology among different prehistoric aboriginal groups. Unfortunately, Webb's samples can only occasionally be controlled for time-depth. He reports that one well-defined early sample from the terminal Pleistocene Period exhibits comparatively low rates of enamel hypoplasia and porotic hyperostosis compared to more recent groups. He also reports that rates of pathology of several kinds (infections, porotic hyperostosis, enamel hypoplasias) are relatively high in those recent populations that were thought to have lived in large, permanent (supposedly more civilized and affluent) settlements.

In short, although the data are mixed, the preponderance of existing evidence suggests that the Broad Spectrum Revolution was most often accompanied by declining stature, declining nutrition, and steady or increasing rates of episodic stress. Given F. Hassan's (1981) estimates of declining rates of population growth in the Mesolithic Period of the Old World (see below), this economic revolution may even have been associated with a temporary decline in reproductive success.

Paleopathology and the Adoption of Farming

When hunting and gathering populations are compared to subsequent farming populations in different parts of the world, studies are more numerous and samples are generally better. Most of the samples discussed below involve cemetery samples of natural populations rather than aggregates, and most involve samples of 100 to 200 or more individuals from each period compared. A number of trends emerge.

First, rates of infection and infectious disease observable on bone almost invariably seem to increase as human settlements increase in size and permanence. Quantitative trends can be observed for frequencies of non-specific skeletal lesions – periostitis and osteomyelitis (usually thought to be associated with staphylococcus and streptococcus bacteria) – as well as for specific infections such as treponematosis (yaws/syphilis) and tuberculosis.[7] Working with mummies from Peru, Allison (1984) has been able to show an increase in intestinal parasites associated with sedentism, although the mummies display no comparable increase in respiratory infection.

A second common trend is that farmers usually appear to have been less well nourished than the hunter-gatherers who preceded them. For example, rates of porotic hyperostosis are almost universally higher among farmers in a region than among earlier hunter-gatherers.[8] The increase in porotic hyperostosis after the adoption of agriculture was once commonly thought to represent a decline in the quality of the diet associated with cereal (particularly maize) agriculture (see, for example, El Najjar, 1977). Now, it is increasingly thought to represent anemia secondary to parasite infestation of one sort or another, alone or in combination with cereal diets and altered cooking techniques (D. C. Cook, 1984; Stuart-Macadam, 1986; Walker, 1986).

Other independent measures of nutrition are less widely reported but most often seem to suggest a decline in the quality of nutrition accompanying the adoption or intensification of agriculture. For example, bone cortical area and maintenance are often reduced among farmers in comparison to earlier hunter-gatherers in the same region (Cassidy, 1984; D. C. Cook, 1984; A. Goodman et al., 1984a; Nelson, 1984; Pfeiffer, 1984; Smith et al., 1984; Stout, 1978). Individual childhood growth is often retarded among farmers (D. C. Cook, 1984; A. Goodman et al., 1984a; Martin et al., 1984). The stature, size, and robusticity of adult individuals is often reduced (Angel, 1984; Haviland, 1967; Kennedy, 1984; Larsen, 1984; Meiklejohn et al., 1984; Nickens, 1976; Rose et al., 1984 for one of two regional comparisons; but cf. J. Rose et al. reporting on a second regional comparison, as well as Bridges, 1983; Saul, 1972). Specific skeletal dimensions such as pelvic inlet depth and skull base height are reduced among early farmers in Greece (Angel, 1984), and the size of deciduous teeth declines with the Advent of farming in Georgia over a time span too brief to reflect genetic evolution (Larsen, 1983). Incidentally, some specific vitamin and mineral deficiencies such as scurvy and rickets, which become common in the early civilized world or during medieval times, are remarkably infrequent among hunter-gatherers and early farmers as well. (Compare Meiklejohn et al., 1984, and Zivanovic, 1982.)

Most studies comparing rates of Harris lines in hunting and gathering and subsequent farming populations have found the lines to be more common in the earlier groups, apparently indicating that later populations experienced fewer bouts of biological stress (Cassidy, 1984; D. C. Cook, 1984; A. Goodman et al., 1984a; Perzigian et al., 1984; Rose et al., 1984; cf. Rathbun, 1984).

In contrast, enamel hypoplasias and microscopic enamel defects (Wilson bands) almost invariably are reported to have become more frequent and/or more severe as farming replaced hunting and gathering in different parts of the world.[9]

The apparent contradiction between hypoplasia and Harris line trends can be explained in one of several ways. One possibility is that the two stress indicators represent stress events of different cause, severity, or duration. Perhaps hunter-gatherers traded frequent mild stress events (recorded as Harris lines) for less frequent but severe stresses (recorded as hypoplasia) when they adopted sedentary agriculture. Cassidy (1984), for example, suggests that seasonal hunger may have been more frequent for hunter-gatherers, starvation and epidemics more frequent for prehistoric farmers.

A second possibility is that the different trends reflect the different age of development of teeth and long bones. Because teeth develop over a relatively short and early portion of the life span, hypoplasia rates are particularly sensitive to weaning age stress, which apparently increased with the adoption of sedentism and farming. Harris lines provide a more general record of stress episodes throughout childhood. However, two other differences need to be considered. First, as suggested above, Harris lines mark recovery from stress, not the stress itself. The dense line of bone is created by growth acceleration following the stress episode. In contrast, hypoplasia represents the stress itself. In theory, malnourished individuals would be less likely to record a Harris line than well-nourished individuals; and tests with rhesus monkeys seem to confirm that individuals with better background nutrition are more likely to record stress events in their bones (Murchison et al., 1983). Given other evidence that hunter-gatherers often were comparatively well nourished, their high Harris line frequency may reflect superior recovery rather than more frequent stress. In addition, Harris lines in bone are erased or remodeled during the subsequent growth of the individual. Hypoplasias are not. If farmers were more likely to resorb or remodel lines than hunter gatherers the contradiction would be explained. Cereal-based agriculture may in fact be associated with increased bone turnover (Stout, 1978) and with cortical thinning of bone as discussed above. This may explain the low rate of Harris lines in farming populations.

In short, various interpretations of these contradictory data are possible, but none implies that the adoption of agriculture was marked by a significant decline in episodic stress. Most suggest the contrary. Hypoplasia of deciduous ("baby") teeth represent stress in utero and therefore reflect maternal health and nutrition. Three studies explicitly compare rates of deciduous tooth hypoplasia between hunter-gatherers and later farmers in the same region: Cassidy (1984) found higher rates in farmers than in earlier hunter-gatherers in Kentucky; Sciulli also (1977) found higher rates among farmers than among hunter-gatherers in Ohio; Cook and Buikstra (1979), comparing hunter-gatherers and farmers in Illinois, found no difference in rates of hypoplasia but did suggest that stressed infants were more likely to die in the later group.

Paleopathology and the Emergence of Complex Societies

Although samples from recent complex societies — urban civilizations and complex chiefdoms — are potentially large and well preserved, health trends in these populations have as yet received less systematic attention than the health of early farmers. Existing studies suggest strikingly contradictory results. Angel (1984), for example, suggests that nutrition and health rebounded in Bronze Age Greece following the bottoming out of most health trends in the Neolithic Period, although he also notes that in the Bronze Age conspicuous health differences are to be found between kings and commoners. In contrast, Martin et al. (1984) and Rudney (1983) indicate that nutrition and health in Sudanese Nubia declined in proportion to the intensification of agriculture and the inclusion of Nubia in the sphere of larger political societies. They argue that Nubians may have lost more nutritionally than they gained during episodes of political unification. And Smith et al. (1984) observe that in the Levant signs of anemia, cortical thinning of bone, and enamel hypoplasia often appear most severe in Chalcolithic, Bronze Age and later Arab populations. In Europe, signs of infectious disease and nutritional stress are most common after the Iron Age (Meiklejohn et al., 1984; Steinbock, 1976; Wells, 1975; Zivanovic, 1982).

Among New World populations complex societies also display contradictory health patterns. D. C. Cook (1984), Buikstra (1984), and Buikstra and Van der Merwe (1986) suggest that Mississippian Period health (that is, the health of the most recent and largest prehistoric populations) was comparatively good in the Illinois Valley despite high rates of porotic hyperostosis, associated with the appearance of a "tuberculosis like" pathology that had not occurred earlier. Similarly, Powell (1984) found that Mississippian Period health was comparatively good at the major site of Moundville in Alabama, despite the common presence of low-grade infection; and Blakely (1977) found health to be good at Mississippian Period Etowah in Georgia. (However, Koerner and Blakely (1985) and Blakely and Brown (1985) have also reported that health and nutrition were not as good among commoners in relatively central — and predominantly agricultural — Etowah as among those living in the contemporary outlying — and predominantly hunter-gatherer — King site within the same political network.)

In contrast, A. Goodman et al. (1984a) suggest that almost all indicators point to a continuing decline of nutrition, health, and longevity extending into the Mississippian Period population at Dickson Mounds in Illinois. They attribute this in part to Dickson's marginal position in regional trade networks of the period. Other workers in the eastern United States have also reported high rates of biological stress of various kinds in Mississippian

Period sites (Cassidy, 1984; Eisenberg, 1985, 1986; Perzigian et al., 1984; Robbins, 1978; Storey, 1985). Stodder (1986) has recently reported that health and survivorship declined significantly in the later prehistory of the Anasazi Pueblo region of the American southwest.

In Mesoamerica, Rebecca Storey (1985) has reported exceptionally high levels of biological stress (involving maternal malnutrition, stillbirth, and fetal growth retardation) associated with urbanization at Teotihuacan, the great Mesoamerican metropolis. Also, in Mesoamerica, various sources (Haviland, 1967; Nickens, 1976; Saul, 1972) report a decline in stature and presumed increase in dietary stress continuing through the florescence of Mayan civilization − a decline apparently not shared by Mayan elites − and White (1986) has reported that the highest rates of porotic hyperostosis within the long sequence of the Mayan site of Lamanai in Belize occur during the most recent periods of the site's occupation.

What may be emerging in these data is a pattern of health and nutrition in the early civilizations sharply divided by class and location. Low social status and/or a weak position in the trade network appears to work against the health and nutrition of individuals. Large, urban settlements appear sometimes to benefit from trade and sometimes to act as foci of disease and malnutrition, in which case their populations − like those of historic European cities − display rates of pathology unequalled in earlier, less "civilized" groups.

Taken as a whole, the paleopathological data reviewed seem to suggest that the quality of nutrition declined (and/or the synergistic effects of infection and malnutrition increased) as hunter-gatherers became farmers in most parts of the world. The emergence of early civilizations appears to have had mixed effects at best, effects sharply partitioned by social class and trade. Neither ethnographic evidence nor archeological data support the common assumption that malnutrition or starvation were particularly common among early and/or "primitive" human groups.

Must the Slow Growth of Prehistoric Populations Reflect Malthusian Constraints?

As I suggested at the outset of the paper, the apparent slow growth of the human species is often assumed to reflect Malthusian constraints − starvation or disease − which we have only lately overcome. In order to evaluate this assumption it is necessary to review something of what is known about population growth rates and the factors that affect them.

Archeologists' estimates of world population in prehistory usually suggest that as recently as 10,000 years ago there may have been no more than 10 to 15 million people on earth (see, for example, F. Hassan, 1981). The implication is that, in the Old World at least, the species must have expanded very slowly, at a rate of less than 0.01 percent per year, in contrast to recent population growth of 1 or 2 percent per year or more. Hassan, for example, estimates that the human population grew at a rate of 0.01 percent per year during the Upper Paleolithic Period; grew at a rate of only 0.0033 percent per year during the Mesolithic; and accelerated to rates averaging 0.1 percent per year after the adoption of farming during the rise and decline of the early civilizations. (In contrast, the New World may have been peopled relatively rapidly.) We tend to assume that the very slow, early growth of population before the advent of agriculture must represent either extremely low average life expectancy or relatively frequent population crashes resulting from famine or epidemics.[10]

But the assumption of extremely high mortality — constant or sporadic — may be unfounded. Epidemic and even chronic disease would certainly have been a less serious risk for small isolated populations than for later, denser, sedentary communities linked by increasingly rapid trade (Black et al., 1974; Cohen and Armelagos, 1984; McNeill, 1975).[11] And neither the ethnographic observations nor the osteological evidence reviewed above shows a greater frequency of starvation in primitive than in civilized prehistoric populations. If mortality was indeed high in early groups, it may have been because the strains of mobility itself eliminated individuals. Given equal or even lower rates of trauma, malnutrition, or disease, the selective strain of mobility might have led to higher mortality than among the settled counterparts of mobile groups because less help could be given to the disabled. Observations of twentieth-century populations do find that mortality rates go down — at least temporarily — in spite of declining health and nutrition, when mobile groups settle down. (See Harpending and Wandsnider, 1982; Roth and Ray, 1985; cf. Hitchcock, 1982.) But judging by longer term trends visible in the archeological record, and discussed below, the advantages may rapidly be lost in face of other disadvantages associated with prolonged sedentism.

Mortality of Contemporary Hunter-Gatherers

In a landmark study of hunter-gatherer demography, Nancy Howell (1979) estimated that the !Kung San foragers of the Kalahari lost approximately 20 percent of their infants during the first year; lost 35 to 50 percent by age 15; and had life expectancies of 35 years overall at birth and of 35–40 years at age 15 — values that were surprisingly good by historic standards. (Life expectancy at birth, she suggested, had probably risen recently from a longer-term average value of 30 years.) A range of reports by other authors in other locations suggest that her figures for infant and child mortality, at least, are about average among hunter-gatherers (Cohen, 1989). These figures in turn are comparable to a large part of Europe in the eighteenth century, and much of the nineteeth century as well.

Estimated life expectancies at age 15 for other contemporary foraging groups are often lower, ranging from 20 to 40 years and averaging about 28 years (Cohen, 1989). These values are probably skewed downward by the marginal circumstances of modern groups (several of the best reported groups are Eskimo); and by the effects of historic and modern epidemic diseases spreading outward from civilization, the most commonly reported cause of death in "primitive" groups outside the arctic. Exogenous epidemic diseases should have a disproportionately great effect on adult mortality in isolated groups, which lack continuous exposure to the diseases so that immunity is not promoted in childhood. In any case, hunger does not appear to be a major cause of adult deaths outside the arctic.[12]

Estimates of life expectancy at birth for different modern foraging groups range from the 20s to 50. Combined averages for adult and childhood mortality suggest that life expectancy at birth in such groups averages between 25 and 30 years, a figure not as low by historic standards as we might expect.[13]

Paleodemographic Reconstruction of Prehistoric Groups

Direct reconstruction of paleodemography from prehistoric cemetery samples lends some further credence to the argument that population

Table 3.3   Life expectancy at birth (e_0^0)

Group	Source	Estimate of e_0^0
San	Howell, 1979	30–5
San	Tanaka, 1989	40
Andaman	Man, 1885	20[a]
Asmat	Van Arsdale, 1978	25
Hadza	Dyson, 1977	30
Australians	F. L. Jones, 1963	50
Pygmies	Cavalli-Sforza, 1986	17[b]
Pygmies	Turnbull, 1961, 1965	High[a]
New Guinea tribes[c]	Wood, 1988	26–35

[a] Casual observation.
[b] A population manifestly in negative growth.
[c] Isolated, highland, primarily horticultural tribes.

growth need not have been limited primarily by extremely high mortality prior to the origins of agriculture. Such reconstruction is difficult and fraught with potential sources of error or bias of three main types: cemetery populations may be an incomplete and biased sample of deaths in the community; the community from which they come may fail to meet the requirements for stable (let alone stationary) populations on which most modeling is based; and skeletal analysis permits only rough, relative aging of adult individuals and almost certainly underestimates older adult ages at death.[14]

These caveats notwithstanding, the largest and most complete samples at our disposal representing prehistoric hunter-gatherers display rates of infant mortality (ca. 20 percent) and overall child mortality before the age of 15 (ca. 40–50 percent) which are consistent with those recorded ethnographically among hunter-gatherers, moderate by historic standards, and often lower than those of subsequent prehistoric populations in the same regions.

There are a few archeological sites representing prehistoric hunting and gathering populations with large skeletal samples and large populations of children from which infant and child mortality can be calculated. In these samples, infant and child mortality rates appear to be relatively low (in keeping with the ethnographic values for hunter-gatherers reported above) and often lower than those of subsequent societies in the same or nearby locations (Buikstra and Mielke, 1985; Cassidy, 1984; A. Goodman et al., 1984; Lovejoy et al., 1977; Mensforth, 1985, 1986.)

In addition, despite the difficulty of aging adult skeletons, a great deal of fragmentary evidence hints that life expectancy at age 15 – or at least the average age at death of adults – although low among prehistoric huntergatherers, often is not strikingly low in relation to other prehistoric populations and may actually exceed that of later (and presumably faster-growing) groups. There is little to suggest that adult longevity improved when population growth accelerated with the adoption of farming.[15]

In the Old World, average adult ages at death generally appear to have declined in the Neolithic. Adult ages at death then often rebounded to higher levels during the Bronze Age and later times, although the later trend is irregular and improvements in adult life expectancy are not shared by many (particularly urban) areas (Acsadi and Nemeskeri, 1970; Angel, 1984; Weiss, 1973).[16] In the New World, adult ages at death also appear to decline with the adoption of farming but the rebound is less clearly evident.

In contrast to adult ages at death, there is no evidence either from archeological samples or from the comparison of archeological, ethnographic, and historical samples to suggest that child mortality improved over hunter-gatherer levels until relatively recent history.

Table 3.4 Observed infant and child mortality in New World prehistoric hunter-gatherer cemeteries (percent)

Site	Source	N	IMR	% infants[b] % children[b]
Indian Knoll, Kentucky	Cassidy, 1984	295	23	45
Indian Knoll, Kentucky	Johnston and Snow, 1961	1000	20	41–54
Eva/Cherry, Tennessee	Magennis, 1977	8–14	8–14	22–34
Libben, Ohio[a]	Lovejoy et al., 1977	1327	18	47
Carlston-Annis, Kentucky[a]	Mensforth, 1985	354	22	38
Carrier Mills, Illinois	Bassett, 1982	28	28	34
Klunk, Illinois	Asch, 1976	12	12	34
Dickson, Illinois[a]	A. Goodman et al., 1984	351	13	35
Illinois (Archaic)	Blakely, 1971	23	23	49
Illinois (Woodland)	Blakely, 1971	14	14	26

[a] sites treated by their excavators/analysts as complete representations of mortality — others are not.
[b] These numbers may under-represent childhood mortality if children are not brought faithfully to cemeteries; but along with the ethnographic observations described above they represent the only real data that we have on the loss of children by hunter-gatherers. Neither source (archaeology or ethnology) suggests extremely high rates of child mortality among these groups.

The Probable Balance of Fertility and Mortality Before the Neolithic Revolution

An alternate explanation of the slow growth of pre-farming populations — one which accords better with existing evidence — is that early human populations were naturally (or by regulation) low-fertility populations with only moderately high mortality. According to this model, population growth accelerated after the adoption of sedentism and farming because human fertility increased and/or different birth-control choices were made.

In her demographic study of the !Kung San, Howell (1979) calculated that San women had a low natural completed fertility, averaging only 4.6 children per woman who lived to complete reproduction. She calculated that given a relatively late age of menarchy and low observed fertility, the San would need to maintain a life expectancy of approximately 30 years at birth to prevent long-term population decline. (In contrast, a life expectancy of 20 years could balance modern Third World total fertility rates averaging about seven live births.)

If prehistoric hunter-gatherers produced on the average no more than 4–5 children on a schedule similar to that of the !Kung San, then they must have maintained an average life expectancy of 30 years at birth or more to have been as successful as they were, even if their populations never crashed. If we assume, in addition, that prehistoric populations were particularly susceptible to periodic crashes then they must in the normal course of things have enjoyed somewhat higher life expectancy for populations to grow even very slowly over the long run.

The key question is whether San fertility is typical of hunter-gatherers – a question that requires both theoretical and empirical evaluation. Low San fertility has been explained as a function of nursing patterns associated with hunter-gatherer activity and the absence of cereal gruels (Konner and Worthman, 1980; Lee, 1980). It has also been explained as a function of the exercise associated with the hunting and gathering life (Bentley, 1985) and as a function of low levels of body fat associated with lean diets and exercise (Howell, 1979, 1986). There is some evidence from other populations such as Australian Aborigines, African pygmies, and horticultural groups in highland New Guinea to suggest that one or more of these mechanisms may be at work (Bailey and Peacock, in press; Elphinstone, 1971). Whether any of these arguments could be applied by extrapolation to Pleistocene populations (or even to populations not inhabiting a desert and enjoying a richer, easier life than the San) is not clear.[17] On the other hand, there is ample suggestion that artificial means including abortion and infanticide are brought to bear to space children as necessary among the San and other hunter-gatherer groups (Birdsell, 1968; Dickeman, 1975; F. Hassan, 1981). Hassan, in particular, has argued that the adoption of farming increased the marginal utility of additional children, altering birth-control or infanticide decisions in favor of larger families.

Reports on a variety of other hunter-gatherers do suggest that completed fertility is most often of the order of 4–6 babies, although it is not always clear whether natural or controlled fertility is implied. Moreover, there are numerous indications that hunter-gatherer fertility is lower than that of their neighbors and/or rises as they become more sedentary.[18]

Some reports of fertility among hunter-gatherers, however, indicate higher values ranging up near modern Third World averages, including one population (the Agta of the Philippines) in which women are very active hunters (M. Goodman et al., 1985). These latter data seem to suggest that, although observed hunter-gatherer child production is often below world averages, there is no universal biological mechanism inherent in hunting and gathering per se that limits fertility to the San level. On the other hand, there is nothing in the data to suggest that hunter-gatherers enjoy extremely high fertility and could therefore have endured extremely low life expectancies, as some authors have suggested (Acsadi and Nemeskeri, 1970; C. Rose, 1960, 1968).

In sum, it cannot be proved that natural low fertility comparable to that of the !Kung San characterized early human populations. But observed hunter-gatherer groups do seem to have average rates of child production somewhat below modern Third World averages; and given observed average child production of fewer than seven children among hunter-gatherers, life expectancy at birth probably averaged more than 20 years.

The extant data (ethnographically observed fertility and mortality, and fragments from paleodemography including the relatively higher adult ages at death among hunter-gatherers than early farmers) are consistent with the assumption that fairly low fertility, below modern Third World levels, in combination with moderately high mortality – life expectancy at birth of 25–30 years – restrained the growth of early prehistoric groups. Population growth appears to have accelerated with the adoption of farming more as a function of increased fertility than of reduced mortality.

Summary and Conclusion

I have suggested that a critical look at the social revolutions leading to civilization need not imply improvements in human nutrition or in the capacity of our species to buffer itself against hunger and starvation. I have also suggested that the problem is an empirical one which can only be approached by triangulation from two different and admittedly imperfect sources of data: ethnographic examples of contemporary hunter-gatherers and archeological evidence of prehistoric starvation and malnutrition. The ethnographic evidence suggests that the simplest human societies enjoy varied and generally well-balanced diets, in which caloric intake is moderate to low by our standards but protein and vitamin intake are commonly healthy. Clinical signs of malnutrition are in fact relatively rare. Under-nutrition may be more common, and hunger and starvation undoubtedly occur, but they occur primarily in extreme environments such as deserts or the arctic in which other populations do not even attempt to survive. There is no evidence that hunger is regularly a bigger problem for hunter-gatherers than for more sedentary populations in similar environments.

The archeological evidence also suggests that qualitative nutrition was relatively good in the earliest hunter-gatherer populations in any region, more commonly declining than improving with agriculture. The effects of civilization appear to be mixed and patchy, dependent on social class and one's position in the trade network. Seasonal hunger (represented by Harris lines in the skeleton) may have become less common after the appearance of agriculture – unless the Harris lines are misleading. More severe stresses represented by enamel defects of teeth commonly appear to have become more common in later prehistory.

Evidence on the fertility and mortality of living hunter-gatherers and fragmentary evidence from skeletons suggests that we need not rely on the assumption of extremely high mortality (constant or cyclic) to explain the slow early growth of the human population. The data summarized best fit the assumption that early human groups were relatively well nourished (although with a different balance of calories and other nutrients to that we obtain) and well buffered against starvation, their numbers being limited as much by low fertility as by starvation or other Malthusian checks.

NOTES

1 For example, the adoption of domestic crops sometimes precedes, sometimes follows the adoption of sedentism; and some populations such as the Indians of California achieved many of the trappings of large and complex society ("civilization") by utilizing plentiful wild resources which they never managed to domesticate. See Fagan, 1986; Price and Brown, 1985.

2 Efficiency tests of the type referred to above suggest that these improvements in weapons may not offset the loss of efficiency associated with the decline of larger game. Hunting large animals with spears appears to be more efficient in terms of caloric returns for time spent than hunting small animals with nets, snares, bow, blow-guns, and in some cases even primitive firearms. Hunting large game is also more efficient than getting and processing most vegetable foods, particularly small seeds such as cereals. For a more complete review see Cohen, 1987, 1989.

3 For Africa see: Bailey and Peacock, in press; Blackburn, 1982; Harakao, 1981; Ichikawa, 1983; Lee, 1968; Metz et al., 1971; Tanaka, 1980; Woodburn, 1968. For India see: ARNIN, 1969; Bose, 1964; Dutta, 1978; Furer-Haimendorf, 1943; Gardner, 1972; Man, 1885; Morris, 1982; Radcliffe-Brown, 1984; but cf. B. J. Williams, 1974. For southeast Asia see: Dunn, 1975; K. Endicott, 1979; K. L. Endicott, 1980; Schebesta, 1928. For the Philippines see: Bion Griffin, 1984; Eder, 1978; J. T. Peterson, 1981. For Australia see: Bonwick, 1870; C. E. Cook, 1970; Curr, 1886; Eyre, 1845; Gould, 1967; C. W. Hart and Pilling, 1964; Hodgkinson, 1845, R. Jones, 1980; Lumholtz, 1889; McArthur, 1960; McBryde, 1978; McCarthy and McArthur, 1960; Meehan, 1977a, 1977b; Moore, 1979; O'Connell and Hawkes, 1981; Spencer and Gillen, 1927; Thomson, 1975; Tonkinson, 1978; Turner, 1974; Warner, 1937. For South America see: Flowers, 1983; Hawkes et al., 1982; Hill and Hawkes, 1983; Holmberg, 1969.

4 For Africa see: Hitchcock, 1982; Jelliffe et al., 1962; Metz et al., 1971; Silberbauer, 1981; Truswell and Hansen, 1976; but cf. Tobias, 1966. For India see ARNIN, 1969. For Australia see: Curnow, 1957; Davidson, 1957; Davis et al., 1957; Elphinstone, 1971; Wilkinson et al., 1958; but cf. Gould, 1969b. Compare descriptions of Third-World populations by: Basta, 1977; N. Hassan and Ahmad, 1984; May, 1970.

Hunger in Prehistoric Societies

5 However, low caloric intake can hardly explain the small size of the Hadza reported by Woodburn (1968) and by Hawkes and O'Connell (personal communication), who are clearly well fed; nor that of the Ache (Hawkes et al., 1982), who eat enormous amounts of food. (See table 3.1.)

6 See also ARNIN, 1969; Blackburn, 1982; Bonwick, 1870; Bose, 1964; Cook, 1970; Dunn, 1975; K. L. Endicott, 1980; Eyre, 1845; Flowers, 1983; Furer-Haimendorf, 1943; Gardner, 1972; Goodale, 1970; Hart and Pilling, 1969; Hill, et al., 1984; Hodgkinson, 1845; Hurtado and Hill, 1987; McBryde, 1978; Marshall, 1976; Morris, 1982; O'Connell and Hawkes, 1981; Radcliffe-Brown, 1948; Schebesta, 1928; Silberbauer, 1981; Spencer and Gillen, 1927; Tanaka, 1980; Thomson, 1975; Tonkinson, 1978; Turnbull, 1961, 1965, 1983.

7 For rates of infection in prehistoric populations in the New World, see: Cassidy, 1984; D. C. Cook, 1984; A. Goodman et al., 1984a; Hartney, 1981; Norr, 1984; Perzigian et al., 1984; Pfeiffer, 1984; Robbins, 1978; J. Rose et al., 1984; Ubelaker, 1984. For the Old World; see: Bennike, 1985; Meiklejohn et al., 1984; Zivanovic, 1982; cf. Rathbun, 1984.

8 For rates of porotic hyperostosis in prehistoric populations in the New World, see: Cassidy, 1984; D. C. Cook, 1984; A. Goodman et al., 1984a; Norr, 1984; Palkovich, 1984 (cf. Walker, 1985); Perzigian et al., 1984; Smith et al., 1984. For the Old World, see: Angel, 1984. In Europe porotic hyperostosis does not become common until the Bronze Age or later (Meikeljohn et al., 1984; cf. Grauer, 1984; Steinbock, 1976.)

9 For rates of enamel hypoplasia/enamel defects in prehistoric populations in the New World, see: Allison, 1984; Cassidy, 1984; D. C. Cook, 1984; A. Goodman et al., 1984a; Perzigian et al., 1984; Rose and Boyd, 1978; Sciulli, 1978; Ubelaker, 1984. For the Old World, see: Angel, 1984; Brothwell, 1963; Kennedy, 1984; but cf. Molnar and Molnar, 1985; Smith et al., 1984 and Y'edynak and Fleisch, 1983.

10 Arguing against the presumption of constant high mortality and slow growth among prehistoric populations, Ammerman (1974) suggested that population crashes among primitive populations might occur as a result of high rates of environmental stress and resource failure, an explanation that does not appear to fit the evidence available (although it might better apply to an ice-age environment in which a large proportion of the human species lived in arctic or subarctic conditions). He also pointed out, however, that very small populations might crash purely as a result of random demographic fluctuations (such as freak sex ratios or coincidental deaths of key individuals), a kind of demographic "drift" associated with very small group size but independent of exogenous stresses.

11 However, A. Goodman et al. (1975) suggested that zoonotic diseases might have played a role in limiting prehistoric populations. These diseases, carried by animals and only accidentally transmitted to human hosts, are likely to have been infrequent in occurrence compared to community-borne diseases; but they are likely to have had severe consequences once contracted. Diseases which normally coexist with a specific host become adapted to that host and

the virulence of their attack declines. Diseases which are accidentally introduced to a new host often have devastating effects. Moreover, given the small size of hunter-gatherer groups, the accidental infection of one productive adult might have had disproportionately negative effects on the rest of the group. (See the description by Elphinstone (1971) of a group of Australian Aborigines that had lost some of its able hunters.)

12 Howell (1979) and Laughlin et al. (1979), among others, note the major importance of infectious disease (much of it epidemic disease exogenous to isolated groups) as a cause of deaths recorded. Laughlin also notes that adult life expectancy among Aleuts declined significantly from the time of the first records in the nineteenth century until the middle of the twentieth century, a trend he associated with exogenous diseases. Most observations cited (done since the nineteenth century) were clearly undertaken in populations already significantly exposed to such diseases.

13 e_0^0 of 25 to 30 years is well above the figure considered minimally necessary to maintain a population in modern times. It is considerably over that of India in 1920; and not markedly below much of Europe as late as the eighteenth century. A life expectancy at birth of 25 to 30 years appears to be made up of a different balance of childhood and adult mortality to that normally recognized in historic populations.

14 Problems in paleodemographic analysis are debated by Boquet-Appel and Masset, 1982, 1985; Buikstra and Konigsberg, 1985; F. Hassan, 1981; Howell, 1982; Lovejoy et al., 1977; Sattenspiel and Harpending, 1983; Van Gerven and Armelagos, 1983. Hassan and Bocquet-Appel and Masset, in particular, argue for the underestimation of adult ages at death.

Sattenspiel and Harpending point out that if population growth rates accelerate, the average age at death in a cemetery will go down even if there is no change in mortality or individual life expectancy. Accelerating population growth means that each new cohort of babies is larger than the last and each cohort therefore has more individuals at risk of death. Even if the percentages of each age who die remain the same, the larger cohorts will account for an increasing proportion of the cemetery, producing a declining average age at death.

For this reason, in any one cemetery an apparent decline in average age at death could paradoxically reflect an increase in fertility, not a change in mortality. However, to have a noticeable effect on average age at death the acceleration of population growth has to be fairly marked (far greater than the average acceleration from near zero to 0.1 percent per year growth postulated for the Neolithic – see tables in Coale and Demeny, 1983). Since the perceived decline in average age at death in the Neolithic is so widespread (involving so many populations which must, in sum, have accelerated only by this small average amount) it seems unlikely that the pattern can be explained entirely by this mechanism. Some real increase in mortality and decline in life expectancy must also have occurred.

15 Estimates of adult age at death from skeletons are notoriously crude. Many paleodemographers agree that we have difficulty recognizing older adults.

Because the aging of adult skeletons measures progressive degeneration rather than genetically programmed growth, we have a better sense of relative age than absolute age. Probably for these reasons estimates of average adult age at death or adult life expectancy are consistently lower in archeological samples than in comparable samples from ethnographic reports, and archeological life tables may fail to match those of historic groups. Moreover they appear to be unrealistically low (see, for example, F. Hassan, 1981; Howell, 1982; Weiss, 1973: cf. Lovejoy et al., 1977; Mensforth, 1985, 1986). They are primarily valuable for comparison to each other. Moreover, because aging skeletons involves some subjectivity, the best comparisons are those in which the same individual or team has made age estimates on two or more populations. As an example of the relative ages at death, Angel (1984) suggests an average value for adult age at death of 35 years (m) and 31 (f) for paleolithic populations. But his estimates for later Neolithic farming groups are only 33 and 29. Bronze Age values are only slightly higher (high 30s, low 40s), and for the period between 1400 and 1800 AD his estimates of average age at death are below those of the Paleolithic, at 34 (m) and 28−31 (f).

At Dickson Mounds, Illinois, A. Goodman et al. (1984) suggest the earlier hunter-gatherer population had an expectation of life at age 15 of a further 23 years; in the later agricultural population at the site, e_{15}^0 was only 18 years. In Kentucky, Cassidy (1984) has suggested that an archaic (hunting and gathering) population had an expectation of life at age 15 of 20 years (m) and 18 years (f), whereas a later agricultural population had e_{15}^0 of 14 years (m) and 16 (f). In Georgia the average age at death for adults dropped from about 31 years to about 26 years with the adoption of farming, according to figures provided by Larsen (1984).

Welinder (1979) reports that in Scandanavia life expectancy at age 15 dropped from 25−6 years to 13−20 years with the adoption of farming. Kobayashi (1967) suggests a two- to five-year drop in the average age at death with the adoption of rice farming in Japan. Kennedy (1984) is less explicit in describing a decline in adult ages at death with the advent of farming in India.

In more eclectic samples, Acsadi and Nemeskeri (1970) report life expectancies at age 20 of 24, 27, and 36 years for men and 17 and 23 years for women in Old World pre-Neolithic (that is, hunting and gathering) populations; and of 16 and 21 for men, 14 and 17 for women, in Neolithic (early farming) populations. The same authors suggest that Copper Age populations had e_{20}^0 of 27−9 (m) and 21−7 (f); Bronze Age values were 22−6 (m) and 18−20 (f); and Iron Age values are given as 32 years (m and f).

Weiss (1973) reports e_{15}^0 of 15, 16, and 17 years for pre-Neolithic populations and of 12, 14, 15, 15, 17, and 29 for Neolithic populations. Among Copper Age populations he reports values of 13, 21, 18, and 23 years. For Ancient Greece he suggests a value for e_{15}^0 of 22 years and for Roman Britain a value of 24 years. Yugoslavia and Hungary in the tenth to twelfth centuries had e_{15}^0 of 31−2 years. However, a sample from medieval Sweden had a life expectancy at age 15 of only 17 years.

While noting that adult ages are likely to be underestimated in archeological samples, F. Hassan (1981) argues that prehistoric populations are unlikely to have exceeded contemporary hunter-gatherers in life expectancy. He cites an average e^0_{15} of 26 years for contemporary hunter-gatherers, based on figures provided by Weiss which did not include the higher San, Hadza, and Aleut values subsequently reported. I would argue contrary to Hassan that prehistoric groups are likely to have outlived their modern counter-parts and that archeological age estimates are even more misleading than he believes. I suggest this for several reasons: the contemporary examples (especially those available to Weiss) live in marginal environments; they are living in areas in which the richest resources, large game, are largely depleted; their tools are not markedly more efficient than Stone Age counterparts; and, most important, they are exposed to a variety of epidemic diseases that would not have affected their forebears.

16 In European cities, life expectancies often remained at Stone Age levels. Acsadi and Nemeskeri (1970) estimate the e^0_0 was 15 to 16 years in Ancient Rome and that e^0_{20} was an additional 15 to 20 years. Weiss (1973) suggests that e^0_{15} in Classical Athens was about 19 years, only slightly higher than his estimates from archeological samples for the Paleolithic and well below the average he reports for contemporary hunter-gatherers.

17 If low caloric consumption returns and/or high rates of activity are associated with low rates of fertility among contemporary hunter-gatherers, we cannot necessarily assume that the same applied in the past (cf. Howell, 1986). The evidence cited above for diminishing returns for labor and declining nutrition in the Mesolithic period suggests that human fertility might have been restricted by these means in the Mesolithic (perhaps explaining the declining population growth rate postulated by F. Hassan, 1981). But it also suggests that similar mechanisms would not have worked among earlier, apparently better-nourished Paleolithic populations. If, however, the spacing of children among hunter-gatherers is associated with nursing and the difficulties of weaning a child without domestic cereals, tubers, or animal milk, or is associated with the difficulty of carrying young children on foraging rounds, or with the low marginal utility of children among foragers, then the arguments would apply equally to earlier prehistory.

18 A number of sources suggest that hunter-gatherer fertility goes up when they become sedentary or that the fertility of neighboring sedentary populations is higher than that of mobile groups. See Hitchcock, 1982; Howell, 1979: but cf. Harpending and Wandsnider, 1982. See also Binford and Chasko, 1976; Gomes, 1978; Hill et al., 1984; F. L. Jones, 1963; Roth and Ray, 1985; Serjeantson, 1975; Sharp, 1940. For discussion see also Handwerker, 1983; Roth, 1985; Roth and Ray, 1985; cf. Early, 1985; Campbell and Wood, in press.)

REFERENCES

Acsadi, Gy. and Nemeskeri, J. 1970: *History of Human Lifespan and Mortality.* Budapest: Akademei Kiado.

Allen, Harry 1974: The Bagundji of the Darling Basin. *World Archaeology*, 5, 309–22.

Allison, Marvin 1984: Paleopathology in Chilean and Peruvian populations. In Cohen and Armelagos (1984), 515–30.

Ammerman, A. J. 1975: Late Pleistocene population dynamics: An alternate view *Human Ecology*, 3, 310–34.

Angel, J. L. 1984: Health as a crucial factor in the changes from hunting to developed farming in the Mediterranean. In Cohen and Armelagos (1984), 51–74.

Annegers, J. E. 1973: Seasonal food shortages in West Africa. *Ecology of Food and Nutrition*, 2, 251–8.

ARNIN 1969: Health Survey of the Onge tribe on the Andaman and Nicobar Islands. *Annual Report of the National Institute for Nutrition*, 99–100.

Asch, D. L. 1976: *The Middle Woodland Population of the Lower Illinois Valley: A Study in Paleodemographic Method.* Evanston: Northwestern University Archaeological Program Scientific Papers No. 1.

Bailey, R. C. and Peacock N. in press: Efe pygmies of northeast Zaire: subsistence strategies in the Ituri Forest. In I. de Garine and G.A. Harrison (eds), *Uncertainty in the Food Supply*, Cambridge: Cambridge University Press.

Basedow, Herbert 1925: *The Australian Aboriginal.* Adelaide: F. W. Preece and Sons.

Bassett, F. 1982: Osteological analysis of Carrier Mills burials. In R. Jeffries and B. Butler (eds), *The Carrier Mills Archaeological Project*, Carbondale: Southern Illinois University Center for Archaeological Investigations, Research Paper 33, 1029–114.

Basta, S. S. 1977: Nutrition and health in low income urban areas of the Third World. *Ecology of Food and Nutrition*, 6, 113–24.

Beisel, W. R. 1982: Synergisms and antagonisms of parasitic diseases and malnutrition. *Review of Infectious Diseases*, 4, 746–55.

Benfer, Robert 1984: The challenges and rewards of sedentism: The preceramic village of Paloma, Peru. In Cohen and Armelagos (1984), 531–58.

Benfer, Robert 1986: Middle and Late Archaic adaptation in Central Coastal Peru. Paper presented to the Annual Meeting of the Society for American Archaeology, New Orleans.

Bengtsson, T. et al. 1984: *Preindustrial Population Change.* Stockholm: Almquist and Wiksell.

Bennike, Pia 1985: *Paleopathology of Danish Skeletons.* Copenhagen: Academisk Forlag.

Bentley, G. 1985: Hunter-gatherer energetics and fertility: A reassessment of the !Kung San. *Human Ecology*, 45, 243–72.

Binford, L. R. and Chasko, W. J. 1976: Nunamiut demographic history, a provocative case. In E. Zubrow (ed.), *Demographic Anthropology*, Albuquerque: University of New Mexico, 63–144.

Bion Griffin, P. 1984: Forager resource and land use in the humid tropics: The Agta of Northeastern Luzon, the Philippines. In Schrire (1984), 95–122.

Birdsell, Joseph 1968: Some predictions for the Pleistocene based on equilibrium studies among recent hunter gatherers. In Lee and Devore (1968), 229–40.

Black, F. L. 1975: Infectious diseases in primitive societies. *Science*, 187, 515–18.

Black, F. L. et al. 1974: Evidence for persistence of infectious agents in isolated human populations. *American Journal of Epidemiology*, 100, 230–50.

Blackburn, Roderic H. 1982: In the land of milk and honey: Okiek adaptations to their forests and neighbors. In Leacock and Lee (1982), 283–306.

Blakely, Robert 1971: Comparison of mortality profiles of Archaic, Middle Woodland, and Middle Mississippian populations. *American Journal of Physical Anthropology*, 34, 43–54.

Blakely, Robert 1977: Sociocultural implications of demographic data from Etowah, Georgia. *Proceedings of the Southern Anthropological Society*, 11, 45–66.

Blakely, Robert and Brown, A. B. 1985: Functionally adaptive biocultural diversity in the Coosa chiefdom of 16th century Georgia. *American Journal of Physical Anthropology*, 66, 146.

Blakely, R. L. and Detweiler, B. 1986: Odontological evidence of differential stress at the King and Etowah sites in 16th century Georgia. *American Journal of Physical Anthropology*, 69, 176

Bleek, D. F. 1928: *The Naron*. Cambridge: Cambridge University Press.

Bonwick, James 1870: *Daily Life and the Origins of the Tasmanians*. London: Samson, Low.

Boquet-Appel, J.–P. and Masset, C. 1982: Farewell to Paleodemography. *Journal of Human Evolution*, 11, 321–33.

Boquet-Appel, J.–P. and Masset, C. 1985: Paleopathology: Resurrection or ghost. *Journal of Human Evolution*, 14, 107–111.

Bose, Saradindu 1964: The economy of the Onge of little Andaman. *Man in India*, 44, 298–310.

Boserup, Ester 1965: *The Conditions of Agricultural Growth*. Chicago: Aldine.

Boyden, S. V. (ed.) 1970: *The Impact of Civilization on the Biology of Man*. Canberra: Australian National University.

Bridges, Patricia 1983: Subsistence activity and biomechanical properties of long bones in two Amerindian populations. *American Journal of Physical Anthropology*, 60, 177.

Bronte-Steward, B., Budtz-Olsen, D. E., Hickley, J. M., and Brock, J. F. 1960: The health and nutritional status of the !Kung Bushmen of southwest Africa. *South African Journal of Laboratory and Clinical Medicine*, 6, 188–216.

Brothwell, D. R. 1963: Macroscopic dental pathology of some earlier human populations. In D. R. Brothwell (ed.), *Dental Anthropology*, Oxford: Pergamon, 271–88.

Brunt, P. A. 1971: *Italian Manpower 225 BC to 14 AD*. Oxford: Clarendon.

Buikstra, Jane (ed.) 1981: *Prehistoric Tuberculosis in the Americas*. Northwestern University Archaeological Program Scientific Papers, No. 5.

Buikstra, Jane 1984: The Lower Illinois river region as a prehistoric context for study of diet and health. In Cohen and Armelagos (1984), 217–36.

Buikstra, Jane and Cook, D. C. 1980: Paleopathology: An American account. *Annual Review of Anthropology* 9, 433–70.

Buikstra, Jane and Konigsberg, L. 1985: Paleodemography: Critiques and controversies. *American Anthropologist*, 87, 316–33.

Buikstra, Jane and Mielke, James, 1985: Demography, diet and health. In Gilbert and Mielke (1985), 360–422.

Buikstra, J. and Van der Merwe, N. 1986: Diet, demography and health: Human adaptation and maize agriculture in the Eastern Woodlands. Paper presented to the Nineteenth Chacmool Conference, University of Calgary.

Buikstra, J., Konigsberg, L. and Bullington, J. 1985: Diet sedentism and demographic change: The identification of key variables. *American Journal of Physical Anthropology*, 66, 151.

Bunting, A. H. 1970: *Change in Agriculture*. London: Duckworth.

Campbell, K. and Wood, J. W. in press: Fertility in traditional societies. To appear in P. Diggory, M. Potts, and S. Teper (eds), *Natural Human Fertility: Social and Biological Mechanisms*. London: Macmillan.

Carr-Saunders, A. M. 1922: *The Population Problem*. Oxford: Clarendon.

Cassidy, C. M. 1984: Skeletal evidence for prehistoric subsistence adaptation in the central Ohio River Valley. In Cohen and Armelagos (1984), 307–46.

Cavalli-Sforza, L. L. 1986: *African Pygmies*. New York: Academic.

Chafkin, S. H. and Berg, A. D. 1975: The innocent bystander: Some observations on the impact of international financial forces on nutrition. *Ecology of Food and Nutrition*, 4, 1–4.

Childe, V. G. 1950: *Man Makes Himself.* New York: Mentor.

CIBA 1977: *Health and Disease in Tribal Societies*. Amsterdam: Elsevier.

Clark, Colin and Haswell, Margaret 1970: *The Economics of Subsistence Agriculture*. London: Macmillan, fourth edition.

Cleland, Burton 1930: Notes on pathological lesions and vital statistics of Australian natives in Central Australia. Adelaide University Collected Papers, No. 6, reprinted from *Medical Journal of Australia*.

Coale, A. and Demeny, P. 1983: *Regional Model Life Tables and Stable Populations*. New York: Academic, second edition.

Cockburn, T. A. 1971: Infectious diseases in ancient populations. *Current Anthropology*, 12, 45–62.

Cohen, M. N. 1977: *The Food Crisis in Prehistory*. New Haven: Yale University Press.

Cohen, M. N. 1987: The significance of long term changes in human diet and food economy. In M. Harris and E. Ross (eds), *Food*, Philadelphia: Temple University Press, 261–84.

Cohen, M. N. 1989: *Health and the Rise of Civilization*. New Haven: Yale University Press.

Cohen, M. N. and Armelagos, G. J. (eds) 1984: *Paleopathology at the Origins of Agriculture*. New York: Academic.

Colchester, Marcus 1982: The economy, ecology and ethnohistory of the Sanema Indians of Southern Venezuela. Oxford University: unpublished dissertation.

Condran, G. A. and Crimmins-Gardner, E. 1978: Public health measures and mortality in U.S. cities in the late 19th century. *Human Ecology*, 6, 27–54.

Cook, C. E. 1970: Notable changes in the incidence of disease in Northern Territory Aborigines. In A. Pilling and R. Waterman (eds), *Diptrodon to Detribalization*, Lansing: Michigan State University Press, 116–50.

Cook D. C. 1984: Subsistence and health in the lower Illinois Valley: Osteological evidence. In Cohen and Armelagos (1984), 237–70.

Cook, D. C. and Buikstra, J. 1979: Health and differential survival in prehistoric populations: Prenatal dental defects. *AJOA*, 51, 649–64.

Cowlishaw, G. 1982: Family planning: A post contact problem. In J. Reid (ed.), *Body, Land and Spirit: Health and Healing in Aboriginal society*, St. Lucia: University of Queensland Press, 31–48.

Curnow, D. H. 1957: The serum protein of Aborigines in the Warburton Range area. *Medical Journal of Australia*, 2, 608–9.

Curr, E. M. 1886: *The Australian Race*. Melbourne: J. Ferres.

Dando, W. A. 1976: Man made famine: Some geographical insights from an exploratory study of a millennium of Russian famines. *Ecology of Food and Nutrition*, 4, 219–34.

Davidson, W. S. 1957: Health and nutrition of Warburton Range natives of Central Australia. *Medical Journal of Australia*.

Davis, R. E. et al. 1975: Some hematological observations on aborigines in the Warburton Range area. *Medical Journal of Australia*, 2, 605–10.

Dennett, Glenn and Connell, John 1988: Acculturation and health in the Highlands of New Guinea. *Current Anthropology*, 29, 273–99.

Dickel, David 1985: Growth stress and central California pre-historic subsistence shifts. *American Journal of Physical Anthropology*, 63, 152.

Dickel, David, Schulz, P. O., and McHenry, H. M. 1984: Central California: Prehistoric subsistence changes and health. In Cohen and Armelagos (1984), 439–62.

Dickeman, Mildred 1975: Demographic consequences of infanticide. *Annual Review of Ecology and Systematics*, 11, 107–38.

Draper, H. H. 1977: The aboriginal Eskimo diet. *American Anthropologist*, 79, 309–16.

Dunn, F. L. 1975: *Rainforest Collectors and Traders*. Kuala Lumpur: Royal Asiatic Society of Malaysia.

Dutta, P. C. 1978: *The Great Andamanese*. Calcutta: Anthropological Survey of India.

Dyson, Tim 1977: The demography of the Hadza in historical perspective. *African Historical Demography* (proceedings of a seminar at the University of Edinburgh Centre for African Studies), 139–54.

Early, John D. 1985: Low forager fertility: Demographic characteristic or methodological artifact. *Human Biology*, 57, 387–99.

Eder, James F. 1978: The caloric returns to food collecting: Disruption and change among the Batek of the Philippine tropical forests. *Human Ecology*, 6, 55–69.

Eisenberg, L. E. 1985: Bioarchaeological perspectives on diseases in a "marginal"

Mississippian population. *American Journal of Physical Anthropology*, 66, 166–7.

Eisenberg, L. E. 1986: The patterning of trauma at Averbuch: Activity levels and conflict during the late Mississippian. *American Journal of Physical Anthropology*, 69, 197.

El Najjar, M. Y. 1977: Maize, malarias and the anemias in the pre-Columbian New World. Yearbook of *Physical Anthropology*, 28, 329–37.

Elphinstone, J. J. 1971: The health of aborigines with no previous association with Europeans. *Medical Journal of Australia*, 2, 293–303.

Endicott, Karen L. 1980: *Batek Negrito Sex roles: Behavior and Ideology*. Lavalle: Second International Congress on Hunter Gatherers, 625–70.

Endicott, Kirk 1979: *Batek Negrito Religion*. Oxford: Clarendon.

Evans, I. 1937: *The Negritos of Malaya*. Cambridge: Cambridge University Press.

Eyre, E. J. 1845: *Journals of Expeditions of Discovery into Central Australia and Overland from Adelaide to King George's Sound*. London: T. and W. Boone.

Fagan, Brian 1986: *People of the Earth*. Boston: Little Brown.

Fenner, Frank 1970: The effects of changing social organization on the infectious diseases of man. In Boyden (1970), 48–76.

Flinn, Michael 1981: *The European Demographic System*. Baltimore: Johns Hopkins.

Flood, Josephine 1976: *The Moth Hunters*. Canberra: Australian Institute for Aboriginal Studies.

Flowers, Nancy M. 1983: Seasonal factors in subsistence, nutrition and child growth in a central Brazilian Indian community. In Hames and Vickers (1983), 357–90.

Frayer, David 1981: Body size, weapon use and natural selection in the European upper paleolithic and mesolithic. *American Anthropologist*, 83, 57–73.

Fried, Morton 1967: *The Evolution of Political Society*. New York: Random House.

Furer-Haimendorf, C. von 1943: *The Chenchus*. London: Macmillan.

Gardner, P. M. 1972: The Paliyans. In M. Bicchieri (ed.), *Hunters and Gatherers Today*, New York: Holt Rinehart, 404–47.

Gaulin, Stephen and Konner, Melvin 1977: On the natural diet of primates including humans. In R. J. Wurtman and J. J. Wurman (eds), *Nutrition and the Brain Vol. 1*, New York: Raven.

Gilbert, R. I. and Mielke, J. 1985. (eds) *The Analysis of Prehistoric Diets*. New York: Academic.

Gomes, Albert 1978: Demographic and environmental adaptations: A comparative study of two aboriginal populations in west Malaysia. Kuala Lumpur: SEAPRAP Research Report No. 35.

Goodale, J. C. 1970: An example of ritual change among the Tiwi of Melville Island. In Pilling and Waterman.

Goodman, A., Lallo, J., and Armelagos, G. J. 1975: The role of infectious and nutritional diseases in population growth. Paper presented to the 74th annual meeting of the American Anthropological Association.

Goodman, A. et al. 1984a: Health changes at Dickson Mounds, Illinois (AD 950–1300). In Cohen and Armelagos (1984), 271–306.

Goodman, A., Martin, D., Armelagos, G., and Clark, G. 1984b: Indications of stress from bone and teeth. In Cohen and Armelagos (1984), 13–50.

Goodman, Madeleine et al. 1985: Menarche, pregnancy, birth spacing and menopause among the Agta women foragers of Cagayan Province, Luzon, the Philippines. *Ann. Hum. Biol.*, 12, 169–78.

Goubert, P. 1984: Public hygiene and mortality decline in France in the nineteenth century. In Bengtsson et al. (1984), 151–60.

Gould, Richard 1967: Notes on hunting, butchering and sharing of game among the Ngatatjara and their neighbors in the Western Central Desert. Kroeber Anthropological Society Papers, 56, 41–66.

Gould, Richard A. 1969a: Subsistence behavior among the Western Desert Aborigines of Australia. *Oceania*, XXXIX, 253–74.

Gould Richard A. 1969b: *Yiwara: Foragers of the Australian Desert*. New York: Chas. Scriberners Sons.

Gould, Richard A. 1982: Comparative ecology of food sharing in Australia and Northwest California. In Harding and Teleki (1982), 422–54.

Grauer, Anne 1984: Health and disease in an Anglo Saxon cemetery population from Raunds, Northamptonshire, England. *American Journal of Physical Anthropology*, 63, 166.

Grey, Sir George 1841: *Journals of Two Expeditions of Discovery in North-west and Western Australia, During the Years 1837, 1838, and 1839*. London: Boone.

Hames, R. B. and Vickers, W. T. (eds) 1983: *The Adaptive Responses of Native Americans*. New York: Academic.

Handwerker, W. P. 1983: The first demographic transition: Analysis of subsistence changes and reproductive consequences. *American Anthropologist*, 85, 5–27.

Harakao, Reizo, 1981. The cultural ecology of hunting behavior among Mbuti pygmies in the Ituri Forest, Zaire. In Harding and Teleki, (1981), 499–555.

Harding, R. S. O. and Teleki, G. (eds) 1981: *Omnivorous Primates*. New York: Columbia University Press.

Harlan, Jack 1967: A wild wheat harvest in Turkey. *Archaeology*, 20, 197–201.

Harpending, H. C. 1976: Regional variation in !Kung Populations. In Lee and Devore (1976), 152–65.

Harpending, H. C. and Wandsnider, L. 1982: Population structures of Ghanzi and Hgamiland !Kung. In M. H. Crawford and J. H. Mielke (eds), *Current Developments in Anthropological Genetics*. Vol. 2, New York: Plenum, 29–50.

Harris, Marvin 1977: *Cannibals and Kings*. New York: Random House.

Hart, C. W. M. and Pilling, A. R. 1964: *The Tiwi of Northern Australia*. New York: Holt Rinehart.

Hart, John 1978: From subsistence to market: A case study of the Mbuti net hunters. *Human Ecology*, 6, 325–54.

Hartney, P. C. 1981: Tuberculosis in a prehistoric population sample from southern Ontario. In Buikstra (1981), 141–60.

Hassan, Fekri 1981: *Demographic Archaeology*. New York: Academic.

Hassan, N. and Ahmad, K. 1984: Studies on food and nutrient intake by rural populations of Bangladesh and comparisons between intake of 1962–4, 1975–6, and 1981–2. *Ecology of Food and Nutrition*, 15, 143–58.

Hausman, Alice and Wilmsen, E. N. 1985: Economic change and secular trends in the growth of San children. *Human Biology*, 57, 563–72.

Haviland, William 1967: Stature at Tikal, Guatemala: Implications for ancient Maya demography and social organization. *American Antiquity*, 32, 316–25.

Hawkes, Kristen and O'Connell, J. F. 1985: Optimal foraging models and the case of the !Kung. *American Anthropologist*, 87, 401–5.

Hawkes, Kristen, Hill, K., and O'Connell, J. F. 1982: Why hunters forage: The Ache of eastern Paraguay. *Am. Ethnol.*, 9, 379–98.

Hayden, Brian 1981a: Research and development in the Stone Age. *Current Anthropology*, 22, 519–48.

Hayden, Brian 1981b: Subsistence and ecological adaptations of modern hunter/gatherers. In Harding and Teleki (1981), 344–422.

Hill, Kim 1982: Hunting and human evolution. *Journal of Human Evolution*, 11, 521–44.

Hill, K. and Hawkes, K. 1983: Neotropical hunting among the Ache of eastern Paraguay. In Hames and Vickers (1983), 139–88.

Hill, K., Kaplan, H., Hawkes, K., and Hurtado, A. M. 1984: Seasonal variance in the diet of Ache hunter gatherers in Eastern Paraguay. *Human Ecology*, 12, 101–37.

Hitchcock, Robert K. 1982: Patterns of sedentism among the Basarwa of eastern Botswana. In Leacock and Lee (1982), 223–68.

Hodgkinson, Clement 1845: *Australia from Port Macquarie to Moretown Bay with Description of the Natives*. London: Boone.

Holmberg, Allen R. 1969: *Nomads of the Long Bow*. New York: American Museum.

Howell, Nancy 1979: *Demography of the Dobe !Kung*. New York: Academic.

Howell, Nancy 1982: Village composition implied by a paleodemographic life table: The Libben site, Ohio. *American Journal of Physical Anthropology*, 59, 263–70.

Howell, Nancy 1986: Feedback and buffers in relation to scarcity and abundance: Studies of hunter gatherer populations. In David Coleman and R. Schofield (eds), *State of Population Theory*, London: Basil Blackwell, 156–87.

Hufton, Olwen 1985: Social conflict and the grain supply in eighteenth century France. In Rotberg and Rabb (1985), 105–31.

Hurtado, A. and Hill, Kim 1987: Early dry season subsistence ecology of the Cuiva (Hiwi) foragers of Venezuela. *Human Ecology*, 15, 163–87.

Huss Ashmore, R., Goodman, A. H., and Armelagos, G. J. 1982: Nutritional inference from paleopathology. *Advances in Archaeological Method and Theory*, 5, 395–474.

Ichikawa, M. 1981: Ecological and sociological importance of honey among Mbuti net hunters of Eastern Zaire. *Kyoto University African Studies Monographs*, 1, 55–68.

Ichikawa, M. 1983: An examination of the hunting dependent life of the Mbuti pygmies of eastern Zaire. *Kyoto University African Studies Monographs*, 4, 55–76.

Jacobson, Thorbild and Adams, Robert McC. 1958: Salt and silt in ancient Mesopotamian agriculture. *Science*, 128, 1251–8.

Jelliffe, D. F., Woodburn, J., Bennett, F. J., and Jelliffe, E. F. P. 1962: The children of the Hadza hunters. *Journal of Paediatrics*, 60, 907–13.

Johansson, S. R. and Horowitz, S. 1986: Estimating mortality in skeletal populations: Influence of the growth rate on the interpretation of levels and trends during the transition to agriculture. *American Journal of Physical Anthropology*, 71, 233–50.

Johnston, F. and Snow, C. E. 1961: The reassessment of the age and sex of the Indian Knoll skeletal population: Demographic and pathologic considerations. *American Journal of Physical Anthropology*, 19, 237–44.

Jones, F. L. 1963: *A Demographic Survey of the Aboriginal Populations of the Northern Territory with Special Reference to Bathurst Island Mission.* Canberra: Australian Institute for Aboriginal Study.

Jones, Rhys 1980: Hunters in the Australian coast savanna. In D. Harris (ed.), *Human Ecology in Savanna Environments*, New York: Academic, 107–47.

Kennedy, Kenneth 1984: Growth, nutrition and pathology in changing paleodemographic settings in South Asia. In Cohen and Armelagos (1984), 169–92.

Kobayashi, K. 1967: Trend in length of life based on human skeletons from prehistoric to modern times in Japan. *Journal of the Faculty of Science*, III, 2.

Koerner, B. D. and Blakely, R. L. 1985: Degenerative joint disease, subsistence, and sex roles at the protohistoric King site in Georgia. *American Journal of Physical Anthropology*, 66, 190.

Konner, Melvin and Worthman, Carol 1980: Nursing frequency, gonadal function and birth spacing among !Kung hunter gatherers. *Science*, 207, 788–91.

Krzywicki, Ludwig 1934: *Primitive Society and its Vital Statistics.* London: Macmillan.

Larsen, Clark 1983: Deciduous tooth size and subsistence change in prehistoric Georgia coast populations. *Current Anthropology*, 24, 225–6.

Larsen, Clark 1984: Health and disease in prehistoric Georgia: The transition to agriculture. In Cohen and Armelagos (1984), 367–92.

Laughlin W. S. et al. 1979: New approaches to the pre- and post-contact history of Arctic peoples. *American Journal of Physical Anthropology*, 51, 579–87.

Leacock, Eleanor and Lee, R. B. (eds) 1982: *Politics and History in Band Societies.* Cambridge: Cambridge University Press.

Lee, R. B. 1968: What hunters do for a living or how to make out on scarce resources. In Lee and Devore (1968), 30–43.

Lee R. B. 1979: !Kung Bushman subsistence: An input output analysis. In A. P. Vayda (ed.), *Ecological Studies in Cultural Anthropology*, New York: Natural History Press, 47–79.

Lee, R. B. 1979: *The Kung San: Men, women and work in a foraging society.* Cambridge: Cambridge University Press.

Lee, R. B. 1980: Lactation, ovulation, infanticide and women's work: A study of hunter-gatherer population regulation. In M. N. Cohen, Roy S. Malpass, and Hal Klein (eds), *Biosocial Mechanisms of Population Regulation*, New Haven: Yale University Press, 321–48.

Lee, R. B. and Devore, I. (eds) 1968: *Man the Hunter.* Chicago: Aldine.

92   *Hunger in Prehistoric Societies*

Lee, R. B. and Devore, I. (eds) 1976: *Kalahari Hunter Gatherers*. Cambridge, Mass.: Harvard University Press.
Livingstone, Frank B. 1984: The Duffy blood group, vivax malaria and malarial selection in human populations: A review. *Human Biology*, 56, 413–25.
Lovejoy, O., Meindl, R. S., Pryzbeck, T. R., Barton, T. S., Heiple, K. G., and Kotting, D. 1977: Paleodemography at the Libben Site, Ottowa Co., Ohio. *Science*, 198, 291–3.
Lumholtz, Carol 1889: *Among Cannibals*. London: John Murray.
McAlpin, M. B. 1983: *Subject to Famine*. Princeton: Princeton University Press.
McArthur, Margaret 1960: Report of the nutrition unit. In Mountford (1960), 1–13.
McBryde, Isabel (ed.) 1978: *Records of Times Past*. Canberra: Australian Institute for Aboriginal Studies.
McCarthy, Frederick D. and McArthur, Margaret 1960: The food quest and the time factor in Aboriginal economic life. In Mountford (1960), 145–94.
McHenry, Henry 1968: Transverse lines in the long bones of prehistoric California Indians. *American Journal of Physical Anthropology*, 29, 1–18.
McNeill, William 1975: *Plagues and Peoples*. Garden City: Anchor.
Magennis, Ann 1977: Middle and late Archaic mortuary patterns. Knoxville: University of Tennessee. Master's thesis in anthropology.
Malhotra, M. S. 1966: People of India including primitive tribes: A survey on physiological adaptation, physical fitness, and nutrition. In P. T. Baker and J. S. Weiner (eds), *The Biology of Human Adaptability*, Oxford: Clarendon, 329–56.
Man, E. H. 1885: On the aboriginal inhabitants of the Andaman Islands. *Journal of Anthropology in India*, 12, 69.
Mann, G. V., Roels, A., Price, D. L., and Merrill, J. M. 1962: Cardiovascular disease in African pygmies. *Journal of Chronic Diseases*, 14, 341–71.
Marshall, Lorna 1976: *The Kung of Nyae-Nyae*. Cambridge: Cambridge University Press.
Martin, Debra, Armelagos, G. J., Goodman, A. H., and Van Gerven, D. P. 1984: The effects of socioeconomic change in prehistoric Africa: Sudanese Nubia as a case study. In Cohen and Armelagos (1984), 193–216.
May, Jacques 1970: *The Ecology of Undernutrition in Eastern Africa and Four Countries in Western Africa*. New York: Hafner.
Meehan, Betty 1977a: Hunters by the seashore. *Journal of Human Evolution*, 6, 363–70.
Meehan, Betty 1977b: Man does not live by calories alone: The role of shellfish in a coastal cuisine. In Allen, J., Golson, J., and Jones, R. (eds) *Sunda and Sahul*, London: Academic, 493–532.
Meiklejohn, C., Schentag, C., Vanema, A., and Key, P. 1984: Socioeconomic change and patterns of pathology and variation in the mesolithic and neolithic of Western Europe: Some suggestions. In Cohen and Armelagos (1984), 75–100.
Mensforth, Robert 1985: Relative long bone growth in the Libben and Bt-5

prehistoric skeletal populations. *American Journal of Physical Anthropology*, 68, 247–62.

Mensforth, Robert 1986: The pathogenesis of periosteal reactions in earlier human groups: Diagnostic, epidemiological and demographic considerations. Paper presented to American Association of Physical Anthropologists, Albuquerque.

Mensforth, Robert, ms: Paleodemography of the skeletal population from Carlston Annis (Bt-5).

Metz, J. D., Hart, D., and Harpending, H. C. 1971: Iron, folate, and vitamin B12 nutrition in a hunter gatherer people: A study of !Kung Bushmen. *American Journal of Clinical Nutrition*, 24, 229–42.

Molnar, S. and Molnar, I. 1985: Observations of dental diseases among prehistoric populations of Hungary. *American Journal of Physical Anthropology*, 67, 51–63.

Moore, David 1979: *Islanders and Aborigines at Cape York*. Canberra: AIBS.

Morris, Bryan 1982: *Forest Traders: A socioeconomic study of the hill Pandarem*. London: Athlone.

Mountford, Charles P. (ed.) 1960: *Records of the American-Australian Scientific Expedition to Arnhem Land. Vol. 2: Anthropology and Nutrition*. Melbourne: Melbourne University Press.

Murchison, M., Owsley, D. W., and Riopelle, A. J. 1983: Transverse line formation in protein-deprived rhesus monkeys. Paper presented to the Paleopathology Association, Indianapolis.

Nelson, D. A. 1984: Bone density in three archaeological populations. *American Journal of Physical Anthropology*, 63, 198.

Nickens, Paul R. 1976: Stature reduction as an adaptive response to food production in Mesoamerica. *Journal of Archaeological Science*, 3, 31–41.

Norr, Lynette 1984: Prehistoric subsistence and health status of coastal peoples from the Panamanian Isthmus of lower Central America. In Cohen and Armelagos (1984), 463–90.

Norr, Lynette 1986: Skeletal responses to stress in prehistoric Panama. *American Journal of Physical Anthropology*, 69, 247.

Nurse, George T. 1975: Seasonal hunger among the Ngoni and Ntumba of Central Africa. *Africa*, 45, 1–11.

Nurse, George T. and Jenkins, Trefor 1977: *Health and the Hunter-gatherer*. Basel: Karger.

O'Connell, James and Hawkes, Kristen 1981: Alyawara plant use and optimal foraging theory. In Winterhalder and Smith (1981), 99–125.

O'Connell, James, Hawkes, K., and Blurton Jones, N. 1988: Hadza scavenging: Implications for Plio/Pleistocene hominid subsistence. *Current Anthropology*, 29, 356–63.

Ogbu, John 1973: Seasonal hunger in tropical Africa as a cultural phenomenon. *Africa*, 43, 317–32.

Ortner, Donald and Putschar, W. 1981: Identification of pathological conditions of human skeletal remains. Smithsonian Contributions in Anthropology, 28.

Palkovich, Ann 1984: Agriculture, marginal environments and nutritional stress in the prehistoric southwest. In Cohen and Armelagos (1984), 425–38.

Paolucci, A. M., Padone, M. A., Pennetti, V., and Cavalli-Sforza, L. L. 1969: Serum free amino acids patterns in a Babinga Pygmy adult population. *American Journal of Clinical Nutrition*, 22, 1652−9.

Pelto, Gretel H. and Pelto, Perti J. 1985: Diet and delocalization: Dietary change since 1750. In Rotberg and Rabb (1985), 309−30.

Perez Diez, A. A. and Salzano, F. M. 1978: Evolutionary implications of the ethnography and demography of Ayoreo Indians. *Journal of Human Evolution*, 7, 253−68.

Perzigian, A., Tench, P. A., and Braun, O. J. 1984: Prehistoric health in the Ohio River Valley. In Cohen and Armelagos (1984), 347−66.

Peterson, J. T. 1981: Game, farming and interethnic relations in Northeastern Luzon, Philippines. *Human Ecology*, 9, 1−22.

Peterson, W. 1981: Recent adaptive shifts among the Palanan hunters of the Philippines. *Man*, 16, 43−61.

Pfeiffer, Susan 1984: Paleopathology in an Iroquoian ossuary with special reference to tuberculosis. *American Journal of Physical Anthropology*, 65, 181−9.

Polgar, Stephen 1964: Evolution and the ills of mankind. In S. Tax (ed.), *Horizons of Anthropology*, Chicago: Aldine, 200−11.

Polunin, Ivan 1953: The medical natural history of Malay aborigines. *Medical Journal of Malaysia*, 8, 55−174.

Powell, M. L. 1984: Health, disease, and social stress in the complex Mississippian chiefdom at Moundville, Alabama. *American Journal of Physical Anthropology*, 63, 205.

Price, D. L., Mann, G. V., Roels, O. A., and Merrill, J. M. 1963: Parasitism in congo Pygmies. *American Journal of Tropical Medicine and Hygiene*, 12(3), 83−7.

Price, T. D. and Brown, J. A. (eds) 1985: *Prehistoric Hunter Gatherers: The emergence of social and cultural complexity*. New York: Academic.

Radcliffe-Brown, A. R. 1948: *The Andaman Islanders*. Glencoe: Free Press.

Rathbun, T. A. 1984: Skeletal pathology from the paleolithic through the metal ages in Iran and Iraq. In Cohen and Armelagos (1984), 137−68.

Robbins, L. M. 1978: The antiquity of tuberculosis in prehistoric peoples of Kentucky. *American Journal of Physical Anthropology*, 48, 429.

Rose, Frederic C. 1960: *Classification of Kin, Age Structure, and Marriage among the Groote Eylandt Aborigines*. Oxford: Pergamon.

Rose, Frederic C. 1968: Australian marriage, land owning groups and initiations. In Lee and Devore (1968), 200−8.

Rose, Jerome and Boyd, L. F. 1978: Dietary reconstruction utilizing histological observations of enamel and dentin. *American Journal of Physical Anthropology*, 48, 431.

Rose, Jerome, Burnett, B. A., Nassaney, M. S., and Blauer, M. W. 1984: Paleopathology and the origins of maize agriculture in the lower Mississippi Valley and Caddoan culture areas. In Cohen and Armelagos (1984), 393−424.

Rose, J., Condon, K., and Goodman, A. H. 1985: Diet and dentition: Developmental disturbances. In J. Buikstra and J. Mielke (eds), *The Analysis of Prehistoric Diets*, Orlando: Academic Press, 281−306.

Rosenberg, I. H. et al. 1976: Interaction of infection and nutrition: Some practical concepts. *Ecology of Food and Nutrition*, 4, 203—6.

Rotberg, Robert I. 1983: *Imperialism, Colonialism and Hunger*. Cambridge: Cambridge University Press.

Rotberg, Robert I. and Rabb, T. K. (eds) 1985: *Hunger and History*. Cambridge: Cambridge University Press.

Roth, E. A. 1985: A note on the demographic concomitants of sedentism. *American Anthropologist*, 87, 38—82.

Roth, E. A. and Ray, Ajit 1985: Demographic patterns of sedentary and nomadic Juang of Orissa. *Human Biology*, 57, 319—26.

Rudney, Joel 1983: Dental indicators of growth disturbance in a series of ancient lower Nubian populations: Changes over time. *American Journal of Physical Anthropology*, 31, 295—302.

Sahlins, Marshall 1972: *Stone Age Economics*. Chicago: Aldine.

Sattenspiel, Lisa and Harpending, H. 1983: Stable populations and skeletal age. *American Antiquity*, 48, 489—98.

Saul, Frank P. 1972: *Human Skeletal Remains from the Altar de Sacrificios*. Harvard: Peabody Museum Papers.

Schebesta, Paul 1928: *Among the Forest Dwarfs of Malaya*. London: Hutchinson.

Schrire, Carmel (ed.) 1984: *Past and Present in Hunter-gatherer Studies*. New York: Academic.

Sciulli, P. W. 1977: A descriptive and comparative study of the deciduous dentition of prehistoric Ohio Valley Amerindians. *American Journal of Physical Anthropology*, 47, 71—80.

Sciulli, P. W. 1978: Developmental abnormalities of the permanent dentition in prehistoric Ohio Valley Amerindians. *American Journal of Physical Anthropology*, 48, 193—8.

Sen, A. 1981: *Poverty and Famines*. Oxford: Oxford University Press.

Sen Gupta, P. N. 1980: Food consumption and nutrition of regional tribes of India. *Ecology of Food and Nutrition*, 9, 93—108.

Serjeantson, Susan 1975: Marriage patterns and fertility in three Papua New Guinea populations. *Human Biology*, 47, 399—413.

Sharp, Lauriston 1940: An Australian Aboriginal population. *Human Biology*, 12, 481—507.

Sibajuddin, S. M. 1984: Reproduction and consanguinity among Chenchus of Andhra Pradesh. *Man in India*, 64, 181—92.

Silberbauer, George 1981: *Hunter and habitat in the Central Kalahari*. Cambridge: Cambridge University Press.

Sinha, D. P. 1972: The Birhors. In M. Bicchieri (ed.), *Hunters and Gatherers Today*, New York: Holt Rinehart, 371—403.

Smith, Patricia, Bar-Yosef, Ofer, and Sillen, A. 1984: Archaeological and skeletal evidence for dietary change during the late Pleistocene/early Holocene in the Levant. In Cohen and Armelagos (1984), 101—36.

Spencer, Baldwin, and Gillen, F. J. 1927: *The Arunta*. London: Macmillan and Co.

Steinbock, R. T. 1976: *Paleopathological Diagnosis and Interpretation*. Springfield: C. C. Thomas.

Stodder, A. W. 1986: The paleoepidemiological transition in the Mesa Verde region Anasazi, AD 600–1725. *American Journal of Physical Anthropology*, 69, 260.

Storey, Rebecca 1985: An estimate of mortality in a pre-Columbian urban population. *American Anthropologist*, 87, 519–35.

Stout, Sam 1978: Histological structure and its preservation in ancient bone. *Current Anthropology*, 19, 600–4.

Stuart-Macadam, P. 1986: Nutrition and anemia in past human populations. Paper presented to the Nineteenth Chacmool Conference, University of Calgary.

Sweeny, G. 1947: Food supplies of a desert tribe. *Oceania*, 17, 289–99.

Tanaka, Jiro 1980: *The San: Hunter gatherers of the Kalahari*. Tokyo: University of Tokyo Press.

Thomson, Donald 1975: *Bindibu Country*. Melbourne: Thomas Nelson Ltd.

Tilley, L. A. 1985: Food entitlement, famine and conflict. In Rotberg and Rabb (1985), 136–51.

Tobias, Phillip 1966: The people of Africa south of the Sahara. In P. T. Baker and J. S. Weiner (eds), *The Biology of Human Adaptability*, Oxford: Clarendon, 111–200.

Tonkinson, Robert 1978: *The Mardudjara Aborigines*. New York: Holt Rinehart.

Townsend, P. K. 1971: New Guinea sago gatherers. EFN, 1, 19–24.

Truswell, A. S. and Hansen, J. D. 1976: Medical research among the !Kung. In Lee and Devore (1976), 166–95.

Turnbull, Colin 1961: *The Forest People*. New York: Simon and Schuster.

Turnbull, Colin 1965: *Wayward Servants*. Garden City: Natural History Press.

Turnbull, Colin 1983: *The Mbuti Pygmies: Change and adaptation*. New York: Holt Rinehart.

Turner, David H. 1974: *Tradition and Transformation: A study of aborigines in the Groote Eylandt area, northern Australia*. Canberra: AIBS.

Ubelaker, Douglas 1984: Prehistoric human biology of Ecuador: Possible temporal trends and cultural correlations. In Cohen and Armelagos (1984), 491–514.

Van Arsdale, P. W. 1978: Population dynamics among Asmat hunter gatherers of New Guinea: Data, methods, comparisons. *Human Ecology*, 6, 435–67.

Van Gerven, D. P. and Armelagos, G. J. 1983: Farewell to paleodemography: A reply. *Journal of Human Evolution*, 12, 352–66.

Walker, P. L. 1985: Anemia among prehistoric Indians of the American southwest. In C. Merbs and R. J. Miller (eds), *Health and Disease in the prehistoric Southwest*, Arizona State University: Archaeological Research Papers No. 34, 139–64.

Walker, P. L. 1986: Porotic hyperostosis in a marine dependent California Indian population. *American Journal of Physical Anthropology*, 69, 345–54.

Walker, P. L., ms: Enamel hypoplasia during 5000 years of southern California prehistory.

Walker, P. L. and de Niro, M. 1986: Stable nitrogen and carbon isotope ratios in bone collagen as indices of prehistoric dietary dependence on marine and terrestrial resources in Southern California. *American Journal of Physical Anthropology*, 71, 51–62.

Warner, W. L. 1937: *A Black Civilization*. New York: Harper and Bros.

Webb, Stephen 1984: Prehistoric stress in Australian Aborigines. Department of Prehistory, Australian National University: unpublished thesis.

Wehmeyer, A. S., Lee, R. B., and Whiting, J. M. 1969: The nutrient composition and dietary importance of some vegetable foods eaten by the !Kung Bushmen. *South African Tydskrif vir Geneeskunde*, 95, 1529–30.

Weiss, K. M. 1973: Demographic models for anthropology. Memoir, Society for American Archaeology, No. 27.

Welinder, Stig 1979: Prehistoric demography. *Acta Arch. Lundensia*. Series IN8 Minore no. 8.

Wells, Calvin 1975: Prehistoric and historical changes in nutrition, disease and associated conditions. *Progress in Food and Nutrition Science*, 1, 729–79.

Wenlock, R. W. 1979: Social factors, nutrition and child mortality in a rural subsistence economy. *Ecology of Food and Nutrition*, 8, 227–40.

White, Christine 1986: Mayan diet and health status at Lamanai, Belize. Paper presented to the Nineteenth Chacmool Conference, University of Calgary.

Wilkinson, G. K. et al. 1958: Serum proteins of some central and south Australian Aborigines. *Medical Journal of Australia*, 2, 158–60.

Williams, B. J. 1974: A model of band society. *American Antiquity*, 39(4), 2 (Memoir, Society for American Archaeology).

Williams, J. A. 1985: Evidence of pre-contact tuberculosis in two Woodland skeletal populations from the northern plains. *American Journal of Physical Anthropology*, 66, 242–3.

Wilmsen, Edwin 1978: Seasonal effects of dietary intake on the Kalahari San. Federation Proceedings, 37, 65–72.

Wilson, E. O. 1975: *Sociobiology*. Cambridge, Mass.: Harvard University Press.

Wilson, W. 1953: A dietary survey of aborigines in the Northwest Territory. *Medical Journal of Australia*, 2, 599–605.

Winterhalder, Bruce and Smith, E. A. 1981: *Hunter Gatherer Foraging Strategies*. Chicago: Chicago University Press.

Wittfogel, Karl 1957: *Oriental Despotism*. New Haven: Yale University Press.

Wood, James 1988: Comment. *Current Anthropology*, 29, 290.

Wood, James et al. 1985: Lactation and birth spacing in highland New Guinea. *Journal of Biosocial Science*, Supplement 9, 158–73.

Woodburn, James 1968: An introduction to Hadza Ecology. In Lee and Devore (1968), 49–55.

Wrigley, E. A. and Schofield, Roger 1981. *The Population History of England, 1541–1871*. Cambridge, Mass.: Harvard University Press.

Wurm, H. 1984: The fluctuation of average stature in the course of German history and the influence of the protein content of the diet. *Journal of Human Evolution*, 13, 331–9.

Y'edynak, Gloria and Fleisch, Sylvia 1983: Microevolution and biological adaptability in the transition from food collecting to food production in the Iron Gates of Yugoslavia. *Journal of Human Evolution*, 12, 279–96.

Yengoyan, Aram 1972: Biological and demographic components in Aboriginal Australian socioeconomic organization. *Oceania*, XLIII, 85–95.

Zivanovic, S. 1982: *Ancient Diseases*. London: Methuen, English translation.

Part III
Hunger in Complex Societies

The millennial era, spanning the period from 6000 BC to AD 1400, witnessed innovations in agriculture and the proliferation of permanent settlements, the emergence of urban centers in the great city-states, the development of hierarchical social structure, and broadly ranging trade. The Working Group focuses on a tracing of these historical and cultural trends through intensification of agriculture in Mesopotamia, determinants of hunger in the ancient Graeco-Roman world, and population growth and decline in the Europe of the Middle Ages. Chapter 4 emphasizes causes and consequences of food shortage, poverty, and deprivation, and the development of social hierarchies. Peter Garnsey discusses secular and sacred responses to food crises in the ancient Mediterranean. Robin D. S. Yates reports on war, siege, and relief measures in China from the Shang and Western Chou Dynasties through the Han Dynasties. B. L. Turner presents perspectives on the immense growth and then still unsolved, mysterious collapse of the Classic Mayan civilization of the Yucatan Peninsula from 1000 BC to AD 800. While there is still much to understand about ancient civilizations, these chapters document complex societal responses to problems of food shortage, and suggest that it is seldom only a result of natural disaster, or indeed of a relation of population increase to limited resources, but often a crisis of human origin.

4

Agricultural Intensification, Urbanization, and Hierarchy

LUCILE F. NEWMAN, ALAN BOEGEHOLD, DAVID
HERLIHY, ROBERT W. KATES, AND KURT
RAAFLAUB

Introduction

Millennial era studies range from the metropolis of Ur in Sumer of six thousand years before the present, to the feudal lands of Europe six hundred years ago. They address the question of hunger, from the further intensification of agriculture to the emergence of urban centers, hierarchical social structure, and trade, that set the stage for the development of a world economy.

The social achievements of the millennial era were permanent settlements leading to urbanization and the organization of specialized human functions. This included land differentiated by special purposes − the separation of production spaces from population living spaces. It marks a difference from hunting-gathering societies with extensive land use, wide-ranging gathering of food plants, and seasonal following of animal herds, to a more sedentarized life. Intensification of agriculture included flood control (notably in Egypt with use of the annual inundation of the Nile), complex irrigation systems such as those of Sumer and the Classic Maya, the definition of "field" as exclusive agricultural space, and seasonal patterns of productive and fallow periods. The result of these innovations, including plant and animal domestication, was production beyond subsistence toward what Boserup (1981) has termed "population surplus."[1] The combination of increased population required by and supportable from increased food production, and specialization of work in trade, in localized workshops and manufactures, and in priestly and administrative functions, were all contributors to the process of localization of population centers, settled communities, hierarchical social organization, and ultimately urbanization. The centralization of large numbers of people in one place required attention not only to food production, but also to food distribution, food storage, and, in times of dearth, trade and importation of grain from external suppliers. Trade in this period ultimately united the entire Mediterranean area. The control of grain markets for particular urban areas along with wide-ranging grain trade could be considered a major feature of the millennial era.

The history of hunger in the millennial era is derived from many kinds of evidence. These include written sources such as epics, histories, dramas, archives, inscriptions; material sources such as walled cities, stele, inscribed monuments, sculpture, granaries, ships, pottery; human burials and memorials; grain and other food substances that have been found in jars and storage spaces; the remains of irrigation structures, terracing, channelized raised fields, and the remains of animals that had become domesticated. The evidence so far available indicates human activities including agricultural intensification, building of significant structures, storing and distribution of food resources, transport of people and products over great distances, and development of the centralized religious and political organization to support these activities. The literatures of this era represent the views of the elite and powerful, and seldom reflect the concerns of the people. The voices of those who lived through hunger events are often voices of public officials driven to comment on human tragedy, or inadvertent references to hunger and starvation in daily accounts or records of transactions. There is no voice for the common people in the ancient world.

Hunger and plenty are described circumstantially by early Greek authors, such as Homer in (probably) the eighth century BC and the prose writers in the fifth and fourth centuries − Herodotus, Thucydides, Demosthenes, and later Galen, among others. These authors suggest that hunger, while sometimes resulting from climatic forces, water shortage, and crop failure, was also attributable to human actions. Food resources often went to supply armies, and in wartime the strategies of siege, embargo, and destruction of irrigation systems were already in use in these early periods (see chapter 6). Intentional limitation by families of their number of children, and out-migration in times of scarcity both characterize human responses to hunger and the threat of hunger in this era.

While Malthus and Boserup concentrated on increased resources and technological change as two main forces contributing to the carrying capacity of society, there must also be identified a third force, the human element of administration or management that also increased the capacity of communities to secure a food supply. The complex organization of urbanization, colonization, and establishment of fixed settlements itself may be seen as a technological innovation. The characteristic that most describes the millennial era is the social organization that led to hierarchical differentiation of classes of citizenship − of religious and political leaders, bureaucracies and government workers, farmers, slaves, and foreigners, and enlargement of spheres of activity through widespread trade.

The political economy of management as seen in the evidence of this era includes the function of *establishing control* over contiguous territories through cooperation or subjugation, involving the sharing or appropriation of resources, the control of waterways and irrigation, and the establishment of food systems. A subsequent function is then *maintaining control* through hierarchical social structure, the perquisites and entitlements of citizenship (as in the Greek city-state), appropriation of the labor of both free and enslaved peoples, maintenance of peaceful relations, and storage and distribution of food. Responsiveness to drought, flood, and other natural disasters, as well as to human invasions, was enhanced by centralization of population and maintenance of order. Finally, the evidence of this era includes *expansion*, migration into unoccupied territories, protection of trade routes, and deportation of surplus population in times of stress, as well as war and the establishment of control over other communities.

The relations of food production and scarcity are described in this chapter, including agricultural intensification in Mesopotamia; land use, the development of resources, and the determinants of hunger in the ancient Graeco-Roman world to the third century AD; and population growth and decline in the Europe of the Middle Ages. We then turn to causes of hunger, and preventive and ameliorative measures throughout this era. This chapter serves also as an introduction to three intensive studies – Peter Garnsey's 'Responses to food crisis in the Ancient Mediterranean World' (chapter 5); Robin D. S. Yates's 'War, food shortages, and relief measures in early China' (chapter 6); and B. L. Turner's 'The Classic Maya: The rise and fall of population and agriculture' (chapter 7).

Agricultural Intensification in Mesopotamia from the Sixth Millenium BC

Mesopotamia, the land between the rivers Tigris and Euphrates, has its heartland in present day Iraq and its uplands in Syria, Turkey, and Iran, the fertile crescent where the Neolithic Revolution in food production may have first begun. The heartland, the floodplain of the Tigris-Euphrates, requires irrigation to maintain a significant population. The earliest traces of organized irrigation date to about 6000 BC, and were found on the northwest border of the plain in the foothills of the Zagros mountains.

Within the floodplain, there have been two and a half cycles of population rise and decline over the past six thousand years (figure 4.1). Yet, in many ways, the essentials of life have been remarkably stable throughout the

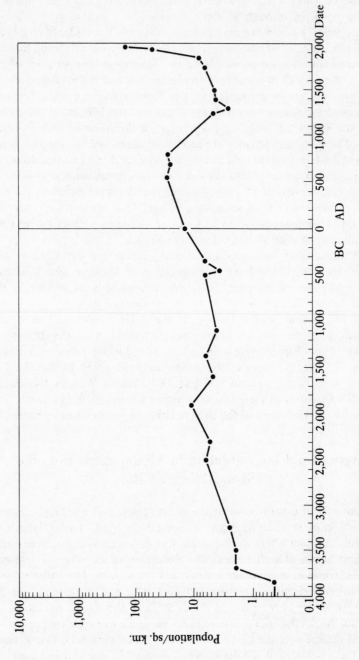

Figure 4.1   Population density of the Tigris-Euphrates floodplain over 6,000 years

period, with a cereal-based agriculture produced in ox-ploughed, irrigated, and fallowed fields. The first population increase was characterized by the rise of urban settlements and the Sumerian and Akkadian empires. A combination of archeological and historical evidence can be employed to examine the period (Flannery, 1965). The dependence on irrigation and the widespread distribution of old river courses and canal spoilbanks provide a type of roadmap to early settlement. An imaginative archeological effort has used these to survey the overall settlement of the plain (Adams, 1981). And the early invention of cuneiform writing on clay tablets has preserved, in the dry climate, the written materials of this society in a way not comparable to any other ancient one.

In the Mesopotamia of the early dynastic period, social differentiation, organized around separate production units, included extended family or kinship corporate units, the private estates of the elite public officials, and the public institutions of palace and temple (Zagarell, 1986). Land rights were specialized in the separation of levels of ownership and attribution of field cultivation rights. The temple mode of production included free individuals, some of whom occupied important positions within the temple — palace hierarchy and had ties to community kin groups. Some free individuals served as foremen, in the temple, and received field cultivation rights for their services. Under them were workers who were dependent to different degrees, not fully understood at the present time — ranging from being tied to state/temple lands but retaining family-life and land-use rights, to being deprived of family life and receiving the rations enumerated in the inscribed tablets found throughout this area. "Such encumbered laborers have been classified as helots or slaves depending on whether or not they were deprived of family life and could be separated from the land and bought and sold" (Zagarell, 1986: 417). The lowest level of the social hierarchy was made up of those who tilled the soil and produced the food.

Hunger Conditions

Food Shortage Given the prevalence of war and natural hazard in the eastern Mediterranean, food-short hunger resulting in famine was common. The water systems provided the essential ingredient for maintaining a food supply, but the climate and the morphology of the major rivers made flood and drought a recurrent hazard. Military strategy often sought to annex a neighboring state's water supply before undertaking a frontal assault on the enemy kingdom or to cut its supply as a major strategy in an attack. And siltation and salinization posed frequent threats to the utilization and maintenance of the system.

There are some direct references to hunger in the texts, most commonly in reference to sieges, a time when the scribes themselves might be expected to hunger. Describing the fall of Ur in 2004 BC, a Sumerian laments: "In its places, where the festivities of the land took place, the people lay in heaps ... Ur — its weak and strong perished through hunger" (quoted in Roux, 1980:168). But as with all written history of hunger the record is sparse, and there is no easy source or compilation of such textual references. Thus at this time the evidence is mainly indirect: geomorphic and actual historical experience with drought, flood, sedimentation, and salinization; much textual evidence of the enormous effort to maintain silt-free irrigation channels; some evidence of a long-term decline in yields; and archeological survey data reflecting the rise and fall of regional populations within the floodplain (Jacobson and Adams, 1958).

Food Poverty Evidence for chronic hunger or food poverty today relies on three major methods: food availability as compared to a currently standardized requirement; symptoms of undernutrition or malnutrition; and behavioral expressions or adjustments. In current practice the availability/requirement ratio is measured, most crudely by an overall food/population ratio, somewhat better by a food resource (in money or self-provision)/requirement ratio, or best by a direct measure of household or individual consumption. While there are no overall food production statistics utilizable for the first approach, nor household budget surveys for the third approach, there are three different types of evidence that suggest the basic adequacy of common diets in Mesopotamia. These include data on rations given to temple or palace dependents in return for their labor, wages for daily labor in irrigation construction, and the size of farm required to support an average family. If these constitute the Mesopotamian safety net, what is not readily available are data of the number who received less than the ration amount, customary daily wage, or leaseholding area, or the many times that the system, under stress or corruption, failed to meet its own standards.

Nonetheless, the evidence as shown in table 4.1 and corroborated by other information suggests basic protein—calorie sufficiency. The data were obtained by Ellison (1981) from tablets inscribed with lists of rations, mainly in the form of barley (at times with other foods), and given to "dependent" workers in palace or temple estates. The size of the rations varies by occupation, age, and gender, and in that sense they mirror differentials found in modern dietary requirement lists. There is some uncertainty in the establishment of standard measures invariant over 1,600 years, and there is a question as to whether some of the larger allowances were wages or intended for sharing with dependents. Nonetheless, data from many different periods suggest that Mesopotamians knew what it took

Table 4.1   Daily energy supply standards estimated from barley ration lists

Date (BC)	Period	Average calories
3000–2400	Early Dynastic	3,152
2400–2200	Agade	4,320
2100–2000	Ur III	2,880
2000–1600	Old Babylonian	4,140
1600–1400	Nippur	2,880
1600–1400	Nuzi	3,600
Mesopotamian average		3,495
Modern Iraq (FAO estimate)		2,790

Source: Ellison, 1981: 40–3

to feed an adult and for the most part attempted to provide it at a scale just recently realized in modern Iraq. That they were able to do so is not entirely surprising, for at its peak (2400 BC) barley had a yield comparable to modern North American standards.

However, barley is not in itself sufficient for an adequate diet. Vitamin A and C deficiencies may have been serious and there are frequent textual references to blindness and scattered references to what might have been a scurvy-like disease (Ellison, 1981, 1983).

Food Deprivation   The barley rations data also suggest the possibility of trying to identify the adequacy of intrafamilial distribution based on gender and age differentials. In particular, the rations for children do not appear adequate for their needs, many children receiving the equivalent of only 900 calories per day (Ellison, 1981:30). And while the averages for both men and women seem adequate, there are still frequent listings of both men and women below the requirement for an active life. A benign explanation for such differentials is not apparent.

Responses   The long-term adaptations to coping with hunger are primarily irrigation, storage, redistribution, and the social organization required to do these, as well as population movement and control. The supply adaptations – irrigation, storage, and redistribution – are well documented, while the population restrictions are evidenced through settlement site development or abandonment and through immigration by other cultures. What is less known are the adjustments to hunger – the short-term changes and emergency responses. One extraordinary measure is documented in a series of "siege documents" detailing the sale of children, almost all girls, by their parents into slavery for a token payment and for the promise that the child would be fed (Oppenheim, 1955).

Population Dynamics

In addition to the common questions of hunger history, the exploration of population regulation, as well as theories of population growth and decline, includes hunger as a major causative variable. The 6,000-year population history of the Tigris-Euphrates floodplain (figure 4.1) suggests a dynamic oscillation very different from the conventional view of continual progress (as does chapter 3). And within the region itself subregions and city-states evidence oscillation in growth and decline including extinction.[2]

These population fluctuations have been compared with three sources of perturbations: environmental fluctuation, political events (empire formation, invasions, civil war and revolts), and technological innovations. No single set seems to correlate easily with population. Indeed, population oscillations that span millennia have been little studied and have no ready explanation.

If one considers Boserupian innovation, Malthusian collapse, and Marxist exploitation as potential prime movers, there is evidence in this long history of particular roles for each of these processes. But there is no clear evidence to award a leading role either to population growth as requiring irrigation intensification, or to irrigation intensification as permitting more rapid population growth, or to the requirements of surplus extraction as requiring the intensification of irrigation and the massive population needed to execute it. Rather, these population dynamics appear as a resultant of the interaction of all these forces. In addition, the emergence of hierarchical social structure had an impact on both land use and food distribution.

Food Production and Trade in the Graeco-Roman World

The City-State and Social Hierarchy in Greece of the Fifth and Fourth Centuries BC

"Ancient Greece" denotes a number of widely dispersed land areas around the Mediterranean Sea, whose traditional center is roughly the Peloponnesos taken together with much of the peninsula to its north. The population of Attica at this period was made up of 20,000 to 30,000 citizens. Wives and children of citizens added another 50,000 to 60,000 souls, and then there was an unknown number of resident aliens (metics), plus an unknown number of slaves. The high point of population in the fifth century BC, before the Peloponnesian War, is estimated at 250,000–300,000 (Garnsey, 1988:90).

In Attica and other mainland areas of this period, the "state" did not own land as such. Only citizens could own land. They worked the land themselves along with any slaves they had. The metics, a class of resident non-citizens, worked at commerce and banking. They could not own and bequeath land, but they could rent. Outside of those metics whose activities were wholly mercantile, and whatever slaves happened to be employed in manufacturing, construction projects, or mining, everyone contributed to food production.

Continuous labor would be given to family gardens of vegetables, thus making families self-sufficient in this respect. Attica has thin soil. The main fruits grown there are olives and grape vines, both of which require concentrated work at given seasons, but little attention at other times. Athens was not self-sufficient, however, in grain production. The city was always an importer of grain. Cereals were mainly imported from areas around the Black Sea and Egypt. Some grain may have been cultivated on the plain east of Mt Hymettos and in the Thriasian Plain. There was not much grazing land for cattle. Sheep and goats grazed on hillsides, and cheese was an important element in the diet, but herding seems not to have been a principal Attic occupation.

Citizens were mainly divided into rich and poor. There are intimations of the old Solonian system of four timocratic classes based on annual income, but in effect, the division is "haves" vs "have-nots." All citizens were eligible to be allotted to the Council of Five Hundred, a body that prepared the agenda for the *ekklesia*, and all had a vote in the *ekklesia*, where final decisions were made on all the most important business of the city. Citizens also served in the lawcourts where, in panels of 500 or 1000 or more, they judged disputes and crimes and monitored the accounts of retiring officials. When a foreign potentate made a gift of grain to the state, the distribution went to the citizens. The city democracy of Athens has been likened to a political guild (Polanyi et al., 1957). Resources gained, such as tribute or payments from confederate cities, were distributed among the citizens, as was conquered land. Cleruchies, or overseas settlements of citizens, were strategically placed sometimes to enhance the grain supply and sometimes to protect trade routes. And finally, the city paid from the proceeds of its political activity for allotments of grain as well as for jury duty, religious rites, and preparation of actors for theatrical performances.

Certain lands were delimited as belonging to a given hero or god. Such a lot was called *temenos*. It could be rented and whatever income it realized would go to the hero or god; that is, to the priests who administered it. In times of need the people (the state) could borrow gold or silver from the god. Sacred calendars show a great number of feast days. On these days people got meat from lambs, kids, and pigs that were sacrificed. For some it was the only meat in their diet. Presumably the hero's or god's treasury helped finance these sacrifices. In the calendars available, prices are listed for various sacrificial animals.

Inasmuch as the population of Attica remained more or less constant during the years under consideration here, and much grain was imported, there seemed to be no need for radical advances in technology. The agricultural intensification of Egypt and Mesopotamia was not characteristic of this area. Where need was felt – until about 350 BC, that is – the response might have been more grain-carrying ships or grain-storage areas at Eleusis, in Piraeus, or in the Agora. There was no known experimentation with new grains or grasses, crop rotation, or the like, although development of treated products such as cheese, olive oil, and wine enabled maintenance and storage of food resources from one season to another.

A few well-known and handsomely adorned springs provided water for public consumption. Shallow (7 to 10 m) wells provided water for families. The archeological record, however, shows evidence of drought not only at Athens but elsewhere in the Greek world some time around the middle of the fourth century. Demosthenes reported in 361 BC that "my land not only produced no crops, but that year, as you all know, the water even dried up in the wells, so that not a vegetable grew in the garden" (from Demosthenes' oration against Polykles, chapter 61; quoted in Camp, 1982).

References to grain shortages found in literature and decrees during the following 25 years or so establish a diminished food supply (Jameson, 1983). A convincing element of the archeological record is one sort of technological change. Athenians, pressed by drought, discovered new springs and accordingly provided them with fountain houses, and later, under further pressure, they developed a bottle-shaped cistern, 3 to 7 m deep, that was sunk into the ground and provided with channels to catch rainwater from roofs. Increased gifts of grain, financed by private citizens or admiring neighbor-states, were a previous and subsequent response to food shortages (Camp, 1982). In fact it may be said generally of the Greek world that response to troubles of many sorts was characteristically set in motion by private and individual energy and funds.

Responses to Hunger and Food Shortage in the Roman Empire

The Roman Empire comprised the entire Mediterranean area from Spain to Syria and from the Rhine and Danube to Egypt. Total population in the early empire was about 50–60 million, and in the first and second centuries AD the population of the city of Rome was roughly 1 million.

Food shortages in the city are documented with some frequency, particularly in times of civil disturbances and wars, but they rarely reach a critical stage in this period, in contrast to early Rome and late antiquity (Garnsey, 1983). Occasionally famine was reported, but chronic hunger is hardly attested at all, which may be true for the entire Roman Empire in this period due to general peace and prosperity. There are no detailed descriptions of hunger like that of the plague in Thucydides or that quoted from a late antique source (see chapter 5). Due to the nature of the sources the focus is almost entirely on the political aspects or consequences of food shortage: the complaints or riots of the population forcing the emperor to take drastic measures. Beginning in the late Republic, cheap or even free grain was distributed to the urban poor, not for social or humanitarian but for political reasons, to keep the dissatisfaction level low and gain political support in upcoming elections. Like the evidence of other social and economic aspects of life, hunger certainly was not thought a subject worth detailed study in itself.

Apart from natural disasters and diseases, which played a significant role in early Roman history, food shortages were mostly the result of human actions: wars, civil wars, piracy, failure to transport food to where it was needed, speculation. Therefore there is little evidence for food shortages in times of peace and well-functioning government. Moreover, the social organization prevailing in the Roman empire was such that, with the few exceptions of very large cities (Rome, Alexandria, Antioch), food supply was organized regionally and locally. Throughout the ancient Mediterranean world, official strategy for preventing food shortage was control of the grain market. Although there had been a free grain market in earlier Rome, by the late empire grain was controlled. The grain supply of Rome was termed the *annona*. The *annona* served to restrict speculation and in case of a famine to authorize subsidized distribution of grain. The controls were binding to ship owners and administered through officials in Rome as well as in the port of Ostia. Later personified as the daughter of the goddess Ceres, Annona appeared on coins throughout the period of the empire (Rickman, 1980). The practice of control of grain supplies was used in many outlying areas as well as in the major urban centers.

The Roman Empire was characterized by a high density of urbanization, but most cities were small and agricultural. It has been estimated that no more than 10–15 percent of the entire population was non-agricultural. Resources were therefore distributed widely, both socially and geographically. All citizens could own land. Although in some areas (such as North Africa) land was largely concentrated in a few hands, particularly in the huge estates owned by the emperor and wealthy senators, most of the population was still working in agriculture as tenants or laborers. Just as in Rome the Senate and later the emperor assumed responsibility for distributing food to the population, on the local level in the provinces the aristocracy were responsible for supplying food whenever necessary. Munificence and individual philanthropy were here, as in Attica, an established condition for office-holding and promotion into the imperial aristocracy.

The Concept of Land Tenure and Appropriation of Resources   In Rome just as in Greece land tenure was valued very highly: from the earliest time, the patrilineal clan or *gens* was the most important landholding social group, and its representative was the individual household. Children were important for long-term sustaining of land and family home. Continuity of the household and its obligations was confirmed by having male children to carry on the lineage and female children to marry into the community of citizens. It was a citizen's privilege, and at the same time landed property or the income thereof served as a basis for the citizen's rights and duties, including service in the army.

The concept of citizen as farmer and fighter can be traced back to the archaic period and appears down to the first century BC. Only when the area controlled by Rome extended around the entire Mediterranean did this system fall into disuse. At this time, there appeared professional armies composed of proletarian volunteers replacing the landowning citizen militia. In close parallel there emerged the large slave-run latifundia (large estates producing profitable crops such as oil and wine rather than grain), because land remained the only reputable form of investing the riches gained in the empire. Consequently landless proletarians flocked in great numbers to the cities and eventually to Rome, swelling the population of the capital and forcing the gradual introduction of measures to feed them. Nevertheless, small and middle farmers continued to exist in large numbers in Italy and throughout the empire. Typically, veterans were discharged after their military service with a "pension" ideally consisting of land; we therefore see large-scale distribution of land in the age of civil wars (during the periods of Sulla, Pompey, and Augustus). The senatorial government of the republic was unable ideologically and practically to cope with these problems. Only the emerging centralized government of the dictator Caesar and the emperor in disguise, Augustus, proved able to do so: they aimed at solving the immediate crisis by settling hundreds of thousands of soldiers on confiscated or bought land, reducing the numbers of persons in need of food support by exporting enormous numbers of veterans and civilians from Rome to colonies in the provinces, and putting into place the structures necessary to secure a steady and sufficient food supply (granaries, harbor facilities, officials in charge of food supply, control of speculation, encouragement and emergency support for grain traders, ship captains, etc.). These measures, however, were kept to the necessary minimum; the financial capacity of the empire did not allow more, and the prevailing ideology did not want more. The army of 300,000 troops, though small in comparison to the size of the empire, devoured much of the existing resources. The food resources therefore were mostly left in private hands, except that the emperor disposed of the resources of the provinces to support the population of Rome and the army. Except for times of emergency the Roman citizens did not pay any taxes during this period.

Beginning in the late second century AD and increasingly in late antiquity, all this changed for various reasons. Massive outside pressure and increasing expenses for the army forced the emperor to institute and later to increase taxes. Wars and civil wars brought large-scale disruption and devastation. The need to supply the armies became a tremendous burden for the areas in which those armies were garrisoned or fought. There were therefore increasing food shortages and increasing government intervention such as mandatory corporations of bakers, ship owners, and similar essential professions, families tied to the soil or to their professions, and wages and prices regulated by imperial decree. These habits of rule became institutionalized throughout late antiquity and in the Europe of the early Middle Ages, with land and wealth concentrated in the hands of an aristocracy, continuing professionalization of the armies, development of peasant farming, and a proletariat engaged in production and trade of transportable goods.

Population Growth and Decline in Medieval Europe

The Middle Ages represent a fairly long period of well-documented change in population growth and decline (Herlihy, 1985). Though the epoch remains very much a part of the "pre-statistical age," some statistics have survived, and indirect evidence on medieval social experiences is very abundant. It is therefore a period that invites the testing of hypotheses on the relationship between population movements, resource utilization, plenty, and penury. We look here at three hypotheses: Ester Boserup's argument that a high level of population density provokes a move to more intensive agriculture; and the current views of both Malthusianists and Marxists concerning the crisis of the fourteenth century.

Land Tenure in the Early Middle Ages

The system of agriculture practiced in the European north in late antiquity and the early Middle Ages seems to correspond well with Boserup's model of a long-fallow, semi-migratory agricultural system. To be sure, the Romans in conquering Gaul and Britain introduced more intensive methods, but it is not known how well Roman villas survived the tumult of the barbarian migrations. The barbarians themselves certainly relied principally on long-fallow systems (Barker, 1985).

By about 750, a short-fallow system, based on permanent homesteads (known most commonly as *mansi*) and estates (manors), had come to dominate northern agriculture. This move to more intensive methods also marks the emergence of the European peasantry as a historic class. The remarkable aspect of this change is that the Germanic migrants did not impose their own extensive methods on the former Roman provinces – a common result of similar migrations, according to Boserup. Rather, they adopted short-fallow agriculture, and the methods were taken into Germany itself, never part of the Roman Empire.

Do growing population densities chiefly explain this transition? This is difficult to discern. *Penuria hominum*, a shortage of people, seems to have been the bane of the late empire. And the initial reaction of the barbarians themselves to hunger was migration. The more powerful (or at least the more visible) stimulus to change seems to have been the emergence of barbarian kingdoms, based on a highly stratified social structure, with kings, warrior elites, and priests ruling over a now settled and fully "peasantified" population. The barbarians either took over or had to compete with well-organized states, the heirs of the ancient empire. A further factor was the growing reliance on heavy cavalry as the chief instrument of warfare – a change which was making war more expensive and therefore the preserve of the warrior elite. Eager to marshal resources for the support of armies and monasteries, the elites seem to have required the common freeman to remain fixed upon the land. Probably because the freemen were inefficient farmers, the elites taxed them in time – the one resource the cultivators possessed in abundance. By about 750, the typical dependent cultivator would spend half his time (three days a week) working on the lord's manor. Now a full-time cultivator, he ceased to be a fighter; he thus lost this as his chief claim to status and freedom. He became, in sum, a peasant and a serf. The establishment of a peasant economy in Europe north of the Alps in the early Middle Ages was a decisive change, but its relationship with population densities remains obscure and questionable.

Peasant Economy and the Late-Medieval Crisis

The new peasant economy did, however, show a remarkable capacity for growth, perhaps because the dues the lord could claim from the peasants were fixed by custom; the peasants therefore could increase their own share of output by greater effort or by enlarging the areas of cultivation. In contrast, the slave economy of the ancient world seems to have powerfully repressed demographic growth. For example, the population of ancient Italy seems to have grown hardly at all between the third and first centuries BC (according to Brunt, 1971). The medieval peasant economy rather favored expansion. At least there is no doubt that the numbers of Europeans grew substantially, from at least the year 1000, and were at very high levels when struck by the great plague of 1348.

Interpretations of Population Decline

The plague introduced a period of radical population decline, and Malthusians and Marxists have proposed divergent interpretations of the causes of this great debacle. According to the Malthusian view (well represented by the late M. M. Postan in England and Emmanuel Le Roy Ladurie in France), the small population of the early Middle Ages enjoyed an abundance of resources. Cheap and plenteous food launched and sustained a long wave of expansion (the first phase of a "long-term agrarian cycle"). But by about 1300, increasing human numbers and exhaustion of new lands became the continent's nemesis. A deepening crisis of over-population is manifest in recurrent famines, devastating epidemics and violent competition (wars and revolts) over diminished resources. There ensued, roughly between 1350 and 1420, a horrendous population collapse, probably by as much as two-thirds. The population then stabilized at very low levels, but did not begin to grown again until around 1480, when the long-term agrarian cycle started anew.

Marxist historians, represented by Robert Brenner in America and Guy Bois in France, agree with the data but see the crisis as rooted in the collapse of "feudal rents." The feudal economy could expand only extensively, by taking new lands under cultivation, but the good soils had all been claimed by about 1250. Diminishing returns set in, and the first to suffer from the new penury were the lords. The peasants, many of whom were crowded onto marginal lands, simply could not sustain high levels of rent. Faced with declining rents, the lords took to direct expropriation (pillage) or collective expropriation (wars) to repair their failing fortunes. The heightened levels of social violence increased vulnerability to hunger and epidemics.

The two views invite the following comments: the Malthusian model does not seem to correspond very well with actual population movements. The plagues and famines did not strike against a vigorously expanding population. Rather, Europe's population seems to have remained stable, though at very high levels, a century before 1350. If fourteenth-century plagues and famines were a Malthusian reckoning, they should have occurred a hundred years earlier. And the Marxist model, as outlined above, seems itself to have a Malthusian basis, as it is the growing reliance on poorer soils and the diminished returns to the cultivators that provoke the crisis in feudal rents.

Most recently, historians have been developing a different concept, one not of Malthusian crisis, but of Malthusian deadlock or stalemate. Europe's population by the late thirteenth century had reached a stunning size, and famines were widespread and recurrent. Yet the remarkable aspect of these famines is the slight impact they had on absolute numbers of people. Even the great north-European famine of 1315–17 seems to have produced no considerable and lasting reduction in human numbers. When compared with the impact of epidemics, its consequences appear trivial. Many Europeans in this large population doubtless went hungry, but the community successfully maintained its size until plague overwhelmed it. This Malthusian deadlock might have held on indefinitely within Europe. The plague broke its grip, and ultimately made possible a profound reorganization of the European economy. (See chapter 8)

Causes of and Responses to Hunger throughout the Millennial Era

All of the known civilizations from antiquity to the Middle Ages were characterized by functional specialization leading to hierarchical social systems. Agricultural intensification and the growth of non-agricultural labor resulted in high status for the non-agricultural sector, particularly those who owned the means of production or were in roles of political or religious leadership. Low status for agricultural sectors of society is seen from Mesopotamian temple laborers, to the farmer-warriors of the Roman Empire, to the Middle Ages with their development of peasant economies tied to the land and to food production. At the same time, other ways of acquiring foodstuffs were developed. Trade and protection of trade routes initiated both the safety net of alternate sources of food, and colonization and warfare to secure the sources. It is in this setting that excess appropriation as a cause of hunger emerges, and creates an endemic food poverty.

Causes of Hunger: Excess Appropriation

Appropriation, closely linked to social stratification, refers to the acquisition of resources other than through ownership, production, or exchange. It includes appropriation of the means of production such as labor or land or food itself, or of surplus value in the form of taxation. Appropriation of labor can be through colonization of peoples, through raiding of "barbarian tribes," by tribute, by debt, through peonage, and through slavery. Tribute resulted from subjugation of a people and the requirement of labor from colonies. Those in debt eased their indebtedness through sale of children or young people into indentured servitude. Peonage refers to those individuals bound to the land and allowed to maintain a family, while those in slavery were attached to their owner without benefit of a family themselves. Hierarchical social structure was the cause and in turn the result of excess appropriation of labor and taxation.

The decline of population in the Roman Empire of the first century AD has complex and controversial origins, but food poverty, want, and hunger figure significantly in most analyses (see chapter 5). The connection in the first century between food productivity and excess appropriation, and the constant threat and frequent reality of hunger, resulted from the fragility of productivity. With a few exceptions, Roman agriculture was unable to generate consistent surpluses, sometimes sustained serious failures, and continually suffered from inadequate land transport (Evans, 1981). Not only was food production and distribution fragile, but in many areas there were appropriations − obligations imposed centrally − that proved overwhelming. The historian Rostovtzeff defined the problem as internally driven − the pressure of government on the people − "the supremacy of the interests of the state over those of the population" (1957:377−8). A loss of productivity provided difficulty to the urban dwellers who demanded to be fed, but it proved disastrous to the peasantry. Excess appropriations were variously described as the predations of moving armies on peasant communities in their path, the continuing oppression by neighboring standing armies of the food resources of communities in peace time, or the appropriation of harvests by urban dwellers. While each was a legitimized entitlement of Roman citizenship, direct appropriation of food left the peasantry hungry and without recourse. Galen's AD 148 description of the appropriations of city dwellers is graphic:

> For those who live in the cities, in accordance with their habit of procuring sufficient grain at the beginning of summer to last for the entire coming year, took from the fields all the wheat, barley, beans and lentils, leaving the other legumes to the *rustici*, although they even carted off no small portion of these to the city as well. Consequently the peasantry of these districts, having consumed during the winter whatever was left, were literally compelled for the rest of the year to feed on noxious plants, eating the shoots and tendrils of trees and shrubs, the bulbs and roots of unwholesome plants (quoted in Evans, 1981).

The maintenance of a standing army meant an unrelenting fiscal drain upon already fragile resources, and "involved many in personal contact with a soldiery whose behavior too often ranged from crudely extortionate to openly murderous" (Evans, 1981:439). The other side of this description is provided by Brunt, who noted that in this era, even in peace time, only three of five soldiers lived to return home (Brunt, 1971).

Responses to Hunger and the Threat of Hunger

Food Shortage: Migration and Other Strategies   Consequences of the hardships of food shortage must always have involved dispersal of people to "greener pastures," sometimes voluntarily, sometimes by decree. Successful migration and the establishment of colonies in new areas created center–periphery relationships making possible development of new areas for food production and protection of transport, and enhancing trade relationships.

One of the most effective forms of warfare was to block the movement of a population or the transport of their food by siege (see chapter 6). It was as if the walled city, designed for protection against enemies, became their agent, causing either starvation or capitulation.

Short-term adjustment to the fear of food poverty and long-term adaptation to food shortage have sometimes differed in motivation and pursued opposing objectives. In the Rome of the empire, families in fear of food poverty were known to limit the number of their children, thereby limiting the number of mouths to feed. Government response to food need, on the other hand, was often enlargement of the army and colonization, resulting in official exhortation to have more children, and including entitlement programs targeted to large families, or support of poor families through direct monetary gift.

Food Poverty: Citizen Entitlement Programs   Entitlement in the urbanized ancient world was generally legitimated through citizenship, itself dependent on parentage and residence. While entitlement refers to access to and control over resources, it also refers to exemption from obligation. Citizens were often exempt from taxation but benefited from taxation of the colonies. Levels of citizenship and some form of entitlement characterized all known ancient communities from Sumer and Greece to Rome, and included those landless laborers and slaves resulting from labor appropriation. Their dependent (as opposed to free) status entitled them to food rations, as seen in the Sumerian tablets, to public distributions of grain, as in Attica, or to dispensation from the public granaries of Rome.

In Rome, an entitlement program under the *lex frumentarium*, or grain law, was established by Gaius Gracchus in 123 BC, in which fixed amounts of grain were made available to citizens at subsidized prices. Subsequent political exigencies first limited and then increased the number of citizens who might benefit, and the program was still functioning by the time of Trajan. At its peak in 46 BC, an estimated 320,000 Roman citizens were enrolled, entitling them to purchase subsidized grain. A large number of inscriptions to officials and local dignitaries indicate the extent and importance this program attained (Rickman, 1980).

Food Poverty: Intentional Family Limitation On the family level, adjustment to hunger or the fear of hunger has often taken the form of intentional limitation of the number of children a family would have (Newman, 1972). The prevalence of references by early authors to abstinence, contraception (Preus, 1975), abortion (Dickison, 1973), exposure (Patterson, 1985), and infanticide (Ben Khader et al., 1987; Engles, 1980; Pomeroy, 1983) in times of want, suggest that these were strategies that were known and used in households for spacing between children or to limit the total number of offspring.[3] While the extent of their use has been a subject of question, and is not known with any assurance, their variety and the explicit descriptions of their use in conjunction with lack of consistent reference to large families, except for the very wealthy, give some indication of their acceptance.

In ancient Greece, the most frequent reference to postnatal family limitation strategy was to exposure of a newborn infant, either in an open place where it might be found and "taken up," and possibly sold into slavery, or by placing the newborn in a well or "in some distant place" where it probably would not be found.[4] Many were discovered in Angel's excavations of wells in Attica (Angel, 1945). Effective life was seen to begin with citizenship, signaled by acceptance into the family by the father − there is a specific term, *brephos*, that refers to a fetus and newborn until the ceremony of acceptance. Exposure was one of the ways of choosing the timing, number, and gender of offspring.

According to Patterson (1985) the most cogent and usual reasons for exposure were illegitimacy, a visible defect in the infant, too many children in the family already, or gender selection. Legitimacy was particularly important in a society where citizenship, civil status, and heritage were central issues, and the infant born at an inappropriate time or to inappropriate parents was particularly problematic (Patterson, 1985). Exposure left the possibility of the infant being found. Although this was a part of literary and theatrical tradition, it is not clear how extensively exposure was practiced or how realistic was the expectation of an exposed infant becoming a foundling or even being sold into slavery.

Gender selection also provided a motivating factor in exposure. An estimate of the rate of female infanticide at Athens places exposure of female infants at 10 percent or more of those born (Golden, 1981). The evidence of inscriptions on the Delphinion at Miletus, naming newly en-franchised mercenary soldiers and their families, indicated among the children a ratio of boys to girls of four to one. Pomeroy concludes "the people whose names appear on the Delphinion gave preference to males and exposed or neglected their female offspring, and such practices were not anomalous in Hellenistic Greece" (1983:218). A more subtle and more pervasive form of gender selection may well have been special care of male children as opposed to female. While this practice is difficult to document, it has been perceived in many societies, from the Indus Valley to the western reaches of the Roman Empire (Harris, 1986; Miller, 1981; Wemple, 1981). Differential treatment affects births in the next generation in that it limits the number of females surviving, and may have contributed to lack of population growth in this period.

The further development of Christianity and its interpretations in the Middle Ages introduced a changing set of values and caveats. While exposure and infanticide were unacceptable to Christians, other forms of family limitation became evident in the Middle Ages. As LeRoy Ladurie notes from religious sources in a Christian village in France in the thirteenth and fourteenth centuries: "The documents concerning Montaillou, like others, exhibit both male and adult chauvinism, omitting to mention the existence of some daughters, the presence of young babies or the death of children who perished very early" (1979:77). He indicates also widespread knowledge of herbal medicine for contraceptive purposes. In this era, the practice of withdrawal or coitus interruptus is also documented. The exhortation "*Si non caste tamen caute*", "If not chastely, at least cautiously", was found by Biller as early as 1049; by the thirteenth century it was a commonplace. He derives evidence of coitus interruptus from the writings of the confessors, who consistently condemned the practice, and cites the Savoyarde Peter de Palude: "referring to the married man who engages in contraceptive coitus interruptus, he writes that he does this in order to avoid having children 'whom he cannot feed' (*quos nutrire non possit*)" (1982:24).

Food Deprivation: Family Entitlement Strategies   In Rome at the time of the empire, the *alimenta* was a government entitlement program (modeled on earlier private initiatives) devised under Trajan to provide cash payments for poor children outside Rome in the states and municipalities (Garnsey, 1968; Veyne, 1965). An inscription at Veleia announced distribution in that area to 263 boys, 35 girls, and 2 illegitimate children. A total of 46 such inscriptions has been found in different municipalities. The *alimenta* entitlement program was well known as the subject of a bas-relief at Beneventum and on a series of widely distributed coins.[5]

Conclusion

Agricultural intensification, urbanization, and the complex social organization to support them have been the dominant historical themes in this era. This review has focused on the causes and consequences of hunger, and strategies for its prevention or amelioration. Examples of particular societies have included a discussion of agricultural intensification in Mesopotamia from 6000 BC, land use and citizenship in the Graeco-Roman world from the fifth century BC to the third century AD, and population growth and decline in medieval Europe. All of the examples have dealt with questions of the balance of population and food resources. Permanent settlements and sedentarization of hunting-gathering populations made possible the surplus production that could support non-producers of food, the special-ization of function that led to social stratification. The causes of hunger have ranged from drought, flood, and other natural disasters that curtail food production, to hierarchical social structure with its rules of inclusion and exclusion that limit the distribution of food and wealth, to the excess appropriation of surplus value that characterized the empires of antiquity in their relationships with subject peoples. The consequences of hunger have resulted first in changes in food habits, hoarding, and attempts at restraint of the supply of food. In circumstances of greater need, the consequences of hunger have included food riots against those in political power, raids and warfare against those with resources, out-migration when possible. Strategies of prevention have differed depending on whether there is fear of food shortage at the societal level, or fear of food poverty at the level of the family. All of the societies have undergone periods of plenty and periods of famine, of growth and decline, and long periods of stagnation and barely enough.

NOTES

1   Technology, in Boserup's first work *The Conditions of Agricultural Growth* (1965), referred to agricultural innovation. In *Population and Technological Change* (1981), the reference is to population-related technologies, including not only agricultural methods, but also sanitary methods, literacy, and administrative techniques. This last group is emphasized in this chapter as social organization for population surplus.

2   Some of the best indicators of rise and decline of populations are from arche-
    ological sites of continuous residence for millennia, such as Gomolava on the
    Sava River in present-day Yugoslavia, which was earlier part of the Roman
    Province of Pannonia (Museum of Voivodina, 1986), or Esbus in Transjordan,
    also a Roman outpost (LaBianca, 1987). Rather than suggesting a continuing
    progress, both sites indicate alternating periods of fertility and drought, of
    wealth and poverty, of population density and fewer numbers. Chapter 7 describes
    such an oscillation and ultimate decline of the Mayan civilization of the Yucatan
    Peninsula.

3   Written evidence for the use of fertility regulation in the ancient world is
    derived from a number of sources. The later Hippocratic authors (probably
    fourth to third centuries BC) included abortion in a treatise on the diseases of
    women, suggesting that methods of abortion were known and practiced at that
    time. Aristotle, in the *Politics*, differentiated on the basis of prenatal movement
    between the "unformed fetus" and the "formed" one, thus establishing indicators
    of an acceptable timing for abortion. The herbal compendium of Dioscorides
    Pedanius of Anazarbus (first century AD), *De Materia Medica*, included a large
    number of emmenagogues and abortifacients. Soranus of Ephesus, in the
    second century AD, recommended against such abortifacients "unless they were
    necessary," also suggesting use.
        Contraceptive methods from a number of these sources included herbal
    infusions of roots, barks, leaves, flowers, pessaries (often with a honey base),
    and douches of brine or vinegar. Many of the methods enumerated have
    symbolic or religious value, but no contraceptive effectiveness. Some, however,
    particularly those creating an acidic environment for sperm (such as those
    including citrus, vinegar or honey), can be effective spermicides. Others have
    been found to be oxytocics, muscle relaxants, or plant estrogens, and theoretically
    are capable of impeding conception (Himes, 1963; Hopkins, 1965−6; Newman,
    1985; Riddle, 1985).

4   There is controversy as to the extent of exposure in antiquity between British
    investigators, who note widespread nuclear family structure with close-knit
    family ties (on the basis of tombstones with inscriptions), and French investigators,
    such as Veyne, who consider exposure to have been ubiquitous in antiquity and
    familial love to have appeared only with the advent of Christianity. Veyne writes
    of private life in the Roman Empire: "The story is told in sufficient detail to
    bring out the dramatic contrast with Christianization." He then describes "the
    transition from 'civic man' to 'inward man'" and later asserts that "the Roman
    family, just to take one example, has little in common with its legendary image
    or with what we would call a family" (1987:1−2).

5   Interpretations of this program vary greatly. *The Oxford Classical Dictionary*
    asserts "Its primary object was to increase the birth-rate among the poorer
    classes, partly, as Pliny suggests (*Panegyricus* 26), with a view to the recruiting of
    the Roman legions" (Hammond and Scullard, 1978:45). The ratio of males to
    females would support this view. Evans, on the other hand, suggests "in Italy at
    least, the incidence of malnutrition-related exposure and infanticide seems to
    have been of sufficient magnitude that late in the First Century AD the imperial

government, following local precedent, designed a program to counteract it: the celebrated and much-discussed *alimenta*" (1981:429).

REFERENCES

Adams, Robert McC. 1981: *Heartland of Cities: Surveys of ancient settlement and land use on the central floodplain of the Euphrates.* Chicago: University of Chicago Press.

Angel, J. L. 1945: Skeletal material from Attica. *Hesperia*, 14, 249–63.

Barker, Graeme 1985: *Prehistoric Farming in Europe.* Cambridge: Cambridge University Press.

Ben Khader, Aicha Ben Abed, and Soren, David 1987: *Carthage: A mosaic of ancient Tunisia.* New York: The American Museum of Natural History and W. W. Norton.

Biller, P. P. A. 1982: Birth-control in the West in the thirteenth and early fourteenth centuries. *Past and Present*, 94, 3–26.

Boserup, Ester 1965: *The Conditions of Agricultural Growth.* London: Allen and Unwin.

Boserup, Ester 1981: *Population and Technological Change.* Chicago: University of Chicago Press.

Brunt, P. A. 1971: *Italian Manpower 225 BC to AD 14.* London: Oxford University Press.

Camp II, John McK. 1982: Drought and famine in the fourth century BC. *Hesperia*, Supplement 20, 9–17.

Campbell, Bruce M. S. 1982: Population pressure, inheritance and the land market in a fourteenth-century peasant community. In Richard M. Smith (ed.), *Land, Kinship and Life-Cycle*, Cambridge: Cambridge University Press.

de Jong, J. W. 1985: The overburdened earth in India and Greece. *Journal of the American Oriental Society*, 105, 397–400.

Dickison, Sheila K. 1973: Abortion in antiquity. *Arethusa*, 6, 159–66.

Ellison, Rosemary 1981: Diet in Mesopotamia: The evidence of the barley ration texts, (c.3000–1400 BC). *Iraq*, 45, 35–45.

Ellison, Rosemary 1983: Some thoughts on the diet of Mesopotamia from c.3000–600 BC. *Iraq*, 45, 146–50.

Engles, Donald 1980: The problem of female infanticide in the Graeco-Roman world. *Classical Philology*, 75, 112–20.

Evans, J. E. 1981: Wheat production and its social consequences in the Roman world. *Classical Quarterly*, 31, 428–42.

Feen, Richard Harrow 1983: Abortion and exposure in ancient Greece: Assessing the status of the fetus and 'newborn' from classical sources. In William B. Bondeson, H. Tristram Engelhardt, Jr, Stuart Spicker, and Daniel H. Winship (eds), *Abortion and the Status of the Fetus*, Dordrecht: D. Reidel, 283–300.

Flannery, Kent V. 1965: The ecology of early food production in Mesopotamia. *Science*, 147, 1247–56.

Garnsey, Peter 1968: Trajan's *alimenta*: Some problems, *Historia*, 17, 381.

Garnsey, Peter 1983: Famine in Rome. In Peter Garnsey and C. R. Whittaker (eds), *Trade and Famine in Classical Antiquity*, The Cambridge Philological Society, supplementary vol. 8, 56–65.

Garnsey, Peter 1988: *Famine and Food Supply in the Graeco-Roman World: Responses to risk and crisis.* Cambridge: Cambridge University Press.

Garnsey, Peter, Gallant, T., and Rathbone, D. 1984: Thessaly and the grain supply of Rome during the second century BC. *The Journal of Roman Studies*, 74, 30–44.

Golden, Mark 1981: The exposure of girls at Athens. *Phoenix*, 35, 316–31.

Hammel, E. A. and Howell, Nancy 1987: Research in population and culture: An evolutionary framework. *Current Anthropology*, 28, 141–60.

Hammond, N. G. L. and Scullard, H. H. (eds) 1978: *The Oxford Classical Dictionary*. Oxford: Clarendon Press, second edition.

Harriss, Barbara 1986: The intrafamily distribution of hunger in south Asia. Helsinki, Finland: Paper for WIDER Project on Hunger and Poverty: Seminar on Food Strategies. Draft.

Herlihy, David 1985: *Medieval Households*. Cambridge Mass.: Harvard University Press.

Himes, N. E. 1963: *Medical History of Contraception*. New York: Gamut Press (first published 1936).

Hopkins, M. K. 1965–6: Contraception in the Roman Empire. *Comparative Studies in Society and History*, 8, 124–51.

Jacobson, Thorbild and Adams, Robert McC. 1958: Salt and silt in Mesopotamian agriculture. *Science*, 128, 1251–8.

Jameson, Michael 1983: Famine in the Greek World. In Peter Garnsey and C. R. Whittaker (eds), *Trade and Famine in Classical Antiquity*, The Cambridge Philological Society, supplementary vol. 8, 6–12.

La Bianca, Oystein Sakala 1987: Sedentarization and Nomadization: *Food System Cycles at Hesban and Vicinity in Transjordan.* Winona Lake, Indiana: Andrews University Press.

Lee, Ronald Demos 1986: Malthus and Boserup: A dynamic synthesis. In David Coleman and Roger Schofield (eds), *The State of Population Theory*, New York: Basil Blackwell.

LeRoy Ladurie, Emmanuel 1979: *Montaillou: The promised land of error.* New York: Vintage Books, translated by Barbara Bray.

Lucas, Henry S. 1930: The great European famine of 1315, 1316, and 1317. *Speculum: A Journal of Medieval Studies*, 5, 343–77.

Miller, Barbara D. 1981: *The Endangered Sex*. Ithaca, NY: Cornell University Press.

Museum of Voivodina 1986: *Gomolava: Prehistory to the Middle Ages*. Novi Sad, Yugoslavia.

Newman, Lucile F. 1972: Birth control: An anthropological view. Addison-Wesley Modular Publications, 27, 1–21.

Newman, Lucile F. (ed.) 1985: *Women's Medicine: A Cross Cultural Study of Indigenous Methods of Fertility Regulation*. New Brunswick, NJ: Rutgers University Press.

Oppenheim, A. L. 1955: Siege documents from Nippur. *Iraq*, 17, 69–89.

Patterson, Cynthia 1985: "Not worth the rearing": The causes of infant exposure in ancient Greece. *Transactions of the American Philological Association*, 115, 103–23.

Polanyi, Karl, Arensberg, Conrad M., and Pearson, Harry W. (eds), 1957: *Trade and Market in the Early Empires: Economies in theory and history.* Glencoe, Ill.: The Free Press.

Pomeroy, Sarah 1983: Infanticide in Hellenistic Greece. In A. Cameron and A. Kuhrt (eds), *Images of Women in Antiquity*, London: Croom Helm, 207–22.

Preus, Anthony 1975: Biomedical techniques for influencing human reproduction in the fourth century BC. *Arethusa*, 8.

Rickman, Geoffrey 1980: *The Corn Supply of Ancient Rome.* Oxford: Clarendon Press.

Riddle, John M. 1985: *Dioscorides on Pharmacy and Medicine.* Austin: University of Texas Press.

Rostovtzeff, M. 1957: *The Social and Economic History of the Roman Empire.* Oxford: Clarendon Press, second edition revised by P. M. Fraser.

Rouche, Michel 1973: La faim à l'époque carolingienne: essai sur quelques types de rations alimentaires. *Revue Historique*, 295–320.

Roux, Georges 1980: *Ancient Iraq.* Harmondsworth: Penguin Books, second edition.

Saller, Richard P. and Shaw, Brent D. 1984: Tombstones and Roman family relations in the principate: Civilians, soldiers and slaves, *The Journal of Roman Studies*, 74, 124–56.

Veyne, P. 1965: Les "Alimenta" de Trajan. In *Les Empereurs Romains d'Espagne*, Paris: Editions du Centre National de la Recherche Scientifique, 169–70.

Veyne, Paul, (ed.) 1987: *A History of Private Life: from Pagan Rome to Byzantium.* Cambridge, Mass.: The Belknap Press, translated by Arthur Goldhammer.

Wemple, Suzanne Fonay 1981: *Women in Frankish Society: Marriage and the cloister 500 to 900.* Philadelphia: University of Pennsylvania Press.

Zagarell, Allen 1986: Trade, women, class, and society in ancient western Asia. *Current Anthropology*, 27, 415–30.

5

Responses to Food Crisis in the Ancient Mediterranean World

PETER GARNSEY

The potential for hunger in the form of food crisis was a regular feature of Mediterranean society from Homer to Justinian (eight century BC–sixth century AD).[1] The causes were both natural and human. Food crises, then as now, issued from a sharp reduction of available food, not of food produced. Its origins are therefore to be found, on the one hand, in the climate, the physical environment, and the state of agricultural technology, and on the other, in the conditions of transport and trade, and the disruption of the movement of essential foods through human intervention in the form of war, piracy, maladministration, or profiteering.

Food crises vary greatly in intensity. It is helpful to think in terms of a food crisis spectrum with scarcity at one end and disastrous famine at the other, where the two key terms are given the following working definitions (cf. Bennett, 1968; Sen, 1981:39–40):

> Food scarcity is a short-term reduction in the amount of available foodstuffs, as indicated by rising prices, popular discontent, and hunger, in the worst cases bordering on starvation.

> Famine is a critical shortage of essential foodstuffs leading through hunger to starvation and a substantially increased mortality rate in a community or region.

The most serious food crises, those belonging at the famine end of the spectrum, were a consequence of a succession of harvest failures, wars of long duration, sieges, or the conjunction of harvest shortfall and epidemic disease. In terms of impact rather than cause, symptoms of famine as opposed to scarcity include, in addition to the sharp rise in mortality rates which is the main defining characteristic of famine, the following: severe food price inflation; dramatic action by government, including food rationing and the expulsion of sections of the population (slaves, gladiators, foreigners);

and drastic reactions among ordinary people, including emigration, suicide, sale of children, and the consumption of strange foods.

Most of these features are visible, for example, in the crisis of AD 312– 13 suffered by the people of Palestine as recorded by Eusebius, or in the crisis of AD 499–501 at Edessa, northern Mesopotamia, in the extended narrative of Pseudo-Joshua (Garnsey, 1988:3–6, 34–5). Both these food crises were most definitely famines. Many others, however, are not so easily classified. The explanation for this lies in the sketchy treatment of the ancient sources. Food crises were not an object of interest in themselves to the historians and biographers of antiquity. Where they do enter the historical record, it is usually because a superstitious people ascribed to them religious significance as portents, or because they gave rise to important political events, or because they illustrate the character, the virtues and vices, of an emperor or other high-ranking politician. At the same time, judicious source-criticism can take us quite a long way in assessing "famine narratives" within single works and in making cross-comparisons from one work to another. Formal inscriptions on stone, a second major source of relevant information, equally fail to provide in-depth analysis of food crises; their purpose is usually to glorify or honor an individual for his generosity to the state and its citizens. But the shortcomings of this form of evidence, as of the literary sources, do not prevent qualitative evaluations of the crises to which they refer. Finally, the cumulative data furnished by the various kinds of source convey the following message about the frequency and severity of food crises. Briefly, famine was rare, the outcome of abnormal conditions, whereas scarcity was common.

The Pattern of Food Crises

Food Crises Were Frequent

The frequency of food crisis is easily illustrated with reference to the best-known communities of antiquity, Athens and Rome. Romans suffered food crisis more than one year in nine between 509 and 384 BC (the early Republic) and about one year in five between 123 and 50 BC (the late Republic). Athenians experienced about one food crisis every six years between 403 and 323 BC. However, frequency of food crisis can be illustrated also from other states, and with the aid of sources which are few in number and narrow in range but nonetheless qualitatively impressive.

The island of Samos, just off the west coast of modern Turkey, is a pertinent case. The coverage of the literary sources is poor. If it has proved possible to write a history of the island (Shipley, 1987), this is because the non-literary sources (archeology, epigraphy, and coins) go some way towards filling the gaps left by literature. Two inscriptions are enough to prove the vulnerability of Samos to food crisis in the third century BC (Austin, 1981:113, 116). The first of them is a decree of the local council and assembly in honor of a local benefactor, by name Boulagoras. It is carved into marble and is 60 lines or over 600 words in length. What benefits did Boulagoras confer on Samos around the middle of the third century BC? The decree begins by recording a spectacular act of diplomacy. Boulagoras recovered for Samos from the Seleucid king Antiochus Hierax, in whose sphere of influence Samos lay at the time, a valuable strip of territory on the mainland (the Anaia) traditionally belonging to Samos but lost from time to time to neighbouring states, and now taken over by courtiers of the king. Boulagoras did not secure a royal audience at Ephesos, but he pursued the king to Sardis and won his approval for the return of the lands against the opposition of the courtiers. The Anaia was an important source of agricultural wealth; Samians (including perhaps Boulagoras) owned property there, and the tithes from the temple estate of Hera in the Anaia provided the grain for the distributions set up in Samos a generation later (see below). The inscription goes on to describe Boulagoras' services to the people with regard to the food supply on three separate occasions. Once he "advanced all the money required for a reserve fund as the people had resolved." Another time, he "promised to equal the contributions of those who provided the most;" this followed another call from the people for contributions to a grain-purchase fund. Rather than advance the whole amount, Boulagoras tried to stimulate some activity among his peers. The third occasion was a more complicated affair:

> He not only contributed from his own pocket all the money for the reserve fund, but also, when the grain had been brought to the city and the grain commissioner was negotiating a loan for it, he came forward in the assembly and promised that, since there were no resources available to refund the money, he himself would pay back the loan on behalf of the city, together with the interest and all other expenses, and he did this quickly and refunded the creditor without imposing any written contract for these sums on the city, and without requesting the nomination of guarantors, but attaching the greatest importance to the common good and the enjoyment of abundance by the people.

It appears that the sum made over by Boulagoras in advance turned out to be insufficient to purchase the grain required. Grain prices were perhaps higher than had been anticipated. The grain commissioner was forced to look for further loans to pay the traders, who were demanding payment before they would release the grain. Loans were negotiated. At some later stage, presumably when the loans were due to be repaid, Boulagoras intervened again and settled the account. If he had hoped that the city's finances would recover sufficiently to pay back those loans, which carried interest, as well as his own, which may or may not have carried interest, he was disappointed. It may be noted in passing that Boulagoras, for all the talk of patriotic zeal, dealt only in loans, not in gifts, whether of cash or of grain. Moreover, the inscription does not state that his loans were interest-free, as some parallel inscriptions do, or, in the first two instances, that he had written off his loans. For present purposes, however, the essential point is that the city faced at least three food crises within the political career of one Samian.

The second inscription comes from the turn of the third century, that is, a little over a generation later than the honorific decree for Boulagoras. It is a law establishing a permanent grain fund for Samos, and setting out the arrangements for controlling it and acquiring and distributing the grain purchased from the fund. The contents, after the opening lines which are missing, may be summarized as follows:

1   The people grouped by tribes are to elect the managers of the grain fund and approve securities and guarantors provided by the managers.
2   The managers are to collect interest from the borrowers of the sums donated and pay it over to special grain officials.
3   The special grain officials are to purchase grain from the returns of the 5-percent tax on the temple estates of Hera on the Anaia at a minimum price of 5 drachmas 2 obols.
4   Any money not spent in the purchase of grain should be handed over by the special grain officials either to their successors or to the elected grain commissioner for further purchases, as the people decide.
5   The grain commissioner is to purchase the extra grain from the Anaia or elsewhere, as the people decide. The matter is to be discussed in an assembly meeting in the month of Artemision every year.
6   At the magisterial elections each year, the first to be appointed after the regular magistrates are two men, one from each tribe, to be special grain officials, each with property of at least three talents. Their task is to receive interest from the managers, pay for the grain and measure it out.
7   At the same assembly a grain commissioner is to be appointed, with property worth not less than two talents.
8   The money from interest does not have to be spent on grain by the grain commissioner; it can be lent on provision of suitable security and guarantors to others to get grain more advantageously. This is the responsibility of the special grain officials.

9   Distribution is to resident citizens by tribe, monthly, at two measures each, to begin in the month Pelusion, and to continue until the grain runs out.
10 Managers can serve up to five times in succession if elected.
11 If borrowers fail to pay back the money, then the tribe concerned must find the money from the sale of security and from the guarantors; if the managers take the money they are supposed to lend and keep it for themselves, they are liable to a fine of 10,000 drachmas; if the managers do not pay over the interest to the special grain officials, they are to forfeit 10,000 drachmas, and the tribe does not receive the grain that is its due unless its members provide the money themselves; if the funds are directed to other purposes, the guilty parties are to pay a fine of 10,000 drachmas.
12 List of subscribers: 98 persons gave a total of 16,200 drachmas, and there are 31 missing contributors and contributions.

There is much of interest in this remarkable document, not least the elaborate precautionary measures designed to preserve the fund and see that its purposes were not thwarted; hence the multitude of officials and the detailing of offences and sanctions for offenders. The authorities obviously felt that rich Samians (all the officials concerned had to be men of property) were extremely corruptible. The central point is that the Samians would not have bothered to set up a grain fund if the community did not suffer from endemic food supply problems. Here it is worth noting the clause charging the assembly with considering the position as regards the food supply in the month of Artemision, that is to say, every spring.

Famine Was Rare

The next question to discuss is whether the ancient evidence helps us decide whether food crisis often reached famine proportions. While making full allowance for the gaps in the evidence, one can conclude that famines were rare. It is not only that few famines are recorded, though this does count for something in the best-known states at least; but in addition, all the communities of antiquity developed mechanisms, which though rudimentary were nonetheless effective, for heading off famine. Here the example of Samos is more relevant than those of Athens or Rome, whose experiences were singular. Whereas there was only one state in fifth- and fourth-century Greece that both was a democracy and ran an empire, Athens, the Greek world was full of men like Boulagoras of Samos (Gauthier, 1985; Veyne, 1976). In fact, no oligarchic state (and oligarchy was the standard form of government throughout the Mediterranean region after the fourth century BC) could preserve its constitution intact unless members of the ruling class were prepared from time to time to be public benefactors like Boulagoras. What precisely did his, and their, achievement amount to? It was not the prevention of food shortage. On the contrary, food shortages were frequent. Rather their interventions prevented famine evolving out of shortage. No doubt there were some genuine famines, when the rich were unable to shoulder the burdens of the community for one reason or another, perhaps because of a combination of food crisis and disastrous epidemic or war. But the typical food crisis was one of those alluded to in the hundreds of inscriptions celebrating the successful intervention of a public benefactor, whether acting in an official capacity or as a private individual, in arresting the slide from crisis into catastrophe.

Proxy Data

The conclusion that food shortage was common and famine rare is to some extent confirmed by modern agroclimatological data from the Mediterranean region.[2] The general picture provided by such data (rather than the precise details), when transferred to other periods of history marked by comparable climatic conditions, suggests a model of the environmental constraints against the background of which traditional farmers had to operate (Garnsey et al., 1984). It is generally agreed that the Mediterranean climate (or climates) in the modern period and in classical antiquity were broadly similar (Renfrew and Wagstaff, 1982:95ff; Wagstaff, 1981; and chapter 2, this volume).

A well-known feature of the modern Mediterranean climate is the low and variable rainfall which commonly but unpredictably produces a poor or mediocre crop in many parts of the region, particularly in the south and east. There can be little doubt that the inhabitants of the Mediterranean in antiquity experienced essentially similar conditions, even if quantitative data such as are available for the modern period are lacking. The most detailed evidence from antiquity is the data furnished by tree-ring analysis; these demonstrate a pattern of interannual variability in tree growth which implies a corresponding pattern of climate variability in forested areas (Kuniholm and Striker, 1983; Mariolopoulos, 1962).

What can be divined from the modern data which has relevance to food crisis, its incidence and severity? Rainfall figures for Attica in 1931–60 over the winter months (October to May), the season of growth for the main sown crops, when set against moisture thresholds, produce the following results. The percentage probability of a failure of wheat, barley, and dry legumes was, respectively, 28 percent, 5.5 percent, and 71 percent. That is to say, wheat failed more than one year in four, barley about one in twenty and legumes almost three years in four.

Attica is generally thought of as one of the drier and less productive

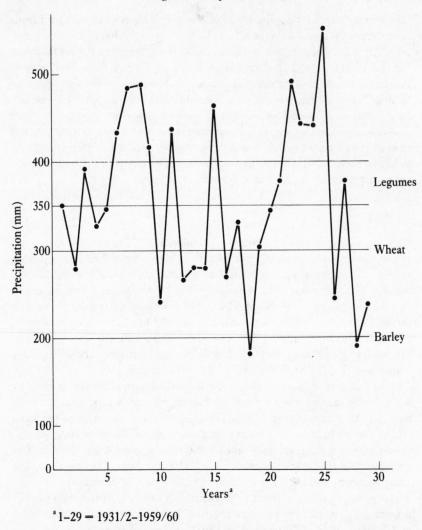

Figure 5.1 Winter precipitation in Attica against crop moisture requirements.

areas of Greece. Thessaly is supposed to be more fertile. Yet the modern data show that wheat performs no more reliably in the plain of Larisa, the centre of Thessalian cereal production, than in Attica, and barley less so (for the years 1911, 1926–36, 1955–6, and 1959–80): the failure rate is more than one year in four for wheat and one year in ten for barley; dry legumes fail more than four years in ten. Thessaly owes its reputation as a

Table 5.1 Percentage probability of crop failure in Athens and Larisa

	1 year	2 years in succession
Athens		
Wheat	28.0	7.8
Barley	5.5	0.3
Larisa		
Wheat	28.5	8.1
Barley	5.5	0.3

cereal producer to the fact that it offers extensive areas of arable land and large surpluses in good years (Garnsey et al., 1984).

The modern data have implications for repeated as well as one-off crop failure. The probability of a poor harvest in successive years is much lower than in single years (see table 5.1).

The modern data, therefore, confirm the picture provided for antiquity by the contemporary sources: in so far as harvest failure underlies most food crises, and repeated harvest failures prepare the ground for famine, then, on the one hand, food shortage will be frequent, and on the other, famine will be infrequent.

In the rest of this paper, I analyse responses to food crisis among ancient populations. How did Mediterranean communities cope with the problem of food crises, given that they occurred frequently, without being precisely predictable? Two sets of responses are analyzed, the first secular and the second religious. There are two preliminary comments to be made. First, as with secular so with religious responses, my present interest is in *communal* disaster and response. This means that I am passing over the whole field of individual misfortunes, and the explanations and responses of private individuals, especially of a magical nature, that were rooted in popular culture.

Secular Responses

Peasants

A rounded view of the peasantry in antiquity is difficult to arrive at. The attention of the literary sources, which emanate from the cultured urban elite, is seldom drawn to lower-class society, apart from slaves, who were valuable property. Galen, the second-century AD physician and philosopher from Pergamum in Asia Minor, is exceptional for his interest in ordinary countryfolk. Sometimes his information is conveyed in the form of brief digressions in the midst of extended anatomical or physiological discussions. Thus for example, when treating the drawing capacity of things, he tells a story about crafty peasants who try to add weight to the wheat they are bringing to market by hiding a jar of water amongst it, knowing that the wheat will absorb some of the moisture from the jar. The treatise *On the Properties of Foodstuffs*, however, while pervaded by physiological and philosophical doctrine, is at another level a catalogue of foods and drinks consumed in the Roman Empire, with particular attention given to those that formed part of the peasant diet, in both normal and critical times. The following passage nicely illustrates the peasant's resourcefulness and ability to cope in lean times:

Ch. 38: Concerning the fruit of wild plants, among them acorns from oak trees.

All men are accustomed to call those plants wild which grow on the land without the farmer's aid ... Among plants of this kind are the oaks, the cornel tree and arbutus and other trees of this kind, to which one can add shrubs like the bramble, dog-thorn, the wild pears and wild plums and medlars. The fruit of this shrub is called "inedible" in Italy, being bad for the stomach and headache-inducing and quite sour with a slight suspicion of sweetness.

Countryfolk habitually eat the fruit of the cornel tree and blackberries and acorns and the fruit of the arbutus, and rather less those of the other trees and shrubs. But when our land is in the grip of food crisis, and there are plenty of acorns and medlars, countryfolk store them in pits and consume them instead of food from cereals throughout the winter and in early spring. Acorns were previously fed to swine, then when the pigs could not be kept in the winter in the usual way, first they slaughtered them and used them as food, then they opened up their storage pits and began to eat the acorns, preparing them as food in a variety of ways from place to place. Sometimes they boiled them in water, covered them in hot ashes and roasted them moderately. Or else having crushed them and reduced them to a powder, they made a soup out of them, sometimes soaking them in water by itself and throwing in some condiment, sometimes pouring in honey and boiling it with milk.

... Acorns alone of the wild fruits give the body worthwhile nourishment. The fruit of the cornel tree and the plum and the blackberry and white rose, sloe, arbutus, jujube, nettletree, winter cherry, terebinth and wild pear, and so on, give meagre nourishment. They are all productive of bad juices, and some of them are bad for the stomach and have a disagreeable taste. They are pig food, and I am not talking of the domesticated variety, but of those whose habitat is the mountains. They at least get a lot of nourishment from them.

Ch. 39: On nourishment from the plants themselves.

We eat not only the seeds and fruit of plants, but also the plants themselves, often in their entirety, often only the roots or sprigs or new shoots, according as the need is pressing for each. In our part of the world at least, people are used to tearing off the stalk and leaves of turnips ... they sometimes eat them, making do with them when better foods are lacking. They do this too with the same parts of radishes and what in our dialect is called *rapus*. It is what one might call a wild radish. And often when forced by hunger people eat pyrethrum, sia, alexander, fennel, wild chervil, chicory, gum soccory, gingidium, wild carrot, and the tender shoots of a great many shrubs and trees. Some of these they eat even when they are not suffering from hunger, just as some eat the top of rye-grass which they call its head.

Discussions of comparable quality of peasant farming practices, relationships with equals and superiors, and family structure, all matters central to the survival strategy of any peasantry, are not available in the extant literature from antiquity. What follows is a composite picture reconstructed from many fragments of information and tested in the light of comparative evidence (Forbes, 1982; Foxhall, 1986; Halstead, 1984, 1988; Millett, 1984; Scott, 1976; etc.).

Peasants in antiquity, as in other traditional societies, followed a production strategy designed to minimize risk. The essential components of this strategy involved property dispersal, crop diversification, storage of the surplus (and, as Galen testifies, of substitute foods), and "social storage," or the cultivation of reciprocal relationships with, on the one hand, kin, friends, and neighbours, and on the other, patrons. In addition, peasants sought to maintain an equilibrium between family size and economic resources by following various adaptive strategies. These included the adjustment of marriage age and the interval between births, contraception, abortion, and, in particular, infant exposure. The key point is that peasants did not passively await the operation of the Malthusian positive check of famine. On the contrary, they actively pursued adaptive strategies in the shaping of the family, in the process of agricultural production, and in management of social and economic relations.

Urban Communities

A proportion of the residents of cities were consumers who were not at the same time agricultural producers. How were their wants satisfied? Surprisingly, city governments devised very little in the way of permanent institutions for maintaining a regular food supply system and for coping with food crisis.

Athens and Rome break this rule of minimal government intervention, though not in all periods of their history. In the case of Athens, a truly impressive apparatus of laws and institutions to secure the food supply was erected only in the course of the fourth century BC, and collapsed when democracy was suppressed in 322 BC. At some point in the fourth century, the Athenians passed a double-barrelled law encouraging imports: any voyage made by a transport vessel that was financed by a maritime loan negotiated by an Athenian, resident alien, or one in his power (typically, a slave), had to issue in the import of necessities, particularly grain, to Athens; no one who lived at Athens could transport grain to any other port than the Piraeus. The penalty for breach of these laws was death. There were measures backed by the same harsh sanctions to ensure that at least two-thirds of the grain once arrived at the port got onto the market in the city of Athens itself (the rest was apparently held at the Piraeus), to restrict the amount of grain that dealers could buy, and also their profit margins. A college of no fewer than 35 officials named grain-wardens watched over the operation. The Romans, for their part, developed a regular grain supply system for the first time from the turn of the third century BC, when grain began to be exacted as tax from the annexed provinces of Sicily and Sardinia and as rent from confiscated lands in Campania. Moreover, monthly distributions of subsidized grain were instituted in Rome only from 123 BC, and for a minority of the inhabitants of the metropolis. It is important to stress that Athens and Rome were different. They may be the best-known of all ancient states, but they were also the least typical.

A brief glance at the range of potential responses to food crisis highlights the atypicality of Athens and Rome. The main options of states seeking to avoid or soften the impact of food crisis were the following:

1   Increasing food production: extend land under cultivation, raise arable, or raise productivity on existing arable.
2   Imperialism: territorial expansion at the expense of other communities.
3   Colonization: "export" population, so as to reduce aggregate consumption requirements.
4   Supply: obtain staple foodstuffs from domestic producers and from abroad through trade and other methods of exchange.
5   Distribution: allocate foodstuffs throughout the citizen community.

The first option, the extension or intensification of production, was not ordinarily taken up by governments. Decisions as to how much land to cultivate, which crops to sow, and production targets to aim at were customarily left to the individual farmer.

The second and third options were not regularly available to the mass of ordinary cities of the Mediterranean world. Imperialism as a long-term policy was open only to major powers such as Athens in her prime, Macedon, and Rome. Again, colonization could not normally be indulged in with profit by any but the powerful.

There remain two lines of action, the supply of essential foodstuffs and their distribution through the community. How far did governments ordinarily intervene in these areas?

Supply In the matter of supply, instead of taking long-term measures to avoid future food shortage, city authorities tended to react to each crisis as it came. Thus the importing of food from outside was left to private enterprise. Trade in antiquity was in private hands. States neither owned merchant fleets nor employed those who sailed in them. Largely informal contacts were made with traders who were independent and cosmopolitan. In addition, arrangements, again normally informal, were made with neighboring cities, and with others bound by traditional links, such as those existing between mother city and colony. These loose networks of supply were brought into play and supplemented in critical times by special officials appointed for the tasks of finding emergency grain stocks and the money to purchase them – officials like the grain commissioner of the Samos inscriptions.

Similarly, governments did not normally interfere with the distribution of locally produced foodstuffs; this was left in the hands of the landowners themselves and whatever agents they employed for marketing their produce. This meant that the rich could also decide not to market their grain, or to release it too slowly or in quantities insufficient to satisfy demand. Even public benefactors like Boulagoras were not above speculating in vital foodstuffs. They differed from other rich landowners in the degree of willingness they showed to limit their own gains in the interests of the community at large. An inscription honoring one Polykritos of Erythrae is essentially similar to the epigraphic tribute to Boulagoras of Samos; but it contains the following sentence, which carries serious implications about the dual role performed by him and others of his kind as benefactor and grain hoarder: "Later, when because of the grain shortage no one was bringing grain into the market, he promised the people to advance money for a reserve fund to those about to be appointed grain commissioners, and to bring into the market the wheat he himself held so that the people might be fed."

The Boulagoras inscription does not give the game away quite so openly. It should, however, be noted that he never made over grain to the grain commissioners or directly to the people, and apparently charged interest on his loans, unlike Polykritos. One Protogenes from Olbia in the northern Black Sea region had an extraordinary list of benefactions to display in his prodigiously long inscription, but those acts of generosity that concern us are somewhat ambiguous. Protogenes, like Polykritos, put grain on the market in times of food crisis, but still made a healthy profit; the grain was sold (sold, not given) at less than the heavily inflated market rate. Moreover, it is clear that Protogenes was expecting repayment. As in the case of Boulagoras, this was a forlorn hope, and he had to write off the debts: he could well afford to do so (Austin, 1981:97). Moschion of Priene gives a better impression. He twice offered cut-price grain and once gave it away, a very rare occurrence in the epigraphy of the Hellenistic period (third to first centuries BC, to which all the above inscriptions belong). The suspicion has been voiced that he was, or was fearful that he might become, a target of food riots (Veyne, 1976:223). This may be unfair, but it can be agreed that it was above all the danger of civil disturbance or social revolution which moderated the selfishness of the urban ruling classes. Resolutions of the popular assembly and council, extracted from the ruling class by pressure from below, usually induced one or more of its members to act as grain commissioner, advance cash, or release some of the supplies of grain superfluous to their own requirements which they inevitably had in their barns and warehouses.

When appeals from government were unavailing, further steps were sometimes taken which limited the control of local landowners and traders over essential foods. We find both restrictions on the movement of grain, and orders that private grain stocks be released and sold.

Prohibitions on export appear early in the historical record. Solon of Athens passed a law in the first decade of the sixth century BC forbidding the export of all agricultural produce apart from olive oil (Plutarch, *Life of Solon* : 24). The context is unknown but can be reconstructed in the light of other incidents, for example a food crisis in Selybria near Byzantium which produced a law explicitly banning the export of grain, and a similar crisis in Aspendus in Pamphylia (southwest Asia Minor), resolved by the pagan wonder-worker Apollonius of Tyana. When Apollonius came to Aspendus: "He found vetches on sale in the market, and the citizens were feeding upon this and on anything else they could get; for the rich men had shut up all the grain and were holding it up for export from the country" (Philostratus, *Life of Apollonius* :1.15). In Solonian Athens landowners had presumably been sending their supplies abroad instead of releasing them on the home market at a time when they were sorely needed.

The same unpatriotic spirit was exhibited in the city of Teos on the Asia Minor coast a little more than a century later. This time the offences are identified as either preventing the import of grain or hoarding grain once it had been imported. An inscription lists curses to be repeated by the magistrates of the city three times each year, among them the following: "If anyone prevents grain from being imported into the territory of Teos by any pretext or device, either by sea or from the mainland, or forces up the price of imported grain, that man shall die, both himself and his family" (Fornara, 1983:63 (corrected translation)).

The regulation from Teos differs from the Solonian law and similar laws elsewhere in that it was not an ad hoc, temporary measure. Permanent legislation passed in the interests of the consumer was a rarity in the Greek world. The Athenians were exceptional in regulating the profits of traders, millers, and bakers. For example, a speech of Lysias of about 386 BC shows that grain dealers were restricted in the quantity of grain they could buy and the amount they could charge above the wholesale price. Rome had an anti-speculation law from the reign of the first emperor, Augustus (27 BC–AD 14), and the law seems to have served as a model for similar regulations in cities founded or promoted by the Romans in the western provinces of the empire (Gonzales, 1986:193). However, there is no sign that such laws were ever enforced, or that others like them were introduced in the eastern empire.

Secondly, governments from time to time ordered the release of private grain stocks and their sale at reasonable prices. In the Roman period this end was achieved commonly through the intervention of outside agents, normally Roman governors and other officials, but also charismatic individuals, whether pagan wonder-workers (such as Apollonius of Tyana) or Christian ascetics. It is difficult to avoid the conclusion that Roman rule reduced the capacity of the subject communities of the empire to cope with food crises and other emergencies, both by making demands of local economies and by reducing political autonomy.

The central message is clear: city authorities took only rudimentary, ad-hoc measures against food hoarders, real or suspect, in the midst of food crisis. Supply of foodstuffs has now been considered; it remains to ask whether governments commonly distributed cheap or free grain to the citizenry on a regular basis.

Distribution   Although some cities possessed grain reserves and special grain-purchase funds, regular grain distributions were very rare indeed. Outside Crete, Samos, some Egyptian towns (in particular periods), and of course Rome, they hardly existed.

Aristotle describes the Cretan communal distributions thus: "Out of the crops and cattle produced from the public lands, and the tribute paid by the serfs, one part is assigned for the worship of the gods and the maintenance of public services, and the other part for the public messtables" (Aristotle, *Politics* : 1272a17). This was an archaic survival, embodying the old ideology, born with the Greek polis itself, that the revenues of the state were the possession of its citizens (Latte, 1968:294ff). The documents show that the Cretan system gradually lost its special character, until under the Romans it consisted of biennial distributions financed by the rich.

The Samian distribution system was apparently also singular. Moreover, it conferred only limited benefits on the people of Samos. The distributions were financed by a public subscription, which was then invested, and produced interest that was put to the purchase of grain each year. The problem is that the sum realized in this way was not nearly enough to feed more than a small fraction of the citizens (as in Crete, only citizens could receive) for part of the year. The grain fund, in other words, was by no means a complete solution to the food supply problem. The system, ironically, worked best in good years, when 5 percent of the harvest from the temple estate was an appreciable amount of grain and could be obtained relatively cheaply. In bad seasons the funds available would have bought much less grain, and Samos would have had to fall back on more orthodox remedies – grain commissioners and benefactors.

For more comprehensive measures in support of the citizenry one looks to democratic and imperial Athens and imperial Rome. Democratic Athenians believed that all citizens had a stake in the revenues of the state, and in the heyday of empire there was wealth to distribute, but it was cash rather than food which was made available, and as a reward for participation in the political, judicial, and economic activities of the state. There were echoes of the old ideology at the birth of the Roman distribution system in 123 BC, but the ruling class at Rome was deeply conservative, and the distributions were maintained, and in time extended, out of political necessity not ideological conviction. Nor were the Romans interested in financing distributions in the subject communities; such systems were therefore exceedingly rare.

The weak and ad hoc nature of the official, institutional response to subsistence crisis requires an explanation. The key is to be found in the social, economic, and political power of the local aristocracies. The crucial role in the resolution of food crises was played by members of the elite, whether as magistrates, performers of regular public services, or private benefactors. Appointed as grain commissioners, they collected funds and sought emergency food supplies, while as private individuals they themselves put up cash or cut-price grain. However, the public generosity of the wealthy was institutionalized by the rich in their own interests. The grain stocks of the community were in their barns and could be released as it suited them; that is why the class that produced philanthropists also produced profiteers. Also, through philanthropy and the performance of unpaid services, the few competed with one another for office, prestige, and honor. In so doing, they avoided the less attractive alternative of financing necessary expenditures through regular tax-payments to the civic treasury. Treasuries were always virtually empty; wealth was private. The rich opted for a system where they made contributions that were irregular and enhanced their reputations, rejecting the alternative, regular, and obligatory transfers that brought no credit to the giver. In this way they effectively preempted the possibility of regular state-funded supply and distribution schemes.

This discussion is primarily relevant to oligarchy, but oligarchy was the standard form of government in the cities of the Graeco-Roman world. It is sometimes forgotten how rare and short-lived democracies were in antiquity. In any case, democracies also drew on the resources of the wealthier citizens. Even Athens looked to the propertied class for the performance of expensive services that were considered vital for the functioning of the community: the equipping of warships, the training of dramatic choruses, and so on. However, Athens, because of the resources of empire, was able to avoid recourse to philanthropy and private patronage by the rich (Millett, 1989), which were the salvation of the typical city-state.

Religious Responses

The secular/religious divide is highly artificial and misleading as concerns antiquity. (If I have adopted this distinction in this paper, it is for convenience of analysis.) This is especially obvious in the matter of communal response to disaster. The ancients did not face the dilemma of seventeenth-century European settlers in north America, for some of whom practical measures against natural disaster, notably epidemic disease, were seen as interference with the Divine Providence (Hopkins, 1983). Fate, immutable and predetermined, figures in Greek and Roman religious conceptions. However, in practice, the idea that the gods can be persuaded appears to have prevailed. Thus it is incorrect to assume that religious and non-religious responses were seen as different in kind, the one symbolic, the other practical, let alone that the two classes of response were in some way mutually incompatible. Christians and Jews, moreover, held a similar world-view. They have less in common with Puritan New Englanders, or medieval Europeans reacting to plague (Biraben, 1976; Dols, 1977), than with, for example, Christian leaders of modern times who lead the faithful in public prayers for rain.

As with secular so with religious responses, we should be on the look out for both short-term, ad-hoc and long-term, institutional responses. Sometimes they took the same form, as with the Pharmakos or scapegoat ceremonies (Bremmer, 1983; Burkert, 1979:59ff). Every year, on the first day of the Thargelia (the Athenian early-summer festival in honour of Apollo), two ugly men were selected, one for each sex, and ritually expelled from the city, perhaps with violence, carrying with them the guilt of the community. Something similar occurred in many other cities. Plutarch as chief magistrate of Chaeronea in Boeotia presided over one such ritual:

> There is a traditional rite of sacrifice, which the archon performs at the public hearth but everyone else at home, called the driving out of bulimy. They strike one of the servants with wands of *agnus castus* and drive him out, chanting, "Out with Bulimy, in with Wealth and Health." When I was archon, a larger number than usual participated in the public rite. After we had completed the ritual acts and returned to our places at table we discussed first the term bulimy, then the formula which they repeat as the servant is driven out, and especially the affliction itself and the particulars of a case of it. The name, we thought, signified a great or general famine. (Plutarch, *Moralia* :693)

Such rites were also available for emergency use, in the midst of famine, plague, or some other disaster. At Marseilles, in time of epidemic disease, a poor man was feted and then driven out of the city. It is likely enough that the ad-hoc use of rituals of this kind preceded their installation as a regular festival with an apotropaic function.

The Thargelia or the Boulimos ceremony was only one of a complex series of rituals which made up the religious calendar of a people, whether they were organised as a polis, or, like the Jews, as an *ethnos*. Significantly, the major festivals appear to have been attuned to the agricultural year. The Athenians had a succession of festivals to Demeter (and other gods – Brumfield, 1981), the Jews the three pilgrimage festivals, Passover, Shavout, and Sukkot, falling respectively in the spring, at the end of the barley harvest and the beginning of the wheat harvest, and at the end of the harvest. (Encycl. Jud., 1971; Schauss, 1938). At Sukkot, the rituals looked ahead to the next agricultural year. On the first day the people took up and shook the palm-branch, together with its accessories, the citron, myrtle, and willow, in a traditional rain-making ritual (cf. Loewe, 1981:348ff). On the seventh day, Hoshana Rabba, prayers for a good harvest to come were recited in the course of a procession. Finally, special ceremonies of "water libation" were associated with the same festival. These festivals in the course of time received politico-historical explanations and justifications; their origin, however, was in the agricultural cycle and the uncertainties of production in a semi-arid zone.

As I have already hinted, the assumptions behind pagan, Jewish, and Christian ritual were similar. The prosperity and continuity of the community were held to depend upon the good will of the gods (or God). Divine favor therefore had to be cultivated and maintained by regular cult acts and demonstrations of piety.

The common ground between pagans and Christians on this issue is exemplified in the exchange between Symmachus and Ambrose in AD 384. The Christian emperor Gratian, under pressure from Ambrose, bishop of Milan, had cut off the subsidies of the traditional pagan state cults and priesthoods. In pleading for their reinstatement, Symmachus stressed the social consequences of Gratian's act of disestablishment, claiming that "universal famine" replaced prosperity. There was in fact a food shortage in Rome in AD 383. Ambrose's defence is interesting. He does not deny the plausibility of the causal sequence: human acts, divine displeasure, famine. His line of defence is that there was not "universal famine," no global food shortage, merely local difficulties (Croke, 1982:39–40).

Natural disasters pose a major dilemma for all religions. As Geertz has shown, religion serves the function of synthesizing a people's view of the world and ideas of order (Geertz, 1963). Thus, odd, painful, or disastrous happenings spread anxiety among a people: "Man depends upon symbols and symbol systems with a dependence so great as to be decisive for his creatural viability, and as a result, his sensitivity to even the remotest indication that they may prove unable to cope with one or another aspect of experience raises within him the gravest sort of anxiety." How did a people cope with the doubts thrown on the religious system by the odd or the disastrous? This was the function of the scapegoat rituals and other responses: religious innovations (new cults, gods, temples); consultations of oracles or sacred books; public prayers, processions, and fasting (North, 1976; Patai, 1939; etc.).

Such remedies did not always achieve the desired results. Heaven did not always obligingly cloud over when importuned by a rabbi, or plagues cease after a pilgrimage to the Delphic oracle. Thucydides had this to say about the behavior of Athenians when smitten with epidemic disease at the beginning of the great war with Sparta: "The supplications made at sanctuaries, or appeals at oracles and the like, were all futile, and in the end, men desisted from them, overcome by the calamity" (Thucydides, *The Peloponnesian War* :2.47.4,53). Thucydides goes on to describe the collapse of religious and moral standards in Athens.

Outbreaks of scepticism in consequence of natural disaster were presumably not unusual. David Hume gives some examples from antiquity in his discussion of the origin and nature of polytheistic religions (Hume, 1963). He notes that Augustus refused to carry Neptune in procession with other gods after storms had destroyed two of his fleets, and that Romans showed their anger at the death of Germanicus by stoning the gods in their temples and renouncing all allegiance to them. Of these two reactions, that of Augustus is the more significant, because the leaders of a community, if no one else, had the responsibility of, and vested interest in, propping up the religious system rather than undermining it.

Conclusion

This is the point at which the two broad categories of responses I have been discussing come together. The public generosity of the rich frequently takes place against a background of religious ceremonial (Gordon, 1989). That is appropriate. The elite through their contributions of food and money were performing a dual function: at one level, they were protecting the poor and hungry from starvation; at another, they were shoring up the religious system and enabling it to continue to play its role of shielding the community from disaster. It was vital, as much for the continuous rule of the elite as for the future of the community, that both these functions be performed.

In sum, while food crises were frequent, famine was rare – in large part because of human anticipation and adaptability. Secular responses to and religious recognition of the vulnerability of populations led to increases in agricultural production, emergency imports and food distribution, and individual philanthropy in support of all of these, as well as ritual acts of prevention and response.

NOTES

1   A fuller account of matters treated in all but the last section of this paper is presented in my book (Garnsey, 1988). I have had profitable discussion with Richard Gordon on the subject of religious responses.

   For further reading consult: Gallant, 1989; Garnsey and Morris, 1988; articles in Garnsey and Whittaker, 1983, by Garnsey, Jameson; Rickman, 1980; Virlouvet, 1985.
2   This section embodies some preliminary results from a research project undertaken by myself with T. Gallant (who is responsible for figure 5.1 and table 5.1) on the agroclimatology of the Mediterranean region, funded initially by the Economic and Social Research Council, latterly by the British Academy.

REFERENCES

Austin, M. M. 1981: *The Hellenistic World from Alexander to the Roman Conquest.* Cambridge: Cambridge University Press.
Bennett, M. K. 1968: Famine. *International Encyclopedia of the Social Sciences. Vol. 5.* New York: MacMullan and Free Press, 322–6.
Biraben, J.-N. 1976: *Les Hommes et la Peste en France et dans les Pays Européens et Méditerranéens. Vol. 2: Les Hommes face à la Peste.* Paris: Ecole des Hautes Etudes en Sciences Sociales.
Bremmer, J. 1983: Scapegoat rituals in ancient Greece. *Harvard Studies in Classical Philology,* 87, 299–320.

Brumfield, A. C. 1981: *The Attic Festivals of Demeter and their Relation to the Agricultural Year*. New York: Arno Press.

Burkert, W. 1979: *Structure and History in Greek Mythology and Ritual*. Berkeley, Cal.: University of California Press.

Croke, B. 1982: *Religious Conflict in Fourth Century Rome: A documentary study*. Sydney: Sydney University Press.

Dols, M. W. 1977: *The Black Death in the Middle East*. Princeton: Princeton University Press.

Encycl. Jud. 1971: *Encyclopedia Judaica*. Jerusalem: Keter, 16 vols.

Forbes, H. A. 1982: Strategy and soils: technology, production and environment in the peninsula of Methana, Greece. University of Pennsylvania: unpublished Ph.D. dissertation.

Fornara, C. W. 1983: *Archaic Times to the End of the Peloponnesian War: Translated documents of Greece and Rome. Vol.1*. Cambridge: Cambridge University Press, second edition.

Foxhall, L. 1986: Greece ancient and modern – subsistence and survival. *History Today*, 36, 35–43.

Gallant, T. W. 1989: Crisis and response: Risk-buffering behavior and subsistence crises in Hellenistic Greek communities. *Journal of Interdisciplinary History*, 19(3), 393–414.

Garnsey, P. 1983: Famine in Rome. In Garnsey and Whittaker (1983), 118–30.

Garnsey, P. 1988: *Famine and Food Supply in the Graeco-Roman World: Responses to risk and crisis*. Cambridge: Cambridge University Press.

Garnsey, P. and Morris, I. 1988: Risk and the polis: the evolution of institutionalised responses to food supply problems in the ancient Greek state. In Halstead and O'Shea (1988).

Garnsey, P. and Whittaker, C. R. (eds) 1983: *Trade and Famine in the Graeco-Roman World*. Cambridge: Cambridge Philological Society.

Garnsey, P., Gallant, T., and Rathbone, D. 1984: Thessaly and the grain supply of Rome during the second century BC. *Journal of Roman Studies*, 74, 30–44.

Gauthier, Ph. 1985: *Les Cités grecques et leurs bienfaiteurs*. Paris: Bulletin de Correspondance Hellénique, suppl. vol.12.

Geertz, C. 1963: Religion as a cultural system. In M. P. Banton (ed.), *Anthropological Approaches to the Study of Religion*, London: Tavistock, 1–46.

Gonzales, J. 1986: The Lex Irnitana: A new copy of the Flavian municipal law. *Journal of Roman Studies*, 76, 147–243.

Gordon, R. 1989: The veil of power: emperors, sacrificers and benefactors. In M. Beard and J. North (eds), *Pagan Priest*, London: Duckworth.

Halstead, P. 1984: Strategies for survival: an ecological approach to social and economic change in the early farming communities of Thessaly, N. Greece. University of Cambridge: unpublished Ph.D. dissertation.

Halstead, P. 1988: The economy has a normal surplus: Economic stability and social change among early farming communities of Thessaly, Greece. In Halstead and O'Shea (1988).

Halstead, P. and O'Shea, J. (eds) 1988: *Bad Time Economics: Cultural Responses to Uncertainty*. Cambridge: Cambridge University Press.

Hopkins, D. R. 1983: *Princes and Peasants: Smallpox in history*. Chicago and London: University of Chicago Press.

Hume, David 1963: *Hume on Religion*. Edited by R. Wollheim. London: Collins.

Jameson, M. 1983: Famine in the Greek world. In Garnsey and Whittaker (1983), 6–16.

Kuniholm, P. and Striker, C. 1983: Dendrochronological investigations in the Aegean and neighbouring regions, 1977–1982. *Journal of Field Archaeology*, 10, 411–20.

Latte, K. 1968: Kollektivbesitz und Staatsschatz in Griechenland. *Kleine Schriften zu Religion, Recht, Literatur und Sprache der Griechen und Römer*, 294–312.

Loewe, R. 1981: "Salvation" is not of the Jews. *Journal of Theological Studies*, 32, 341–68.

Mariolopoulos, E. G. 1962: Fluctuation of rainfall in Attica during the years of the erection of the Parthenon. *Geofisica Pura e Applicata*, 51, 243–50.

Millett, P. 1984: Hesiod and his world. *Proceedings of the Cambridge Philological Society*, 30, 84–115.

Millett, P. 1989: Patronage and its avoidance in Athens. In A. Wallace-Hadrill, *Patronage in Ancient Society*, London: Routledge.

North, J. 1976: Conservatism and change in Roman religion. *Papers of the British School at Rome*, 44, 1–12.

Patai, R. 1939: The "control of rain" in ancient Palestine. *Hebrew Union College Annual*, 14, 251–86.

Renfrew, C. and Wagstaff, J. M. (eds) 1982: *An Island Polity: The archaeology of exploitation in Melos*. Cambridge: Cambridge University Press.

Rickman, G. 1980: *The Grain Supply of Ancient Rome*. Oxford: Oxford University Press.

Schauss, H. 1938: *The Jewish Festivals from their Beginnings to our Own Day*. New York: American Hebrew Congregation.

Scott, J. C. 1976: *The Moral Economy of the Peasant: Rebellion and subsistence in southeast Asia*. New Haven: Yale University Press.

Sen, A. 1981: *Poverty and Famines: An essay on entitlement and deprivation*. Oxford: Oxford University Press.

Shipley, G. 1987: *History of Samos 800–188 BC*. Oxford: Oxford University Press.

Veyne, P. 1976: *Le Pain et le Cirque; Sociologie historique d'un pluralisme politique*. Paris: Editions du Seuil.

Virlouvet, C. 1985: *Famines et émeutes à Rome des origines de la République à la mort de Néron*. Rome: Ecole française.

Wagstaff, J. M. 1981: Buried assumptions: some problems in the interpretation of the Younger Fill raised by recent data from Greece. *Journal of Archaeological Science*, 8, 247–64.

6

War, Food Shortages, and Relief Measures in Early China

ROBIN D. S. YATES

Introduction

In the last two centuries, China experienced unprecedented population growth that was accompanied by massive famines occasioned by disastrous floods and droughts, so much so that China was dubbed the "Land of Famine" (L. Li, 1982:687; Mallory, 1926; Nathan, 1965; Teng, 1958:1). It has been only recently that the country has managed to limit the effects of natural disasters and has more or less been able to feed its now massive population; but even so it has had to call upon international agencies to help it overcome the Yangtse flooding in 1980 and 1981 (Oka, 1981; Weisskopf, 1981; Xue, 1982:424−6). Of course, in the lean years following the Great Leap Forward, it did not seek help from the outside to save the numerous victims of famine and it took a number of years to recover from poorly designed water-control projects initiated in that burst of enthusiasm, projects which actually resulted in the deterioration of the environment at the local level, rather than improving it (Shalom, 1984:46−63; Smil, 1984; Volti, 1982:123−4). What do we know of earlier times? In a recently published symposium on "Food, Famine, and the Chinese State" Lillian Li drew a general conclusion

> "that the traditional Chinese state, particularly in the Qing period, played a significant role in the feeding of the population. The articles presented here focus primarily on the ability of the state during the high Qing, roughly the eighteenth century, to affect the movements of the population, to distribute resources among regions, to regulate the use of land and water, and finally to control the circulation of grain. These articles reinforce the widely held view of the eighteenth century as a period of unprecedented political stability and economic prosperity for Chinese society. The population explosion, which is assumed to have been a result of these favorable conditions, in turn led to the decline of state power and the end of the era of prosperity. In the nineteenth century,

population pressure rendered ineffective the power of the state to perform the same functions of regulation, or at least intervention, that it apparently had done so well in the previous era. Without this degree of state authority, the articles imply, food crises and famines multiplied in the nineteenth and twentieth centuries". (L. Li, 1982:689)

What was the situation at the beginning of Chinese history? How and why did the state develop its interventionist techniques? Did the Chinese suffer from famine to the same degree then as they did in the last two centuries, and were the reasons for famine the same then as in the recent past? The aim of this paper is to explore some of these questions and to provide some answers to the age-old problem of famine in China.

Before we begin this inquiry, it is important to note that there are serious impediments to drawing a complete and accurate portrayal of starvation and the efforts to alleviate it in early China. These impediments take the form of inadequate or nonexistent statistics on famine victims; prior to AD 2, there are also no population statistics, even though we know that censuses were initiated several centuries before (Bielenstein, 1947; Chen Chi-yun, 1984; Kuan, 1979; Tu, 1983; Yates, 1987;). All the documentation we have comes from the central authorities: there are no local sources of information as there were (in the form of local gazetteers) in Sung and later Chinese history (Leslie et al., 1975). Thus whatever was not reported to the center does not appear in our sources; and the lack of complete records of climatic conditions from different parts of China, most notably north and south of the Yangtse river, makes it impossible at the present time to confirm or deny the existence of the eigenvectors and periodicities of drought and flood analyzed by Wang and Zhao for the last six hundred years (Wang and Zhao, 1985:274).

An additional difficulty in evaluating famine in early China is that we do not know by how much the average daily intake of a peasant had to drop for the government to proclaim a famine. Some evidence on starvation rations does exist, however, and it will be presented below. In addition, the way natural disasters are recorded is abbreviated: "there was a famine, or great famine, a drought or flood, or plague of locust-like insects and so-and-so many people died (the figures being given in round numbers, if at all) or people ate each other," an all too frequent trope that was frighteningly real (des Rotours 1963, 1968; cf. Bielenstein, 1954:61−3). We do now, however, have evidence from Han and some earlier tombs of the types of food and even of dishes eaten by the elite, and archeologists have been able to reconstruct in considerable detail the extensive food resources of Neolithic, Bronze and Iron Age Chinese (K. C. Chang, 1977a, 1977b; Yü Ying-shih, 1977). Although this lack of information is serious, yet I do believe that we can make some headway in understanding famine in early China.

Nevertheless, studies of nutrition patterns, the stature of the different classes in the population, the effects of disease, and other issues relevant to the analysis of the causes and effects of malnutrition and famine, which have received considerable attention in the west (see, for example, the excellent essays in Rotberg and Rabb, 1986), have barely begun in the China field. It is hoped that this essay will stimulate further research in these most important topics, most particularly because the Chinese primary data – that generated by Chinese archeologists currently working in the field and that transmitted through traditional historical records – is exceedingly rich and potentially an invaluable source for comparative analysis.

The period I wish to discuss, the late second millennium BC to the fall of the Han dynasty in AD 220, can be divided into three distinct phases for the purposes of this study. The first is that of the high Bronze Age, the Shang and Western Chou dynasties, roughly 1500–700 BC. The second is the end of the Bronze through the early stage of the Iron Age, the Eastern Chou dynasty to the Ch'in empire which unified China in 221 BC and fell shortly after the death of the First Emperor in 210 BC. The third phase is that of the early empire, the Western and Eastern Han dynasties, 206 BC to AD 220.

In all of these periods, it is important to note that food was not merely considered to be fuel for the human machine. Rather the sharing of food bound individuals indissolubly together in spirit. The sharing of the cooked and uncooked meats, wine, and grain of the Bronze Age sacrifices to the ancestors ritually symbolized the creation of an extended community of the living and the dead, and willingness to participate indicated recognition of the religious and political legitimacy of the group initiating the sacrifice (cf. Keightley, 1978).

By the second period, we find the Ch'in dynasty laws proclaiming that if a husband committed a crime, his wife was considered to have knowledge of the crime and be equally culpable if she shared meat with him (Hulsewé, 1985a:125, D 15). Moreover, according to the military texts of the followers of Mo-tzu (the Mohists), the leaders of a defense of a city or town under attack gave wounded defending soldiers packages of meat and wine to help them recover, and thereby at the same time cemented their loyalty to the cause of defense (Yates, 1980:492–4, fragment 99). Finally, grain bound the peasants to their family and fellow village members in its production, to the government and their superiors in the form of taxes, and to their ancestors in the form of cooked offerings and sacrificial wine. It was a condensed symbol of society. Therefore the abstention from grain consumption and production symbolized complete rejection of society and its norms. In addition, probably by late Warring States times (fourth–third centuries BC) and certainly by Han times, it was believed that the grain-borer bug, which chewed the heart of such grains as millet and sorghum when government officials were corrupt, also could infest the body. It ravenously ate away at the extremities, such as the nose and fingers, teeth and gums, so that they would eventually fall off. The pathology of the disease strongly suggests that it was leprosy, but it too could be halted by abstention from grains (Harper, 1982:305–8, xviii, Recipe 77; McLeod and Yates, 1981:152–3, 5.18; Maspero, 1950:98–100). Thus the Taoist transcendent beings from the third century BC on achieved physical immortality by "abstaining from the five types of grains;" they survived by merely supping on the sweet dew of heaven, the etheral *ch'i* or ether which was believed to be the primary or basic constituent of the universe.

Not all abstention from food consumption, therefore, implied famine in China. Conscious abstention was a ritual or religious act intended to sever relations with one's fellow man, one which also had medical implications. It signified freedom to ascend to the higher level of the cosmic forces and the celestial deities and enabled the individual to live forever. But, of course, most individuals who abstained from food consumption were forced to do so by natural disasters or human activity – most particularly in times of war. If grain supplies failed, and the government refused or was unable to alleviate the crisis, then the cement binding society was cracked and social norms could be legitimately broken. The peasants could legitimately attack higher authorities and seek redress, and cannibalism could be resorted to. Through the centuries the texts are full of incidents, and Arab visitors, as well as Marco Polo, noted the prevalence of this custom in times of famine induced by war (des Rotours, 1963, 1968).

Finally, it is important to observe how the Chinese themselves defined famine. As Greenough points out, Lillian Li "observes that in Chinese thought famines are distinguished from floods and droughts, the former being a 'result of the interaction of human and natural forces,' the latter belonging to a category of "heavenly calamities'" (Greenough, 1982:795). This is in the late imperial period. The situation was somewhat different in early times, as will become apparent in the course of the discussion.

Period I: The Bronze Age
(Shang and Western Chou Dynasties)

Climate and Environment

In the Bronze Age, all the evidence suggests that the climate and environment in north China was somewhat different to what it is today. The average temperature was 2–4°C warmer and the rainfall seems to have been more abundant (K. C. Chang, 1980:138–42; Chu, 1972:16–18), Indeed, K. C.

Chang suggests that the area around An-yang in the late second millennium BC could have even enjoyed the effects of the monsoon, for rains are recorded in the Shang oracle bones as lasting up to eighteen days in one case (K. C. Chang, 1980:141; Hu, 1945). However, toward the end of the period, at the beginning of the Western Chou, but perhaps starting as early as ca.1500 BC, there seems to have been a cooling and drying trend before a resumption in period II of warmer and moister conditions (Hinsch, forthcoming). In the first part of period I, warmer and moister conditions permitted subtropical species of animals and plants to live further north and there is evidence for the existence of the following animals (not an exhaustive list): water buffalo, boar, elaphure, dog, pig, cattle, bamboo rat, tapir, rhinoceros, and elephant. Much of the north China plain seems to have been marshy and the hills thickly forested; bamboo grew near the Yellow River, whereas from the end of the thirteenth century AD it has not been possible to raise bamboo commercially this far north (Chu, 1972).

In the central Yangtse valley, the evidence suggests that Tung-t'ing and other lakes extended over a much wider area than they do today, and in this region was also the vast Yun-meng marsh (cf. Bodde, 1978; Huang, 1981). Therefore the effects of excessive snowmelt from the Tibetan massif flowing down the Yangtse could be dissipated in the complex of lakes east of the gorges on the Szechuan–Hupei border, and the Yangtse did not flood to such a disastrous extent as it has done in the recent past.

Thus there is a considerable difference in the origin or cause of floods in the early period from those discussed by Perdue (1982; cf. Perdue, 1987) for Hupei and Hunan in the late eighteenth and nineteenth centuries. Floods were *not* caused by local lineages illegally creating dikes and polders at the lower elevations and encroaching on the lakes and rivers, diminishing their surface area and restricting or redirecting the flow of the waters. And they were not caused by excessive deforestation at the higher elevations of the drainage basin, deforestation that allowed greater run-off with heavy silt content which blocked the lower channels (cf. Smil, 1984:9–77). Human activity simply had not reached a level of intensity that caused the environment to deteriorate substantially.

Nevertheless, throughout the centuries from the Neolithic period preceding the Shang, through the Shang to later times, the pace of human activity increased. In addition, the rivers, especially the Yellow and Yangtse, continually brought down silt from the highlands to the west, and gradually filled in the marshes and lakes, eventually creating fertile plains which humans then proceeded to exploit and further modify.

But initially, in the first thousand years of recorded history (roughly periods I and II), the Chinese did not engage in extensive, centrally coordinated irrigation projects. Rather, local communities drained marsh land for their own use. In other words, Karl Wittfogel is wrong to maintain that the Chinese despotic state emerged out of the necessity for centrally controlled irrigation projects which brought water to parched fields that provided the subsistence base for the population (Wittfogel, 1957; cf. Bailey and Llobera, 1981; R. Cohen, 1978; Wright, 1978). The great water works only developed *after* the founding of centralized states and the empire.

Population

It is not possible to estimate the Bronze Age population; there were no censuses, for the state apparatus did not have sufficiently developed bureau-cratic techniques, nor the power or even desire, to inquire of numbers at the local level. Indeed, some argue that its control only existed where the king was physically located, and the king had to be constantly active in war and sacrifice, to be constantly redistributing his wealth among his erstwhile allies, to maintain his prestige and his throne (Keightley, 1983). We do have some numbers, however, for military campaigns: the largest is one led by the wife of one of the Shang rulers, in about 1200 BC, which consisted of 13,000 men all told (K. C. Chang, 1980:195). But most armies were much smaller than this and casualties in war often numbered in the tens. It is therefore not possible from the Chinese evidence to support Robert Carneiro's hypothesis that the state emerged as a result of competition for scarce resources in restricted environments (Carneiro, 1970). Chinese resources were abundant and defeated groups could always move away, and, in fact, apparently did.

Causes of Food Shortages

Because the historical records are limited for the Shang and Western Chou dynasties, it is not possible to estimate the number or severity of famines and food shortages in the first period, although they clearly did occur. Thus, although certainly there was fissioning of villages and colonization of empty or newly emerging territory, or territory occupied by bands or tribes living at a lower level of social-cultural integration, there is no real evidence that population pressures were the cause of famine in period I. The evidence from the oracle bones rather suggests that there were two main reasons for failure to gather crops. The first was that the fields were attacked and destroyed, or the harvest was gathered by, the enemies of the Shang state. The second is that the crops were subject to the vagaries of the weather. We know this from the Shang oracle bones dating from the late second millennium BC and found at An-yang, just north of the Yellow

River, in Honan province, where there are several thousand requests for rain or snow. The largest number of those that are dated are in the first five months of the year when grain would have been sown (Chu, 1972; Hinsch, forthcoming).

Droughts obviously were of crucial significance to the Shang people. It seems that they believed they were caused by Ti, the highest god, or by the god of the Yellow River, who might have been conceived as a kind of alligator or dragon (Allan, 1984:528; Glum, 1982; Tsung-tung Chang, 1970:211−14). At least by Western Chou times and possibly as early as the Shang, it was also believed that the affliction was initiated by a drought demoness called *han-po* (Glum, 1982:257; Karlgren, 1950a:224−5); she was described in late period II and III texts as being bald and hairless with eyes on top of her head (Schafer, 1951:162−9). A major method of relieving droughts was either to burn or expose to the heat of the sun a probably naked shamaness (*wu*) or a deformed person with a pigeon-chest and protruding stomach (*wang*) (Ch'en Meng-chia, 1956; Qiu, 1983−5; Schafer, 1951). Other scholars suggest that the victims were slaves or shamanesses (Hu Hou-hsuan, 1974), prisoners-of-war (Yao, 1979), or slaves (Yü Hsing-wu, 1979:7−8, 380), but the interpretation of shamanesses or witches is probably correct. It is possible that the shamaness was conceived of as impersonating the offending spirit, or that, since shamanesses had immediate and direct access to the suffering the people were enduring, she was a sacrifice to the spirit.

The practice of ritual exposure continued right through the historical period and into the present century, for nudity was supposed to demonstrate the individual's spiritual power and removal from ordinary Chinese society. Thus we find in funeral ritual in periods II and III the mourners, especially the chief mourner, stripping bare in the course of the ceremony (Granet, 1922). Even emperors and officials could threaten to burn or expose themselves to bring down fructifying rain (Schafer, 1951:138−43).

Other deities were thought to be able to intercede on behalf of the Shang people in times of drought or excessive rain, and prayers and rain dances, probably including drumming in certain instances, were offered to various gods of lesser rivers, mountains, the four directions, the clouds, the god of the earth, the spirit of a constellation in the sky, and the royal ancestors (Glum, 1982:242−3; Granet, 1959:482; Tsung-tung Chang, 1970:178−205). Prayers and sacrifices also seem to have been addressed to clay figurines of dragons, which were conceived to be rain deities (Glum, Qiu 1982: 1983−5).

Finally, it is extremely important to point out the close connection between sacrifice, war, and agriculture in period I. A statesman in the *Tso Chuan*, a text which was written down in late period II but reflects the conditions of late period I and early period II, put it succinctly: "The great affairs of state are sacrifice and warfare. At sacrifices one presides over cooked meat, and in war one receives raw meat: these are the great ceremonies of the spirits" (Kierman, 1974:28). As Kierman states, "Warfare was part of the system of ritual which kept the society in touch with the ancestral spirits and the cosmic order."

There are several points to note here. First, meat, especially, as far as we know, for the elite, was a much more important article of consumption than it later became (Schafer, 1977:98–9). Second, the word for hunting and agriculture was the same, *t'ien* (Hsu Chung-shu, 1944). Hunting itself was a military activity: not only was it conceived of as training for soldiers but also war was conceived of as a kind of hunt. Specifically, the Shang went on many expeditions either to kill or capture human victims as offerings to their ancestral spirits. If enemies were captured, they were returned to Shang territory and offered along with other forms of meat, such as cattle and wild animals, in large quantities to the Shang ancestors. It is not at all unlikely that the cooked flesh of these human victims was actually consumed by the participants in the rite together with the fresh flesh of the animals.

Agriculture was still at a fairly primitive stage of development and probably most tools were still made of stone, although some may have been of bronze (Bray, 1978). What the Shang practiced was a modified form of slash-and-burn farming. The king personally sent out groups, probably of lineage members numbering from 100 to 300, to hunt in a specific area; they would set nets, light fires, and first catch the animals fleeing the flames. Once this had been accomplished, the land was cleared and the ashes of the burned vegetation were used as fertilizer for the subsequently created fields (Bray, 1978; Chang Cheng-lang, 1973; K. C. Chang, 1980:220–30; Hu, 1945; Keightley, 1969:98–125).

Not infrequently it is recorded that the king's farmer-soldiers were sent into territory previously not under his control. Eventually, the colonists were able to incorporate the land into the Shang kingdom. The grain thus gathered was used to feed the Shang population, to offer to the ancestors, and to create an alcoholic beverage which was consumed in large quantities in the course of ancestral worship. The people who conquered the Shang, the Chou, specifically criticized their defeated enemies for their drunkenness (Karlgren, 1950b:43–6).

It is important to note that the king personally divined by means of oracle bones about war and agriculture, for herein lies the origin of the later Chinese state's interest in the welfare of the people. The king had access to the divine powers and claimed to be the only one who had such access (Hu, 1957; cf. K. C. Chang, 1983). The spirits could affect the weather and the outcome of war, and therefore the king's ability to manipulate them by sacrifice was crucial. Should he not be able to influence them at all, or should they send down natural disasters, this would indicate that he was morally and religiously inadequate; he would lose the legitimate right to rule and he could be replaced by someone with greater access to the divine.

Indeed, later myths of the founding of the two earliest dynasties, the Hsia and the Shang, emphasize this point. In the first case, the previous ruler was shown to be inadequate because a great inundation had flooded the plains. Yü then worked himself so hard that the hairs on his body were rubbed off while he was channeling the waters so that they could drain away into the eastern sea. Thus was he able to bring about social and cosmic order. In the second, T'ang, after overthrowing the last Hsia ruler, exposed himself as or like a shaman as a sacrifice to halt the five- or seven-year drought that had ensued, took upon himself the guilt for human moral failings, and thereby ended the disaster and founded a new dynasty (Allan, 1984).

Period II: The Eastern Chou and Ch'in Dynasties

Much more data is available to us for period II than for period I and the methods for relieving food shortages become much more sophisticated and explicit. Let me review briefly some of the historical developments affecting food production and the prosecution of war.

First of all, the Western Chou, which had defeated the Shang probably in 1046 or 1045 BC, itself succumbed to a coalition of enemy tribespeople and rebelling vassals in 770 BC and was forced to move from its homeland in the Wei River valley, Shensi, in the northwest, to Loyang in the central plains of the lower middle Yellow River — the modern province of Honan. Subsequent to this time, until its final destruction in 256 BC, the Chou, now known as the Eastern Chou, ruled only in name; they possessed ritual authority, but not political or military power. The states that had been their vassals fought increasingly bitter campaigns against each other, attempting to gain more and more territory, until one, the Ch'in, finally succeeded in eliminating all its rivals and founded the unified empire in 221 BC.

In order to compete with other states, each found it necessary to develop what eventually came to be highly centralized and bureaucratized polities and to create larger and larger armies. In addition, in order to support the increasingly complex state structure and burgeoning numbers of officials and to keep the armies provisioned, it became necessary for the states to become intimately involved in agricultural and handicraft production. The state that eventually won, the Ch'in, was most successful in these ventures.

What general trends can be perceived? First of all, the peasant population came to be incorporated for the first time into the state and social hierarchy that had been previously reserved for aristocrats. The state needed the peasants to provide corvée labor for construction projects, the building of palaces, roads, walls, and eventually water-control and irrigation projects; it required their bodies for military conscription as infantry, and their taxes in the forms of grain, hay, and straw, and of part of the products of the mountains, marshes, rivers, lakes, and sea that they gathered. From the fourth century BC a head or poll tax was also levied, usually in cash or its cloth equivalent.

Initially, land was owned by the states or the major lineages in the state, even though ultimate ownership was claimed to reside in the Chou kings. It was divided into three grades of quality, best, medium, and worst, and the state periodically (every three years or so altogether) reassigned or rotated the plots so that no one family would get rich at the expense of another which had poorer land (T'ien, 1986). In the mid-fourth century, the Ch'in adopted the policies and philosophy of the so-called "Legalist" statesman Shang Yang, who reorganized the laws and social and political forms of the Ch'in state, thus laying the foundations for its eventual success a century later. Briefly, the Ch'in only valued agriculture and war, and all secondary occupations, such as trade, were discouraged. Peasants could gain aristocratic rank by cutting off heads in battle: one head gained one rank, two heads two ranks, or the rank could be returned to the government in exchange for a low-level official position. Ranks could also be awarded if an individual turned in to the state a large amount of grain or arrested a criminal. The advantage of rank was that the individual who possessed it was punished less severely for crimes, and could redeem family members from slavery or punishment. He could also receive from the government land to farm and slaves to help him work it − in other words, the means of subsistence.

Shang Yang encouraged immigration into the Ch'in from other, more populous areas by offering tax exemptions for newcomers. In addition, the Ch'in put convicts and slaves to work in government-run factories for the production particularly of weapons and cast-iron tools, including plowshares, which in turn would increase productivity. It seems to have cultivated large tracts of land directly too, using convict and slave labor (Hulsewé, 1985b).

Reasons for Food Shortages

Under these historical conditions, what were the reasons for famines and what were the responses of the state governments?

(1) Natural disasters occurred. The records become more extensive with the appearance in period II of annalistic histories and commentaries, in-

cluding the *Spring and Autumn Annals*, said to have been edited by Confucius himself, and its associated commentaries, most notably the *Tso Chuan*, or commentary of Tso Ch'iu-ming, the *Bamboo Annals* of the state of Wei, the *Discourses of the States (Kuo Yü)*, and the annals of the various states compiled by Ssu-ma Ch'ien in his *Records of the Grand Historian (Shih Chi)*. But even though the data are fragmentary and not very reliable, Teng Yun-t'e has been able to determine that there were at least five floods and eight droughts in the Shang dynasty, for a total of 13 natural disasters, and in the Western and Eastern Chou there were 16 floods, 30 droughts, 13 infestations of locust-like insects, 5 damaging hailstorms, 1 epidemic, 9 earthquakes, 7 cases of untimely frost and snow and 8 other famines, for a grand total of 89 death-inducing disasters (Teng, 1958:40; cf. 1–7).

(2) There began to be population pressure in certain areas, most notably in north-central China. Evidence for this may be found in section 15 of the *Book of Lord Shang*, which may have been written in about the middle of the third century BC. It is a disquisition directed at the ruler of the state of Ch'in, trying to persuade him to adopt policies that would encourage the population of the Ch'in's enemy neighbors to the east, the states of Han, Wei, and Chao in north-central China, to migrate westwards, thus damaging economically Ch'in's rivals and increasing the human resources of his own state. Ch'in, he argued, lacked a sufficiently large population to exploit its fertile open lands, rivers, and mountains, whereas the enemy

territory is narrow, but their population is numerous; their dwellings are built higgledy-piggledy, and they live close together; their grain production is small and merchants charge interest.

The people, on the one hand, do not have their names registered, and, on the other hand, have no fields or houses, so that for subsistence they rely on evil occupations and pursuits of minor importance [i.e. trade], with the result that those who are exempt from taxation because they live in steep and inaccessible places, in morasses and by streams, are more than half the population. Therefore it would appear that a condition where the territory is not sufficient to support the population is still worse than that where, as in the case of Ch'in, the population is insufficient to fill the territory. (Duyvendak, 1963:266–7).

Unfortunately, we do not possess independent evidence to confirm the author's observations, but it is generally agreed by historians that one of the reasons for Ch'in's success in unifying China was that it was able to attract migrants into its territory: it may indeed have exempted such immigrants from taxes for three generations, as the author of the section quoted above strongly advocated. Did the three Ch'in (Han, Wei, and Chao) suffer from more famines than other states because of pressure from overpopulation?

This is very hard to determine, not least because the first emperor of Ch'in ordered the destruction of the historical records of his opponents.

(3) Fields were abandoned by the population, either because they were being terrorized by bandits or enemy forces, or because of poor harvests, or because they did not wish to pay taxes or be conscripted either for labor or military service by their respective governments: corrupt and immoral government frequently resulted in peasant migration. One may also note here that the population seems to have been highly mobile in this period (Keightley, 1977), and I would speculate another reason for this was that the population did not own the fields they cultivated: they had no reason to stay when conditions deteriorated.

While this is not the place to discuss the highly complex issue of changes in land-tenure practice in the late Warring States and Ch'in periods (Cho-yun Hsu, 1971:110−16), it is important to note that there is little or no evidence in the newly discovered Ch'in laws to support the contention made by Han Confucians that the economic and legal changes instituted by Lord Shang in the fourth century immediately resulted in the buying and selling of land, and that the poor peasants were gradually forced out of their ownership rights by greedy and wealthy merchants and aristocrats (Kao, 1979:148−70; cf. Hulsewé, 1985b:215−18). No doubt there was *some* private ownership of land by the peasants in period II, but the vast bulk of the land under the Ch'in seems to have been owned by the state and either cultivated by it directly, using slave or convict labor, or leased out to free peasants, who paid for their rights of use by taxes in kind, including grain, hay, and straw, and by corvée labor service. In neither Ch'in nor Han law is there any evidence that land was an item which could be stolen (Hulsewé, 1988).

(4) There was actual physical destruction of the farming population during the course of the many campaigns leading up to the unification of China in 221 BC. Figures are very unreliable here, but the historical records do mention occasions when surrendered armies were summarily butchered. For example, the Ch'in is said to have murdered more than 400,000 men of Chao who had surrendered in the mid-third century BC, and some scholars have estimated that two million men died in the battles for unification (Kuan; cf. Cho-yun Hsu, 1971:67).

The precise size of the population cannot be gauged accurately because census figures are not extant from these times; and even if they were, the bureaucratic techniques of census taking did not begin to be developed until the later part of period II. Nevertheless, on the basis of some round numbers given for the size of Warring States armies, and reckoning that each household contained six people, Kuan estimates that the maximum size of the total population before the wholesale destruction in the wars began was approximately 25 million for the whole of China. Further huge loss of life occurred in the rebellions that accompanied the fall of the Ch'in and the civil wars that led to the foundation of the Han. Kuan concludes that the population had dropped to 8 million by the beginning of the Han (Kuan, 1979:655), but it should be remembered that much of the loss may be the result of the disruption of local government and the inability of officials to keep the registration records accurate: the people were still alive, but had fled or their names were not inscribed on the registration tablets (cf. Chen Chi-yun, 1984).

The Mohists, who were the most active of all the groups in late period II in condemning offensive warfare, made a particular point of the waste and destruction of war, not least because it deprived the spirits of both the supplies for and the officiants of the sacrifices in their honor (Yi-pao Mei, 1973:102−3; cf. Yates, 1979). Indeed, these followers of the philosopher Mo-tzu specialized in the defense of towns besieged in these great wars (Yates, 1979, 1980). They put the citizens and rural refugees under military law, gathered in all material and food supplies that could be used in the defense, required that the population keep three years' worth of provisions in case of crop failure due to drought and flood, and even wrote down detailed rules for grain distribution in time of severe grain shortage. These rules are interesting, for they confirm K. C. Chang's (1977a:7) observation that the Chinese divided food into the categories of grains and starches (*fan*) and vegetables and meats (*ts'ai*), and that grain was the more important of the two. They also provide us with data regarding what was considered to be minimal grain intake. Unfortunately, the text does not speak of famine (*chi*), but rather of an austerity (*yueh*), so this does not resolve the question posed above as to the level to which the grain supplies had to drop before the government declared there to be a famine. The text reads as follows (1 *sheng* = 199.687 cc; 1 *tou* [10 *sheng*] = 1.996 litres; 1 *shih* [10 *tou*] = 19.968 litres):

If [grain] rations are a *tou* [per day], at the year's end 36 *shih* [will be consumed]. If the rations are divided into three (and two-thirds consumed per day), 24 *shih* [will be consumed] at the year's end. If divided into four (and one-half are consumed per day), 18 *shih* [will be consumed] at the year's end. If divided into five (and two-fifths consumed per day), 14 *shih* 4 *tou* [will be consumed] at the year's end. If divided into six (and one-third consumed per day), 12 *shih* [will be consumed] at the year's end. At the ration of a *tou*, 5 *sheng* will be eaten [per meal]; at the ration of thirds, 3⅓ *sheng* will be eaten; at the ration of quarters, 2½ *sheng* will be eaten; at the ration of fifths, 2 *sheng* will be eaten; at the ration of sixths, 1⅔ *sheng* will be eaten. Two meals per day [are eaten]. At a time when [you are trying] to save [the population] from death, [the rations are]: 20 days at 2 *sheng* per day, 30 days at 3 *sheng* per day, and 40 days at 4 *sheng* per day. If you calculate at this rate, the people will avoid an austerity lasting ninety days. (Yates, 1980:576, slightly modified)

In contrast to these starvation rations, the newly discovered Ch'in legal statutes dating from the mid-third century BC specified the amount of grain to be issued to convicts working off hardlabor punishments. Grain was given to them depending on their age, whether they were working or not, the degree of difficulty of the work, the time of year, and their status.

The most serious offenders were called "*Ch'eng-tan*" "builders of walls" (male) and "grain-pounders" (female), the next "*li-ch'en-ch'ieh*" "bond-servants and bond-women", the next "(gatherers of) firewood for the spirits" (male) and "(sifters of) white rice" (female), the next "robber-guards," and the lightest "watchmen." Infants with no mother as well as infants whose mothers were working were given ½ *shih* of grain a month. Girls up to the age of 6 or 7, who were categorized as bond-women and grain-pounders, were issued 1 *shih* a month; non-adult bond-women and grain-pounders (aged from ca.7 to ca.16 years) working for the government were given 1 *shih* ½ *tou* a month; whereas male *ch'eng-tan* and bond-servants were given more, 1½ *shih*. Adult female convicts (grain-pounders and bond-women) were given the same rations as non-adult males, 1½ *shih* a month: if they were engaged in heavy construction work, however, grain-pounders, grain-pounder-robber-guards, and (sifters of) white rice received ⅓ *tou* in each of the two meals per day — in other words 2 *shih* a month. Adult males (the statute specifies bond-servants) were given 2 *shih* a month, but if they were performing agricultural labor, from the second to the ninth months, they were issued 2½ *shih* a month. Similarly, *ch'eng-tan* engaged in construction work or other labor equal in hardship were given ½ *tou* (0.998 litres) in the morning and ⅓ *tou* in the evening meal, for a total of 2½ *shih* a month.

Finally, one rule seems to imply that imprisoned convicts were starved on rations of ⅓ *tou* per day. Perhaps this is the figure the government used to determine whether a famine was in progress; if the peasants were reduced to ⅓ *tou* per day, a famine was declared. As the Ch'in alternated short months of 29 days with long months of 30 days, and as the rations were calculated on the basis of the 30-day month, the Ch'in authorities required that officials store the rations for each of the extra days of the 29-day months and issue them as regular rations in the intercalary month which was inserted after the ninth month: four such months had to be inserted every ten years according to the calendar the Ch'in were using (Hulsewé, 1985a:31–3).

Both the *Mo-tzu* and the Ch'in rations were presumably calculated in husked grain, rather than unhusked grain. The Ch'in "Statutes on Granaries" specified the ratios of husked to unhusked grain for different types:

Grain (untreated) weighing one *shih* constitutes 16⅔ *tou* of husked grain. One *shih* of husked grain becomes 9 *tou* of polished grain. 9 *tou* of polished grain become 8 *tou* of refined grain. Rice weighing one *shih* constitutes 20 *tou* untreated grain; when pounded this becomes 10 *tou* of (refined) grain. Ten *tou* of refined grain (when further pounded produce) 6⅔ *tou* of refined rice. 10 *tou* of barley are equal to 3 *tou* of coarse flour. 15 *tou* of beans, peas, or hemp are equal to one *shih*. When issuing refined grain or rice, 10 *tou* are equal to one *shih* (Hulsewé, 1985a:A 29, slightly modified).

A famous passage in the *History of the Han Dynasty* by Pan Ku records a calculation made by Li K'uei (424−387 BC), minister of marquis Wen of the state of Wei, of a typical peasant's yearly income and expenditure. The text itself may not be from Li's hand, but it is still of interest, for the author reckons that the peasant would expect to provide 1½ *shih* (probably of unhusked grain) a month for each of the five members of his family, and would end with a deficit of 450 cash per year: he would produce 150 *shih*, worth 30 cash per *shih*, of grain on 100 *mu* (acres) of land, 10 percent of which would be taken for land tax, and he would have to pay for clothes and the costs of village festivals and sacrifices (Duyvendak, 1963:43; Cho-yun Hsu, 1980:68; Swann, 1950:142). Although the calculation is supposed to date from about a hundred years before the Ch'in legal statutes, it still seems somewhat unlikely that the Ch'in state would supply its convicts with more grain rations than the average free peasant could expect. So perhaps Li K'uei was exaggerating to make a point about the peasant's plight and the average daily intake was higher than Li K'uei claimed.

It is from this period that instances of cannibalism are first recorded (des Rotours, 1968:2−8). Later, in the T'ang dynasty (to take one example among many), at the time of An Lu-shan's rebellion in AD 755, one city, Sui-yang, suffered such famine that out of an army of 10,000 men and a population of about 30,000 only 400 remained at the end. The rest had died and had been eaten (des Rotours, 1968:27−8).

(5) Grain supplies were destroyed in the endemic wars. The Mohists argued that

The rulers and lords of to-day are quite different from the sages of the past who ruled by morality. They all rank their warriors and arrange their boat and chariot forces; they make their armour strong and weapons sharp in order to attack some innocent state. *Entering the state they cut down the grain fields and fell the trees and woods*; they tear down the inner and outer walls of the city and fill up the ditches

and ponds; they seize and kill the sacrificical animals and burn down the
ancestral temple; they kill and murder the people and exterminate the aged and
weak; they move away the treasures and valuables (Yi-pao Mei, 1973:108 – my
italics).

Sun-tzu, the great military strategist, also specifically advocated the
destruction of grain supplies as one sure way that would help defeat the
enemy (Griffith, 1973:141), and this tactic is discussed in many other contemporary military treatises.

(6) Finally, increasing social stratification and hierarchization, urbanization
and the gradual commercialization of the economy created differential
access to food supplies. Endowment entitlements to food supplies (Sen,
1982) also changed markedly in late period II. These developments undoubtedly affected who actually suffered the most and died in any of the
famines of both periods II and III, but we lack the kind of data to provide
detailed analyses of specific early Chinese famines that scholars have been
able to make in studying western and recent African and Indian famines
(Tilly, 1986; Sen, 1982).

We do know, however, that not only did officials receive greater amounts
of grain as salaries the higher up the bureaucracy they climbed, but rich
traders were able to make fortunes in the sale of food and grain. This was a
trend that continued into the third period. With regard to the merchants,
Ssu-ma Ch'ien noted that in the breakdown of the Ch'in (late period II),
and the first hundred years of the Han (period III), "They gained their
wealth in the secondary occupations [particularly trade and craft production]
and held on to it by investing in agriculture; they seized hold of it in times
of crisis and maintained it in times of stability" (Watson, 1968, vol.
2:498–9). One such individual was Jen of Hsuan-ch'u, a Ch'in official in
charge of the granary at Tu-tao. He apparently embezzled the grain in the
civil war at the end of the Ch'in and made a fortune when the two armies
of Han and Ch'u, which were locked in combat for the final victory, were
stalemated at Jung-yang. The price of the grain rose to 10,000 cash per
picul (*shih*) and, because the fighting prevented the peasants from plowing
their fields and planting their crops, he made enormous sums, accepting
the gold and jewels purloined by the opposing commanders in exchange for
grain for their troops. This capital Jen's family invested in agriculture,
buying up all the really good-quality and valuable land while others purchased
the cheapest fields and pasture lands (Watson, vol. 2:497–8). Thus, in the
period of chronic political instability between the Ch'in and the Han, many
peasants found their crops either destroyed or commandeered, and were
forced to abandon their fields or to sell them. Reduced to penury, they

even had to go so far as to sell their children and other family members into slavery to avoid starvation, while Jen and his ilk grew fat and prosperous.

As for the increasing social stratification and hierarchization, we have already noted that the Ch'in gave ranks and the use of fields to males in exchange for actions beneficial to the state. Lord Shang advocated the policy of giving an official position at the salary of 50 piculs (*shih*) per year (instead of one degree of rank) for one head cut off in battle, if the successful soldier so desired, and a position at 100 piculs for two degrees of rank. And he also speaks of heads of counties (prefects, *hsien-ling*) being given salaries of 700, 800 or 1,000 *shih* per year and being attended by 70, 80, and 100 swordsmen respectively. (Hsiung, 1985, vol. 2:447; Duyvendak, 1963:196–7). Eventually, by the middle of the Han, salaries of the top government officials reached 10,000 *shih* per year, and the monthly salary ranged from 8 *hu* (159.74 litres) to 350 *hu* (6988.8 litres) of grain per month, according to An Tso-chang and Hsiung T'ieh-chi (1985, vol. 2:449). The difference between these amounts and those available to the average peasant given above is obvious and depressing.

Although there were a few cities founded in period I, urbanization developed dramatically, especially after 770 BC, and some of the cities reached enormous sizes. Lin-tzu, for example, the capital of the state of Ch'i on the eastern coast, could boast of a population of 70,000 households (Cho-yun Hsu, 1971:137) and many of the other state capitals were of a comparable size. While remaining religious and administrative centers, cities and towns also became commercial centers with thriving markets and industrial facilities, usually controlled by the governments of their respective states. Legalist statesmen, such as Lord Shang, mistrusted the volatility of the petty tradesmen and artisans and even proposed that merchants not be allowed to buy grain or peasants to sell it (Duyvendak, 1963:177). But economic progress could not be stopped that easily: the states found it to their economic advantage to control the markets by registering merchants and tradesmen on separate rosters from the rest of the population, to have officials regulate buying and selling practices and prices and collect taxes on commerce in the markets and customs posts – a practice strongly condemned by the Confucian philosopher Mencius – and Ch'in law even required price tags to be placed on all items offered for sale worth one cash or more. One of the Statutes on Currency reads "When there is buying as well as selling, to each [object] the price is to be attached. To small objects, each not worth one cash, it must not be attached" (Hulsewé, 1985a, A 46:53).

Although cities did contain some open areas where crops could be grown, such large urban agglomerations had to rely on long-distance trade as well as produce from the nearby fields to meet their needs. Whenever trade was disrupted by war or there were crop failures close at hand, it was obviously the urban poor who, lacking the means to grow their own food, suffered most immediately and most severely. The rich merchants and artisans and the officials, the administrative elite, doubtless possessed the cash reserves to weather dramatic price fluctuations. Although few details are available, evidence from the Ch'in legal documents suggests that indeed prices did fluctuate considerably, despite the government's best efforts to prevent this happening, for two items record the value of stolen property. In one case, the value dropped from 660 cash to 110; in the other, it rose from 110 cash to 660. Officials were required to price the goods at the time of the thief's capture: if they failed to carry out this procedure, and the goods were priced only at the time of the trial and these fluctuations had occurred, the officials were punished (Hulsewé, 1985a, D 27 and D 28:129–31). Steep drops in prices are, of course, just as dangerous as price increases for those living at the subsistence level. Thus the development of the market economy, while being of benefit to some, must also, in times of crisis, have adversely effected the rural and the urban poor's ability to survive.

Relief Measures

In period II, the Eastern Chou and Ch'in, two different techniques or procedures for relieving food shortages due to natural disasters in the short term, or precluding their possibility in the long term, were developed. These were administrative, and ritual and religious in nature, but both resulted from an ideological orientation. The administrative techniques were developed primarily by practical statesmen whose ideas were influenced by "Legalist" thinking, whereas the ritual and religious procedures derived more from Confucian thinking. In actual practice, however, rulers tended to use both, believing that whatever was efficacious should be employed.

The administrative techniques appear most clearly in the Ch'in legal documents where we find the following:

1 Immediate reporting of disaster-affected areas to the central authorities, including the type of disaster, the acreage affected, and the extent of the disaster.
2 Establishment of minutely detailed rules for agricultural activities, including the amount of grain to be sown per acre, each type of grain having its own rule.
3 Establishment of agricultural officials and regular inspection procedures, including those for draft animals.

4 Creation of a system of government granaries, with exceedingly detailed rules concerning all forms of accounting, including disbursement and receiving procedures and the preservation of the stored grain.
5 Physical movement of the population from disaster-affected areas and relocation in more prosperous or less affected regions.
6 Beginnings of the cutting of canals and irrigation ditches to facilitate grain distribution and interregional trade, as well as to bring previously infertile areas under cultivation, and to prevent seasonal flooding. A road network also began to be developed.
7 Distribution of grain in times of famine and the reward of grades of rank to rich people who supplied the government with large stores of grain.
8 Remission of taxes in times of hardship or for those who opened up previously unoccupied or abandoned territory.

Confucian influence was most readily apparent in the development of the idea that it was the ruler and his officials who were morally and practically responsible for natural disasters and the consequent misery suffered by the people. The ruler stood in the position of being father and mother to the people and therefore he was morally obliged to think first of their welfare, even before the satisfaction of his own desires or needs. Furthermore, it was believed that there was a direct correlation between the human and the natural world, and ill-conceived or morally corrupt official actions could bring about almost immediate response from the natural order. Thus famines were not distinguished from floods and droughts as they were in late imperial times. Natural portents warned the ruler of his failings. If he refused to heed these warnings, he would be criticized by his officials, or even removed if he stubbornly rejected the obligation to mend his ways.

These developments can be seen first of all in the late period II text *Lü-shih Ch'un-ch'iu* (*Spring and Autumn Annals of Lu Pu-wei*, the prime minister of the First Emperor of Ch'in before the conquest). This incorporated a calendar known as the *Monthly Ordinances* (*Yueh Ling*), which was later placed in the Confucian ritual canon, the *Li Chi*. In it, the ruler is advised that he must wear robes of a certain color, eat certain foods, and only permit certain actions according to the season: if he acted otherwise, dire consequences would ensue. For example, the text in the section devoted to spring reads:

If, in this last month of spring, the governmental proceedings proper to winter were observed, cold airs would constantly be prevailing; all plants and trees would decay; and in the states there would be great terrors. If those proper to summer were observed, many of the people would suffer from pestilential diseases; the seasonable rains would not fall; and no produce would be derived from the mountains and heights. If those proper to autumn were observed, the sky would be full of moisture and gloom; excessive rains would fall early; and warlike movements would be everywhere arising. (Legge, 1885:266–7)

The ritual requirements for each month of the year are followed by similar warnings of natural and human disasters.

Furthermore, the followers of Mo-tzu criticized excessive expenditure by the rulers, aristocrats, and the wealthy, arguing that anything above and beyond the bare essentials in food, clothing, weapons, and transportation was contrary to the rules laid down by the ancient sage kings and injurious to the welfare of the people. Everything has its proper use, they said, and thus "wealth is not wasted and people's resources are not exhausted, and many are the blessings procured" (Yi-pao Mei, 1973:118). But by the rulers' levying heavy taxes, the "people fall into poverty and innumerable persons die of hunger and cold" (ibid.: 119). The Mohists even went so far as to condemn elaborate funerals and music, both dear to the hearts of Confucians:

> Outlining the rules for funerals and burials, Motse said: The coffin shall be three inches thick, just sufficient to hold the rotting bones. Of shrouds there shall be three pieces just enough to hold the rotting flesh. The pit shall be dug not so deep as to strike water, and not so shallow as to allow the odour to ascend. The mound shall be be just high enough to be identified (by the mourners). There may be weeping on the way to and from the burial. But upon returning they shall engage in earning the means of livelihood. Sacrifices shall not be neglected in order to express one's filial piety to parents. Thus the rules of Motse neglect the necessities of neither the dead nor the living. (ibid.: 134)

Although Mohism was widely accepted and followed in late period II, it was, however, Confucian practices that eventually dominated in the Han, and sometimes children ruined themselves financially in order to provide their parents with a socially acceptable and sufficiently magnificent funeral. Even in the Warring States, immense wealth was conspicuously destroyed by being consigned for the use of the dead in the underworld. While this may have reduced the amount of wealth available for the living, we would know much less about the material life of the ancient Chinese if Mo-tzu's ideas on simplicity in funerals had actually been carried out.

Next, the Confucians strongly argued that the government should not take away peasants from their agricultural pursuits for corvée and military duties except during the off-season: wall building, other construction work, and wars, therefore, should only be carried out or prosecuted in the autumn or winter, when the cosmic force of *yin*, the cold, dark, and female power, was dominant, not in the spring and summer when *yang*, the hot, light, and male power, was in the ascendant.

Rulers of states also prayed and sacrificed to the deities of the mountains and rivers of their particular states, a practice that undoubtedly originated in the earlier Bronze and Neolithic periods. In the *Tso Chuan*, it is recorded for the year 641 BC (Duke Hsi, year 19) that there was a great drought in the state of Wei, so divination was made and sacrifices were made to the mountains and rivers; and in the year 541 BC (Duke Chao, year 1) the text reads, "as for the Spirits of the Mountains and Rivers, when there are calamities of floods, drought, epidemics, then one makes *yung* deprecatory sacrifices to them" (Karlgren, 1968:26, slightly modified).

Yet another rite to end a drought, in addition to exposing a shamaness or the king (Chang Ch'un-i, 1959:21–22), was to move the markets. The reason for this was that markets were conceived of as being *yin*. By moving the markets, the people were symbolically moving the wet, quiescent *yin* principle and encouraging the rain to fall (Forke, 1962:329–30 — Wang Ch'ung, the first-century AD Confucian who records this custom, ridicules it, saying that it is impossible to affect the weather by moving the markets).

By the late Warring States and Ch'in times, late period II, all these techniques, procedures, and ideas were available to the rulers. In any given circumstance, they could elect to adopt one alone or many of these in combinations to try to alleviate the people's suffering.

Period III: The Han Dynasty

Before we pass on to period III, it should be noted that, after the cooling and drying trend at the beginning of the first millennium BC of period I, the climate of period II into the first half of period III seems to have been more temperate than it is today: the growing season in north China seems to have been 30–40 days longer. Beginning from about the turn of the millennium, China seems to have suffered considerable deterioration of its climate, a condition that reached its nadir in the late third century AD and that lasted for 700–800 years, when amelioration set in once again (Chu K'o-chen, 1972).

These natural conditions are reflected in the now much more abundant historical sources. Li Chien-nung (1962:162–4) calculates that the Western Han dynasty (205 BC–AD 9) had 32 years when disasters struck and 182 years without calamities. Of the disasters, 7 were floods from excessive rain, and there were also 6–7 devastating breaks in the banks of the Yellow River; 13 were droughts; 7 were plagues of locusts; 3 were of drought combined with plagues of locusts; and 2 of unseasonable frost and snow. In the 195 years of the Eastern Han, which ended in AD 220, the balance shifted. There were 119 disasters and only 76 years without calamities. He counts 55 floods, 25 windstorms, 57 droughts, and 37 plagues of locusts; there were 6 years when 3 disasters struck, 2 disasters in each of 31 years, and 82 years with one type of disaster. Ma Fei-pai (1935) also observes that sickness that killed off the oxen used in agriculture struck particularly in the first hundred years of the Eastern Han dynasty.

Apart from these natural disasters, we should also note other major reasons for famine. First and foremost was the collapse of central orderly government at the end of the Ch'in dynasty and the beginning of the Han (roughly 209–203 BC). The collapse of the Wang Mang interregnum in AD 23 was accompanied by truly devastating rebellions, and the Yellow Turban rebellion occurred in AD184. From the last date to the final abdication of the Han in 220, warlords and rebels marched over the land, killing, burning, and destroying. In these periods of civil disorder, there was great loss of life. In the Ch'in–Han transition, in some areas it was said that 80–90 percent of the population perished, although this may be an exaggeration (Chi-yun Chen, 1984). Conditions deteriorated to such an extent that the Han emperor had to permit people to sell their children into slavery and migrate to safer regions, such as Szechuan. There were also, however, other military reasons for deprivation and starvation.

The *Discourses on Salt and Iron* purports to record a lengthy discussion on imperial government policy in 81 BC. There were two factions involved. One was led by Sang Hung-yang, the government spokesman, a merchant who had organized government monopolies of salt, iron, and liquor from 119 BC and who had developed a system called "equable marketing." Under this system, the state created granaries throughout the land, bought grain when prices were cheap, and sold it when prices rose, to prevent grain merchants from making excessive profits and manipulating the market, and to enable the poor to have some reliable source of nutrition when times were hard. The monopolies and granary system was also intended to provide the financial means whereby the Han could expand their territory far into Korea in the northeast, into the north and northwest deserts, where they drove back the nomadic Hsiung-nu peoples and created the Silk Road to the west, and to the south into Vietnam. Sang Hung-yang was the representative of statesmen who advocated strong government involvement in economic and strategic matters, and was a direct heir of the "Legalist" line of the Ch'in state a hundred years before.

Opposed to him were men who represented more of a Confucian approach to government. They were men of letters who were not government officials, who advocated retrenchment on all fronts, and who rejected the idea that the state should compete over wealth with members of its population. "Back to basics" was their slogan: and this meant back to agricultural self-sufficiency.

While Sang Hung-yang argued that the reason people were underfed was that the rich hoarded grain and the poor lacked adequate iron tools to cultivate their fields, the men of letters unequivocally claimed "it is the long drawn-out service of our troops in the field and ceaseless transportation for the needs of the commissariat that cause our soldiers on the marches to suffer from hunger and cold abroad while the common people are burdened at home" (Gale, 1973:6).

Sang Hung-yang attempted to defend the expansionist policies by declaring that "ever since the frontier expeditions under Han Wu-ti, the common people have had access to fine horses and delicacies such as oranges, whereas before, though they wore themselves out, they did not have enough to eat." To which the men of letters retorted that before the labor conscriptions and military levies, the people had more than enough to eat and there was no need to rely on barbarians and foreign foodstuffs. "But later on, because of innumerable military expeditions, there was a lack of such battle-horses, that mares and cows were despatched to the front. *Colts and calves were now born on battle-fields*, while the six domestic animals were not raised at home; the five cereals were not cultivated in the countryside, and the people had not even enough husks and chaff to go around. How could they feast upon oranges and pumaloes? *Following a great war*, says the Chuan, *recovery is slow to come even after several generations*" (Gale, 1973:92–3).

And the disputants pointed out further problems; for example, the rich avoided tax burdens and corvée labor duty, forcing the burden to fall even more heavily on the poor, because the officials still required the tax quotas to be delivered in full. Furthermore, Sang Hung-yang declared that famine brings about moral depravity among the population and it is therefore the government's duty to feed the population, while the Confucians claimed that official, imperial, and rich men's extravagance and corruption brought on famine. The debate ended in essentially a stalemate, although some concessions to the men of letters' criticisms were made: the liquor monopoly was abandoned, but the salt and iron monopolies continued to operate for at least another 50 years or so.

Certainly, we can see that the Han imperial dynasty devoted enormous amounts of effort and financial resources to irrigation and water-control projects, and continued to practice the same types of relief measures for famine victims as we saw in period II. To the list I have given, I would add that on the occasion of major flooding in 119 BC, local rich men were forced to provide loans to the starving (Cho-yun Hsu, 1980:28), but this was not sufficient and 725,000 famine victims were moved from their homes in the east to the newly opened northwest frontier commanderies, away from the floods. The emperor also distributed his own personal landed estates to the poor in other hard times, but eventually this resource was expended (Cho-yun Hsu, 1980:31).

This points to another major development in the Han which had a direct effect on the ability of the peasant population to survive in famines. Starting in late Warring States times (that is, in late period II), land began to be bought and sold, and by the middle of the Han, rich local families and lineages, as well as imperial favorites, were able to buy up or encroach upon the holdings of individual peasant households. Many of the independent peasants were forced into tenancy, outright dependency, or slavery on their richer neighbors' property and those that remained free bore the increasing tax burden of those protected from paying by their patrons or landlords (Cho-yun Hsu, 1980; Dubs, 1946).

In addition, the quite extensive development in agricultural technology, including the use of an impressive array of iron implements, such as the turn-plow with its associated seed-drill, and two new methods of cultivation, the ridge-and-furrow system and pit cultivation, could only be satisfactorily employed on larger estates with adequate capital and labor resources. Thus the independent peasant did not benefit from them once the government was unable financially to support them with seed and animals (Bray, 1979–80; 1984; Mazumdar, 1985–7; cf. Cho-yun Hsu, 1980).

Finally, we may note that the interpretation of the responsibility for famines and natural disasters that the Confucians and others had developed in period II became official state ideology. It was the emperor and his officials who were held responsible for them. It was their moral inadequacy or ritual imperfection or practical policies that caused imbalances in the cosmic forces of *yin* and *yang*, which in turn led to natural disasters. Even rebellions were interpreted in this fashion. Nevertheless, Wang Ch'ung, whom we have encountered before, rejected this interpretation, saying that floods and droughts were the result of certain movements of the planet Jupiter, of the moon and the sun, of *yin* and *yang*. They had nothing to do with government policies, and the performance of rain sacrifices had no direct effect on the weather, though they should still be performed to salve human consciences and show respect (Forke, 1962:327–88). Wang Ch'ung's ideas were, however, generally disregarded in the Han.

Conclusion

What we may conclude, I believe, from the period III evidence, is that the development of technology in the Han to increase production and reduce the ravages of natural disasters, in the sense of both administrative and material technology, was offset by two main factors. First was the hopelessly extravagant military expansion, following the aggressively expansionist and interventionist government policy of the Legalist line. Second was the expansion of private property and the encroachment of rich landlords on the holdings of the poor peasants. The government, after a while, simply was unable to mediate disputes at the local level and to act as a fair redistributor of wealth.

Eventually, the incapacity of the central government to be perceived to be as moral as it claimed and to act fairly led to a loss of legitimacy and to the development of a whole series of popular religious movements, which desired to create new utopias. The members of these inspired groups eventually rebelled and were put down with enormous loss of life and destruction of property. This led in turn to a drop in the population and abandonment of fertile fields and water-control and irrigation projects. In addition, it enabled nomadic peoples of the steppe land to the north to encroach upon the farmland. They turned fields into pastures. Great waves of migration of the Han people to the south occurred. Only very much later did the Northern Wei, itself a Turkish dynasty, attempt to return to the system prevalent in periods I and II of claiming the government's right to land ownership and to redistribute it more equally among the adult populace. But this system had its own flaws and was eventually abandoned.

Finally, from what has been said it can be seen that most of the ways the Chinese state used to alleviate famine in the last few centuries were developed in the early period of Chinese history. Let me add that there were just a few other innovations.

First, by the fifth century AD, the Chinese government took it upon itself to punish recalcitrant rain deities for failing to provide the needed moisture (A. Cohen, 1978). This punishment could take various forms depending on the extent to which the deity was remiss. The image of the deity could be exposed to the sun or even flogged if no rain fell. Further unwillingness could result in the emperor decreeing that the deity be demoted in the celestial hierarchy. The ultimate punishment was to banish the deity altogether or, even worse, to destroy the deity, either by throwing his effigy in the local river or smashing it with hammers or bare fists. If this had to be resorted to, another deity would be invited to replace the former, incompetent one.

Secondly, and perhaps more practically, the Chinese government relied not only on the "ever-normal" public granaries to provide back-up supplies in time of crop failure, but also encouraged local gentry and their landowners to stock private and charitable community-owned granaries, and urged them to disburse their holdings in time of grain shortage. Often this succeeded, but at the same time there was a certain conflict of interest; it was often the rich landowners who forced the grain prices up in time of distress, not infrequently shipping supplies out of the district in order to realize greater profits in areas where the prices were higher (L. Li, 1982).

We can thus see that the origins of famine in China and the responses to it were highly complex. The people interacted with their environment in special and unique ways. While they could not solve the difficult problems of feeding their population adequately in all circumstances and responding to natural and human-induced disasters, yet they laid the foundations for the system of state involvement in providing for the basic needs of the general population. It is hard to imagine that China's population could have reached the size it is today without the long historical experience of developing complex techniques to cope with food shortages.

NOTE

I would like to thank Bret Hinsch for his invaluable research assistance in gathering data for this chapter. I am also most grateful to David N. Keightley and Lillian M. Li for reading the draft and making a number of important suggestions and corrections.

REFERENCES

Allan, Sarah 1984: Drought, human sacrifice and the mandate of heaven in a lost text from the *Shang Shu. Bulletin of the School of Oriental and African Studies*, 47, 523–39.

An Tso-chang and Hsiung T'ieh-chi 1985: *Ch'in Han kuan-chih shih-kao*. Tsinan: Ch'i Lu shu-she, 2 volumes.

Bailey, Anne M., and Llobera, Josep, R. (eds) 1981: *The Asiatic Mode of Production: Science and politics*. London and Boston: Routledge and Kegan Paul.

Bielenstein, Hans 1947: The census in China during the period 2–742 AD. *Bulletin of the Museum of Far Eastern Antiquities*, 19, 125–63.

Bielenstein, Hans 1954: The Restoration of the Han Dynasty, vol. I. *Bulletin of the Museum of Far Eastern Antiquities*, 26, 1–209.

Bodde, Derk 1978: Marshes in *Mencius* and elsewhere: A lexicographical note. In David T. Roy and Tsuen-hsuin Tsien (eds), *Ancient China: Studies in Early Civilization*, Hong Kong: Chinese University Press, 157–66.

Bray, Francesca 1978: Swords into plowshares: A study of agricultural technology and society in early China. *Technology and Culture*, 19, 1–31.

Bray, Francesca 1979–80: Agricultural technology and agrarian change in Han China. *Early China*, 5, 3–13.

Bray, Francesca 1984: *Science and Civilisation in China. Vol. 6: Biology and Biological Technology. Part II: Agriculture*. Cambridge and London: Cambridge University Press.

Carneiro, Robert L. 1970: A theory of the origin of the state. *Science*, 169, 733–8.

Chang Cheng-lang 1973: Pu-tz'u p'ou-t'ien chi ch'i hsiang-kuan chu wen-t'i. *K'ao-ku hsueh-pao*, 1, 93–120.

Chang Ch'un-i (ed.) 1959: *Yen-tzu ch'un-ch'iu chiao-chu*. *Chung-kuo ssu-hsiang ming-chu*, ts'e 8, Taipei: Shih-chieh shu-chü.

Chang, K. C. (ed.) 1977a: *Food in Chinese Culture, Anthropological and Historical Perspectives*. New Haven and London: Yale University Press.

Chang, K. C. 1977b: Ancient China. In K. C. Chang (1977a), 23–52.

Chang K. C. 1980: *Shang Civilization*. New Haven and London: Yale University Press.

Chang, K. C. 1983: *Art, Myth, and Ritual: The path to political authority in ancient China*. Cambridge, Mass., and London: Harvard University Press.

Chang, Tsung-tung 1970: *Der Kult der Shang-dynastie im Spiegel der Orakelinschriften: Eine paläographische Studie zur Religion im archaischen China*. Wiesbaden: Otto Harrassowitz.

Chen Chi-yun 1984: Han Dynasty China: Economy, society, and state power. A review article. *T'oung Pao*, 70.1–3, 127–48.

Ch'en Meng-chia 1956: *Yin-hsu pu-tz'u tsung-shu*. Peking: K'o-hsueh ch'u-pan she.

Chu K'o-chen 1972: Chung-kuo chi-wu-ch'ien-nien-lai ch'i-hou pien-ch'ien ti ch'u-pu yen-chiu. *K'ao-ku hsueh-pao*, 1, 15–38.

Cohen, Alvin P. 1978: Coercing the rain deities in ancient China. *History of Religions*, 17.2–3, 244–65.

Cohen, Ronald 1978: Introduction. In Ronald Cohen and Elman R. Service (eds), *Origins of the State: The anthropology of political evolution*, Philadelphia: Institute for the Study of Human Issues, 1–20.

des Rotours, Robert 1963: Quelques notes sur l'anthropophagie en Chine. *T'oung Pao*, 50.4–5, 386–427.

des Rotours, Robert 1968: Encore quelques notes sur l'anthropophagie en Chine. *T'oung Pao*, 54.1–3, 1–49.

Dubs, Homer H. 1946: Wang Mang and his economic reforms. *T'oung Pao*, 35, 205–19.

Duyvendak, J. J. L. (trans.) 1963: *The Book of Lord Shang: A classic of the school of law*. Chicago: University of Chicago Press.

Forke, Alfred (trans.) 1962: *Lun-Heng. Part II: Miscellaneous Essays of Wang Ch'ung*. New York: Paragon Book Gallery, second edition.

Gale, Esson M. (trans.) 1973: *Discourses on Salt and Iron: A debate on state control of commerce and industry in ancient China, Chapters I–XXVIII*. Sinica Leidensia, Vol. II. Taipei: Ch'eng-wen Publishing Company.

Glum, Peter 1982: Rain magic at Anyang? Speculations about two ritual bronze vessels of the Shang Dynasty filled with revolving dragons. *Bulletin of the Museum of Far Eastern Antiquities*, 54, 241–72.

Granet, Marcel, 1922: Le langage de la douleur d'après le rituel funéraire de la Chine classique. *Journal de Psychologie*, 19, 97–118.

Granet, Marcel 1959: *Danses et Légendes de la Chine Ancienne*. Paris: Presses universitaires de France. Ministère de l'éducation nationale, Annales du Musée Guimet, Bibliothèque d'études, new edition.

Greenough, Paul R. 1982: Comments from a south Asian perspective: Food, famine, and the Chinese state. *Journal of Asian Studies*, 41.4, 789–97.

Griffith, Samuel B. (trans.) 1973: *Sun Tzu: The art of war*. Oxford: Oxford University Press.

Harper, Donald J. 1982: The "Wu Shih Erh Ping Fang", translation and prolegomena. University of California: unpublished Ph.D. dissertation.

Hinsch, Bret, forthcoming: Climatic change and history in China. *Journal of Asian History*.

Hsu, Cho-yun 1971: *Ancient China in Transition: An analysis of social mobility, 722–222 BC*. Stanford: Stanford University Press.

Hsu, Cho-yun 1980: *Han Agriculture: The formation of early Chinese agrarian economy (206 BC–AD 220)*. Edited by Jack Dull. Seattle and London: University of Washington Press.

Hsu Chung-shu 1944: Ching-t'ien chih-tu t'an-yüan. *Chung-kuo wen-hua yen-chiu hui-k'an*, 4, 121–56.

Hu Hou-hsuan 1945: Pu-tz'u chung so-chien chih Yin-tai nung-yeh. *Chia-ku-hsueh Shang shih lun-ts'ung. Vol. 2*. Ch'eng-tu: Ch'i Lu ta-hsueh kuo-hsueh yen-chiu-so.

Hu Hou-hsuan 1957: Shih'Yü i-jen'. *Li-shih yen-chiu*, 1, 75–8.

Hu Hou-hsuan 1974: Chung-kuo nu-li she-hui ti jen-hsun ho jen-chi (hsia p'ien). *Wen-wu*, 8, 56–67, 72.

Huang Hsi-chou 1981: An outline of China's marshes. In Lawrence J. C. Ma and Allen G. Noble (eds), *The Environment: Chinese and American views*, New York and London: Methuen for the Ohio Academy of Science, 187–96.

Hulsewé, A. F. P. 1985a: *Remnants of Ch'in Law: An annotated translation of the Ch'in legal and administrative rules of the 3rd century BC discovered in Yün-meng Prefecture, Hupei Province, in 1975*. Sinica Leidensia, Vol. XVII. Leiden: E. J. Brill.

Hulsewé. A. F. P. 1985b: The influence of the 'Legalist' government of Qin on the economy as reflected in the texts discovered in Yunmeng county. In Stuart R. Schram (ed.), *The Scope of State Power in China*, Hong Kong: School of Oriental and African Studies, University of London/The Chinese University Press, 211–35.

Hulsewé, A. F. P. 1988: The wide scope of *tao*, "theft," in Ch'in-Han law. *Early China*, 13, 166–200.

Kao Min 1979: *Yun-meng Ch'in-chien ch'u-t'an*. Hsin-cheng: Ho-nan jen-min ch'u-pan she.

Karlgren, Bernhard 1950a: *The Book of Odes*. Stockholm: Bulletin of the Museum of Far Eastern Antiquities.

Karlgren, Bernhard 1950b: The Book of Documents. *Bulletin of the Museum of Far Eastern Antiquities*, 22, 1–81.

Karlgren, Bernhard 1968: Some sacrifices in Chou China. *Bulletin of the Museum of Far Eastern Antiquities*, 40, 1–31.

Keightley, David N. 1969: Public work in ancient China: A study of forced labor in the Shang and Western Chou. Columbia University: unpublished Ph.D. dissertation.

Keightley, David N. 1977: Peasant migration, politics, and philosophical response in Chou and Ch'in China. Unpublished paper presented to the Berkeley Regional Seminar in Confucian Studies, University of California, Berkeley.

Keightley, David N. 1978: The religious commitment: Shang theology and the genesis of Chinese political culture. *History of Religions*, 17.2–3, 211–25.

Keightley, David N. 1983: The late Shang state: When, where, and what? In David N. Keightley (ed.), *The Origins of Chinese Civilization*, Berkeley and Los Angeles: University of California Press, 523–64.

Kierman, Frank A., Jr 1974: Phases and modes of combat in early China. In Frank A. Kierman, Jr and John K. Fairbank (eds), *Chinese Ways in Warfare*, Cambridge, Mass.: Harvard University Press, 27–66.

Kuan Tung-kuei 1979: Chan-kuo Ch'in Han ch'u ti jen-k'ou pien-ch'ien. *Chung-yang yen-chiu-yuan li-shih yü-yen yen-chiu-so chi-k'an*, 50.4, pp. 645–56.

Legge, James (trans.) 1885: *The Sacred Books of China: The Texts of Confucianism. Part III: The Li Ki, I–X. The Sacred Books of the East, vol. XXVII* F. Max Muller ed. Oxford: Clarendon Press.

Leslie, Donald D., Mackerras, Colin, and Wang Gungwu (eds) 1975: *Essays on the Sources for Chinese History*. Columbia, South Carolina: University of South Carolina Press.

Li Chien-nung 1962: *Hsien-Ch'in Liang Han ching-chi shih-kao*. Peking: Chung-hua shu-chü.

Li, Lillian M. 1982: Introduction: Food, famine, and the Chinese state. *Journal of Asian Studies*, 41.4, 687–707.

McLeod, Katrina C. D. and Yates, Robin D. S. 1981: Forms of Ch'in Law: An annotated translation of the *Feng-chen shih*. *Harvard Journal of Asiatic Studies*, 41.1, 111–63.

Ma Fei-pai 1935: Ch'in Han ching-chi shih tzu-liao-(san) – nung-yeh, *Shih-huo yueh-k'an*, 3.1, 9–31.

Mallory, Walter H. 1926: *China: Land of famine*. New York: American Geographical Society.

Maspero, Henri 1950: *Mélanges Posthumes sur les religions et l'Histoire de la Chine. Vol. 2: Le Taoisme*. Publications du Musée Guimet. Bibliothèque de diffusion, 58, Paris: Civilisations du sud.

Mazumdar, Sucheta 1985–7: Review of Francesca Bray, *Science and Civilisation in China, vol. 6, Part II: Agriculture* (Cambridge: Cambridge University Press, 1984). *Early China*, 11–12, 276–82.

Mei, Yi-pao (trans.) 1973: *The Ethical and Political Works of Motse*. Westport, Conn.: Hyperion Press.

Nathan, Andrew James 1965: *A History of the China International Famine Relief Commission*. Harvard East Asian Monographs 17, East Asian Research Center, Harvard University, Cambridge, Mass.

Oka, Takashi 1981: China copes with Sichuan flood with post-Mao candor. *Christian Science Monitor*, July 21, 4.

Perdue, Peter C. 1982: Official goals and local interests: Water control in the Dongting Lake region during the Ming and Qing periods. *Journal of Asian Studies*, 41.4, 747–65.

Perdue, Peter C. 1987: *Exhausting the Earth: State and peasant in Hunan, 1500–1850*. Cambridge, Mass.: Council on East Asian Studies, Harvard University.

Qiu Xigui 1983–5: On the burning of human victims and the fashioning of clay dragons in order to seek rain in the Shang Dynasty oracle-bone inscriptions. Translated by Vernon K. Fowler. *Early China*, 9–10, 290–306.

Rotberg, Robert I. and Rabb, Theodore K. (eds) 1986: *Hunger and History: The impact of changing food production and consumption patterns on society*. Cambridge: Cambridge University Press, originally published in *The Journal of Interdisciplinary History*, xiv.2 (Autumn, 1983).

Schafer, Edward H. 1951: Ritual exposure in ancient China. *Harvard Journal of Asiatic Studies*, 14, 130–84.

Schafer, Edward H. 1977: T'ang. In K. C. Chang (1977a), 87–140.

Sen, Amartya 1982: *Poverty and Famines: An essay on entitlement and deprivation*. Oxford: Clarendon Press.

Shalom, Stephen Rosskamm 1984: *Deaths in China due to Communism: Propaganda versus Reality*. Occasional Paper No. 15, Center for Asian Studies, Arizona State University, Tempe, Ariz.

Smil, Vaclav 1984: *The Bad Earth: Environmental degradation in China*. Armonk, New York: M. E. Sharpe.

Swann, Nancy Lee (trans.) 1950: *Food and Money in Ancient China*. Princeton: Princeton University Press.

Teng Yun-t'e 1958: *Chung-kuo chiu-wang shih*. Peking: Sheng-huo tu-shu hsin-chih san-lien shu-tien.

T'ien Ch'ang-wu 1986: T'an Lin-i Yin-ch'üeh-shan chu-shu-chung ti t'ien-chih wen-t'i. *Wen-wu*, 2, 57–62.

Tilly, Louise A. 1986: Food entitlement, famine, and conflict. In Rotberg and Rabb (1986), 135–51.

Tu Cheng-sheng 1983: 'Pien-hu ch'i-min' ti ch'u-hsien chi ch'i li-shih i-i — pien-hu ch'i-min ti yen-chiu chih i. *Chung-yang yen-chiu-yuan li-shih yü-yen yen-chiu-so chi-k'an*, 54.3, 77–111.

Volti, Rudi 1982: *Technology, Politics, and Society in China*. Boulder, Colo.: Westview Press.

Wang Shao-wu and Zhao Zong-ci 1985: Drought and floods in China, 1470–1979. In T. M. L. Wigley, M. J. Ingram, and G. Farmer (eds), *Climate and History: Studies in past climates and their impact on man*, Cambridge: Cambridge University Press, 271–88.

Watson, Burton (trans.) 1968: *Records of the Grand Historian of China translated from the Shih Chi of Ssu-ma Ch'ien*. New York and London: Columbia University Press, 2 vols.

Weisskopf, Michael 1981: U.S. gives cash to China for flood victims. *Washington Post*, September 10, A13.

Wittfogel, Karl A. 1957: *Oriental Despotism: A comparative study of total power*. New Haven and London: Yale University Press.

Wright, Henry T. 1978: Toward an explanation of the origin of the state. In Ronald Cohen and Elman R. Service (eds), *Origins of the State: The anthropology of political evolution*, Philadelphia: Institute for the Study of Human Issues, 49–68.

Xue Muqiao, (ed.-in-chief) 1982: *Almanac of China's Economy with Economic Statistics for 1949–1980*. Hong Kong: Modern Cultural Co. Ltd. Compiled by the Economic Research Centre, The State Council of the People's Republic of China and the State Statistical Bureau.

Yao Hsiao-sui 1979: Shang-tai ti fu-lu. *Ku-wen-tzu yen-chiu*, 1, 337–90.

Yates, Robin D. S. 1979: The Mohists on warfare: Technology, technique, and justification. *Journal of the American Academy of Religion*, Thematic Issue 47.3S, "Studies in Classical Chinese Thought," 549–603.

Yates, Robin D. S. 1980: The City under siege: Technology and organization as seen in the reconstructed text of the military chapters of Mo-tzu. Harvard University: unpublished Ph.D. dissertation.

Yates, Robin D. S. 1987: Social status in the Ch'in: Evidence from the Yün-meng legal documents, part one: Commoners. *Harvard Journal of Asiatic Studies*, 47.1, 197–237.

Yü Hsing-wu 1979: *Chia-ku wen-tzu shih-lin*. Peking: Chung-hua shu-chü.

Yü Ying-shih 1977: Han. In K. C. Chang (1977a), 53–83.

7

The Rise and Fall of Population and Agriculture in the Central Maya Lowlands: 300 BC to Present

B. L. TURNER II

The ancient Maya civilization developed and flourished in its tropical lowland domain for nearly 2,000 years before it collapsed some time between AD 800 and 1000. The central Maya lowlands, the so-called heartland of the Classic Period civilization, were virtually abandoned. A vast tropical forest established itself over the region, literally covering the giant pyramids and palaces, settlements of all sizes, and the various "farmscapes." For 1,000 years, the central lowlands were ephemerally occupied at best. Even today the region remains sparsely settled in contrast to its past occupation. Considerable attention has been given to the collapse of the Classic Maya civilization; *hunger*, or the inability to feed the population, is central to many, if not most, of the collapse explanations. Much less attention has been given to the millennium-long depopulation spiral in the central Maya lowlands apparently kicked off by this collapse.

The history of Maya studies is replete with population "overshoot" and other Malthusian-like explanations of the collapse and depopulation (Adams, 1973). I suspect that a comparison would reveal that for no other civilization collapse and, perhaps, for only one other major depopulation, that in nineteenth century Ireland, have such explanations been so commonly invoked by professionals and lay experts alike.[1] Why this is so may have more to do with the biases of individual interpreters, ill-conceived and general notions about tropical agricultural soils, or the desire of many to find simple, mechanistic solutions to problems in prehistory, than with the actual evidence. To my knowledge, no study documents and compares the temporal and regional patterns of population and agriculture in the central Maya lowlands – an obvious requirement for the analysis of the explanations in question. Studies of other early civilizations rarely, if ever, support simple "population overshoot" hypotheses. Why then the persistence of such explanations for the Maya case?

As detailed elsewhere (B. L. Turner, 1983a) this persistence is attributed, in part, to the myths of Maya uniqueness − myths involving the presumed hostilities or fragilities of tropical environments for agriculture and the presumed rudimentary levels of cultivation. These myths have been largely dismissed as specialists have directed their attention to them. Nevertheless, the Classic Period civilization collapse and the depopulation spiral that lasted about a millennium have yet to be demonstrated adequately let alone explained. A "lost" civilization and a destroyed and unrecovered population invite interpretations of environmental catastrophes brought on by a population pressing its food supply.

The principle objective of this study is to examine the relationships between population and agricultural food production change in the central Maya lowlands from 300 BC to the present by means of direct evidence. This is accomplished primarily by merging the rather detailed work on Maya agriculture with a recent attempt to reconstruct the population (B. L. Turner, 1986).[2] The results are used to evaluate the various Malthusian-like explanations of the Maya collapse and the longer-term depopulation of the central lowlands, again emphasizing the direct evidence.

This exercise illuminates several factual and interpretive issues that question the validity of these explanations for the ancient Maya. First, the direct evidence suggests a broad correspondence between the patterns of population growth and the development of the spatial scales and types of agriculture. The projected maximum size of regional population is consistent with agricultural practices employed; the population and its food base were within the sustainable range of Maya technology and the lowland environs. Second, the evidence is too ephemeral to support any conclusions linking Maya-induced environmental degradation to the collapse and depopulation. Third, the overall evidence suggests to me that the ancient Maya of the central lowlands were not unique among their peers in terms of population, food, or environmental problems and solutions. Finally, explanations of the collapse of the Classic Maya do not account for the scale of the depopulation spiral that continues for one half century or more before the Spanish arrive to sustain that spiral into modern times.

Central Maya Lowlands: An Outline

The central Maya lowlands is neither a physiographically nor culturally defined region. Rather it corresponds to the so-called "core region" or "heartland" of the Classic Maya civilization, centered on northeastern Peten, Guatemala, and southern Quintana Roo and Campeche, Mexico (Culbert, 1973; Ford, 1986; Rathje, 1972; B. L. Turner, 1983a). The region shares a composite of cultural and environmental characteristics that

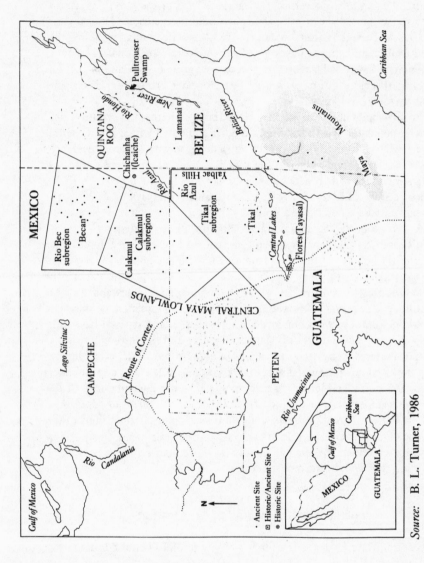

Source: B. L. Turner, 1986

Figure 7.1   The central Maya lowlands

distinguish it from the rest of the surrounding lowlands. The density of ancient Maya settlements, both nucleated sites (or centers) and clusters of individual dwellings, is high, and the chronology of settlement is relatively similar throughout, including a depopulation between AD 850 and 1000. The region is largely restricted to the interior ridge lands – a physiographic zone of uplands (constituting about 65 percent of the terrain) interspersed with seasonally inundated depressions (bajos). Elevations range from 50 m to 300 m above sea level, and no permanent or navigable rivers exist. This region corresponds well with three archeological zones or subregions, defined architecturally and demonstrated by use of the nearest neighborhood statistic (Adams and Jones, 1981). From north to south these are the Rio Bec, Calakmul, and Tikal subregions (figure 7.1), comprising about 4,780 sq. km, 5,335 sq. km, and 12,600 sq. km respectively.

As defined here, the central Maya lowlands is some 22,715 sq. km in area, constituting from 6 to 9 percent of the entire Maya lowlands, depending on demarcations. The north–south extension of the central region is about 360 km beginning in east central Campeche and extending to the edge of the savanna zone in central Peten. The east–west axis ranges from 80 to 120 km between the Hondo and Belize rivers in the east and the Usumacinta and Candelaria rivers in the west.

Archeologically, the Calakmul and Tikal subregions are more similar to one another than they are to the Rio Bec subregion (Adams, 1981). Differences include settlement patterns and local chronologies. For these reasons, population calculations are provided at both the regional and subregional levels.

Population

The central Maya lowlands have had an exceptionally varied occupation that can be traced at least to 3000–2000 BC. From that time until about AD 850–1000, this region, and the Maya lowlands in general, witnessed the development of one of the most advanced New World civilizations – the Classic Maya – and the growth of apparently "exceptional" levels of population, perhaps 2–3 million in the central region alone. After this time, the Classic Period civilization collapsed, and massive depopulation of the central region occurred. Remnants of the occupation were encountered by the Spanish explorers in the sixteenth century, and by the nineteenth century the region was almost "vacant." The population has yet to recover to any appreciable size, although current rates of growth are the highest known in the region. Much of the central lowlands remain as expansive tracts of tropical forests, beneath which the litter of ruins abound.

The reconstruction of the population of the region produces a rather unusual curve – one long wave of growth and decline followed by a very recent rise. The long wave is minimally 2,100 to 2,800 years in duration. It is undoubtedly longer, but the data for reconstructions previous to 1000–300 BC do not exist. The reconstruction shows a steady population increase until about AD 600, a rapid growth that crests about AD 800, and a decline that lasts for 1000 years.

Data and Reconstruction Procedures

Surprisingly little attention has been given to the reconstruction of ancient Maya populations at the regional level, given the significance of the topic to understanding the civilization, its collapse, and the extended depopulation of much of the Maya lowlands. Of course, problems abound in such attempts, and these and the reconstruction procedures can only be briefly discussed here (see B. L. Turner, 1986, forthcoming). Drawing upon several estimation procedures and censuses, this regional population reconstruction is based on three subregional reconstructions.

Prehistoric Period   The reconstruction of the prehistoric population relies largely on settlement surveys and excavations, knowledge of site locations and approximate sizes (for example, Adams, 1981; Adams et al., 1984; Graham, 1967; Rice and Puleston, 1981), and attempts to place settlements in rank order (Adams and Jones, 1981).[3] Settlement surveys typically provide data for a *house-count procedure* of estimation for a spatially "bounded" condition (center of a site, periphery of a site, away from site), and can be best used to estimate "rural" population densities.[4] A *rank-order procedure* of estimation must be used for "nucleated" settlements or sites because so many exist, but so few have been surveyed. This procedure, based on untested assumptions, assumes that the mass of architecture at the center of site is analogous to the size of contemporary Central Business Districts (E. S. Turner et al., 1981). This mass is used as a surrogate of population size. Here, these two procedures have been merged into a *composite procedure* to account for the discrepancies between site and rural population densities.[5]

Historic and Modern Periods   Population information for the central Maya lowlands from AD 1500 to the late nineteenth century is slim. The Spanish simply payed little attention to this "tropical forest" zone with little immediate riches for the taking, as attested by Cortez's tortuous trek through Peten in 1524 (figure7.1). Archival and other data have been evaluated by Thompson(1967) and others (see Bolland, 1977; Hellmuth, 1977; Jones, 1977, 1983). From AD 1500 to 1850, the population was undoubtedly so small that even a large error factor, which is unlikely, would not change the population estimates much. Modern censuses for Peten begin in 1880 and those for Campeche and Quintana Roo begin in 1900 and 1930, respectively.

Population Reconstruction Evidence of the existence of a paleolithic population in the region has recently been uncovered, but its relationship with the neolithic Maya is not understood at this time. The Maya appear as a full-blown agricultural society between 2000 and 1000 BC, but regional population reconstructions cannot be traced back that far. Owing to the paucity of early data, regional reconstructions begin at 300 BC (table 7.1).

Prehistoric Reconstruction The initial population estimate for the central lowlands is 242,000, and that for the end of the prehistoric period is about 104,000 (AD 1500). Between these two figures exists one dramatic wave of population growth and decline which may have obtained a maximum population of some 3.4 million (figure 7.2).

The Rio Bec subregion is not in phase with the other two subregions, and as a result the population curve is more complex than a continuous trend of growth and decline. After a 600-year growth trend for the entire central lowlands, a 300-year stabilization in population apparently occurred (0.18 percent per annum growth), created in part by a decline in the population of the Rio Bec subregion. This stabilization is consistent with the proposed cultural "hiatus" (Willey, 1974) for the central lowlands, and suggests that the other two subregions may have witnessed a population decline as well, as indicated by Ford (1986).

From AD 600, the three subregional curve trends correspond, with a 200-year growth spurt (0.45–0.58 percent per annum growth) culminating in a population peak of 2.6–3.4 million. This range is again created by the phasing of the Rio Bec data and the discrepancies between the rural and "urban" trends for that region (see Ball, 1983; Thomas, 1981; B. L. Turner, 1983a, forthcoming). The population of the central Maya lowlands begins a major decline thereafter, first at a decline rate of nearly 1 percent per annum and then within the 0.3 percent per annum range.

Historic Reconstruction This population decline continues during the post-AD 1500 period (table 7.2), as portrayed in the sixteenth-century maps of central Yucatan in which much of the Rio Bec and Calakmul subregions is vacant (Andrews, 1984; Clendinnen, 1987:43; Gerhard, 1979; Roys, 1965:660). The only major population was around the central lakes of Peten where the last vestiges of the Itza Maya survived (Roys, 1965:661; Thompson, 1967:28). It is estimated that the entire Cehache area, which is

Table 7.1 Prehistoric population reconstructions: central Maya lowlands (1300 BC–AD 1500)

	300 BC	AD 300	600	700	800	1000	1200	1500
Tikal	125,339	271,187	401,750	–	1,521,533	278,561	184,226	50,912
Calakmul	44,676	119,609	173,413	–	656,616	120,191	79,306	21,981
Rio Bec	–	629,142	502,671	1,432,520	485,512/1,257,707	137,866	–	–
Raw totals	–	1,019,938	1,077,834	–	2,663,661/3,435,851	536,618	–	–
Estimated totals	242,000	1,020,000	1,077,000	–	2,663,000/3,435,000	536,000	285,000	104,020
Population density (per sq. km)	10.6	44.9	47.4	–	117.2/151.2	23.6	12.5	4.6
Growth/decline rates (%/annum)	–	+0.24	+0.018	–	+0.45/+0.58	−0.89/ −0.93	−0.32	−0.34

Source: After B.L. Turner, 1986

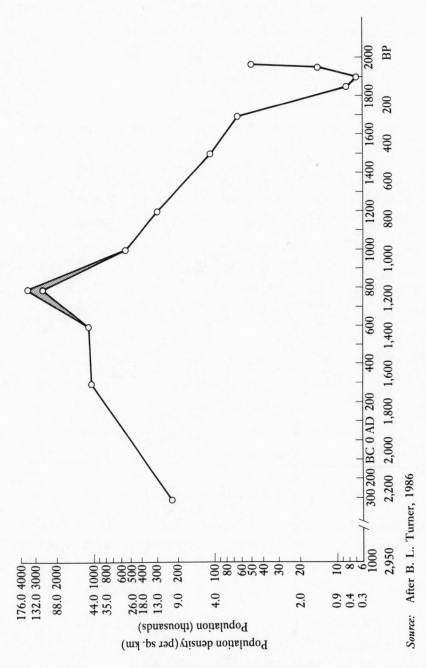

Source: After B. L. Turner, 1986

Figure 7.2 Population reconstruction for the Central Maya lowlands

Table 7.2 Complete population reconstruction: central Maya lowlands (300 BC–AD 1500)

Christian calendar Geologial	300 BC 2,250 BP	AD 300 1,650	600 1,350	700 1,250	800 1,150	1000 950	1200 750	1500 450	1700 250	1850 100	1900 50	1950/60	1970
Total population (thousands)	242	1,020	1,077	–	2,663/ 3,435	536	285	104	62	8	6.8	14.8	48.7
Population density (per sq. km)	10.6	44.9	47.4	–	117.2/ 151.2	23.6	12.5	4.6	2.7	0.4	0.3	0.7	2.1
Growth/decline rates (% per annum)	–	+0.24	+0.018	–	+0.45/ +0.58	–0.89/ –0.93	–0.32	–0.34	–0.26	–1.4	–0.33	+1.4	+7.9

Source: After B. L. Turner, 1986

larger than the central Maya lowlands as defined in this study, had only 5,000 to 6,000 inhabitants (Roys, 1965:661).

While the evidence for the seventeenth century is slim (Lange, 1971:122; Thompson 1967:31), Thompson (1967:28) calculates that Tayasal had 3,000 people in 1618 and that by 1695 the total population was 24,000–25,000, centered on the lake region.[6] It follows that the Tikal subregion had about 2.0 people per sq. km, and the density may have been lower for the Calakmul and Rio Bec subregions.[7] Tayasal and the Itza were conquered in 1697, and the population declined further during the next century. The entire Peten had only 2,555 people in 1778 (Thompson, 1967:28). The areas to the north probably did not have one-half that number, as supported by the reconstructions for Quintana Roo by S. F. Cook and Borah (1947:137–51).

By 1850, the Itza had dwindled to 800 souls, and a general pattern of population decline continued throughout the central lowlands. The decline may have been briefly stabilized by immigrants from the Caste Wars — an 1847 uprising by the northern Maya against the Spanish in Yucatan. An immigrant center, Chichanha (1853–60; later named Icaiche – see figure 7.1), is estimated to have had as many as 8,000 people (Bolland, 1977). This population pushed south in the late 1800s along the Yalbac Hills of the Belize–Peten border (Bolland, 1974, 1977). Assuming that part of the Chichanha population immigrated into the central Maya lowlands proper, the 1850 population is estimated as not more than 8,000 people, a figure supported by the 1800 Guatemala census, which places the total population of the Peten at this same number (table 7.2).[8] Peten reached its nadir in population about 1893 (see Jones, 1977). The forces of decline were so strong, including diseases introduced by the Spanish, that even immigration could not stop the overall depopulation trends.

Modern Period The low point for the population of the central Maya lowlands occurred at the turn of the nineteenth century (table 7.2) – 6,800 people and 0.3 persons per sq. km.[9] Before 1950, the population apparently grew modestly, and since that time, a virtual explosion in population has ensued, reaching growth rates of 7.9 percent per annum. By 1970, the central Maya lowlands had 48,700 inhabitants, including many immigrants. This new rise in population reverses a 1,200-year decline trend, but the overall populations fall well short of those in prehistoric times.

Comments on the Population Reconstruction

The broad pattern of the rise and fall of population in the central Maya lowlands in the long wave of several millennia's duration is difficult to refute. This boom—bust trajectory is itself of critical significance regardless of the actual population numbers involved. Controversy, however, has focused primarily on the actual size of the population before its decline and on the eve of Spanish penetration of the region. This controversy may be largely semantic as the population estimates of those arguing for an "unvacated" region are so low by comparison to those experienced in the populations of the eighth and ninth centuries that the region was indeed comparatively "vacant." Others argue that the maximum prehistoric populations were not nearly as large as has been suggested. This is so because of their sheer sizes or densities and because the catastrophic declines are unusual by Old World standards (for example, Ford, 1986; Petersen, 1975).

Past estimates of the maximum population for the entire Maya lowlands range from 1 to 13 million (table 7.3).[10] Most such assessments were based on some maximum carrying capacity estimate derived from studies of agriculture in northern Yucatan. Estimates based on surveys and house counts from the central Maya lowlands have produced raw accounts that greatly exceed these capacities, despite the reductions of the raw estimates by as much as 75 percent to make them "realistic" (B. L. Turner, 1976; 1978, 1983a). More recent estimates based on field studies have not applied this traditional reduction (for example, Adams, 1981; Rice, 1978), prompting serious critiques (Ford, 1986; Sanders, 1973, 1981).

Proponents of the high estimates note that the population reconstructions do have parallels elsewhere and that the sheer number of Maya dwellings and tests of the variables used to generate population figures as yet do not indicate that reductions in the estimates are warranted. These estimates have ranged to well over 300 people per sq. km (for example, Adams, 1981). The critics apparently want the population data to be comparable to that of the prehistoric Old World or the tropics in general. For example, Sanders' (1981) and Ford's (1986) criticisms of the high estimates for the Maya draw on analogues from elsewhere.

The high estimates produced in this study do not exceed the population densities found for other great civilizations (Whitmore et al., forthcoming). Comparisons between the central Maya lowlands and the Basin of Mexico illustrate this. From 300 BC to AD 300 the central Maya lowlands apparently did not exceed 10—11 people per sq. km (table 7.1). During the next 300 years, this figure rose to the mid—40s range, and by AD 800 it may have reached 150—60 people per sq. km. This high density fell to the low 20s range by 1000, and continued to fall to a nadir below 1.0 person per sq. km during the nineteenth century. These density figures are consistent with those reconstructed for the population of the Basin of Mexico in prehistoric times (Sanders et al., 1979).

Table 7.3   Population estimates for the Classic Maya

Source	Density (per sq. km.)	Total population
Thompson (1954:29)	4.0	1,000,000
Termer (1951:106)	6.6	1,650,000
Stevens (1964:299)	6.6	—[b]
Thompson (1950:17)	12.0	3,000,000
Termer (1953:152)	12.0	—[b]
Morley and Brainerd (1956:47)	12.0	—[b]
Hester (1954:121)	23.0	4,500,000
Sanders (1962:95)	30.0	—[b]
Spinden (1928:6511)	31.0	8,000,000
Brainerd (1954:78)	19.0–31.0	5–8,000,000
Ricketson and Ricketson (1937:23)	51.0[a]	13,000,000
Morley (1946:316)	51.0[a]	13,000,000

[a] Based on the assumption that the ancient Maya employed some form of intensive agriculture.
[b] Citation provides neither a total estimate nor an area with which to derive a total
Source: Turner, 1986

Another check on the estimates involves the resulting rates of population growth and decline. The highest annual growth rate projected here for prehistoric times is about 0.6 percent (doubling rate of 115 years) for 200 years (table 7.2). This rate is well within the range for a paleolithic, agrarian population. Higher rates have been projected for the Basin of Mexico, some 0.77 for about 250 years (Whitmore and Turner, 1986).

The highest rate of decline for the central lowlands is about 0.9 percent per annum for AD 800 to 1000, involving as much as an 85-percent reduction in the population. Such rates of decline and magnitude of depopulation have few parallels. They are matched or exceeded by other reconstructions for the sixteenth-century New World, but these reconstructions are themselves the subject of much controversy (for example, Petersen, 1975).[11]

Finally, the extrapolation of the population densities estimated for the central region to the Maya lowlands in general is hazardous. The latter includes some 300,000 to 500,000 sq. km, depending on the boundaries used, and the extrapolation would obviously lead to some rather astronomical estimates (see Adams, 1981:250).[12] The evidence does not yet suggest that the entire Maya region contained population densities of the magnitude found in the central region. Also phasing and settlement characteristics varied across time and space (for example, Willey, 1982), suggesting that growth in one region or subregion may have been offset by losses in another (for example, Ford, 1986). Indeed, as the subregional evidence improves, it is suspected that the population estimates produced here might well decline.

Agriculture

The literature on ancient Maya agriculture is rather substantial and need not be reiterated here in detail. Interpretations of the data, of course, are controversial, although a general consensus seems to have emerged among Mayanists. Until the last 10 to 15 years, the Maya were held as an exception to the other great civilizations in that they were thought to have maintained themselves primarily through extensive forms of swidden or slash-and-burn agriculture, commonly referred to as *milpa* (B. L. Turner, 1978, 1983a).[13] Subsequently an interdisciplinary assault on the subject has produced data indicating that, previous to AD 1000, the Maya in the central lowlands and its peripheries practiced a range of agricultures involving a large number of cultigens and several sophisticated forms of slope and wetland transformations. It appears that Maya agriculture was elaborated and intensified through time, reaching a zenith with the Classic civilization, and then "collapsed" to an extensive form that largely remains today. The major source of controversy among the scholars of the subject focuses on the precise forms of cultivation used and intensities obtained, and the distribution of these agricultures in space and time.

Data and Reconstruction

Prehistoric Period Fossil pollen of maize has been recovered from lake cores in the central lowlands at depths which suggest a considerable antiquity of cultivation in the area. Unfortunately, radiocarbon dating is difficult in the high carbonate environment. It is generally thought, however, that these finds represent incipient Maya cultivation. The fossil pollen record can be compared with botanical macrofossils (carbonized seeds, stems, and so forth) taken directly from Maya features and studied together with agricultural relics (such as terraces) to produce a relatively accurate picture after this time (table 7.4, figure 7.3).

Apparently before 1000 BC the Maya were practicing various forms of swidden cultivation involving burning and land rotation for the production of maize and other cultigens, including a large number of fruits (such as avocado: B. L. Turner and Miksicek, 1984), perhaps as part of an agro-forestry system (Gordon, 1969; Wilken, 1971; Wiseman, 1985). This interpretation is based on finds from Cuello (on the periphery of the central lowlands in Belize) and elsewhere of botanical remains, on the extensive nature of the settlement patterns, and on the lack of evidence of alternative cropping strategies at that time. Swidden was probably supplemented by house and orchard gardens.

Experimentation with wetland agriculture – a system of raised and channelized fields – perhaps limited to the edges of wetlands, may have begun between 1000 and 300 BC. This is supported by radiocarbon and ceramic dating of relic fields along the Rio Hondo and at Pulltrouser Swamp (Bloom, Pohl, and Stein, 1985; B. L. Turner and Harrison, 1983). Again the evidence is from the peripheries of the central lowlands, and controversies exist over precise interpretations. Swidden or various fallow systems, supplemented as noted above, probably dominated most agriculture. Evidence of the full array of Maya cultigens can be found by this time period (Miksicek et al., 1981; B. L. Turner and Miksicek, 1984). While densities in population were increasing, evidence of widespread wetland or other agrotechnologies has not yet been found which dates to this time.

From about 300 BC to AD 250/300, it is assumed that the trends towards intensification and technological elaboration of cultivation continued. Short fallow may have been practiced on uplands, presumably with various procedures to maintain soil fertility. Ceramic data from channelized fields along Pulltrouser Swamp suggest expansion of that form of wetland culti-vation. Small-scale irrigation may have been practiced in a few locales, but probably not in the central Maya lowlands (Crane, 1986; Matheny, 1979; Scarborough, 1986).

Between AD 300 and 800, the Maya were apparently engaged in large-scale use of various agrotechnologies indicative of intensive agriculture (table 7.4). During this time, raised fields in the interior of wetlands were used along the eastern and northeastern peripheries of the central lowlands, and terraces on upland slopes were used on the southeastern periphery and

Table 7.4 Chronology of evidence of Maya agriculture: central lowlands and periphery

Date	Evidence	Interpretation
3000 BC	Fossil pollen of maize from lake cores, undated but assumed to be from this time or earlier	Probably long-fallow swidden
2000/1000 BC	Macrofossils of maize, cucurbits, and fruit trees, dated by ceramic association, Cuello, Belize	Probably house gardens and varied types of swidden
1000 BC	Radiocarbon dating from a presumed wetland field along Rio Hondo, Albion Island, Belize	Some form of levee or river edge cultivation, perhaps initial use or experimentation with riverine fields (channelized)
300 BC	Radiocarbon dating of a channelized field, Pulltrouser Swamp, Belize	Some form of swamp/bajo edge cultivation, perhaps initial use of channelized fields
AD 250/300	Mixed ceramics from channelized fields at Albion Island Multiple dating of a small canal, field system at Cerros, Belize	Probably well-developed channelized fields in riverine context, annual cultivation Either irrigation or drainage?
AD 250/300–900	Multiple dating of terraces, Vaca Plateau, Belize	Steep slope and channel terracing, extensive short-fallow/annual cultivation
AD 250–850	Ceramic dating of channelized and raised fields, Pulltrouser Swamp	Considerable use of varying wetland fields and canals for intensive cultivation, double cropping possible
AD 500–830	Ceramic dating of terraces, Rio Bec region, Quintana Roo, and Campeche	Shallow slope terracing, extensive short-fallow/annual cultivation
AD 900/1200	No agricultural features dating to this time	Abandonment of all major agrotechnologies and intensive systems, return to swidden–house garden domination
AD 1521	Spanish accounts of swidden systems with house gardens, some lake edge cultivation	Swidden systems with some intensive infield/gardens
AD 1600–1970	Confirmed swidden systems	Long- and medium-fallow and home gardens
AD 1970s–present	Swidden, cattle raising, government-	

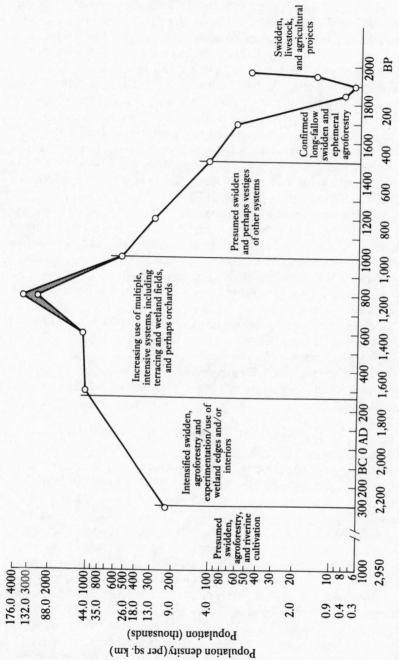

Figure 7.3 Population and agriculture reconstruction for the Central Maya lowlands

throughout the Rio Bec and parts of the Calakmul subregions (for example, Pohl, 1985; B. L. Turner 1983a, 1983b). Reports of terracing in the Tikal region have yet to be confirmed (Schufeldt, 1950). This evidence, in conjunction with the settlement and the environmental data suggestive of mass deforestation (Binford et al., 1987; Wiseman, 1983, 1985), is interpreted to mean that the central lowland Maya had radically altered their homelands and that a land-intensive economy existed. Agriculture was varied in form, but was characterized by labor-intensive systems and, perhaps, strong reliance on tree-crops. Apparently the most important among these were wetland fields and terraces on uplands. The one puzzling element in this interpretation is the sparse evidence of these features to date from the Tikal subregion (Ford, 1986; Pohl, 1985; B. L. Turner, 1985; B. L. Turner and Harrison, 1983).

These intensive systems were abandoned beginning about AD 800, and by AD 1000 there is no evidence of any technically sophisticated forms of agriculture in the central region or its immediate hinterlands. The dating, or lack thereof, of agricultural relics to this time corresponds to the massive depopulation of the central lowlands and its peripheries. An extensive land economy developed, and agricultural pursuits reverted to extensive forms of swidden.

No direct evidence of patterns of agriculture exists for the remainder of the prehistoric period. The pollen record, however, demonstrates that the tropical forest returns as the dominant vegetation of the region (Deevey et al., 1979; Wiseman, 1985). This evidence, coupled with the extremely low population, is highly suggestive that an extensive form of swidden cultivation was followed.

Historic and Modern Periods   The Spanish accounts of agriculture that they encountered in the late 1500s in the central lowlands, in contrast to the coastal zones, is suggestive of fallow systems complemented by house gardens and perhaps orchards (Hellmuth, 1977). Characteristic of these systems was a diversity of cultigens, although maize retained its dominant position.

From this time until very recently, the swidden systems apparently became more extensive as the population reached its nadir in the region. By the turn of the century, *milpa* − long-fallow cultivation based on maize, beans, and squash − dominated agriculture. These systems were slightly intensified near the turn of the century in locales where populations were concentrated, such as around the central Peten lakes. In the 1960s the Rio Bec region was "opened" by the construction of a major highway across the base of the Yucatan Peninsula. Spontaneous frontier farmers followed, as did cattlemen. More recently, the Mexican government has experimented with various agricultural projects on the northeastern edge of the central lowlands, none of which had been successful by the late 1980s.

Comments on Agriculture

In the population reconstruction, care was taken not to use evidence from outside the region designated as the central Maya lowlands. Obviously, this has not been the case for the agricultural reconstruction. Direct evidence of agrotechnologies in the Tikal subregion and the southern one-half of Calakmul subregion during the late Preclassic and Classic periods (300 BC–AD 800) is not yet available. Initial interpretations from the site of Rio Azul in the extreme northeastern part of Peten suggest the presence of wetland cultivation there (Adams, 1986), but otherwise references to terraces are few (B. L. Turner, 1974, 1983a) and ground confirmations of wetland fields are absent, despite provocative radar imagery (Adams et al., 1981).

Several explanations for this situation exist. The densely settled Maya in these parts were indeed exceptional, relying on either some form of agriculture as yet unknown or the massive importation of foodstuffs from the eastern peripheries. Alternatively, the evidence may be masked by the extensive forest cover and special hydrological conditions of the Tikal subregion wetlands (for example, Siemens, 1978). Much of the evidence of relic terraces and wetland fields comes from the more densely settled and utilized peripheries where major ground clearance has taken place of late. Indeed, ground confirmation of wetland fields in the Bajo de Morocoy on the edge of the Rio Bec subregion was not possible until the vegetation was removed by an agricultural project (Gliessman et al., 1985).

The principal issue is that the detailed knowledge of intensive forms of agriculture was possessed by the occupants of the central Maya lowlands, and apparently practiced by some of them. Given the high densities of populations throughout the subregions, which were certainly as high as if not higher than those in the peripheries where relics of intensive agriculture can be found, it is difficult to conclude that the peoples of the Tikal subregion did not also practice intensive cultivation.

Population and Agriculture Summary

The path of population in the central Maya lowlands is one of a steady growth from at least 1000 BC to large numbers and densely settled conditions about AD 800. A major decline ensued lasting over 1000 years and resulting in a nearly "vacated" region. The last few years have witnessed the apparent beginnings of a population recovery. The path of agriculture apparently paralleled that of population. Major land clearance and presumed fallow systems of cultivation mark the early periods of the occupation of the region. Experimentation with wetland agriculture probably began by about 300 BC, as the population moved to regional average densities in the teens. Large-scale intensive systems emerge during the major prehistoric growth period, associated with regional average population densities approaching 130–50 people per sq. km. Evidence of these systems disappears with the depopulation of the region after AD 800, as agriculture apparently disintensified to long-fallow systems which marked the region's history until the advent of recent, government-sponsored agricultural projects.

Malthusian Themes of Maya Depopulation and Collapse

A Malthusian-based explanation is taken to be any that asserts that the demands for sustenance and shelter exceed or severely stress the technological capacity of society, resulting in hunger, starvation, and an involuntary population reduction. Given this meaning, elements of Malthusian-based explanations of the collapse and initial depopulation of the Classic Maya civilization, particularly in the central lowlands, have been dominant and remain the basis of many of the more complex explanations that have been advanced of late.

Mayanists typically merge the collapse of the Classic Maya civilization with the depopulation that accompanied it, so that explanations of the collapse imply depopulation. In actuality, the collapse of the civilization may have been due to forces that were only indirectly linked to depopulation. Indeed, it has been suggested that a depopulation did not accompany the collapse, at least not at the scale that has been projected here (Sidrys and Berger, 1979). The evidence to support this contention is drawn, in part, from the coastal areas peripheral to the central Maya lowlands, areas which were never thought to have experienced the same scale of depopulation as the central region. Here we draw upon all relevant explanations, regardless of their initial purpose, whether to explain the civilization collapse or the depopulation.

The relationships between population and resources are, perhaps, the most commonly employed elements of collapse and depopulation themes. Not all these relationships are Malthusian-based, in the meaning used in this study. For example, short-term and acute environmental, "big bang," natural hazards are events that are beyond the control of any society and need not involve population growth pressing on food production capabilities. Therefore, explanations focusing on environmental change (Huntington,

1917), earthquakes, and hurricanes (Brewbaker, 1979; Bronson, 1978; Saul, 1973) are not considered, unless they are placed in the context of population and food stress prior to the triggering events.

Malthusian-based explanations that have been applied to the events in question involve both simplistic, linear causations and more complex, systemic associations. Each explanation assumes population growth and relates the stresses from it to technology, management, social organization, and the like (table 7.5).

The Explanations

The first set of linear explanations essentially envisions the Maya as never progressing beyond the swidden technology of cultivation. In an attempt to provide for the ever-increasing population, this technology overtaxed the fragile lowland environment, resulting in chronic food shortage. This led to environmental degradation, especially grass invasion, and, ultimately, food shortages and hunger.

The second set is similar to the first, except that the degree of agricultural sophistication and the quality of the lowlands to withstand intensive cultivation are expanded. In these cases, the Maya were able to develop short-fallow systems of cultivation which slowly eroded the environmental base through soil loss and soil nutrient sequestering. Again the consequence is a degraded environment, a collapse in food production, socioeconomic differentiation, and food poverty.

The third set sees the Maya as developing "advanced" forms of agro-technologies, especially in and around wetlands. These systems included raised and channelized fields in the wetlands. In using wetlands and the lands around them, however, intensive agriculture led to soil loss or siltation of the wetlands, destroying the primary production system and the sources of water.

Systemic explanations tend to involve a number of ecological, socioeco-nomic, and ideological factors that interact with one another in various feedback loop arrangements (for example, Willey and Shimkin, 1973). Here only those focusing on population–food relationships as the "prime movers" of the system are considered (table 7.5). Also only those elements related to the Malthusian theme are explored. More comprehensive inter-pretations have been offered elsewhere.

The first such explanation asserts that the central Maya lowlands were resource poor, in agriculture among other things, and the rising population there was dependent on the control of resource imports including food from the peripheries. Once this control was lost, for whatever reasons, a collapse and depopulation had to occur. That is, any sizeable population

Table 7.5 Malthusian elements of explanations of the Classic Maya collapse

Type of explanation	Root cause and result	Keys	Sources
A Linear			
1	Population growth and low level agrotechnology = degraded environment = food collapse	Swidden and fragile environment	D. F. Cook, 1921; Cooke, 1931; Meggers, 1954; Morley, 1946; Sanders, 1962, 1963
2	Population growth and middle-level agrotechnology = degraded environment = food collapse	Swidden and loss of soil/soil nutrients	Deevey et al., 1979; Olson, 1969; Sanders, 1973, 1977
3	Population growth and high-level agrotechnologies = siltation of wetlands = food and water shortage	Wetland systems and their decay	Harrison, 1977; Ricketson and Ricketson, 1937
B Systemic			
1	Population growth, imported resources, and loss of imports = food collapse	Unexplained low-level local food production	Rathje, 1972
2	Population growth and many agrotechnologies = environmental stress = decreased food = increased ideological activity = increased stress = social disruption	Increased vulnerability of system	Hosler et al., 1977; Sharer, 1977
3	Population growth and agriculture exceed socioeconomic management development = environmental stress = food collapse	Underdeveloped state	Lowe, 1985

within the central area could exist only by exceeding the local carrying capacity, with resulting social disorganization.

The second set combines population and food stress with cultural and religious responses to them. Population growth led to the development of multiple systems of cultivation, but over time these led to environmental stress and per capita food declines. Differentiation between elites and commoners introduced differential access to food and families in food poverty. Elite response to the deteriorating conditions was to demand more ceremonial activity, which diverted more labor from food production and land care with concomitant hunger and fear of starvation. The worsening situations gave rise to social disruptions.

The final type of explanation follows closely that just described. Population growth led to intensive agriculture, but without the requisite, complementary development of the sociopolitical economy. As a result, the production systems led to an environmental decay and malnutrition, exacerbating disease and other population-reducing agents associated with inadequate diets (Lowe, 1985). This process presumably would not have happened had the socioeconomic arrangements developed differently.

Assessment of the Explanations

Each of the six groups of explanations in table 7.5 assumes a general trend towards continued population growth in the central Maya lowlands from formative times until the Classic Period collapse. This construction fits well with the reconstruction offered here. Each explanation also assumes that demand for essential resources, which was directly linked to population, exceeded the agricultural abilities of the Maya and/or the sustainability of the central lowlands environs. The direct evidence does not support some of these assumptions and is equivocal on the others.

Those explanations that limit Maya agrotechnology to swidden systems (A1−2 and B1, table 7.5) are incorrect. The evidence of rather elaborate terrace and wetland systems is considerable (for example, B. L. Turner, 1983a, 1983b) and growing with each season of field study. Indirect evidence suggests a variety of other systems may have also been used (B. L. Turner and Miksicek, 1984). It is now believed that these systems emerged through time in conjunction with the rise in population and development of the civilization (figure 7.3).

Evidence of these agrotechnologies exists throughout the Rio Bec and Calakmul subregions. It is surprising that similar evidence is sparse in the Tikal subregion (see B. L. Turner, 1974, 1983b; Adams, 1986). The reasons for this situation may have much to do with the lack of extensive forest clearance in this subregion or with special environmental conditions that prohibited their use (see Ford, 1986; Siemens, 1978).

Those explanations which focus on advanced systems of cultivation which slowly led to soil and soil nutrient loss (A3, table 7.5) are possibly correct, although the data are simply too controversial to draw definitive conclusions. For example, the major geochemical study of a bajo (wetland) in the Tikal subregion concluded that major siltation or in-filling had not occurred (Cogwill and Hutchinson, 1963), and studies from wetlands with agricultural relics elsewhere in the lowlands have yet to uncover such evidence.[14]

The lone documentation of major soil degradation in the central Maya lowlands comes not from a wetland, but from the central Peten lakes, which are surrounded by steep slopes that were once heavily occupied. Analysis of lake cores provides evidence that has been interpreted as follows: forest removal led to increased erosion of topsoils and soil nutrients into the lake, perhaps leaving soils that were less rich organically and in nutrients on the adjacent slopes (Binford, 1983; Binford et al., 1987; Brenner, 1983). This evidence and interpretation is difficult to extend across the region, however, for several reasons. The central lakes are associated with rather large and steep slopes, portions of which were densely occupied, perhaps "urbanized," by the Maya (Deevey et al., 1979). These environmental and settlement characteristics stand in contrast to the "norm" for wetlands (bajos) in general. Indeed, it is questionable whether the steep slopes of the littorals were cultivated, or whether the sedimentation found was attributable to "urbanization" more than agriculture.

The intensive land economy of the Classic Maya in the central region undoubtedly degraded or changed the landscape. At this time, however, the range of this degradation is poorly understood, and the impacts on agriculture are speculative at best. For example, was the amount of sediment lost in the case of the central lakes typical for similar conditions elsewhere in which no depopulation occurred and cultivation continued? Comparative data are sparse indeed.

The core–periphery explanation (B1, table 7.5) seems untenable on energetic grounds alone. Lacking draft animals and waterborne transport into much of the central region, could sufficient food be imported there to support populations of 2,000,000–3,000,000? Inasmuch as relics of intensive agriculture occur in the northern subregions, perhaps the question is better stated as whether 1,500,000 people of the Tikal subregion during the Late Classic Period could be supported, in large measure, by food imports. One intriguing bit of evidence is Wiseman's (1985) find of a short-lived but statistically significant increase in maize in the fossil pollen record from a central Peten lake core. Recognizing problems in dating, he interprets this "maize blip" to be a last-ditch effort by the locals to produce sufficient food, perhaps after having lost control of major food imports from the peripheries.

The explanations that focus on intensification within an underdeveloped political economy (B2-3, table 7.5) must rely on numerous assumptions about ancient Maya social organization and also imply that the agricultural systems were not viable unless led by a managerial elite. Such contentions about other systems elsewhere have generally proven incorrect on detailed examination (for example, Butzer, 1976). No agreement exists about the level of managerial organization needed to sustain the intensive agricultural system used by the ancient Maya (B. L. Turner and Harrison, 1983). It is, of course, plausible that lowland agriculture required a series of "exchanges" of critical inputs − tools, charcoal, mulch − which, if disrupted, would have led to a degradation of the intensive systems. But then the critical question shifts to the sociopolitical agents that disrupted this exchange.

Two broader, generic issues involve the general quality of the central lowlands for agriculture and the evidence for food stress among the classic Maya. While all environments offer constraints on cultivation, the great soil groups that dominated much of the central lowlands, mollisols and vertisols, constitute some of the highest quality soils for agriculture in the tropical world (Sanchez and Buol, 1975). And the Maya had the same skills to cope with environmental and cultivation problems as did their brethren elsewhere in Mesoamerica, none of whom are thought to have collapsed for Malthusian reasons. Evidence of possible food stress in the Maya lowlands has been suggested primarily from analysis of human remains. (See chapter 3.) Some of this evidence has been interpreted to indicate a decline in the quality of nutrition (Haviland, 1967) or health (Saul, 1972, 1973) during the Classic Period, suggesting food shortage and hunger as major factors. The problem with making too much of these claims is the extremely small number of remains on which they are based, the skewed distribution locales from which the remains have been found, and the absence of comparative evaluations. For example, the proposed stature of the Tikal population previous to the collapse (Haviland, 1967) has not been compared to the stature of the Maya for the same period who did not "depopulate." Indeed, the stature of the Maya in the densely settled northern regions has been and remains quite small.

Regardless of their validity, the Malthusian-like explanations of the collapse of the lowland Classic Maya civilization do not adequately account for the longer-term depopulation spiral that was set in motion. For some 500 to 700 years before the arrival of the Spanish, the population of the central lowlands apparently dropped to densities in the range of 5 people per sq. km or smaller. The central lowlands has (had) agriculturally fertile soils which, even if nutrient-depleted during the Classic Period, would have regained their fertility under the forests that grew over them during the period of this study. There are simply no convincing arguments or evidence supporting the case for inadequate technology or excessively constraining environmental conditions that would have steered the population to such low levels. After AD 1500, the continued depopulation of the region is clearly affected by the larger forces of the conquest: disease, slaving, warfare, cultural disillusionment, and Spanish disinterest in this remote "jungle." A reversal of the spiral awaited the nineteenth-century land-intensive conditions in the Mexican and Guatemalan highlands, and armed conflict throughout Central America which has driven large numbers of refugees into the region.

Summary

The reconstruction of the population for the central Maya lowlands indicated one long wave of growth and decline and a recent reemergence of growth. The trajectory is irrefutable, regardless of the error that may exist in the prehistory segment of the reconstruction. Maya occupation apparently began around 2000–1000 BC, the population growing to rather substantial proportions (about 120–60 people per sq. km) by AD 800, doubling in size every 400–50 years. After this time the population entered a 1,200-year collapse in which the region was virtually vacated (average density <1 person per sq. km). Some time during this century, and especially in the second half, the population began to rise dramatically at a growth rate exceeding 7.0 percent per annum (including immigration), creating a current density of about 2 people per sq. km.

The agricultural reconstruction for the central Maya lowlands suggests a long wave of growth and decline which parallels that of the population. From perhaps about 2000 BC, the Maya began to expand and intensify cultivation. By the Classic Period, if not earlier, they had developed systems of raised and channelized fields in wetlands, terrace cultivation over much of the uplands, and numerous other systems compatible with the environmental and socioeconomic conditions of location. These systems were abandoned with the collapse of Classic civilization and depopulation about AD 800 to AD 1000. Consistent with the population, cultivation reverted to extensive swidden systems which remain dominant throughout much of the region today.

Lacking precise chronological control, it is impossible to demonstrate that either population or agricultural changes preceded one another. The best that can be demonstrated is that their growth and decline were in synchrony. Population reached considerable size; agriculture was quite advanced and varied. This relationship can be and has been used by both proponents and opponents of Malthusian-based explanations of the Classic Period collapse.

Complementary data are ambiguous. Pan-regional evidence of major soil erosion, nutrient sequestering, and sedimentation of wetlands — indicators of environmental degradation that could result from population—food crises — do not exist. And chronological interpretations of the evidence of such degradation at specific locales are controversial. For example, is major erosion a product of the abandonment of intensive agricultural systems?

What then are we to make of the validity of Malthusian-based explanations of the collapse? If they are applicable, they are so only within the context of advanced agricultural systems. Beyond this, acceptance or not of these explanations probably says more about the biases of the investigator than about the supporting evidence. My own biases are reflected in a series of works which have led me to conclude that the case of the Classic Maya was not unique or exceptional among early civilizations. Inasmuch as explanations of depopulation of the latter rarely invoke simplistic population overshoot or environmental collapse, it is difficult to accept such for the Classic Maya. Moreover, these explanations and the evidence do not account for the extended depopulation spiral into the historic and modern periods in which nature would have long since overcome any of the environmental impacts attributed to the ancient Maya. Populations and their agricultures were and are much more resilient than the situation described for the central Maya lowlands.

NOTES

1 The Maya case is used as an example of what might happen today if society does not more wisely utilize its resources, protect its environs, and slow its population growth. Lester Brown devoted two pages to the example in his significant book, *Building a Sustainable Society* (1981).

2 The population segment of this study was produced as part of the Millennial Long Waves of Human Occupation Project, sponsored by the National Science Foundation, Geography and Regional Science program (SES 841–3657). The author is indebted to the assistance and advice of the project members — D. Johnson, R. Kates, T. Gottschang, and T. Whitmore — the project's senior advisor, G. R. Willey, and W. M. Denevan, W. E. Doolittle, and R. E. W. Adams.

3 The principal data for this time period are provided by the extensive studies at Tikal (such as Haviland, 1969, 1972) and Becan, Rio Bec (Adams, 1974, 1981; Thomas 1974, 1981), and by the intersite or "rural" surveys in the Tikal subregion (Bullard, 1960; Ford, 1986; Puleston, 1973, 1974; Rice and Rice,

1980, 1981) and the Rio Bec subregion (Eaton, 1975; B. L. Turner 1976, 1983a). Similar guides have not yet been published for the Calakmul subregion which centered between the other two. The similarities between the Calakmul and Tikal subregions have led us to use Tikal-based data and assumptions for the Calakmul reconstruction.

4   The problems inherent in this procedure are well documented (for example, B. L. Turner 1986, forthcoming). Depending on the survey or count locale, site (urban) or intersite (rural), however, the resulting population densities will vary significantly; hence the need for distinguishing between site and intersite population densities.

5   For the most part, the prehistoric reconstruction uses conservative values for the variables in order to err on the side of caution. This is done because of the number of assumptions involved and the general paucity of data for the size of the region. The error factor could be as high as 50 percent, particularly for the earliest and latest prehistoric periods. Even so, the growth and decline of population in the central Maya lowlands was so dramatic that this error factor would not greatly alter the general path of population change described.

6   Jakeman (1938: 128) suggests that Tayasal had 10,000 people in 1626, but apparently he viewed it as an isolated center.

7   A caveat is warranted. Elements of Thompson's (1967) and Jakeman's (1938:128) works suggest that Tayasal may have grown in the mid-seventeenth century, perhaps as a response to Maya escaping the Spanish along the coasts. The data are so sparse, however, that regional estimations for the 1600s are not attempted here. But even had an increase been evident at Tayasal and its hinterlands, the overall numbers would have been quite small, at best constituting only a brief interlude in the overall trajectory of the population decline for this century.

8   The Peten data are for the entire department, whereas this study involves the northeastern quadrant only. Historically, as today, the majority of the Peten population lived in the southern sections and the smaller populations of the north were concentrated primarily around Flores (Tayasal), on Lake Peten Itza. In order not to err in a way that would accentuate the low populations of the historic and modern periods, it is assumed that 50 percent of the Peten population figures pertain to the northeastern segment.

9   The data for Campeche and Quintana Roo are reported by census districts ranging from 3 to 9 per state. Typically, these districts cut sizable paths from the coasts inland to the state's borders, and historically, as today, the large majority of the population has been concentrated in the coastal zones and the larger towns located there. As a rule of thumb, and again not to err on the side that accentuates the low populations, 20 percent of the district census figures are given to the central lowlands. I suggest 10 percent error in the reconstructions for the modern period, largely due to the census boundary problem.

10 Estimates for various regions of the peninsula at the conquest vary considerably. Wagner (1968) estimates the greater Yucatan region to have had 8–10 million people. Lange (1971:133) places the northern Yucatan population in 1528 at about 2.3 million. Jakeman (1938:128–40) argues that the peninsular

region had only about 1.4 million in the fifteenth and sixteenth centuries. And Roys (1965:661) suggests that in the mid 1500s the area from the central Peten lakes northward had no more than 300,000 people!

11 T. Whitmore (Geography, Clark University) is undertaking a detailed study of the validity of proposed major population declines in the Basin of Mexico in light of the criticisms noted in the text.

12 Adams (1981: 250–1) does not provide an estimate per se for the Classic Period. He does, however, demonstrate that by using house-structure methods of estimation, Classic Period populations for Central Yucatan (comparable to the central Maya lowlands) can be obtained that range from about 9 to 14 million (328–511 people per sq. km).

13 The original meaning of the term *milpa*, and that which the Spanish chroniclers apparently intended, was maize or corn field. Therefore any system of cultivation of *Zea mays* could have been designated by then as *milpa*. The dominant system of maize cultivation subsequent to the Spanish conquest has been swidden. Apparently, this maize–swidden form of *milpa* has been interpreted as the system of cultivation to which the early chroniclers referred.

14 Studies from Albion Island in the Rio Hondo of Belize have uncovered evidence of deposition during the Maya occupation. But these are riverine sediments (Bloom et al., 1985).

REFERENCES

Adams, R. E. W. 1973: The collapse of Maya civilization: A review of previous theories. In T. P. Culbert (ed.), *The Classic Maya Collapse*, Albuquerque: University of New Mexico Press.

Adams, R. E. W. (compiler) 1974: *Preliminary Reports on Archaeological Investigations in Río Bec Area, Campeche, Mexico*. Middle American Research Institute Publ. 31. New Orleans: Tulane University.

Adams, R. E. W. 1981: Settlement patterns of the central Yucatán and southern Campeche regions. In W. Ashmore (ed.), *Lowland Maya Settlement Patterns*, Albuquerque: University of New Mexico Press.

Adams, R. E. W. 1986: Río Azul. *National Geographic Magazine*, 169, 420–50.

Adams, R. E. W., Brown, W. E., Jr., and Culbert, T. P. 1981: Radar mapping, archaeology and Ancient Maya land use. *Science*, 213, 1457–63.

Adams, R. E. W., Hall, G. D., Graham, I., Valdez, F., Black, S. L., Potter, D., Cannell, D. J., and Cannell, B. 1984: *Final 1983 Report*. Río Azul Project Reports No. 1. Center for Archaeological Research, University of Texas at San Antonio.

Adams, R. E. W. and Jones, R. C. 1981: Spatial patterns and required growth among Classic Maya cities. *American Antiquity*, 46, 301–22.

Andrews, A. P. 1984: The political geography of sixteenth century Yucatán Maya: Comments and revisions. *Journal of Anthropological Research*, 40, 584–96.

Ball, J. W. 1983: Typological identification and phasing of ceramics from terraced sites. Appendix IV of B.L. Turner II, *Once Beneath the Forest*, Boulder, Colo.: Westview Press.

Binford, M. W. 1983: Paleolimnology of the Peten Lake district, Guatemala. *Hydrobiologia*, 103, 199–203.

Binford, M. W., Brenner, M., Whitmore, T. J., Higuera-Gundy, A., Deevey, E. S., and Leyden, B. 1987: Ecosystems, paleoecology and human disturbance in subtropical and tropical America. *Quaternary Science Review*, 6, 115–28.

Bloom, P. R., Pohl, M., and Stein, J. 1985: Analysis of sedimentation and agriculture along the Rio Hondo, Northern Belize. In M. Pohl (ed.), *Prehistoric Lowland Maya Environment and Subsistence Economy*, Papers of the Peabody Museum of Archaeology and Ethnology, Vol. 77, Harvard University.

Bolland, O. N. 1974: Maya settlements in the upper Belize river valley and Yalbac hills: An ethnohistoric view. *Journal of Belizean Affairs*, 3, 3–23.

Bolland, O. N. 1977: The Maya and the colonization of Belize in the nineteenth century. In G. D. Jones (ed.), *Anthropology and History in Yucatan*, Austin: University of Texas Press.

Brainerd, G. W. 1954: *The Maya Civilization*. Los Angeles: Southwest Museum.

Brenner, M. 1983: Paleolimnology of the Peten Lake district, Guatemala. *Hydrobiologia*, 103, 205–10.

Brewbaker, J. L. 1979: Diseases of maize in the wet lowland tropics and the collapse of the Classic Maya civilization. *Economic Botany*, 33, 101–18.

Bronson, B. 1978: Angkor, Anwradhapra, Prambanon, Tikal: Maya subsistence in an Asian perspective. In P. D. Harrison and B. L. Turner II (eds), *Pre-Hispanic Maya Agriculture*, Albuquerque: University of New Mexico Press.

Brown, L. R. 1981: *Building a Sustainable Society*. New York: W. W. Norton.

Bullard, W. R. 1960: Maya settlement patterns in northeastern Peten, Guatemala. *American Antiquity*, 25, 355–72.

Butzer, K. W. 1976: *Early Hydraulic Civilization in Egypt*. Chicago: University of Chicago Press.

Clendinnen, I. 1987: *Ambivalent Conquests: Maya and Spaniards in Yucatan 1517–1570*. Cambridge: University of Cambridge Press.

Cook, D. F. 1921: Milpa agriculture, a primitive tropical system. *Annual Report of the Smithsonian Institution 1919*, 307–20.

Cook, S. F. and Borah, W. 1974: *Essays in Population History: Mexico and the Caribbean. Vol. 2*. Berkeley, Cal.: University of California Press.

Cooke, C. W. 1931: Why the Mayan cities of the Peten District, Guatemala, were abandoned. *Journal of the Washington Academy of Sciences*, 21, 283–7.

Cogwill, U. M. and Hutchinson, G. E. 1963: El Bajo de Santa Fe. *Transaction of the American Philosophical Society*, 53 (7), 1–51.

Crane, C. J. 1986: Late preclassic Maya agriculture, wild plant utilization, and land-use practices. In R. A. Robertson and D. A. Freidel (eds), *Archaeology at Cerros Belize, Central America. Vol. 1*, Dallas: Southern Methodist University.

Culbert, T. P. 1973: Introduction: A prologue to Classic Maya culture and the problem of its collapse. In T. P. Culbert (ed.), *The Classic Maya Collapse*, Albuquerque: University of New Mexico Press.

Deevey, E. S., Rice, D. S., Rice, P. M., Vaughn H. H., and Brenner, M. 1979: Maya urbanism: Impact on a tropical karst environment. *Science*, 206, 298–306.

Eaton, J. D. 1975: *Ancient Agricultural Farmsteads in the Río Bec Region of Yucatan*.

Contributions of the University of California Archaeological Research Facility Berkeley, No. 27.

Ford, A. 1986: *Population Growth and Social Complexity: An Examination of Settlement and Environment in the Central Maya Lowlands*. Anthropological Research Papers No. 35, Arizona State University.

Gerhard, P. 1979: *The Southeast Frontier of New Spain*. Princeton, NJ: Princeton University Press.

Gliessman, S. R., Turner II, B. L., Rosado May, F. J., and Amador, M. F. 1985: Ancient raised-field agriculture in the Maya lowlands of southeastern Mexico. In J. P. Darch (ed.), *Drained Field Agriculture in Central and South America*, Oxford: British Archaeological Reports International Series 189.

Gordon, B. L. 1969: *Anthropogeography and Rainforest Geology in Bocas Del Toro Province, Panama*. Office of Naval Research Report, Contract 3656 (03) NR 388067. Berkeley, Cal.: Department of Geography, University of California.

Graham, I. 1967: *Archaeological Explorations in El Peten, Guatemala*. Middle American Research Institute Publication 33. New Orleans: Tulane University.

Harrison, P. D. 1977: The rise of the bajos and the fall of the Maya. In N. Hammond (ed.), *Social Process in Maya Prehistory*, London: Academic Press.

Haviland, W. A. 1967: Stature at Tikal, Guatemala: Implications for Ancient Maya demography and social organization. *American Antiquity*, 32, 316–25.

Haviland, W. A. 1969: A new population estimate for Tikal, Guatemala. *American Antiquity*, 34, 424–33.

Haviland, W. A. 1972: Family size, prehistoric population estimates, and the Ancient Maya. *American Antiquity*, 37, 135–9.

Hellmuth, N. 1977: Cholti-Lacondon (Chipas) and Petén Ýtza agriculture, settlement patterns, and population. In N. Hammond (ed.), *Social Process in Maya Prehistory*, New York: Academic Press.

Hester, J. A. 1954: Natural and cultural bases of Ancient Maya subsistence economy. University of California, Los Angeles: unpublished Ph.D. dissertation.

Hosler, D., Sabloff, J. A., and Runge, D. 1977: Simulation model development: A case study of the Classic Maya collapse. In N. Hammond (ed.), *Social Process in Maya Prehistory*, New York: Academic Press.

Huntington, E. 1917: Maya civilization and climatic change. *Proceedings of the 19th Congress of Americanists*, Washington, DC, 150–64.

Jakeman, M. W. 1938: The Maya states of Yucatan (1441–1545). University of California, Berkeley: unpublished Ph.D. dissertation.

Jones, G. D. 1977: Levels of settlement alliance among the San Pedro Maya of western Belize and Eastern Petén, 1857–1936. In G. D. Jones (ed.), *Anthropology and History in Yucatan*, Austin: University of Texas Press.

Jones, G. D. 1983: The last Maya frontiers of colonial Yucatán. In M. J. Macleod and R. Wassertrom (eds), *Spaniards in Southeastern Mesoamerica: Essays on the History of Ethnic Relations*, Lincoln: University of Nebraska Press.

Lange, F. W. 1971: Una reevaluación de la población del norte de Yucatán en el tiempo del contacto español: 1528. *America Indigena*, 31, 117–39.

Lowe, J. W. G. 1985: *Dynamics of Apocalypse: A Systems Simulation of the Classic Maya Collapse*. Albuquerque: University of New Mexico Press.

Matheny, R. T. 1979: Maya lowlands hydraulic systems. *Science*, 193, 639–46.

Meggers, B. J. 1954: Environmental limitations on the development of culture. *American Anthropologist*, 56, 801–24.

Miksicek, C. H., Bird, R. McK., Pickersgill, B., Donaghey, S., Cartwright, J., and Hammond, N. 1981: Preclassic lowland maize from Cusello, Belize. *Nature*, 298, 56–69.

Morley, S. G. 1946: *The Ancient Maya*. Stanford: Stanford University Press.

Morley, S. G. and Brainerd, G. W. 1956: *The Ancient Maya*. Stanford: Stanford University Press.

Olson, G. W. 1969: Data on soils of Tikal, El Petén, Guatemala. Agronomy mimeograph 69. Cornell University, Department of Agronomy.

Petersen, W. 1975: A demographer's view of prehistoric demography. *Current Anthropology*, 16, 227–45.

Pohl, M. (ed.) 1985: *Prehistoric Lowland Maya Environment of Subsistence Economy*. Papers of the Peabody Museum of Archaeology and Ethnology, Vol. 77, Harvard University.

Puleston, D. E. 1973: Ancient Maya settlement patterns and environment at Tikal, Guatemala: Implications for subsistence models. University of Pennsylvania: Puleston, D. E. 1974: Intersite areas in the unpublished Ph.D. dissertation. vicinity of Tikal and Uaxactún. In N. Hammond (ed.), *Mesoamerican Archaeology: New Approaches*, London: Duckworth.

Rathje, W. J. 1972: Praise the gods and pass the metates: A hypothesis of the development of lowland rainforest civilizations in Mesoamerica. In M. Leone (ed.), *Contemporary Archaeology*, Carbondale: Southern Illinois University Press.

Rice, D. S. 1978: Population growth and subsistence alternatives in a tropical lacustrine environment. In P. D. Harrison and B. L. Turner II (eds), *Pre-Hispanic Maya Agriculture*, Albuquerque: University of New Mexico Press.

Rice, D. S. and Puleston, D. E. 1981: Ancient Maya settlement patterns in the Peten, Guatemala. In W. Ashmore (ed.), *Lowland Maya Settlement Patterns*, Albuquerque: University of New Mexico Press.

Rice, D. S. and Rice, P. M. 1980: The Northeast Petén Revisited. *American Anthropologist*, 45, 432–54.

Rice, D. S. and Rice, P. M. 1981: Muralla de Leon: A lowland Maya fortification. *Journal of Field Archaeology*, 8, 273–88.

Ricketson, O. G. and Ricketson, E. B. 1937: Uaxactún, Guatemala, Group E, 1926–1931. *Carnegie Institution of Washington* Publ. 477.

Roys, R. L., 1965: Lowland Maya native society at Spanish conquest. In R. Wauchope (gen. ed.), *Handbook of Middle American Indians*, Vol. III, Part II (ed. G. R. Willey), Austin: University of Texas Press, 659–78.

Sanchez, P. A. and Buol, S. W. 1975: Soils of the tropics and the world's food crisis. *Science*, 188, 598–603.

Sanders, W. T. 1962: Cultural ecology of the Maya lowlands, part 1. *Estudios de Cultura Maya*, 2, 79–121.

Sanders, W. T. 1963: Cultural ecology of the Maya lowlands, part 2. *Estudios de Cultura Maya*, 3, 203–41.

Sanders, W. T. 1973: The cultural ecology of the Lowland Maya: A reevaluation.

In T. P. Culbert (ed.), *The Classic Maya Collapse*, Albuquerque: University of New Mexico Press.

Sanders, W. T. 1977: Environmental heterogeneity and the evolution of Lowland Maya civilization. In R. E. W. Adams (ed.), *Origins of Maya Civilization*, Albuquerque: University of New Mexico Press.

Sanders, W. T. 1981: Classic Maya settlement patterns and ethnographic analogy. In W. Ashmore (ed.), *Lowland Maya Settlement Patterns*, Albuquerque: University of New Mexico Press.

Sanders, W. T., Parsons, J. R., and Santley, R. S. 1979: *The Basin of Mexico*. New York: Academic Press.

Saul, F. P. 1972: *The Human Skeletal Material of Altar de Sacrificios: An Osteobiographic Analysis*. Papers of the Peabody Museum of Archaeology and Ethnology, Vol. 63, Harvard University.

Saul, F. P. 1973: Disease in the Maya area: The pre-Columbia evidence. In T. P. Culbert (ed.), *The Classic Maya Collapse*, Albuquerque: University of New Mexico Press.

Scarborough, V. L. 1986: Drainage canal and raised field excavations. In R. A. Robertson and D. A. Friedel (eds), *Archaeology at Cerros Belize, Central America. Vol. 1*, Dallas: Southern Methodist University Press.

Schufeldt, P. W. 1950: Reminiscences of a Chiclero. In *Morleyana*, Santa Fe: School of American Research and the Museum of New Mexico.

Sharer, R. J. 1977: The Maya collapse revisited: Internal and external perspectives. In N. Hammond (ed.), *Social Process in Maya Prehistory*. New York: Academic Press.

Sidrys, R. and Berger, R. 1979: Lowland Maya radiocarbon dates and the Classic Maya collapse. *Nature*, 277, 269–74.

Siemens, A. H. 1978: Karst and the pre-Hispanic Maya in the southern lowlands. In P. D. Harrison and B. L. Turner II (eds), *Pre-Hispanic Maya Agriculture*, Albuquerque: University of New Mexico Press.

Spinden, H. J. 1928: *The Ancient Civilizations of Mexico and Central America*. New York: American Museum of Natural History, Handbook Series, No. 3.

Stevens, R. L. 1964: The soils of Middle America and their relations to Indian peoples and culture. In R. Wauchope (gen. ed.), *Handbook of Middle American Indians. Vol. 1* (ed. R. C. West), Austin: University of Texas Press, 265–315.

Termer, F. 1951: The density of population in the southern and northern Maya Empires as an archaeological and geographical problem. Chicago: *Proceedings of the 29th International Congress of Americanists. Vol. 1.*

Termer, F. 1953: Die Hochkulture der Maya und ihre Erforschung durch die Moderne Amerikanistik. *Universitas*, 81, 145–59.

Thomas, P. M., Jr. 1974: *Prehistoric Settlement at Becan: A Preliminary Report. Preliminary Reports in the Archaeology of the Rio Bec Region*. Middle American Research Institute, Publ. 31. New Orleans: Tulane University.

Thomas, P. M., Jr. 1981: *Prehistoric Maya Settlement Patterns at Becan, Campeche, Mexico*. Middle American Research Institute, Publ. 45. New Orleans: Tulane University.

Thompson, J. E. S. 1950: *Maya Hieroglyphic Writing. Introduction.* Carnegie Institute of Washington Publ. 589.

Thompson, J. E. S. 1954: *The Rise and Fall of Maya Civilization.* Norman: University of Oklahoma Press, first edition.

Thompson, J. E. S. 1967: The Maya central area at the Spanish conquest and later: A problem in demography. *Proceedings of The Royal Anthropological Society of Great Britain and Ireland for 1966*, 23–37.

Turner II, B. L. 1974: Prehistoric intensive agriculture in the Maya lowlands. *Science*, 185, 118–24.

Turner II, B. L. 1976: Prehistoric population density in the Maya lowlands: New evidence for old approaches. *The Geographic Review*, 66, 73–82.

Turner II, B. L. 1978: The development and demise of the swidden thesis of Maya agriculture. In P. D. Harrison and B. L. Turner II (eds), *Pre-Hispanic Maya Agriculture* Albuquerque: University of New Mexico Press.

Turner II, B. L. 1983a: *Once Beneath the Forest: Prehistoric Terracing in the Rio Bec Region of the Maya Lowlands.* Dellplain Latin American Studies, No. 13, Boulder, Colo.: Westview Press.

Turner II, B. L. 1983b: Comparison of agrotechnologies in the Basin of Mexico and the Central Maya lowlands: Formative to the Classic Maya collapse. In A. Miller (ed.), *Interdisciplinary Approaches to the Study of Mesoamerican Highland-Lowland Interaction*, Washington, DC: Dumbarton Oaks/Harvard University.

Turner II, B. L. 1985: Issues related to subsistence and environment among the Ancient Maya. In M. Pohl (ed.), *Prehistoric Lowland Maya Environment and Subsistence Economy*, Cambridge, Mass.: Peabody Museum, Harvard University.

Turner II, B. L. 1986: Population reconstruction of the Central Maya lowlands: 1000 BC to Present. Technical Paper No. 2, Millennial Long Waves of Human Occupance Project, N. S. F. Grant No. SES 841–3657, Clark University.

Turner II, B. L., forthcoming: Population reconstruction of the Central Maya lowlands: 1000 BC to AD 1500. In T. P. Culbert and D. S. Rice (eds), *Lowland Maya Demography.*

Turner II, B. L. and Harrison, P. D. (eds) 1983: *Pulltrouser Swamp: Ancient Maya Habitat, Agriculture, and Settlement in Northern Belize.* Austin: University of Texas Press.

Turner II, B. L. and Miksicek, C. H. 1984: Economic plant species associated with prehistoric agriculture in the Maya lowlands. *Economic Botany*, 38, 179–93.

Turner E. S., Turner N. I., and Adams, R. E. W. 1981: Volumetric assessment, rank ordering, and Maya civic centers. In W. Ashmore (ed.), *Settlement Patterns in the Maya Lowlands*, Albuquerque: University of New Mexico Press.

Wagner, H. O. 1968: Subsistence potential and population density of the Maya on the Yucatan Peninsula and causes for the decline in population in the fifteenth century. *Verhandlungen des XXXVIII Internationalen Amerikanisten Kongresses, 1968*, 179–96.

Whitmore, T. M., Turner II, B. L., Johnson, D. L., Kates, R. W., and Gottschang, T. R., forthcoming: Long-term population change. In B. L. Turner II et al. (eds), *The Earth as Transformed by Human Action*, Cambridge: Cambridge University Press.

Whitmore, T. and Turner II, B. L. 1986: Population reconstruction of the Basin of Mexico: 1150 BC. to present. Technical Paper No. 1, Millennial Long Waves of Human Occupance Project, N. S. F. Grant 55 No. SES 841–3657, Clark University.

Wilken, G. C. 1971: Food-producing systems available to the Ancient Maya. *American Antiquity*, 36, 432–48.

Willey, G. R. 1974: The Classic Maya hiatus: A "rehearsal" for the collapse? In N. Hammond (ed.), *Mesoamerican Archaeology: New Approaches*, Austin: University of Texas Press.

Willey, G. R. 1982: Maya archaeology. *Science*, 215, 260–7.

Willey, G. R. and Shimkin, D. B. 1973: The Maya collapse: A summary view. In T. P. Culbert (ed.), *The Classic Maya Collapse*, Albuquerque: University of New Mexico Press.

Wiseman, F. 1983: Analysis of pollen from the fields at Pulltrouser Swamp. In B. L. Turner II and P. D. Harrison, (eds), *Pulltrouser Swamp*, Austin: University of Texas Press.

Wiseman, F. 1985: Agriculture and vegetation dynamics of the Maya collapse in central Peten, Guatemala. In M. Pohl (ed.), *Prehistoric Lowland Maya Environment and Subsistence Economy*, Cambridge, Mass.: Peabody Museum, Harvard University.

Part IV
Hunger in the Emerging World System

Exploration and colonialism in the past 600 years united many geographic areas, introducing a broadened world economy, increased international trade, and the emergence of the nation-state. The Working Group seeks the origins of hunger in the depredations of war, sometimes in conflict over the territory of the nation-state, and sometimes in colonization efforts; the effects of industrialization in increasing social status differences among people; and the introduction of commercial crops, diminution of indigenous food crops, and reduced self-sufficiency leading to food shortage and food poverty for many colonies in this period. John D. Post relates food prices to mortality in eighteenth-century Europe, and correlates malnutrition with social breakdown and increased vulnerability to certain epidemic diseases. Christian Pfister introduces a uniquely detailed data set with an in-depth look at farming, farm animals, food storage, and some of the effects of social stratification on food poverty in nineteenth-century Bern, Switzerland. This section emphasizes coping strategies and concerted efforts to reduce food shortage and limit the famines that had been characteristic of the Middle Ages. As effective as these actions were, they did not succeed in diminishing malnutrition or food deprivation.

8

Colonialism, International Trade, and the Nation-state

WILLIAM CROSSGROVE, DAVID EGILMAN, PETER
HEYWOOD, JEANNE X. KASPERSON, ELLEN
MESSER, AND ALBERT WESSEN

Introduction

The literature of the multicentury perspective on hunger is dominated by the story of how the European world coped with and overcame famine since the end of the Middle Ages. These local, regional, and national efforts to combat hunger were not accompanied by international efforts comparable to those of recent decades. Indeed, the spread of European colonialism caused major disruptions in traditional food supplies in many parts of the non-European world. Meanwhile, industrialization impoverished millions of European workers, probably lowering the quality of the average diet for those at the bottom of the economic ladder in the process, while it also destroyed the livelihood of traditional craft producers in the colonized world (Kennedy, 1987:147–50). What is more, no battle against malnutrition comparable to the one against famine occupied the agenda of the emerging European nation-states, and where nutritional improvements occur, they appear to be incidental accompaniments of an improved standard of living. Evidence about hunger from the past few centuries is present in abundance both in narratives and in government records. Very little of it, however, pertains directly to questions of nutritional level, and the research has accordingly focused more on famine. References to famine in one survey of the literature outnumbered references to malnutrition by more than seven to one. For malnutrition, one must rely on "proxy data" (see Herlihy, 1981, for some thoughts on the use of proxy data in historical research), such as the appearance of specific deficiency diseases in early modern times, records of the dietary intake of the working poor, or the use of average heights as in the work of Fogel and his collaborators (Fogel et al., 1985).

The relationship between disease and nutritional level has received widespread attention. Most casual observers take it for granted that the two are linked and that disease and malnutrition have a synergistic relationship in which each exacerbates the effects of the other. Yet the link is not as self-evident as it may seem. In the next chapter John Post shows how careful one must be in making claims that relate malnutrition and disease, and the reader is urged to consult his presentation of the facts and review of the literature.

Civil strife, unrest, and outright war frequently lead to seizure or destruction of food supplies and impoverishment of people, and as a result hunger and war are often intimately linked. Yet the role of violence, including the deliberate withholding of food from groups viewed as hostile, has often been underestimated in the literature on the history of hunger. It is in fact difficult to differentiate among causes when examining historically attested increases in the death rate, the most commonly used index of famine. Golkin, for example, begins her chronology of famines with the following disclaimer: "In most cases, it has not been possible to separate figures for deaths from starvation from estimates of deaths which resulted from epidemic disease, banditry, civil strife, or war" (1987:xi).

We begin with a discussion of the changes that enabled the European nation-states to increase food production more quickly than population, seemingly in defiance of Malthus's predictions. Not only did the food supply grow, but a complex transportation infrastructure and bureaucratic organization developed along with social changes that made the increased food supply available to increasingly high percentages of the citizens of the core states of the European world economy. Related to these organizational and social changes are changing expectations that people have for their lives, expectations that have come to include the right to an adequate food supply.

We then turn our attention to the peripheries of the European world economy, those regions of the globe where colonialism harnessed production for the benefit of the European home markets. A comparison of precolonial and colonial food catastrophes shows the devastating effects of production in large, interconnected markets where distant wealth could command all it needed of scarce resources. Furthermore, the appearance of certain nutritional deficiency diseases, both in Europe and in the colonized world, seems directly related to disturbances of traditional diets introduced in the wake of colonialism.

Given our lack of data on precolonial hunger, it is difficult to decide to what extent seasonal hunger and famine increased in the newly colonized world and to what extent our *awareness* of famine is increased through improvements in communications. We do know of specific instances where the plantation-style cultivation of colonial cash crops, such as sugar cane, coffee, tobacco, tea, and cacao, severely disrupted traditional subsistence agriculture with negative consequences for the indigenous inhabitants of such regions. Scholars such as Mintz (1979:60) argue that the same colonial crops, especially sugar, also had negative nutritional effects on the European populations that consumed them. The argument, though inherently plausible, is based more on anecdotal evidence than on nutritional studies. Hobhouse (1986:47) goes even further and blames increasing sugar consumption for the English addiction to white bread. Since these new consumption patterns did not lead directly to famine, we are led back to the details of nutritional studies and the difficulties surrounding them.

The degree to which various areas of the world were integrated into the European world economy of course varied, even during the height of the colonial period. There were also societies that were relatively unaffected by European colonialism until quite recently: those "external" to the European world economy, to use Wallerstein's terminology (1974:301−44). The best example is China, an advanced civilization with a long history of its own as a center of empire, and one that more or less successfully resisted the encroachments of European colonialism.

During most of the period discussed here, the world market and the infrastructure built by colonial powers served to enhance the well-being of the most developed parts of the world, often to the detriment of colonized peoples. Many features of the systems used to extract surplus from peasant producers can also be used to move food supplies into areas of shortage. It depends on the ideological perspectives of people in power, as we indicate with a few examples. A summarizing statement reiterates the main conclusions to be drawn from the centuries perspective.

Hunger and the Growth of the European World Economy

Food Production and Population Growth

Agricultural production has increased dramatically in the last several centuries. The technological innovations of medieval Europe, such as the moldboard plow harnessed to large teams of oxen or horses, or the three-field system of rotation, were only the beginnings of much more significant changes. These ranged from more intensive use of available land in the Low Countries in the sixteenth century to increasing acreage under cultivation both in Europe and in the European colonies. New crops, especially those useful in manufacturing processes, and better varieties of existing crops were systematically sought out and developed. Kew Gardens is the best known of a vast network of biological resource centers established to obtain, develop, and export new plant resources (Brockway, 1979). The "improvers" of eighteenth-century England initiated the invention of new machines and products that continued with the biochemical and mechanical innovations of the nineteenth century, of which chemical fertilizers, the cotton gin, and the mechanical reaper are perhaps the best known (Slicher van Bath, 1963).

The internationalization of plants was a major feature of both the millennial and the century periods (for example, Harlan, 1976; Hobhouse, 1986). To some extent this was a by-product of new trading patterns, but the Europeans of the colonial period expected to have their traditional kinds of food, especially wheat bread, wherever they went, so they routinely took their familiar plants and livestock along on their colonizing voyages. Crosby (1972, 1986) has chronicled the effects of this "biological imperialism" in great detail. Europeans were constantly on the lookout for productive land to grow exportable crops, but they adapted only slowly to new food sources. Gradually they began to seek out new food plants, though often primarily as food sources for the European poor or for plantation workers. Eventually, plant importation came to be treated as a worthwhile undertaking in its own right. For example, the *Bounty* sailed to Tahiti to obtain breadfruit trees for the Caribbean, where they were intended to become a staple food for the slaves. The spread of maize, cassava, and potatoes in the Old World belongs to a much larger story of biological exchange, part of it a purposeful transfer of familiar plants, part of it the entrepreneurial exploitation of unfamiliar plants, and part of it the accidental transfer of seeds.

Dramatic increases in agricultural production were occurring while Thomas Robert Malthus was writing his famous "Essay" of 1798, in which he hypothesized that unchecked population growth would inevitably outstrip growth in food production. It is one of the ironies of history that the data available in his lifetime tended to support his views even while new modes of production were laying the groundwork for unprecedented increases in population without accompanying mass starvation (Abel, 1977). Not only did Malthus live during the period under review in this chapter, but his views also influenced the responses of statesmen to food crises of the nineteenth century, and the empirical evidence used to argue his hypothesis is typically drawn from early modern European data.

Malthus argued that because population increases geometrically whereas food supply grows arithmetically, one of the "positive checks" on population growth will be famine. Over the last 300 years the population of Europe has grown rapidly, but food supplies have also increased to meet demand. In early modern times, famines occurred with some frequency, but their incidence declined during each century, and major famines have not occurred in Europe in the most recent century except during wars or periods of civil unrest.

Explanations are almost as numerous as authors (Hugo, 1984). In the middle of the twentieth century it was widely believed that public health measures had facilitated European population growth by reducing mortality rates for diseases, but McKeown (1979, 1985) and Kass (1971) deny that medical measures played a major role prior to the introduction of penicillin and antibiotics and argue instead that only expansion of the food supply adequately explains the growth of population in Europe. Boserup (1965, 1985) turns the argument around and claims that population growth itself stimulates agricultural innovation and leads to production increases that more than keep up with the population growth. Similar views have been enunciated for other periods by Simon (1985) and Cohen (1979).

Schofield (1985) and collaborators have continued to find evidence in their data for the view often articulated by historians that there were voluntary controls on fertility, at least in pre-industrial England. Watkins and van de Walle (1985) suggest that famine (as opposed to chronic food shortage) has *never* been a serious check on population growth. McNeill (1976) and others have concluded that epidemics, caused by the introduction of new organisms to virgin population groups that have previously not experienced similar infections, were eliminated not by improvements in nutrition or hygiene, but rather by worldwide adaptation of humans to micro-organisms, and micro-organisms to humans, in the wake of the colonial expeditions of early modern times. Meanwhile, the peoples of the Americas, Australia, and the Pacific Islands paid a high price for the new equilibrium (Crosby, 1986).

Whatever view one adopts on the relation between agricultural production and population growth, two points emerge rather clearly. The population of Europe rose and fell, seemingly in some relation to the available supply of food, prior to about 1800; but after about 1800, fluctuations in local food supplies did not significantly affect population growth. At the same time, hunger persisted in many parts of the world including some where potentially adequate supplies of food were produced.

Sen (1981) presents evidence to suggest that most modern famines result from demand problems and not supply problems. While it would be an overstatement to say that the supply problem (the availability of sufficient quantities of food) has been solved globally, it is certainly true that the entitlement problem (the lack of, or maldistribution of, resources enabling people to obtain adequate amounts and varieties of food) is much further from being solved.

To sum up this discussion, supplies of food and the technical capabilities to distribute them have grown faster than population when we adopt the centuries perspective, and when we focus on the countries of Western Europe or their most developed former colonies. Evidence from other chapters and from other parts of the world suggests that such developments are neither part of a continuous long-term historical trend nor something we can take for granted for the future.

Changes in Political and Social Organization

Sen has made a convincing case for the view that during most famines of the twentieth century, regional and national food supplies have not been inadequate. Population groups have lacked entitlement. Inadequate resources to obtain sufficient food have resulted from the values and legal systems of countries affected by famine. As noted in the previous section, population grew more or less rapidly, or even declined, in early modern Europe along with similar fluctuations in the food supply. Whether the food supply was the primary limiting factor controlling population growth; whether disease, either induced by poor nutrition or not, was the primary factor; or whether populations responded voluntarily to food supply by altering fertility patterns: there seems to be little controversy over the existence of some kind of Malthusian check until the sixteenth, seventeenth, eighteenth, or even nineteenth century in various parts of Europe (Abel, 1977). Limits on population growth, in short, were set by supply problems, though analysis is made even more complex by the massive emigration from Europe that reached its peak in the nineteenth and early twentieth centuries.

If Sen and others who share his views are right, then the past several centuries can be viewed as a period of transition from supply problems to entitlement problems. In pre-industrial Europe food supply appears to have limited population growth, and there are many instances of famines resulting from inadequate supplies of food. During the transition period, the supply of food expanded, but in addition, political processes were set in motion that when completed during the nineteenth and twentieth century protected food entitlements to some degree and largely eliminated famine in some parts of the world.

Two parallel processes thus were at work during the centuries period. The first process involved the introduction of new farming techniques and agricultural products along with a better transportation and distribution network. The second process led to a change in the political acceptability of famine. If governments were to flourish, or even just stay in power, they needed to develop mechanisms through which food could be distributed and famine avoided. The rulers of ancient Rome would not have found this unusual since their citizens expected to be supplied with bread (as noted elsewhere in this volume), nor would rulers in precolonial India, many of whom intervened in market mechanisms when famine threatened (Alamgir, 1980:55). But the rulers of medieval and early modern Europe increasingly tended to regard their subjects primarily as suppliers of the good life for the lords whom they served, and these lords had little need to fear for their existence when some of their suppliers starved to death, however sympathetic they may have been to the fate of individuals.

Mercantilist theories of statecraft did not, however, leave room for such a tolerant view of famine in one's own land. The father of a country was not expected to let his children starve to death, especially if they were to be productive members of a society that wanted to grow and prosper. The decision to take responsibility for one's citizens became easier when overseas colonies and trading partners provided a new supply of peoples for exploitation, peoples who conveniently differed enough in appearance and culture from Europeans so that racial doctrines could be developed to justify their enslavement. The medieval lack of interest in the fate of serfs and other "lower orders" could thus be transferred to foreign lands, and European leaders could begin constructing supply networks within the borders of their own states without worrying whether slaves thousands of miles away were well fed or not. The Europeans, unlike the Romans, were in a position to expand the definition of citizen to include essentially everyone resident in one of the European nation-states, because their slaves were kept busy in far-off lands producing the crops that could satisfy caloric needs at low cost or provide other forms of gratification (see table 8.1).

Citizenship rights were not in fact everywhere extended to everyone, but this simply reflects tenacious barriers of caste and class along with intra-European imperialism. Nonetheless, the growth of administration placed more government officials in direct contact with people at all levels of society. The central government may have remained distant and aloof, but its local representatives were in a position to monitor local food availability.

The overall decline of hunger in the European world between 1600 and

Table 8.1 Increasing British imports of selected products produced by colonial labor, 1700 to 1775

	1700	*1725*	*1750*	*1775*
Coffee (cwt)	35,553	105,029	74,898	401,445
Rum (gallons)	237	9,575	71,962	192,505
Brown sugar (cwt)	667,654	1,182,342	1,269,851	2,667,600
Tea (pounds)	14,398	13,338	482,983	215,159

Source: See note 1.

1900 was associated with the rise of modern states. But the very increase in governmental competence that is a major historical trend of the period also leads to increased information and documentation about food shortages as well as about many other aspects of life. Therefore the overall effect of increased governmental competence may have been to identify many problems unreported in earlier times and hence to obscure the rate of overall progress (especially in the earlier parts of the period). Laslett (1984) offers some useful reflections on this issue in his chapter "Did the peasants really starve?"

Certain changes can create short-term or intermediate-term problems even though they lead to long-term solutions. The growth of a market economy has obviously had many positive effects on the supply and variety of food. Local food sources in a specific area that may lack a trace mineral, such as the iodine needed to prevent goiter, are less likely to have any deleterious effects in a modern food system where foods are shipped both nationally and internationally. In its early stages, however, the market economy may have drawn foodstuffs away from primary producers who lacked money to buy them and thereby caused severe food shortages in areas where there was no supply problem as such. Additionally, national agricultural policies may have encouraged over-reliance on crops, such as maize, that are unable to provide nutritional sufficiency when not supplemented by other food sources. It is a commonplace of modern society, most often exemplified by environmental problems resulting directly or indirectly from actions that helped sustain economic growth and industrialization for the past century and a half, that short-term solutions may create long-term problems; and there are many analogous examples in the history of hunger.

Ironically, the destruction of food supplies as part of war and civil strife, whether deliberate or "accidental," has probably been increasing even as governments have been forced to accept more responsibility for preventing famines among their own people. A typical way for a feudal lord to provoke a fight with a neighboring lord was by burning down a few of the latter's villages. The individual peasant had to live with fear of arbitrary death and destruction at the hands of an attacker. Yet generations could pass without such an attack, and when it came it did not usually involve large numbers of people. As ever-larger formations of foot soldiers organized into national armies became the norm in early modern Europe, civilian suffering increased accordingly. Estimates of the numbers killed in central Europe during the Thirty Years War range as high as one-third of the population in some areas, and many of these deaths were at least indirectly related to food shortages. Appleby notes that war was probably a larger cause of eighteenth- and early nineteenth-century subsistence crises in France than any production shortfalls (1979:846). Yet, while war was becoming increasingly deadly, the destruction of food supplies was usually incidental to the conduct of warfare: armies seized food supplies for their own use, or crops were destroyed or not planted because of military engagements in the area. The deliberate destruction of food supplies is not an invention of modern times, but the increasing size of armies and the technology of modern weaponry have made the effects more and more devastating, whether we are talking about an offensive tactic (Sherman's "march to the sea") or a defensive tactic (Stalin's "scorched earth policy").

Both American and Soviet officials have been quoted as saying that "food is a weapon," and the manipulation of food supplies as a tool for imposing one's will on a hostile population remains a threat that can directly affect the lives of millions. Indeed, one of the worst famines of all time was perpetrated by the Soviet government on its own people in the Ukraine in 1933 as part of the collectivization of agriculture under Stalin (Dalrymple, 1964). So even as governments have come to see it as one of their responsibilities to supply their people with food, they have also been willing to withhold the food supply from segments of their population who are declared "enemies" in order to subdue them.

Changing Expectations

Hunger is a subjective phenomenon at the level of the individual. Some people are hungry when they have to postpone their regular meal for only an hour or two. Others have learned to adapt to much more serious deprivation, whether as part of a ritual of fasting, as an adaptation to food shortage, or both. Cronon has described how the northern New England Indians coped with winter shortages by expecting to eat little in the winter months, to the shock and surprise of European settlers who were inclined to view it as laziness or short-sightedness (1983:39–41). Rationing during times of food shortage is a common technique used by governments to extend the food supply, and abstinence can be viewed as a culturally prescribed individual response to a similar situation.

Laughlin and Brady (1978) have collected a number of examples from various parts of the world that show how altered social circumstances lead to altered expectations, including expectations of what one will eat. To cite just one instance, Bishop (1978:208–30) shows how Northern Ojibwa males resorted to hunting rabbits, a food they previously scorned, after the large game animals they depended on for subsistence and the beavers they trapped for trade goods were killed off in the early nineteenth century. Alternatively, reductions in culturally prescribed abstinence can impose new demands on the food supply. A good example is the decline in Lenten deprivations in eighteenth-century England, which led to year-round demand for meat by the wealthy with a possible concomitant reduction of the grain supply available for the poor.

An important factor in the growth of governmental responses to hunger in recent centuries appears to be hunger or food riots, public demonstrations of discontent in response to actual, anticipated, or rumored food shortages. Similar phenomena occurred in ancient Rome, and it seems plausible to assert that the "hunger riot," however defined, reflects a certain public expectation that an adequate food supply should be available. Some of the early European food riots took place in towns where citizens were outraged at the lack of food at reasonable prices (for example, see Abel, 1980: 168, for Paris in 1692), while others were directed against allowing locally produced food to leave a particular district in times of real or expected shortage (for example, see Hufton, 1985, for eighteenth-century France; Outhwaite, 1978, for England in the sixteenth and seventeenth centuries; Booth, 1977, for England in the late eighteenth century; Tilly, 1985, for some more general considerations).

The existence of some form of market economy appears to be a general prerequisite for food riots, but such riots also indicate the growth of what some scholars call a "public sphere," an arena for debate on issues of the day. The increasing complexity of administration and the amount of information available to ordinary citizens are among the major factors leading to the growth of this public sphere in early modern times (Tilly, 1985), and it is undoubtedly within this public sphere that one finds the growth of expectations that governments were responsible for providing an adequate food supply in times of shortfall and high prices.

Foucault (1979) has vividly described how governments of the *ancien régime* in France reacted violently against those who articulated demands for food too forcefully. The rise of the industrial state, with its view of people as biological cogs in a great productive apparatus, introduced a new mode of punishment, one that focused on training and reform rather than corporal punishment. The implication is that the modern state depended on providing a diet sufficient to keep the biological machines of industrial capitalism running.

Hunger on the Peripheries of the European World Economy

Precolonial Agriculture and Hunger

There can be little doubt that famine and malnutrition were part of everyday life in many parts of the world later colonized by Europeans. As

Eric Wolf (1982) has pointed out, the dichotomy between colonial and precolonial is itself misleading. "Primitive" peoples did not suddenly emerge into history when the Europeans found them. All peoples of the world have their histories, and conquest, subjugation, cultural interchange, trade, borrowing, etc., predate the introduction of "history" by Europeans. At the same time, the scale of exploitation and change introduced by the Europeans created a hiatus for many peoples, and it is useful to consider what kind of a history hunger had for non-Europeans prior to their forced encounter with the new technology of production.

The first problem is one of finding out. We have to rely all too often on European witnesses who were seldom unbiased, on unsystematic recollections of older members of societies who remember precolonial times, or on studies of people not strictly within colonial control but already influenced by trade with colonial powers (Apeldoorn, 1981; Brooke, 1967; Curtin, 1985). Even myths have been interpreted as providing insights into precolonial famine foods as coping mechanisms for dealing with famine (Cove, 1978).

Pankhurst (1966) and Zewde (1976) illustrate how an underdeveloped country (Ethiopia prior to 1900) without a market economy or a modern state can be just as exploitive of its people as any colonial empire when war, drought, insects, or animal disease conspire to create a severe food shortage. Chipungu (1984) and Bryceson (1981) provide similar kinds of arguments from different perspectives about famines in other parts of Africa. Famines were recurrent phenomena in which the people with least entitlement to food suffered most. Durrill (1986) presents a case study for northern Somalia to show how a specific coping system for dealing with drought was upset by the introduction of overseas trading of goods scavenged from offshore shipwrecks. Schmitt (1970) reviews the evidence for famine in Hawaii prior to the American conquest and concludes that war was the cause of the most serious ones. In other cases, shortages were too localized to have serious consequences, and people moved in order to deal with them.

The common thread linking these studies is that the most typical way to cope with the fear of famine was to move in times of shortage, an option that remains a common one, but one that has become more difficult to exercise in a world increasingly divided up into private property marked out by administrative boundaries. The ultimate form of moving is of course emigration to a new land, whether by choice to seek better fortune or by force in the context of the slave trade.

The other main point is that famine tended to be relatively localized. Thousands of people probably suffered severe deprivation every year in different parts of the world, but hunger catastrophes involving millions, such as we have seen in recent centuries in European colonies or in modern states (Bernstein, 1984), were probably the exception, if they ever occurred at all. Thus the centuries period as a whole might be characterized as the period of the delocalization of famine, to borrow a term from Pelto and Pelto (1985). Viewed from the perspective of colonizers, however, the growing coherence of administrative structures, including the delocalization of food supply, incorporated more and more people into systems capable of relieving famine.

The Effect of Colonization on Local Food Supplies

Whatever may be said of the agricultural systems prevailing in various parts of the world prior to European colonization, it can be assumed that most of them had production of food supplies for their inhabitants as a primary goal. This applies to subsistence agricultural systems of the Caribbean islands, to the Incas of the Andes who produced a surplus sufficient to support a vast empire, or to the states on the Indian subcontinent, including some with advanced social organizations, skilled craft workers, long written traditions, and substantial extraction of surplus from the peasant population.

The European colonists had very different interests, as many of the indigenous peoples soon found out. In the thinly populated temperate zones where the Europeans found a compatible climate, this often meant simply that they took over the land to produce their own food and cash crops for export. In India they found a vast labor reservoir and a future market for manufactured goods. In the tropical and subtropical zones of the New World, the Europeans discovered the virtues of plantation agriculture, and they eradicated the native agricultural systems altogether or forced native producers to grow their own food on marginal land while working on the Europeans' plantations. When the supply of local people proved inadequate, the colonists imported additional ones from other parts of the world, and the enslaved peoples either had to grow their own food on subsistence plots or be at the mercy of imported food crops (Dirks, 1978). Watts (1984) describes how this process worked in the West Indies, with a particularly detailed case study of Barbados. The point is not that precolonial agricultural systems were immune to famine — they were not, as noted above — but rather that colonialism introduced a new kind of famine, the famine induced by destruction of indigenous agriculture, including traditional entitlement relations. It converted occasional supply famines of limited scope into entitlement shortages that could become severe and assume regional or national scope for the most disenfranchised members of society.

India offers an especially rich source of information because of the diversity of the subcontinent and the amount of information available. There is disagreement on details among various scholars, but it is commonly thought that both the severity and the scope of famines increased after the imposition of British rule at least until the introduction of the famine codes in the late nineteenth century (Alamgir, 1980; Bhatia, 1967; Murton 1984). Ironically, the construction of a vast infrastructure of railways and administration that helped the British colonizers extract resources to the detriment of millions of Indian peasants also laid the groundwork for the long-term solution (McAlpin, 1983). The ability to monitor local food supplies and move surpluses from one area to another is one of the keys to modern India's success in controlling famine.

Colonial Agriculture, Dietary Changes, and Hunger

The Impact of Crop Diffusion on Dietary Diversification and Hunger The exploration of Africa and the New World by Europeans led to rapid inter-continental diffusions of crop plants and animals from the fifteenth century onwards. The Americas began to grow European wheat, vegetables, and herbs and to support the various kinds of European livestock and poultry. In Latin America, by the end of the sixteenth century, wheat, barley, and European vegetables and herbs along with cattle, goats, sheep, and fowl were well known. Horses, bulls, and asses introduced new forms of traction and transport, facilitating cultivation of the new crops and transport between regions. In North America, British settlers enclosed lands for habitation and agriculture, rapidly taking over the foraging lands of native inhabitants, in the process of introducing European crops and domesticated animals.

Besides their staple crops, animals, and stimulants, Europeans also introduced over the sixteenth to eighteenth centuries hacienda and plantation agriculture in many colonized regions, and directly exploited, often by enslavement, the labor of native inhabitants and imported workers. In their quest for new market crops and market dominance, Europeans began to exhibit the disregard for native nutrition, health, and life which came to characterize the initial period of adjustment to new crops and cropping patterns. Land and labor were appropriated to grow cocoa and indigo in the early Spanish domain. By the eighteenth century, the sugar trade was firmly entrenched, causing misery for the enslaved, malnourished workers who cultivated and cut the cane on tropical New World estates and, plausibly, contributing to short, malnourished lives for the European indus-trial workers who subsisted on sugar as a staple (Mintz, 1985). The large-scale availability of sugar also introduced into Europe for the first time a new nutrition-related disease − dental caries. Indigenous land-use and food systems were seriously disrupted by the new Western-dominated agricultural and herding economies that would eventually feed millions of non-food producing people (see also MacLeod, 1973).

The Spanish, British, and French, returning to the Old World, carried with them maize, which was soon to transform the countryside and diets of whole parts of Europe, and later of Africa. They also transferred the major New World root crops — white potato, cassava and sweet potatoes — to Europe, Africa, and China respectively, where, in turn, each contributed to changing cycles of cultivation and new nutritional patterns. More specifically, during the sixteenth century, Europeans carried maize, cassava, sweet potatoes, groundnuts, tomatoes, and tobacco from the Americas to Africa, where they quickly became established in slash-and-burn agricultural cycles. Tobacco, maize, sweet potatoes, groundnuts, tomatoes, and chili peppers were introduced into China. Tomatoes and, more importantly, chili peppers radically altered the nutritional balance in China, where their introduction, along with that of sweet potatoes, has sometimes been credited with sustaining the rise of population from the sixteenth century onward (but see Lee, 1982, for an opposing view). In Western Europe, the introduction of New World crops was also linked to major population growth during the industrial revolution. The Columbian exchange of food crops has even been credited with changing relationships of people to land and providing the most important condition for sustained population increase. .

Most of the examples of food crop transfer involved single cultigens, lifted out of native production, processing, and consumption contexts. Introduced crops such as maize were grown in monoculture in their new contexts. The new cropping and dietary patterns usually did not include complementary species to sustain their productivity, to ameliorate shortfalls, or to increase the nutritiousness of diets based on them. As a result, at least initially, the spread of new crops, with their changed manners of preparation, storage, and distribution, had the potential to aggravate rather than to alleviate hunger.

Types of Hunger Associated with New Crops   New cropping patterns may lead to localized hunger if they: (a) increase the uncertainty of the food supply, (b) decrease poor people's access to food, or (c) contribute to nutrition-related illness through new dietary patterns based on the new crops. We can ask, for example, whether the transfer of maize or potatoes to wheat-, rye-, barley-, and oat-eating areas, and of wheat to maize areas, resulted in greater vulnerability of the crops in each new area to inclement weather patterns, to pests, or to soil exhaustion. Were the new crops as highly and sustainably productive as the older crops? Any change for the worse, in these circumstances, would mean that people growing the new crops would undergo food shortage over the short to longer term.

The Irish potato famine of 1846−7 provides the most dramatic example of a food shortage resulting from exclusive reliance on a single, new, food crop species, especially one so productive as to contribute to an extended period of population growth. The extensive literature analyzing the Irish famine from many different perspectives (for example, Mokyr, 1983; Schaffner, 1981) makes clear, however, that there were many other issues involved, especially the land tenure system and Ireland's status as a colony of Great Britain.

The potato had become a staple for impoverished Irish tenants largely because it outyielded grain. The tenancy system whereby English landlords rented their land to intermediaries, who in turn sublet ever-smaller plots at great profit to themselves, left small tenants with little choice but to grow potatoes for survival: only potatoes produced enough for subsistence on their extremely small plots. The other side of the coin was, of course, that the potato made survival on small plots possible, and Ireland experienced rapid population growth during the century preceding the potato famine. Then, when the potato crop was destroyed by blight, the effects were immediate and devastating. The underlying political and social relations are evident, however, from the fact that food, mainly grains, continued to be exported from Ireland throughout the famine period, whereas famine relief was usually slow in arriving and inadequate in amount.

In the second instance, people may be food poor as a result of forced changes in crops and cropping systems. Their access to food may be reduced as a result of: taxation, which cuts down their entitlement to the products of their labor; loss of land or loss of other forms of entitlement to factors of production; or crop prices that do not allow producers enough income to live on. In the New World, for example, Spanish collection of taxes payable in cocoa and wheat left indigenous peoples insufficient time and terrain to cultivate their own food crops. Sixteenth-century Spanish records show how cocoa production (for tax payments) interfered fatally with the land and seasonal scheduling requirements of maize, which remained the native food staple (MacLeod, 1973). The early British colonial record was little better, as European settlers appropriated lands that harbored the game animals on which native populations relied for protein (Cronon, 1983).

Policies that appropriated native labor for work in mines or plantations also interfered with native livelihoods. Greedy conquistadors in the Spanish Main, encountering cassava bread for the first time, failed to recognize that a diet based on cassava had to be complemented with fish and animal protein. Losing the freedom to hunt and fish, the indigenous population became ill and died from malnutrition and other newly introduced diseases, as they were forced to work for the Spanish in mines. Records indicate that within a generation, they had lost traditional hunting skills and also the will to live (Sauer, 1966). Three centuries later in Africa, the British were forced to acknowledge a similar finding after interdisciplinary dietary-nutrition studies. Drawing native males off to work in mines interfered with their nutrition and also with the overall levels of food production and nutrition in the rural areas they left behind (Richards, 1939), a problem that continues into current times. Thus, European patterns of land and labor use interfered with native adaptations to land and local foods, and previous entitlements to food.

Finally, new cropping systems may leave people food deprived, as when a meager diet of moldy maize subjected the population subsisting on it to nutrition and health problems. It is during the sixteenth and seventeeth centuries that we note the rise of deficiency diseases associated with the consumption of cereal diets based predominantly on a single grain of inadequate nutritional quality. The most dramatic example is that of niacin-deficiency disease — pellagra — associated with an inadequate maize diet (Roe, 1973).

Maize is approximately 10−12 percent protein and, like the other major cereal grains, short in the essential amino acid lysine, and the vitamin niacin. Pre-Columbian food systems had developed a form of traditional food processing with lime (calcium carbonate) that freed much of the bound niacin, and thereby enhanced the nutritional value of the maize. Production and consumption of maize with beans (mainly *Phaseolus vulgaris*) remedied the lysine deficit in the maize diet. As a result, native populations subsisting on lime-processed maize diets, although occasionally food short, were never reported to have suffered from the nutritional diseases associated with maize in later times and places.

Neither the advantageous native food-processing technology nor the complementary foods of native maize diets, unfortunately, seem to have accompanied maize to its new European locations. While the details of the spread of pellagra in Europe are beyond the scope of this review chapter, one can summarize by noting that it occurred with some regularity in areas where peasants came to rely on maize without adequate dietary supplementation.

It was not until the early twentieth century that public health legislation addressed first nutritional, then economic causes of the disorder. Since 1937, nicotinamide (niacin) has been recognized as the missing vitamin responsible for pellagra. As an additive, it has been suggested as a preventive measure for the poor during seasons when they lack milk, eggs, meat, and fresh vegetables to supplement a predominantly maize diet, and this policy finally spelled the end to pellagra.

While such cheap chemical solutions exist for particular varieties of hunger, such as specific vitamin deficiencies, the root causes remain socioeconomic and cultural. In the United States, poor agricultural populations who relied on sales of cash crops — especially cotton — were thrown back onto subsistence food crops during the severe depression of 1932−4. Under such circumstances of home food production, their nutrition improved. With the resurgence of the national economy and restored demand for cotton, home food production and nutrition again deteriorated in the rural south. Yet, overall, better diets accompanying the working and food-rationing conditions of the Second World War in the United States provided the poor with better diets.

Beri-beri is a disease resulting from thiamine (vitamin B-1) deficiency. People who eat polished rice without adequate dietary supplements are apt to suffer from it. Unlike pellagra, beri-beri appears to have existed in antiquity, and it reminds us that colonial exploitation is not the only source for introducing dietary deficiency diseases. Records in Japan mention it in 808, although interpreters indicate the numbers were probably small as unpolished rice was still the staple. It was not until the Tokugawa period, 1603−1867, that polished rice became the general staple; and this coincided with a high incidence of beri-beri. It reached epidemic proportions in 1691 in Edo (Tokyo). As the custom of eating well-milled rice became widespread in the Meiji period after 1870, the numbers suffering beri-beri surged, peaking in the 1920s, with seasonal mortality peaks August– September. Only after the 1950s, when therapeutic measures became more widespread, was there a sharp decline. In Japan, as elsewhere (for example, the Philippines), decreasing numbers suffering beri-beri have been associated with thiamine enrichment of rice and diversification of diet. Yet, even in the 1960s, farmers accustomed to eating large quantities of polished rice were found to suffer slight deficiencies of vitamin B-1 throughout the year, although beri-beri was unknown.

Hunger in China

China is sometimes referred to in the western literature as the "land of famine". Indeed, this was the title of a book by the head of an international commission investigating the famines of the 1920s (Mallory, 1926). Certainly some of the worst famines of all time have occurred in China, in terms of the numbers of people who perished. But China also contains between a fifth and a fourth of the population of the world, and has done so for as far back as we can make meaningful estimates, if Braudel's assumptions about world population are correct (1981:39−46). It also underwent a population explosion during recent centuries at least as impressive as that of Europe. Severe famines occurred, especially during the periods of upheaval associated with dynastic changes, and the European century of decline, in the seventeenth century, was also a century of stagnation in Chinese population growth.

The eighteenth century, however, saw the numbers of Chinese increasing rapidly with very little evidence of widespread or prolonged, severe food shortages. There is little doubt that the Chinese peasant had a monotonous and barely adequate diet, but the continuity of Chinese agriculture and its efficiency in producing high yields adequate to support an advanced civilization are impressive. The usual explanation has been the relative stability of the Qing dynasty government with its elaborate system of public granaries (Buck, 1982) and an extensive social organization to construct and maintain a flood-control and irrigation system (Perdue, 1982). Improvements in agricultural technology included the introduction of new plants from the Americas. Lee (1982) has shown how early industrialization may have been even more important in one region (the southwest) of especially high growth rates, but the existence of an adequate food-distribution system supplemented by government control measures seems to be presupposed by almost all authors. Wong (1982) shows how food riots played a role in the eighteenth century not dissimilar to their role in Europe.

It was only after the gradual breakdown of authority in the nineteenth century, caused in no small measure by the European attempts to gain a foothold in the Chinese market, that reports of famine and serious food shortages become more widespread (Li, 1982). It is instructive to compare the case of Fukuoka Domain in Japan, as reported by Kalland and Pedersen (1984), where measures adopted in the wake of a severe famine in 1732−3 ensured that subsequent crop failures did not lead to excess mortality. In China the situation grew progressively worse during the nineteenth century, leading to the popular misconception on the part of westerners that China was a traditional "land of famine." None of the contributors to this chapter is a China expert, but our perusal of the literature suggests to us that China is nothing of the sort (and see chapter 6). Chinese civilization has until very recently occupied the most fertile parts of the country, leaving more remote highlands, desert areas, and forests to peoples who were subject to the same kinds of local famines that existed in other parts of the precolonial world. But the mainstream world of Chinese culture has a long tradition of famine-control mechanisms of a scale unequaled anywhere in the Western world. These arose along with a sense of government responsibility for dealing with famine that antedates the same tradition in Europe. We should not be surprised, given the long tradition of Chinese central government, but it is easy to overlook if we focus only on the most recent developments.

Hunger and Ideology

Interpretations of the causes of famine and malnutrition vary according to the ideology of the observer. Reports in the press about the latest technologies that will increase food production suggest that hunger and malnutrition are widespread because we lack the technical means to produce enough food. Others talk about the latest drought that is threatening to cause starvation in the Sahel. The seventeenth-century Englishman who said that: "last yeares famin was made by man and not by God" (quoted in Tilly, 1985:135) implied that human society has the ability to prevent hunger.

The view that hunger results primarily from acts of nature is compatible with a view of society that does not include freedom from hunger as a basic right. If access to food is viewed as a basic human right, then starvation and malnutrition are violations of that right, and governments are expected to strive to eliminate famine and malnutrition. The question then remaining is whether this is a technical question of food production, or a question of providing citizens with the resources that will enable them to acquire food.

The answers society offers to these questions have always influenced the occurrence of famine and malnutrition, and the past few centuries offer some especially striking illustrations of this point. One of the major themes in the history of hunger has been climatic variability and its impact on food supply. Yet similar climatic events have led to different outcomes even when the affected populations seemed otherwise similarly endowed with skills and resources.

Famines were eliminated in many parts of the world in the second half of the twentieth century, while malnutrition persists, and there are also ideological factors at work here. That European governments were accepting the responsibility of coping with inadequate food supplies a century and a half earlier is indicated by their response to the "last great subsistence crisis of the western world" (Post, 1977) in 1816 and 1817. In some countries the relief measures were more effective than in others, but in general the importation of grain from surplus regions mitigated the effects of the production shortfalls. Following revolutions in the United States and France, it had became politically unacceptable to allow famine to run rampant.

Measures to prevent famine have not usually been paralleled by similar efforts to overcome malnutrition. Malnutrition is less visible and its effects require more subtle detection. It results in babies of low birth weight, increases in fetal mortality, slower growing children, smaller adults, and diminished physical activity, work capacity, and social functioning. As Reid (1988:45−50) has pointed out, for example, southeast Asians and Europeans reached approximately the same average adult heights prior to 1800, but the substantial gains since registered by the European middle classes created a diet-based gap between the two groups. Even when recognized, the consequences of malnutrition are apt to be attributed to other causes, such as the alleged inferiority of certain classes of people. Unskilled laborers can put in years of work on diets rich in calories but low in nutritional value, and if they are shorter and less energetic than the well-fed middle classes, whose fault is it?

Ambirajan (1971, 1976) has shown how ideology played a direct role in British responses to famine in colonized India prior to the adoption of famine codes in the late nineteenth century. Administrators influenced by the teachings of Malthus on population growth did not want to intervene to reduce famine because they were convinced that this would only ensure that population would grow even more rapidly. Sir George Couper stated the Malthusian perspective bluntly in a memorandum to the Viceroy, Lord Ripen: "If the famine mortality in 1879 be tested, it will be found that about 80 per cent of the deaths come from the labouring classes, and nearly the whole of the remaining 20 per cent from cultivators owning such minute plots of land as to be hardly removed from laborers ... still they reproduce themselves with sufficient rapidity to overcrowd every employment that is opened to them" (quoted by Ambirajan, 1976:8).

The technological advances of the last several centuries have aided in the elimination of famine. The process has been hindered, however, by ideologies that in some cases prevented governments from utilizing the resources at hand to maximize the distribution of food that could be produced. The reduction of famine in the last few centuries thus depends on a combination of technological advance that provided increased food production for an increasing population, and ideological change that made it politically unacceptable for governments to allow famine to persist in their own lands.

We can observe the beginnings of an ideologically based difference in the approach to malnutrition towards the end of the 300-year period. Sen (chapter 14) has pointed out that the Indian response to famine is dramatic and often related to fierce publicity and to public pressure placed on Indian governments at the first sign of a death from starvation. He also notes, however, that malnutrition is rampant in India even as food exports continue. On the other hand, China with a much larger population and perhaps fewer resources has been able in recent years to deal with both famine and malnutrition, although at times it has dealt more effectively with the latter.

Chinese ideology favors distribution of goods and services in addition to minimum standards of decency (prevention of famine). At the same time, the lack of democracy and the government's interest in maintaining itself and its reputation (and thus in suppressing news of possible failures, famine included) inhibits the government from taking prompt action against famines when they are first noted and can even lead to a major hunger catastrophe, as outlined elsewhere in this volume. A single starvation death in India is an outrage and reaches the public eye and ear immediately. This is not the case in China. Yet the Chinese ideological perspective has favored distributive justice and long-term solutions to the more subtle problem of chronic malnutrition.

Conclusion

The major trend of the past 300 years affecting hunger policy has been the transition in many parts of the world from a feudal or precapitalist market system to a bourgeois liberal capitalist system. This world system produced increased population, goods, and services, but it remained vulnerable to famine if relief measures were not prompt and effective. Famines in turn made the system vulnerable to revolution in a political context where the citizenry had an increasing role in public affairs. Nations adopted poor-laws and appropriate ideological adjustment within the context of growing democracy, though these protections were not readily extended to colonized peoples, as is most graphically illustrated by the Irish potato famine. The adjustments eventually led to the decline of famine in much of the world, but they did not eliminate malnutrition. Malnutrition, though widespread and probably still a contributor to mortality even in the wealthiest developed countries at the end of the 300-year period, has only recently begun to receive a significant amount of attention, especially when it comes to debilitating effects that are not readily visible (Carmichael, 1985). Hunger, a sensation so gnawing that it can stimulate political action, has become ideologically unfashionable to such a degree that worldwide outrage can be mobilized against it.

A second point to emphasize is that the hunger literature of the centuries perspective does not dwell much on changing climate and weather patterns. There is little doubt that production shortages can be linked to weather changes. Drought, excessive rain, and insect plagues continue to cause crop failures, and peoples cut off from alternative supplies or markets suffer accordingly. There is a traditional kind of famine literature that connects bad weather with famine but does not go much further. A good example is Arakawa (1955) discussing Japan in the eighteenth and nineteenth centuries. But even in a prolonged period of colder climate, such as the Little Ice Age of 1550 to 1700, "the crucial variable in the elimination of famine was not the weather but the ability to adapt to the weather"

(Appleby, 1980:83), and in the same vein Dando summarizes 1000 years of Russian famine history by noting that "in essence, all the famines which have occurred in Russia from 971–1970 can predominantly be attributed to human factors" (1976:231).

NOTE

1 Schumpeter, 1960: data taken from table XVI, 52–5. The fluctuations evident in the specific years selected from a complete set of annual data reflect the fragility of the trading system in the days of sailing vessels and European wars, but the general trends are still clear.

REFERENCES

Abel, Wilhelm 1977: *Massenarmut und Hungerkrisen im vorindustriellen Deutschland.* Kleine Vandenhoeck-Reihe, 1352. Göttingen: Vandenhoeck and Ruprecht, second edition.

Abel, Wilhelm 1980: *Agricultural Fluctuations in Europe from the Thirteenth to the Twentieth Centuries.* Translated by Olive Ordish, with a forward and bibliography by Joan Thirsk. New York: St Martin's Press, third edition.

Alamgir, Mohiuddin 1980: *Famine in South Asia: Political Economy of Mass Starvation.* Cambridge, Mass.: Oelgeschlager, Gunn, and Hain Publishers, Inc.

Ambirajan, Srinivasa 1971: Political economy and Indian famines. *South Asia*, 1, 20–8.

Ambirajan, Srinivasa 1976: Malthusian population theory and Indian famine policy in the nineteenth century. *Population Studies*, 30, 5–14.

(Anonymous) 1847: Lessons from the famine. *Blackwood's Magazine*, 61, April: 515–24.

Apeldoorn, G. Jan van 1981: *Perspectives on Drought and Famine in Nigeria.* London: George Allen and Unwin.

Appadurai, Arjun 1984: How moral is South Asia's economy? A review article. *Journal of Asian Studies*, 43, 481–97.

Appleby, Andrew B. 1979: Grain prices and subsistence crises in England and France, 1590–1740. *Journal of Economic History*, 39, 865–87.

Appleby, Andrew B. 1980: Epidemics and famines in the Little Ice Age. *Journal of Interdisciplinary History*, 10, 643–63.

Arakawa, H. 1955: Meteorological conditions of the great famines in the last half of the Tokugawa period, Japan. *Papers in Meteorology and Geophysics*, 6, 101–16.

Bernstein, Thomas P. 1984: Stalinism, famine, and Chinese peasants: Grain procurement during the Great Leap Forward. *Theory and Society*, 13, 339–7.

Bhatia, B. M. 1967: *Famines in India: A study in some aspects of the economic history of India (1860–1965).* Bombay et al.: Asia Publishing House, second edition.

Bishop, Charles A. 1978: Cultural and biological adaptations to deprivation: The Northern Ojibwa case. In Laughlin and Brady (1978), 208–30.

Booth, A. 1977: Food riots in the North West of England 1790–1801. *Past and Present*, 77, 84–107.

Boserup, Ester 1965: *The Conditions of Agricultural Growth: The economics of agrarian change under population pressure*. Chicago: Aldine.

Boserup, Ester 1985: The impact of scarcity and plenty on development. In Rotberg and Rabb (1985), 185–209.

Braudel, Fernand 1981: *Civilization and Capitalism: 15th–18th Century. Vol. I: The Structures of Everday Life: The Limits of the Possible*. Translated by Sîan Reynolds, New York: Harper and Row.

Brockway, Lucile H. 1979: *Science and Colonial Expansion: The role of the British royal botanic gardens*. New York: Academic Press.

Brooke, Clarke 1967: The heritage of famine in central Tanzania. *Tanzania Notes and Records*, 67, 167–76.

Bryceson, D. F. 1981: Colonial famine responses: The Bagamoyo district of Tanganyika 1920–1961. *Food Policy*, 6, 91–104.

Buck, David D. 1982: Imperially inspired philanthropy in the Ch'ing: The case of granaries in the early 18th century. *Bulletin of the Institute of Modern History Academy Sinica* (Taiwan), 11, 225–50.

Carmichael, Ann G. 1985: Infection, hidden hunger, and history. In Rotberg and Rabb (1985), 51–66.

Chipungu, S. N. 1984: Famine and hunger in Bulozi, 1850–1900: Why blame nature? *TransAfrican Journal of History*, 13, 26–30.

Cohen, Mark N. 1979: *The Food Crisis in Prehistory: Overpopulation and the origins of agriculture*. New Haven: Yale University Press.

Cove, John J. 1978: Reflections on the problem of famine in Tsimshian and Kaguru mythology. In Laughlin and Brady (1978), 231–44.

Cronon, William 1983: *Changes in the Land*. New York: Hill and Wang.

Crosby, Alfred W. 1972: *The Columbian Exchange: Biological and cultural consequences of 1492*. Contributions in American Studies, No. 2. Westport, Conn.: Greenwood Publishing Company.

Crosby, Alfred W. 1986: *Ecological Imperialism: The Biological Expansion of Europe, 900–1900*. Cambridge: Cambridge University Press.

Currey, Bruce and Hugo, Graeme (eds) 1984: *Famine as a Geographical Phenomenon*. The GeoJournal Library, ed. Wolf Tietze, vol. 1. Dordrecht: D. Reidel.

Curtin, Philip D. 1985: Nutrition in African history. In Rotberg and Rabb (1985), 172–84.

Dalrymple, Dana G. 1964: The Soviet famine of 1932–34. *Soviet Studies*, 15, 250–84.

Daly, M. E. 1984: *An Economic History of Ireland*. Cork: Cork University Press.

Dando, W. A. 1976: Man-made famines: Some geographical insights from an exploratory study of a millennium of Russian famines. *Ecology of Food and Nutrition*, 4, 219–34.

Dirks, Robert 1978: Resource fluctuations and competitive transformations in West Indian slave societies. In Laughlin and Brady (1978), 122–80.

Durrill, Wayne K. 1986: Atrocious misery: The African origins of famine in Northern Somalia, 1839–1884. *The American Historical Review*, 91, 287–306.

Fogel, Robert W. et al. 1985: Secular changes in American and British stature and nutrition. In Rotberg and Rabb (1985), 247–83.

Foucault, Michel 1979: *Discipline and Punish: The birth of the prison.* Translated by Alan Sheridan. New York: Vintage Books.

Golkin, Arline T. 1987: *Famine: A heritage of hunger. A guide to issues and references.* Claremont, Calif.: Regina Books.

Harlan, Jack R. 1976: The plants and animals that nourish man. *Scientific American,* 235, 88–97.

Herlihy, David 1981: Climate and documentary sources: A comment. In Rotberg and Rabb (1981), 133–7.

Hobhouse, Henry 1986: *Seeds of Change: Five plants that transformed mankind.* New York: Harper and Row.

Hufton, Olwen H. 1985: Social conflict and the grain supply in eighteenth-century France. In Rotberg and Rabb (1985), 105–33.

Hugo, Graeme 1984: The demographic impact of famine: A review. In Currey and Hugo (1984), 7–31.

Kalland, Arne, and Pedersen, Jon 1984: Famine and population in Fukuoka domain during the Tokugawa period. *Journal of Japanese Studies,* 10, 31–72.

Kallgren, Joyce K. (ed.) 1982: Food, famine, and the Chinese state – A symposium. *Journal of Asian Studies,* 41, 685–801.

Kass, Edward H. 1971: Infectious diseases and social change. *The Journal of Infectious Diseases,* 123, 110–14.

Kennedy, Paul 1987: *The Rise and Fall of the Great Powers: Economic change and military conflict from 1500 to 2000.* New York: Random House.

Laslett, Peter 1984: *The World We Have Lost.* New York: Scribner, third edition.

Laughlin, Charles D. and Brady, Ivan A. (eds) 1978: *Extinction and Survival in Human Populations.* New York: Columbia University Press.

Lee, James 1982: Food supply and population growth in Southwest China. *Journal of Asian Studies,* 41, 711–46.

Li, Lillian M. 1982: Introduction: Food, famine, and the Chinese state. *Journal of Asian Studies,* 41, 687–707.

McAlpin, Michelle Burge 1983: *Subject to Famine: Food crises and economic change in western India, 1860–1920.* Princeton: Princeton University Press.

McKeown, Thomas 1979: *The Role of Medicine: Dream, mirage, or nemesis.* Princeton: Princeton University Press.

McKeown, Thomas 1985: Food, infection, and population. In Rotberg and Rabb (1985), 29–49.

MacLeod, Murdo J. 1973: *Spanish Central America: A socioeconomic history.* Berkeley: University of California Press.

McNeill, William H. 1976: *Plagues and People.* New York: Doubleday.

Mallory, Walter H. 1926: *China: Land of famine.* New York: American Geographical Society.

Malthus, Thomas Robert 1798: *An essay on the principle of population as it affects the future improvement of society, with remarks on the speculations of Mr. Godwin, M. Condorcet, and other writers.* London: J. Johnson, Reprinted with notes by James Bonar, Reprints of Economic Classics, New York: Augustus M. Kelley, 1965.

Mintz, Sidney W. 1979: Time, sugar, and sweetness. *Marxist Perspectives*, 2, 56–73.

Mintz, Sidney W. 1985: *Sweetness and Power: The place of sugar in modern history*. New York: Viking.

Mokyr, Joel 1983: *Why Ireland Starved: A quantitative and analytical history of the Irish economy, 1800–1850*. London: George Allen and Unwin.

Murton, Brian 1984: Spatial and temporal patterns of famine in Southern India before the famine codes. In Currey and Hugo (1984), 71–90.

Outhwaite, R. B. 1978: Food crises in early modern England: Patterns of public response. In Michael Flinn (ed.), *Proceedings of the Seventh International Economic History Congress*, Edinburgh: Edinburgh University Press, two vols.

Pankhurst, Richard 1966: The great Ethiopian famine of 1885–1892: A new assessment. *Journal of the History of Medicine and Allied Sciences*, 21, 95–124 and 271–94.

Pelto, Gretel H. and Pelto, Pertti J. 1985: Diet and delocalization: Dietary changes since 1750. In Rotberg and Rabb (1985), 309–20.

Perdue, Peter C. 1982: Water control in the Dongting Region during the Ming and Qing periods. *Journal of Asian Studies*, 41, 747–65.

Post, John D. 1977: *The Last Great Subsistence Crisis in the Western World*. Baltimore: Johns Hopkins.

Reid, Anthony 1988: *Southeast Asia in the Age of Commerce 1450–1860. Vol. I: The Lands below the Winds*. New Haven and London: Yale University Press.

Richards, A. I. 1939: *Land, Labour, and Diet in Northern Rhodesia*. London and New York: Oxford University Press.

Roe, Daphne 1973: *A Plague of Corn*. Ithaca, NY: Cornell University Press.

Rotberg, Robert I. and Rabb, Theodore K. (eds) 1981: *Climate and History*. Princeton: Princeton University Press. First published in Volume 10 of the *Journal of Interdisciplinary History* (Spring 1980).

Rotberg, Robert I. and Rabb, Theodore K. (eds) 1985: *Hunger and History: The impact of changing food production and consumption patterns on society*. Cambridge: Cambridge University Press. First published as a special issue of the *Journal of Interdisciplinary History* (Volume 14, No. 2, Autumn 1983).

Sauer, Carl 1966: *The Early Spanish Main*. Berkeley: University of California Press.

Schaffner, M. 1981: Die irische Hungersnot der Jahre 1845–1849: Eine Analyse von Ursachen und Bedingungen. Paper read at Famine in History, Alimentarium Colloquium, Vevey, Switzerland, July 2–4.

Schmitt, R. C. 1970: Famine mortality in Hawaii. *Journal of Pacific History*, 5, 109–15.

Schofield, Roger 1985: The impact of scarcity and plenty on population change in England, 1541–1871. In Rotberg and Rabb (1985), 67–93.

Schumpeter, Elizabeth Boody 1960: *English Overseas Trade Statistics 1697–1808*. Oxford: Clarendon Press.

Sen, Amartya K. 1981: *Poverty and Famines: An essay in entitlement and deprivation*. Oxford: Clarendon Press.

Simon, Julian L. 1985: The effects of population on nutrition and economic well-being. In Rotberg and Rabb (1985), 215–39.

Slicher van Bath, B. H. 1963: *Agrarian History of Western Europe, AD 500–1850*. London: E. Arnold.

Tilly, Louise 1985: Food entitlement, famine, and conflict. In Rotberg and Rabb (1985), 135–51.

Wallerstein, Immanuel 1974: *The Modern World System, I: Capitalist agriculture and the origins of the European World-Economy in the Sixteenth Century.* Studies in Social Discontinuity. New York: Academic Press.

Watkins, Susan Cott and van de Walle, Etienne 1985: Nutrition, mortality, and population size: Malthus' court of last resort. In Rotberg and Rabb (1985), 7–28.

Watts, David 1984: Cycles of famine in islands of plenty: The case of the colonial West Indies in the pre-emancipation period. In Currey and Hugo (1984), 49–70.

Wolf, Eric R. 1982: *Europe and the People Without History.* Berkeley: University of California Press.

Wong, R. Bin 1982: Food riots in the Qing Dynasty. *Journal of Asian Studies*, 41, 767–88.

Zewde, Bahru 1976: A historical outline of famine in Ethiopia. *African Environment*, Special Report 2, *Drought and Famine in Ethiopia.* London: International African Institute.

9

Nutritional Status and Mortality in Eighteenth-century Europe

JOHN D. POST

Introduction

The recurrent coincidence of food shortage and elevated mortality from epidemic disease in eighteenth-century Europe is well documented and beyond dispute. Whenever the price of grain climbed 50 percent or higher for an extended period of two years or more the morbidity and mortality rates of multiple infectious diseases rose in parallel. Research has established that prolonged undernutrition will exacerbate both the morbidity and case-fatality rates of many common infectious diseases. It is not clear from the historical evidence, however, that the epidemic mortality that marched almost in lockstep with pre-industrial food shortages derived mainly from the demonstrated synergistic relationship between nutritional deficiency and infection. Rather, the eighteenth-century evidence suggests that the epidemics were promoted chiefly by the altered social matrix engendered by famine conditions.

Pre-industrial subsistence crises were invariably preceded by natural calamity, apart from those provoked exclusively by wartime conditions. The shortage of food gave rise to a related series of consequences and phenomena, all of which could transform endemic infections into epidemic diseases. First of all, the antecedent weather, flood, or other misfortune lowered the standards of personal hygiene of the poorer working population and aggravated the already marginal environmental sanitation. The grain harvest shortfalls in turn led to higher food prices, mounting unemployment rates, and an increase in the scale of begging, vagrancy, crime, and social disorder. As an inevitable consequence, these conditions resulted in welfare crises of varying magnitude. The combination of environmental stress, economic hardship, and social disarray tended to foster overcrowding and other changes in normal community spacing arrangements. Thus, the focused issue becomes whether the epidemics that were associated with pre-industrial food shortages resulted primarily from the dysfunctional changes in behavior and the dilution of the normal components of resistance to epidemics, or whether they originated in the biological interaction between undernutrition and infection.

It must be acknowledged at the outset that the degree of synergism between nutritional deficiency and the epidemic diseases that became rife in eighteenth-century subsistence crises cannot be demonstrated by refined statistical analysis. The available medical, demographic, and price data are simply too inadequate and too uneven to test the relationship between nutritional status and immunity.

In order to determine whether changes in nutritional status or the social and economic deprivations invoked by severe subsistence crises were *principally* responsible for the epidemic mortality that coincided with the shortages of food, a cross-national case-by-case examination of the fluctuations in food prices and in the incidence of epidemic infections is carried down, when possible, to the regional level. A considerable body of clinical medical evidence, comparative price data, and demographic time series are available for those years in which mortality waves swept over extensive regions of eighteenth-century Europe, even if in varying degrees of comprehensiveness. From the surviving clinical evidence, it becomes possible to identify the majority of acute infections that became widely epidemic during subsistence crises. Informed by the etiology and epidemiology of the identified disease entities, the relative influence of nutritional status on incidence level can be assessed.

The issue under examination has been investigated previously in a full-length study of the European harvest shortfalls and mortality peaks of the years 1739–42; the findings are summarized below.[1] Here the issue will be reexamined in the light of the economic, demographic, and epidemiological evidence available for the European mortality crises of the early 1770s.

The Interaction between Nutrition and Infection

Most historians concerned with subsistence crises arrived at the conclusion that famine conditions favored the spread of an epidemic, particularly as the consequence of the common practice of beggars and vagrants fleeing the countryside to seek food and work in the towns. Historical research often found that elevated mortality persisted for a year or two after the disappearance of dearth conditions, from which it was hypothesized that diseases propagated by undernourishment continued to drive up death rates.

In the period before the Second World War, physicians and historians alike generally believed that prolonged undernutrition lowered human resistance to virtually all infectious disease. The position that under/ malnutrition inevitably promotes infection has, however, now become the minority viewpoint.[2] Public health researchers working in underdeveloped societies during the postwar decades found a synergistic relationship between malnutrition and many common infections. The synergism seemed most pronounced in young children who were in the process of being weaned from breastfeeding. The high death rates resulted primarily from the medical condition that is termed the diarrhea−pneumonia complex. Medical research indicated that both multiple nutritional deficiencies and protein deficiency produced a synergistic relationship in a large majority of the diseases studied. At the same time, it was found that the relationship between nutrition and infection appeared to be antagonistic in a number of infections. Still, the interaction of under/malnutrition and infectious disease is now well established as synergistic (Scrimshaw et al., 1968).

But the question of the degree to which nutritional deficiency exacerbates the morbidity or case-fatality rates of the epidemic diseases most commonly observed during famine is not resolved. Recent evidence has demonstrated that nutritional stress does not influence all common infections equally. It remains, of course, difficult to determine the causal relationship between nutritional status and infection when human living conditions also involve poor housing, deficient personal hygiene, and inadequate environmental sanitation.[3]

A number of recent medical writers have questioned the finding that undernutrition necessarily leads to more severe or more frequent infections. It has been pointed out that the physiological and microbiological aspects of synergism have not been demonstrated in controlled laboratory studies. Biological research indicates that the failure of the human immune system takes place only when nutritional stress is extreme. Starvation rather than chronic undernutrition precipitates the fatal interaction between infection and nutrition, and then only in the final stages of illness (Carmichael, 1983:250).

Medical observations made in the African famines of the mid-1970s have generated additional doubts whether malnutrition inevitably aggravates infection. John and Anne Murray encountered examples of "grossly malnourished small children, who, though heavily exposed to measles, infectious hepatitis, and polio, either failed to develop the disease or had it in a surprisingly mild form." They have put forth a paradox in the case of human starvation. "Increased resistance to viral infection and at least some bacterial infection exists in the face of an apparent decrease in immune function with the important corollary that increased susceptibility to infection occurs with refeeding when immune function might be expected to be on the mend" (Murray and Murray, 1977:475, 477, 478). The authors suggest that suppression by starvation of "either the primary inflammatory response to an invading microorganism or the secondary hypersensitivity reaction to certain of its constituents" might account for the reduction in symptomatic disease. Indeed, they have suggested that a microorganism requires many of the same nutrients that are essential to human health, and that within some limits undernutrition in humans seems to "decrease susceptibility to infection with viruses, malaria, and some bacteria" (Murray and Murray, 1977:482).

As this discussion indicates, the evidence linking malnutrition and mortality is not unambiguous. The best evidence that supports the view that malnourished rather than well-nourished individuals are more likely to die from infectious diseases derives from studies of contemporary populations in poor, underdeveloped societies. These investigations have been criticized, however, on the grounds that the groups studied were rather small, which made statistically significant estimates of the effect of malnutrition difficult. Even in studies in which the experimental and control groups were matched, differences remained in social variables that are known to affect mortality (cf. Watkins and van de Walle, 1983:218−25). Nonetheless, the results of the studies of underdeveloped societies show that nutrition and mortality are linked in present-day populations suffering from chronic malnutrition. At the same time, it should be noted that the investigations have focused principally on children, not adults, and that elevated death rates among infants and children were not chiefly responsible for the excess mortality that was traceable to epidemic disease in pre-industrial famines. The demographic records indicate that mature, adult age groups accounted for the greatest increase in mortality.

The methodological problem in attempting to assess the influence of nutritional deficiency on epidemic mortality associated with famine is readily apparent. After the antecedent weather calamity and its inevitable consequences of poor hygiene, inadequate sanitation, and overcrowding are removed from famine, what is the residual effect on human resistance to infection? Even in the absence of famine conditions, in the situation of extreme human poverty where human and environmental deficiencies exist together it remains difficult to separate the variables responsible for malnutrition from those responsible for disease from infection. In addition, the historical records clearly demonstrate that several lethal epidemic diseases (influenza, plague, cholera, smallpox) have produced mortality crises apart from malnourished populations.[4]

In support of a possible methodological solution, there is now general agreement that not all common infections are influenced to the same degree by nutritional status, but they in turn may have a significant influence on food deprivation in that they affect the ability to absorb food. Clinical evidence shows, first, that some infections are so virulent that they produce disease regardless of human differences in resistance. In a second category of diseases, the outcome of infection is considered to be only marginally related to nutrition. Among the most important epidemic diseases placed in these two classifications are smallpox, bubonic plague, influenza, malaria, typhoid fever, and typhus fever: all infections prevalent in European pre-industrial famines. Among the common infections believed to be influenced by nutritional status — the third category — are tuberculosis, diarrheal diseases, measles, pertussis, and several respiratory diseases, all also wide-spread in eighteenth-century Europe.

As a consequence, any solution to the question at issue involves the identification of the epidemic diseases that were responsible for the excess deaths in pre-industrial subsistence crises. Epidemic disease cannot be treated as an undifferentiated entity. Thus the connection (if any) with prolonged undernutrition must be demonstrated infection by infection. Each communicable disease has not only its own etiology but in most instances its own epidemiology, which must be reconciled with the prevailing environmental, ecological, and social conditions. Carrying out this procedure entails taking account of the weather, nutritional status, housing conditions, personal hygiene, clothing, environmental sanitation, behavioral changes, alterations in community spacing arrangements, and exposure to disease vectors.

The European Mortality Peaks of the Early 1740s

The mortality wave of the early 1740s, noted above, is an outstanding fact of European population history. Most relevant here, the number of deaths increased 21 percent from 1739 to 1740, and then reached a peak in 1742 at a level 24 percent above the number recorded in 1739. If measured against the low European mortality that predominated in 1735, the number of deaths in 1742 represented a mortality increase of 43 percent. The mortality peak of 1740–2 coincided with a wave of lethal epidemic diseases that spread through the British Isles, France, the Low Countries, the German states, Switzerland, Italy, and Scandinavia. The elevated mortality was ushered in by an extended period of anomalous weather patterns, which began in the second half of 1739 and continued into 1742. Western, northern, and central Europe experienced a series of grain harvest shortfalls. As a consequence, the average price of cereals in these regions rose 60 percent from 1738 to 1740, and prices remained elevated into 1742.

The higher food costs led inescapably to nutritional deficiencies in the

Table 9.1 Rank order increases in grain prices and mortality, Europe 1735–44

	Increase in grain prices from 1737–8 to 1740–1		Increase in mortality from 1735–9 to 1740–2		Change in rank order from grain prices to mortality
	Rank	Percentage	Rank	Percentage	
Low Countries	1	77.0	7	22.3	+6
Denmark	2	71.4	11	10.1	+9
Finland	3	67.1	2	51.8	−1
Sweden	4	60.0	6	22.7	+2
Ireland	5	56.7	3	25.3	−2
Scotland	6	52.9	8	21.1	+2
Germany	7	47.9	12	3.9	+5
Norway	8	44.1	1	81.0	−7
Italy	9	37.2	10	10.4	+1
France	10	35.7	4	24.5	−6
Austria	11	33.7	13	1.9	+2
England	12	32.9	5	23.4	−7
Switzerland	13	30.7	9	17.0	−4

Source: Post, 1985:table I, 32–3; table X, 117.

diets of the poorest working families, who made up more than half of Europe's population, and whose nutritional standards were no more than barely adequate when cereal prices were not elevated. In the relatively poor economies of mid-eighteenth-century Europe, the consumption of food and drink accounted for some 60—75 percent of the household budgets of the laboring population when cereal prices stood at normal levels. In some European locations, the price of grains doubled between 1738 and 1740. Notwithstanding the cumulative European harvest shortfalls, the shortage of food evolved into famine in a limited number of regions during the 1740s. Famine conditions became rife, however, in Ireland, Norway, and Finland, where the shortage of food was exacerbated by military operations of the war fought between Sweden and Russia (Post, 1985:chapters 2—4).

If a synergistic relationship existed between the decline in nutritional standards and the acute infectious diseases of the early 1740s, and if no intervening variables influenced death rates, one would anticipate a correspondence between the magnitude of national increases in grain prices and the amplitude of national mortality peaks. An approximate measurement of the presence or absence of such correspondence is attempted in table 9.1. In the table, thirteen European countries are ranked, first, in order of the magnitude of the increase in grain prices from 1737—8 to 1740—1; second, in order of the amplitude of the increase in mortality from 1735—9 to 1740—2. The final column displays the magnitude of the change in rank order from grain prices to mortality. As seen, in the case of the Low Countries, Germany, and Denmark, there is a lack of correspondence between high-order food price increases and low-order mortality increases. Conversely, England and France registered a moderate increase in food prices but sharp increases in the number of deaths. It seems apparent that variables in addition to prolonged undernutrition influenced the elevated mortality from epidemic disease in the early 1740s.

In order to account for the contrasting outcomes found in table 9.1, it is necessary to assess the relative demographic impact of the several epidemic disease entities that contributed to the mortality wave. The medical evidence distinctly shows that the elevated death rates of 1740—2 derived for the most part from epidemics of dysentery—diarrheal diseases, typhoid fever, and the louse-borne infections of typhus and relapsing fever. Eighteenth-century physicians still perceived fever as a disease rather than as a symptom; consequently, the latter three fevers were often collapsed into a category called "continued fevers." Most critically here, no region of Europe suffered crisis mortality in the absence of major epidemics of dysentery or continued fevers, and usually both diseases became widespread.[5]

The epidemiological evidence available for the early 1740s indicates that the mortality peaks resulted from increases in the morbidity and mortality

Table 9.2 Indexes of annual number of deaths in Europe, 1764–76[a]

Location	1764	1765	1766	1767	1768	1769	1770	1771	1772	1773	1774	1775	1776
England	96	93	108	106	101	99	105	100	102	103	94	99	95
Scotland	94	102	95	96	88	106	115	110	106	97	103	95	94
France	96	104	105	110	100	84	87	98	110	106	102	106	92
Low Countries	104	100	94	92	111	100	96	99	121	103	86	97	97
Germany	98	94	96	105	98	87	90	102	146	110	88	96	92
Austria (Vienna)	76	72	71	80	81	76	112	128	142	113	107	120	122
Switzerland	113	110	110	102	110	98	89	109	104	87	88	91	88
Italy	100	93	91	94	106	98	96	97	100	96	109	121	100
Denmark	111	99	97	96	90	101	102	105	115	124	76	92	92
Norway	101	105	104	84	85	84	92	90	105	184	98	88	80
Sweden	93	95	86	89	95	95	92	99	132	182	77	87	79
Finland	112	102	100	103	92	102	111	97	90	83	84	102	123
Arithmetic averages	100	97	96	96	96	94	99	103	114	116	93	100	96

[a] 1764–76 = 100.
Source: See note 7.

rates of dysentery, typhus, typhoid, and relapsing fevers, and also from epidemics of smallpox and several respiratory diseases, which coincided with an extended period of bad weather and significant harvest shortfalls. It seems almost certain that the majority of the epidemics were promoted by the combination of environmental stress, economic hardship, social disorder, and nutritional deficiencies. Still, the focused question remains: were the epidemics primarily the consequence of the biological interaction of nutrition and infection, or were they the product of the dysfunctional social conditions that developed in the wake of the food shortage? A review of the etiology and epidemiology of the infections that became regional and national epidemics in the 1740s will contribute to a resolution of the issue. But before taking up such an examination, the parallel investigation of the subsequent European mortality crises of the early 1770s will reinforce the controls underpinning a comparative approach.

The European Mortality Peaks of the Early 1770s

The mortality wave of the early 1770s is likewise an outstanding fact of European population history. The crisis mortality, however, was more pronounced in central and northern than in northwestern Europe. Measured from the low level of European mortality that predominated during 1767–9, the number of deaths rose 17 percent during the peak years of 1771–3. But in the more limited European region of the German states, the Habsburg Monarchy, Denmark, Norway, Sweden, and the Low Countries the number of deaths increased 33 percent during the same period. The mortality peak of the early 1770s was also coterminous with a wave of killing epidemic diseases that struck the German-language region, Scandinavia, and the Low Countries, affecting France, Switzerland, and Italy to a lesser degree, and relatively sparing the British Isles, Ireland in particular. As was the case in the 1740s, the mortality peak was preceded by an extended period of abnormal weather patterns, which set in during 1770 and persisted in some locations into 1772. The grain harvest shortfalls proved most severe in central Europe and Scandinavia, but all regions suffered to some degree.[6] Following the decline in cereal yields, the average price of grain in these regions of Europe (omitting Ireland, Norway, and Finland, for which systematic prices are not yet available) climbed 48 percent from 1768–9 to 1771–2. In the German states and Austria during the same period, however, the price of cereals increased by 111 percent, pointing to famine conditions.

Table 9.2 displays indexes of the annual movement of recorded deaths in twelve European countries during the 13-year period from 1764 to

Table 9.3 Indexes of annual grain prices in Europe, 1764–76[a]

Location	1764	1765	1766	1767	1768	1769	1770	1771	1772	1773	1774	1775	1776
England	89	87	110	112	91	81	98	107	118	109	118	87	93
Scotland	92	113	112	107	85	95	94	109	113	110	106	85	81
France	65	73	88	94	103	104	132	128	113	111	98	106	85
Low Countries:	80	96	92	98	101	93	99	121	120	102	104	111	86
Holland	75	85	85	94	100	94	92	120	133	115	103	115	90
Flanders	85	105	96	104	101	96	100	119	117	92	102	100	86
Brabant	79	98	94	95	101	89	106	123	110	100	108	119	82
Germany:	85	90	86	76	76	69	101	193	199	114	72	77	70
Prussia	91	105	97	89	82	65	85	161	156	108	81	91	80
Saxony	73	85	92	n.a.	67	59	90	218	257	98	64	74	67
Bavaria	83	77	74	74	86	79	120	204	218	122	60	56	57
Rhineland	91	94	80	66	67	73	107	190	165	127	82	85	74
Austria	65	67	88	113	102	86	97	153	162	127	82	90	76
Switzerland (Bern)	68	74	101	94	92	94	140	166	119	93	85	87	86
Italy:	109	110	112	100	96	83	87	92	105	116	116	95	77
Milan	77	86	95	104	95	84	86	99	107	129	128	124	86
Florence	88	117	143	95	99	76	83	82	123	131	123	73	62
Naples	161	126	98	102	94	89	91	94	85	89	97	88	84
Denmark (Copenhagen)	96	111	88	97	97	83	93	125	137	112	82	97	85
Sweden	138	111	88	75	72	74	84	128	130	106	86	110	97
Arithmetic averages	89	93	97	97	92	86	103	132	132	110	95	95	83

[a] 1764–76 = 100. The index numbers represent the price of the following designated grains in the national locations: England, wheat; Scotland, oatmeal; France, wheat and rye; Low Countries, wheat and rye; Prussia, rye and barley; Saxony, rye and barley; Bavaria, rye and barley; Rhineland Germany, rye and barley; Austria, rye and barley; Switzerland, wheat, spelt, and rye; Italy, wheat; Denmark, rye, wheat, barley, and oats; Sweden, rye, barley, and oats.
Sources: See note 8.

1776. (Ireland is omitted owing to the unavailability of demographic data; but it is clear from the documentary evidence that the number of deaths did not rise significantly during the early 1770s, even though Ireland experienced a moderate dearth.) The 13−year time period was decided upon because these years comprise the interval between the major European Seven Years War (1756−63) and the intercontinental wars that were touched off by the American Revolution, and thus neither the demographic nor price data were affected by wartime conditions.

Table 9.3 displays the annual grain price indexes for the same years, 1764−76. The countries listed vary from those found in table 9.2, however, because of the unavailability of systematic grain price data for Ireland, Norway, and Finland. Finland, like Ireland, did not experience a significant rise in mortality during the years 1771−3. Norway, by contrast, shared the severe mortality crisis suffered by Sweden during 1773. Table 9.3, at the same time, includes regional cereal prices for the Low Countries, Germany, and Italy, which represent a breakdown of the national index numbers and make comparisons within national territories possible. As table 9.3 shows, the elevated values found during the years 1771−2 parallel similar elevated values found during 1740−1. The index numbers indicate that the shortage of food became most acute in the German-language region and in west-central Europe in general.

Table 9.4 ranks the ten countries included in table 9.3 first in order according to the increase in grain prices from 1768−9 to 1771−2. The third column shows the magnitude of the change in rank order from grain prices to mortality. It is clear that the later period exhibits a more pronounced degree of rank−order correspondence between elevated cereal prices and elevated mortality than the results obtained for the similar comparisons made for the 1730s−1740s (table 9.1). Switzerland (+6) and to a lesser degree England (+3) alone demonstrate a noticeable lack of correspondence. In both cases, a relatively high-order food price increase is associated with a low-order increase in mortality, in Switzerland with a decline in the number of deaths. Another lack of correspondence can be revealed by the comparative calculations, admittedly by a rough-and-ready method. If the increase in mortality is computed as a percentage of the increase in cereal prices (column four), Germany and Austria show the most extreme results. In the case of Germany, which witnessed by far the greatest increase in cereal prices (190.3 percent), the increase in mortality computed as a percentage of the increase in prices amounted to 12.6 percent, whereas in Austria the increase in the number of deaths reached 100.0 percent of the increase in prices. If Switzerland and England are excluded, the remaining six countries listed in table 9.4 experienced increases ranging from 21.0 to 65.2 percent. All the same, it is evident from the matching of the severity of

Table 9.4 Rank order increases in grain prices and mortality, Europe 1764–76

	Increase in grain prices from 1768–9 to 1771–2		Increase in mortality from 1765–9 to 1771–3		Change in rank order from grain prices to mortality	Increase in mortality as percentage of increase in prices
	Rank	Percentage	Rank	Percentage		
Germany	1	190.3	3	24.0	+2	12.6
Sweden	2	76.7	2	50.0	0	65.2
Austria	3	68.1	1	68.4	−2	100.0
Switzerland	4	53.8	10	−5.7	+6	−10.6
Denmark	5	45.6	4	18.6	−1	40.8
England	6	31.4	9	1.0	+3	3.2
Low Countries	7	24.7	5	9.1	−2	36.8
Scotland	8	23.3	6	7.2	−2	30.9
France	9	16.3	7	5.0	−2	30.7
Italy	10	10.0	8	2.1	−2	21.0

Sources: Tables 9.2 and 9.3.

the national food shortages and the national increases in mortality during the 1770s that the results support the position of a synergistic relationship between nutritional deficiency and mortality more decidedly than the results obtained for the early 1740s.

Despite the different degrees of correspondence disclosed by the statistical comparisons, a survey of the evidence will demonstrate that the same epidemic diseases were primarily responsible for the European mortality crises of both the 1770s and the 1740s. In both decades, significant increases in the morbidity and mortality rates of continued fevers, dysentery, and smallpox produced the sharp rise in the number of deaths, with mortality driven higher still by the consequences of starvation in some districts.

In the 1770s as in the 1740s, epidemics of typhoid, typhus, relapsing fever, dysentery, and smallpox struck all regions of Europe, irrespective of acute, moderate, or slight degree of food shortage. During the early 1770s, however, there was a more pronounced tendency for the severity of the epidemics to correspond with the severity of the national food shortages, but not without exception. In Britain, as the tables indicate, the increase in grain prices and the rise in mortality remained moderate compared with the 1740s. Epidemics of continued fever broke out again in the 1770s, but unlike the 1740s the infections remained local contagions and did not develop into regional or national epidemics.[9]

In France also, the increase in cereal prices and the climb in mortality proved more moderate in the 1770s than was the case in the 1740s, in spite of the fact that elevated food prices appeared as early as 1768 and persisted into 1773. Although the prices of grains climbed significantly higher in France than in Britain during 1770–1, the amplitude of the increase in mortality remained lower than in Britain until 1772, when the level of mortality rose somewhat more sharply. Unlike the experience of the 1740s, France escaped severe regional epidemics of dysentery and continued fevers in the 1770s, although a series of local epidemics drove up death rates in several French provinces in the 1770s. Epidemics of putrid, malignant, and "miliary" fever, together with epidemic dysentery and smallpox, dominate the medical accounts.[10]

In the Low Countries, the price of cereals did not rise steeply until 1771; prices remained elevated, however, into 1775. The annual number of deaths did not rise significantly until 1772, when mortality climbed more sharply than in France or Britain. The high cereal price notwithstanding, mortality levels in the Low Countries fell off noticeably both in 1773 and 1774. The mortality peak of 1772 originated chiefly in acute epidemics of "putrid" fever, whose clinical symptoms indicate typhoid fever, and also as a result of epidemic dysentery. The epidemics of fever struck mainly the urban locations of the Low Countries. The evidence suggests that epidemics of typhus and relapsing fever were also prevalent.[11]

By contrast, the price of cereals climbed much more sharply in the Swiss cantons during 1770–1 than was the case in Britain, France, or the Low Countries (as table 9.3 shows), whereas the number of deaths increased only moderately during 1771–2. However, because the price and demographic data derive substantially from western Switzerland, it is probable that the statistical tables understate to a less than critical measure the peaks of both food prices and mortality. The shortage of food and the prevalence of epidemic disease became more acute in the eastern alpine cantons. As elsewhere in northwestern Europe, epidemics of continued fever, dysentery, and smallpox proved chiefly responsible for the rise in mortality. Epidemics of dysentery, it is clear, were more lethal than continued fevers in Switzerland.[12] In Italy, in distinction from northwestern Europe, the price of cereals rose significantly only during 1772–4, and then dearth prices prevailed for the most part in the northern half of the peninsula. The kingdom of Naples, which had suffered a severe famine and crisis mortality in 1764, escaped the harvest shortfalls of the early 1770s. Although the level of mortality rose marginally in northern and central Italy during 1772 and then more sharply during 1774–5, Italy as a region did not experience mortality crises during the early 1770s. As in northwestern Europe, local epidemics of continued fevers, dysentery, and smallpox were common, but regional and murderous epidemics did not develop.[13]

The populations of the German states, the northern region of the Habsburg Monarchy, and Scandinavia endured a much less fortunate demographic outcome. The combination of inclement weather, harvest shortfalls, and food shortage led to famine conditions and widespread epidemic diseases, which in turn produced severe mortality crises. In the western German region, as seen in table 9.3, the price of cereals rose noticeably in 1770 and peaked during 1771–2, at a level nearly three times as high as the low food prices that prevailed during 1767–9. In the central German state of Saxony grain prices did not rise sharply until 1771–2, when they climbed to a peak more than three times higher than during the years 1768–9. In the Prussian provinces, the price of cereals approximately doubled from 1767–70 to 1771–2.

The number of deaths in Germany as a region, as table 9.2 shows, peaked in 1772, reaching a level about 50 percent higher than the death rates that prevailed during the years 1765–9. In Saxony, however, the number of deaths recorded during 1772 (111,822) amounted to about twice the average of the previous five years (54,205), but then fell to approximately the same lower level of 1767–71 during the years 1773–6 (Blaschke, 1967:126). In the kingdom of Prussia, the death rate averaged

30.1 per 1,000 during the five-year period 1767–71, peaked at 42.3 per 1,000 or 40.5 percent higher than in 1772, and then declined to an average of 32.5 during the years 1773–6 (Kisskalt, 1921:460). The mortality peak of 1772 in the German locations other than Prussia and Saxony approximated the same amplitude as in Germany as a region.[14] It should be noted that the mortality peak in Saxony proved about one-third higher than the German average, and that mortality in Prussia remained some 9 percent below the German average.

In all regions of Germany the elevated mortality of 1771–3 resulted primarily from severe epidemics of continued fevers, dysentery, and smallpox, and to a lesser degree from mycotoxins (particularly ergot poisoning) and in some districts from the direct consequence of starvation. The most calamitous German mortality crisis unfolded in the small central autonomous territory of Eichsfeld, located on the northeastern border of the duchy of Saxony. The level of mortality in six Eichsfeld parishes increased fourfold between 1769–70 and 1772 (Abel, 1974:254). According to the district physician, the three major causes of death were epidemic fevers, smallpox, and starvation, the latter reflected in widespread famine edema. The population of the mountainous region of Saxony suffered almost as great a demographic disaster. In the highland districts, 9.3 percent of the population died during 1772, while in the Vogtland district 8.3 percent of the population perished the same year (Blaschke, 1967:128). In these Erzgebirge villages of Saxony as in Eichsfeld, the major causes of death were cited as continued fevers and starvation. In the kingdom of Prussia, death from starvation appears to have been uncommon. The Prussian evidence indicates that epidemics of continued fever, smallpox, dysentery, and respiratory diseases, and probably a rise in deaths from tuberculosis drove up death rates. In Germany as a global region, the epidemiological and clinical evidence points to an increase in mortality from widespread and fatal epidemics of continued fevers, dysentery, smallpox, respiratory diseases, and ergot poisoning.[15]

An equal or perhaps more acute famine and mortality crisis developed in the Habsburg Bohemian lands bordering on Saxony. No systematic price or mortality data are available for Bohemia in the third quarter of the eighteenth century. The fragmentary quantitative data, official accounts, and impressionistic reports, nevertheless, demonstrate that the Bohemian famine of the 1770s produced a crisis reminiscent of the mortality waves that engulfed Ireland and Norway in the early 1740s. The quantitative data available for Austria must serve as an approximation of the price and mortality curves in Bohemia, with the correction that the amplitudes rose higher in Bohemia. Although the price of cereals in Austria increased 68 percent from 1768–9 to 1771–2, neither famine nor starvation became widespread as in Bohemia. As table 9.4 indicates, the level of mortality in Austria likewise rose 68 percent, measured from 1765–9 to 1771–3. Estimates of the increase in the number of deaths in Bohemia during the famine years vary, but the evidence is clear that the crisis mortality proved more severe than in Austria. According to the contemporary historian Franz Martin Pelzel (1817:934), some 250,000 persons died in Bohemia from the epidemic diseases that broke out in the wake of the famine. This statement is of course somewhat imprecise, but the order of magnitude appears to be accurate. Stated differently, some 10 percent of the Bohemian population died during the famine.[16]

The price of cereals did not rise significantly either in Austria or Bohemia until 1771, when they show a steep climb upward, similar to the price curves in Prussia and Saxony. While systematic price comparisons are not possible, the evidence shows that rye prices in Bohemia rose higher than in Austria during 1771–2. Grain prices increased 57.7 percent in Austria from 1770–1; in some Bohemian districts prices rose threefold. In addition, many Bohemian districts suffered from a genuine deficiency of cereals, which was not the case in Austria.[17] In Austria, nonetheless, the number of deaths began to increase sharply in 1770, increasing 47 percent above the figure for the previous year, and then, parallel to the case in Bohemia, the level of mortality in Austria climbed higher still both in 1771 and 1772. In Vienna, the monthly number of deaths became particularly elevated from March, 1771 through June, 1772 (*Wienerisches Diarium*, 1764–76). Epidemics of continued fevers, dysentery, and smallpox were the principal causes of the crisis mortality in Bohemia, Moravia, and Austria; also, in Bohemia as in central and southeastern Germany, deaths from starvation proved common, although this was not the case in Austria and Moravia.[18]

In Scandinavia, the price of cereals did not climb sharply until 1771, when in Denmark and Sweden they increased 34 and 52 percent respectively, and then rose only marginally higher during 1772, remaining slightly elevated during 1773. Grain prices, however, did not rise to the same famine levels witnessed in Germany and the Habsburg Monarchy; rather they increased by a magnitude similar to that experienced in the Low Countries and France, as table 9.3 shows. In Denmark, the increase in the number of deaths also remained moderate during the early 1770s; but Sweden and Norway, after a significant rise in mortality during 1772, both suffered severe crisis mortality during 1773 as epidemics of dysentery, smallpox, and continued fevers drove up death rates. Deaths from starvation also occurred in the Swedish region of Dalecarlia and the Norwegian diocese of Akershus.

Age-specific death rates are known for Sweden during the period under investigation. The data show that the largest increase in mortality during

1772 fell into the mature-adult and adolescent categories, while during 1773 the age groups under ten were most affected, probably as a result of the major smallpox epidemics during that year (Sundbärg, 1905:109–16). Causes of death are also available for Sweden, but not of course with the precision anticipated in the 1980s. The evidence indicates that in 1772 fever epidemics, first, and epidemic dysentery, second, were primarily responsible for the elevated death rates. The number of deaths from dysentery had risen uninterruptedly since 1769. The mortality crisis of 1773 resulted from the intensified diffusion of dysentery, the number of deaths increasing from 9,340 in 1772 to 23,350 in 1773. In addition, the number of smallpox deaths climbed from 5,440 in 1772 to 12,130 in 1773 (Utterström, 1954:160–1). Norway likewise, and Denmark to a noticeably lesser degree, experienced a wave of epidemic diseases during the early 1770s.[19]

The Etiology and Epidemiology of the Reigning Communicable Diseases

The survey of the epidemiological evidence for the mortality peak of the early 1770s shows that, as was the case in the early 1740s, the elevated mortality, which coincided with a shortage of food, derived principally from higher morbidity and mortality rates of the so-called continued fevers (typhoid, typhus, relapsing), dysentery, and smallpox, with deaths from starvation a factor in some locations. But despite a degree of correspondence between the amplitude of national increases in food prices and the magnitude of national increases in mortality from epidemic diseases, the relationships prove by no means invariable and thus the comparative examinations fail to resolve the focused issue: whether the elevated incidence of epidemic disease was primarily the consequence of the biological effects of prolonged undernutrition or was traceable to the sequence of social events provoked by the subsistence crises. The results do suggest, however, that variables in addition to the synergistic relationship between undernutrition and infection influenced the demographic outcomes. In order to advance the resolution of the question, it is necessary to distinguish both the etiology and epidemiology of the several infections that became epidemic in both the 1740s and the 1770s. If nutritional stress fostered higher morbidity rates and/or prejudiced the case outcome of infections, it would be anticipated that the epidemics would be made up mainly of these diseases which are influenced by nutritional deficiencies to either a moderate or a more significant degree.

The etiology of louse-borne typhus and relapsing fevers does not suggest that nutritional deficiency significantly influences either their morbidity rates or case-fatality rates. Although prolonged undernutrition may have some influence on fatality rates, typhus is so virulent that not even good nursing care seems to affect the outcome. Typhus is contracted primarily through the medium of the infected feces of the human body-louse. The act of scratching insect bites allows the pathogenic micro-organisms (*rickettsiae*) to penetrate the skin. The *rickettsiae* can also enter through the mucous membranes of the respiratory tract by means of infected louse feces in dust circulating in the air of unventilated rooms. The less fatal relapsing fever is usually contracted by crushing an infective louse over a bite wound or other abrasion of the skin. In both typhus and relapsing fever the louse becomes infective by ingesting the pathogenic micro-organisms from humans ill with the diseases. In both of these "continued" fevers humans are the reservoir of infection.[20]

As for the epidemiology of louse-borne typhus and relapsing fever, epidemics depend on widespread human infestation with body lice. Typhus epidemics have occurred in Europe in circumstances in which overcrowded populations with poor personal hygiene have promoted the multiplication and dissemination of the louse vector of the disease. Epidemics reach a peak when the weather conditions encourage close indoor personal contact, and at the same time reduce the ability to wash clothing and to bathe – thus usually but not invariably during the winter and spring months. In eighteenth-century European subsistence crises, it is doubtful that destitute persons exhausted by hunger and fatigue bothered much about washing; moreover, whatever clothes they still possessed were worn day and night. A combination of a lack of cleanliness and crowding together for warmth, whether at home or in public shelters, would provide ideal conditions in which lice could multiply and spread rapidly. In such an epidemiological network, a few cases of typhus fever could infect an entire district. The destitute and hungry who often deserted their villages and farms in the face of famine to seek work and welfare in the towns could diffuse the disease wherever they traveled.

Typhoid fever and bacillary dysentery are communicated from person to person by direct or indirect fecal–oral transmission from an infected person, or from an inapparent carrier of infection. Food and water which have been contaminated by human feces or urine have been found to be the most common mode of infection. It is known today that individuals who fail to cleanse contaminated hands or fingernails are primarily responsible for transmission of typhoid fever and dysentery. Both of these bacterial infections tend to be more prevalent in the autumn months, particularly following dry summer seasons.[21] As for human nutritional status, typhoid fever exhibits minimal interaction with nutritional stress. By contrast, both the morbidity and mortality rates of dysentery are believed to be influenced adversely by nutritional deficiencies.[22]

There is agreement that smallpox is not an infection in which under/ malnutrition affects either the morbidity or case-fatality rate.[23] Because smallpox was such a common epidemic infection in the eighteenth century, the extensive and severe epidemics that punctuated both the early 1740s and 1770s could be considered as "fortuitous" events in analyzing the issue under study. At the same time, a striking correspondence between the occurrence of smallpox epidemics and the epidemics of continued fevers and dysentery is apparent from the evidence presented. It is possible that changes in patterns of behavior triggered by subsistence crises, such as work migrations, itinerant vagrancy, and widespread begging, enhanced morbidity rates either by carrying smallpox to communities that otherwise were passing through the normal interval between epidemics, or by exposing isolated communities to the infection. As for the reported increase in respiratory diseases in some locations, it is virtually impossible to identify respiratory disease entities from eighteenth-century clinical descriptions. Nonetheless, there is also agreement that prolonged undernutrition does influence the morbidity and mortality rates of tuberculosis and other respiratory infections. Finally, in the epidemics of the 1770s but not in those of the 1740s, medical commentators, particularly in France and western Germany, identified an elevated incidence of a disease referred to as miliary fever (called *suette miliare* in France and *Friesel* or "the purples" in Germany), which became epidemic in small towns and villages but not in large urban locations, and which was restricted to this region of Europe. According to the standard work of Hirsch, there has been a confounding of typhus, scarlet fever, and other diseases with miliary fever and he concluded that the identification of this infection "must remain an unsettled question" (1883–6: I, 86–8).

In summary, the epidemiological evidence and the present-day medical views on the interaction of nutrition and the disease entities responsible for the epidemics that became rife during the early 1740s and 1770s indicate that prolonged undernutrition probably cannot principally account for the elevated incidence or higher case-fatality rates in the majority of the infections identified. Medical understanding and the evidence do suggest, however, that the widespread epidemics of dysentery can be connected to the food shortages and hunger of the 1740s and 1770s. But even in the case of dysentery, the fact that some locations did not exhibit a strong rank-order correspondence between the increases in food prices and increased mortality from epidemic dysentery suggests that variables other than nutritional deficiency contributed to the elevated morbidity rates of this infection. What appears to be called for is a search for variables that influenced the observed epidemic diseases more uniformly, and also the specification of functional relationships that will connect the shortage of food to the epidemiology of the disease entities.

While it is true that the progression from food shortage to epidemic mortality is not automatic, the evidence indicates that the correspondence between climbing food prices and the rising incidence of continued fevers and dysentery during both the 1740s and 1770s was more than coincidental. It seems more than probable that the combination of meteorological stress, elevated food prices, and large-scale unemployment created a historical matrix that fostered epidemics. The functional relationships that prevailed between the food shortages and the epidemics can be outlined. The harvest shortfalls inevitably led to joblessness, work migrations, an increase in the number of beggars, and elevated levels of vagrancy. The unfortunates involved not only could carry infection from rural to urban locations; they also brought intensified pressure on the marginal welfare systems that existed in eighteenth-century Europe. The public welfare installations that were set up or expanded to meet the increased needs promoted a further breakdown in personal cleanliness. Because of the relative lack of knowledge of the basic principles of public health, these installations frequently became networks for spreading infection. Subsistence crises, moreover, triggered a rise in crimes against property, which led to overcrowded penal facilities. More critically, the practice of abandoning homes and villages and then congregating in urban health, welfare, and penal institutions enhanced exposure to louse-borne, respiratory, and gastro-intestinal diseases. Infections such as dysentery, typhus, and typhoid fever had long been endemic among Europe's working population. These smouldering diseases could become epidemic under conditions that produced economic destitution and social upheaval. All states in the European region under study witnessed a rise in the incidence of vagrancy and mendicancy in the 1740s and 1770s, but the magnitude of the increases varied to a pronounced degree from state to state.[24]

It is true that a conspicuous increase in morbidity rates for dysentery occurred in those states that experienced the most severe and prolonged shortage of food, which suggests the explanation of an interaction of nutrition and infection. In the 1740s, for example, Ireland, Norway, and Finland fell into this category.[25] At the same time, lethal epidemics of dysentery also erupted in Brittany, the southern Netherlands, and other regions that did not experience famine conditions in the 1740s. Rural housing conditions, sanitary practices, and standards of personal cleanliness created a predisposition to permanent endemic dysentery in eighteenth-century Europe. This generalization is borne out in the origin and diffusion of the epidemics that became rife in the southern Netherlands in 1741, described and explained by Bruneel (1977:276–82). Dysentery became universally epidemic in this region only after the drought-like summer of 1741, even though cereal prices had been elevated for two years. The wide diffusion of dysentery in the autumn of 1741 coincided with a wave of begging, vagrancy, and rioting that broke out in the southern Netherlands when welfare systems were overwhelmed by destitute applicants.[26]

In both the 1740s and 1770s a noticeable correspondence obtained between the magnitude of the increase in the number of vagrants and beggars and the increased number of deaths from epidemic disease. Almost without exception those states that passed through the most severe crisis mortality also witnessed a sharp rise in the incidence of unemployment, work migrations, itinerant vagrancy, and mendicancy. Conversely, those states that proved most successful in minimizing the increase in the scale of social upheaval (Denmark and Germany in the 1740s, England and Switzerland in the 1770s) registered a much lesser increase in mortality than in grain prices (see tables 9.1 and 9.4). Accordingly, the evidence indicates that the variable of differential success in minimizing the dysfunctional changes in behavior that followed food shortages must be ranked first in accounting for the varying national demographic outcomes of the crises of the 1740s and 1770s.

Thus it would follow that the most effective method of preventing local outbreaks of continued fever and dysentery from erupting into national epidemics was to preempt the dysfunctional social behavior touched off by the combination of climatic stress, economic destitution, and the shortage of food. The reduction in food consumption together with the inability to maintain minimum standards of housing, home-heating, clothing, and, as a critical consequence, adequate personal hygiene, gave rise to the social phenomena that could provoke a significant increase in the number of deaths. The function of the welfare and assistance programs adopted during the eighteenth century was to compensate in part for the reduction in real income triggered by harvest shortfalls, and thus to offset in some measure the diminished capacity to command minimum food, housing, fuel, and clothing requirements. The primary objective of public grain policies was to prevent the price of cereals from climbing out of proportion to the severity of the harvest shortfalls. The success of welfare responses, however, was not only the function of the ability to prevent hunger and starvation; success also depended on whether the policies and programs pursued were functional or dysfunctional within an epidemiological frame of reference. Public welfare and assistance programs that put downward pressure on the potential rise in unemploymént, migration, vagrancy, begging, crime, and protest demonstrations tended to lower the risk of national epidemics.

National Mortality Crises Avoided and Not Avoided: Explanations

The comparative evidence supports the foregoing conclusions more decisively in the food shortages of the 1740s than in the 1770s. In the subsistence crises of the 1740s, the states of Prussia and Denmark proved particularly successful in inhibiting the spread of epidemic diseases, despite the sharp increases in food prices found in table 9.1. An established system of public granaries together with strict control of grain markets and prices enabled both states to prevent famine conditions. The Prussian state also imported cereal supplies from abroad and carried out a critical program of redistributing food among the provinces within the kingdom. In both Prussia and Denmark, a "feudal" social structure of landlords and subjects made it possible to deliver assistance at home, so to speak, and as a consequence virtually to avoid an increase in the number of vagrants and beggars. The welfare policies of England, France, and the Low Countries proved less successful in minimizing the rise in unemployment and social disorder. Moreover, the policies of these northwestern European states tended to promote the crowding of impoverished and destitute individuals into such public installations as workhouses, hospitals, and soup kitchens. In Ireland and Norway, the combination of severe food shortages and ineffective or absent welfare and relief measures led to the extended crisis mortality of the early 1740s. The policy decisions made by the central governments in London and Copenhagen failed to prevent not only mass hunger but also massive vagrancy and social upheaval. Famine conditions developed in both Ireland and Norway owing to the late arrival or insufficient quantity of transported cereals. The end result in both countries was crisis mortality from national epidemics of dysentery and continued fevers.[27]

The national welfare assistance programs of the 1770s need more examination because of the higher degree of rank-order correspondence between the increases in food prices and mortality (see table 9.4). In the northwestern European states of Britain, France, the Low Countries, and Switzerland, despite pronounced increases in cereal prices and extensive unemployment during the early 1770s, the number of deaths rose far more moderately than in Scandinavia, the German-language region, and Bohemia. The incidence of social disorder also climbed in these northwestern states as food riots, beggars, and vagrants multiplied. The incidence of epidemic disease, however, remained far below that experienced in the other three regions of Europe. This more favorable demographic outcome resulted in part from a less acute shortage of food and thus less daunting welfare crises. But the poor law systems in Britain and a more concentrated level of welfare resources available to public administrations in northwestern Europe also contributed to the lower mortality peaks. The prevailing public assistance programs may appear inadequate by present-day standards, but in north-western Europe they provided a safety net for the destitute fraction of the population, not only in England but also to a significant extent in Scotland, France, and the urban locations of the Low Countries, western Germany, and Switzerland. The combination of public and voluntary assistance and relief measures put downward pressure on vagrancy and mendicancy, an outcome that differed not only from that in central Europe but also from that in northwestern Europe during the 1740s.[28]

In Scandinavia, the demographic outcomes of food shortages varied. In Denmark the death rate rose more moderately than in Sweden and Norway in the 1770s, as was the case in the 1740s, even though grain prices climbed slightly higher in Denmark than in Sweden. Denmark, like Prussia and several Swiss cantons, utilized public granaries to cope with food shortages and elevated prices. Denmark, like East-Elbian Prussia, continued to maintain close control over the movement of the rural population as a corollary of the manorial relationship of lord and peasant. In Copenhagen, the grain storehouses, the magistrates' control over the price and marketing of food products, and the existence of welfare institutions and resources insulated the population in some measure against a sharp decline in living standards.[29] But in the Norwegian half of the kingdom the harvest failures and food shortages translated into famine, epidemic disease, and severe crisis mortality in 1772−3 as in 1741−2. In the 1770s as in the 1740s the relief and rescue operations were tardy. In the principal diocese of Akershus, the royal granaries had been closed in 1764 and were reestablished only in 1772, in connection with the military mobilization triggered by the threat of war in neighboring Sweden. The granaries were transferred to civilian administration only in April 1773, when the danger of war had passed, too late to avoid the famine and mortality crisis. In addition, the civilian administration of the diocese during the early 1770s was disorganized by the personal bankruptcy, resignation, and death of a series of chief admin-istrators. As in the 1740s, the crisis mortality in Norway was traceable to hunger and epidemics of typhus fever, dysentery, and smallpox. The epi-demics were no doubt intensified by the mobilization and demobilization of the military forces during 1772−3.[30]

In Sweden, the will and the capacity to cope with the subsistence crisis were compromised by the political crisis that began in 1770 and was not resolved until Gustav III's coup d'etat of August 19, 1772. The Swedish political instability also compromised the Norwegian relief efforts by provoking the above-mentioned military response. During the famine years of 1771–2, the Swedish Diet was preoccupied with constitutional matters and failed to take remedial steps. An observer in Stockholm claimed that "sufficient measures" had not been "so much as thought of for preventing or relieving the want of corn" (*London Evening Post*, September 10–12, 1772). Although the recently adopted Hospital Ordinances of 1763 had set up a poor-law system funded by rate-payers at the parish level, the number of persons needing assistance became far larger than the resources available for relief. The new king had earlier ordered the purchase of 20,000 tons of grain abroad "for the relief of his poor subjects" (*The Scots Magazine*, April, 1772: 210). At the end of 1772, a voluntary association collected funds to purchase cereals abroad "to be sold 50 percent under the market price, to families who have no annual incomes, employment, shops, and sufficient trade" (*The Scots Magazine*, December 1772: 676). By the second half of 1772, however, the distress had become so severe that these relief measures had little effect on the expanding epidemics. During the winter of 1772–3, work migrations and an intensified scale of itinerant vagrancy drove up the death rates, particularly in the region of Dalecarlia. "Many persons are daily found starved to death in the woods, highways, and in the houses; and this want has occasioned so great an epidemic ... as to be visible to every one" (*Annual Register*, 1773: 84). In all probability the dysentery epidemics of 1772–3 resulted both from the interaction of nutrition and infection and from the diffusion of the infection by the mass of hungry and destitute persons who left their homes in search of food and assistance.[31]

The major reversal of demographic outcomes from the 1740s to the 1770s took place in Germany and in the Habsburg lands of Bohemia and Austria. In the German territories of Eichsfeld and Saxony, where the mortality crises reached calamitous proportions, the evidence is clear that work migrations, vagrancy, and begging increased to an unmanageable scale. In Eichsfeld, a district physician described the social conditions during 1773: "The poor people, as one sees them everywhere on the roads, wander like shades from the grave. They expire from hunger and mortal diseases" (Abel, 1974:255). A clergyman who served the Saxon town of Annaberg has left a similar account: "one sees whole bands of beggars whose legs are swollen and faces withered. They move through the lanes and beg .... Tormented by nagging hunger, they waylay dogs and cats" (Abel, 1974:256). There can be no doubt from these and other contemporary accounts that unemployment and destitution were the rule in the villages and countryside of Eichsfeld and Saxony. It is likewise clear that the welfare resources available or devoted to alleviating the extreme distress proved inadequate to preserve lives, not to mention to maintain well-being.[32] The public authorities in Saxony attempted to reduce the number of beggars through the importation of food and welfare assistance measures,[33] but given the dimension of the crisis the programs proved insufficient.

In Frederick the Great's Prussia, the price of cereals climbed only two-thirds as high as in Saxony during 1771−2, and the increase in the number of deaths in 1772 amounted to only about 40 percent of the increase in Saxony. At the same time, the Prussian mortality peak proved far more severe in 1771−3 than in 1740−2, the consequence of a significant increase in mortality from epidemic diseases during the later period.[34] The Prussian administration in the 1770s again turned to the measures that had succeeded in the past in putting downward pressure on cereal prices. The relative lack of success in the 1770s can be explained in part by the more acute crisis, and in part by the fact that Prussia was still in the process of recovering from the enormous economic and demographic losses incurred during the Seven Years War (1756−63).[35]

Prussia had long pursued a policy of relying on its extensive military cereal storehouses not only to dampen down food prices in case of dearth, but to supply seed-grain to peasants and landowners in case of harvest failure, and also to provide for the subsistence of the urban populations, both civil and military, in the event of food shortage. In addition to the military magazines in the 1770s, a new civilian granary in Berlin provided low-cost bread to the poor and unemployed. In spite of these measures, the Prussian government was unable to maintain the price of rye at the target level of 30 *Groschen* per *Scheffel*. As a consequence, Frederick authorized the purchase of grain in Poland, Lithuania, Livonia, and elsewhere, but only at prices that were unrealistically low in the European markets of 1771−2.

Ultimately Frederick was compelled to turn down requests for assistance from provincial officials, with the explanation either that they were unjustified or that the granaries were nearly empty. Seed-grain needs continued to be met, however, in order to prevent famine conditions from developing, and also to maintain the effectiveness of the army. Bread prices in Prussia, notwithstanding, remained lower than in southern Germany, where cereal prices were twice or three times as high. Large-scale unemployment among industrial workers in the western provinces and in urban locations contributed significantly to the relative failure of the Prussian administration to cope with the subsistence crisis. In addition to Prussian workers migrating in search of employment and assistance, a stream of migrants from neighboring states in search of better opportunities in underpopulated Prussia added to the social disorder. Destitute migrants from famine-stricken districts could only increase the risk of disseminating epidemic diseases. Nevertheless, the Prussian administration did succeed in keeping the increase in mortality lower than the mortality peaks in the central and southern German states, and particularly lower than in neighboring Bohemia.[36]

The acute crisis mortality that unfolded in Bohemia resulted not only from a greater shortage of food and a higher level of unemployment but also from less competent public administration and the relative unconcern of too many manorial landlords for the welfare of their subjects. In addition, the underdeveloped infrastructure and the tardy assessment of the extent of the crisis on the part of the Vienna government contributed to the demographic tragedy. Joseph II, now co-regent, complained in January 1771 that the report forwarded to Vienna by the Bohemian provincial government contained no information beyond the admission of "an almost general dearth and no measures to deal with it, the tyranny of the lords and no control" (Beales, 1987:340). Empress Maria Theresa subsequently dispatched a special commissar to tour the districts of the kingdom of Bohemia and to report on the distress. He found a genuine shortage of cereals, famine-level food prices, massive unemployment (particularly among Bohemia's industrial workers), and inept public officials, together with widespread practices of hoarding, profiteering, and the illegal export of grain to Bavaria and Saxony in search of still higher prices. The commissar also believed that the income of the poor had declined to the point where food could not be purchased at prevailing prices even if available. He blamed the excessive work obligations on manorial land for the plight of the peasantry. Despite intensified efforts by the Bohemian government to alleviate the distress by creating employment through public works projects and by purchasing cereals with public funds, the famine worsened in the course of 1771, causing destitute workers to migrate to Austria in larger numbers. Epidemic fevers became rife both in Prague and rural districts during 1771, and the number of deaths from hunger also multiplied.[37]

In the autumn of 1771, Joseph II decided to tour Bohemia, since, as he wrote, "despite all my protest, nothing is being done to help Bohemia" (Beales, 1987:341). He found that numerous beggars had died of starvation, and he encountered villages on the verge of starvation. He reported to the empress that the Bohemian population also suffered from the practices and decisions of public officials and manorial landlords. Epidemics of continued fevers and dysentery had become common. Rye sold in some Bohemian districts for 7–8 florins per *Metzen*, while the same measure sold for 3–4 florins in the Austrian markets of Linz and St Pollen.

Toward the end of 1771 the Vienna government resolved to provision the Bohemian population by purchasing an entire year's cereal consumption in Hungary, estimated at some half-million *Metzen*(approximately 845,000 bushels), for which one million florins were appropriated, a sum that the Bohemian governments were expected to repay. The Vienna government had already agreed to considerable tax remissions in Bohemia. The Vienna government also found it necessary to increase the public funds available for roadworks and other projects to provide employment in Bohemia. Given the formidable transportation difficulties in shipping massive quantities of grain from Hungary to Bohemia in the 1770s, the heroic provisioning scheme could proceed only slowly. Both mortality and the incidence of epidemic diseases remained elevated in Bohemia throughout 1772, with vagrants and landless day-laborers the chief victims. In the autumn of 1772, the improved harvest outcomes finally brought a decisive change for the better, but the Bohemian population continued to need assistance into 1773.[38]

Crisis mortality also developed in Austria itself, the result largely of the epidemic diseases that followed in the wake of the dearth and unemployment. The stream of migrants from Bohemia added to the number of beggars and vagrants in Vienna and elsewhere, and enhanced the diffusion of the fever epidemics that became rife in Austria during 1771–2. In Austria as in the kingdom of Bohemia, epidemics of typhus, typhoid, and dysentery were primarily responsible for the high death rates.[39]

Conclusion

To sum up, the cross-national and regional examinations of the food shortages, epidemics, welfare crises, and mortality peaks of the early 1740s and 1770s point to the conclusion that the principal link between the shortage of food and epidemic disease was more social than nutritional. That is to say that the epidemic mortality derived more from social disarray than from dangerously lowered resistance to louse-borne infections, typhoid fever, and dysentery. In addition, in light of the simultaneous elevated incidence of a series of contagious diseases, a fraction of the increase in mortality can be traced to a synergism between disease and disease. In eighteenth-century Europe, however, the changes in patterns of behavior and the dilution of the normal components of resistance within societies, such as established human spacing arrangements and standards of hygiene, were primarily responsible for allowing endemic infections to flare into regional and national epidemics.

NOTES

1 The European mortality peaks of the early 1740s have been investigated and reported in Post (1985). The meteorological, demographic, economic, and epidemiological evidence is discussed and displayed in detail, including annual index numbers of European deaths and grain prices for the years 1735–44. The meteorological dimension of the crisis has been focused on in Post (1984); the nutritional issue has been examined in Post (1987).

2 For discussion of the issue, see Taylor (1983), and see also the entire number (14) of the *Journal of Interdisciplinary History* devoted to hunger and history. Several works that appeared in the early 1950s began to question the extent of the influence of nutritional deficiency on infectious disease. Keys et al. (1950) raised doubts about the assumed synergistic relationship based on controlled experiments. Helweg-Larsen et al. (1952), basing their work on experience gained from German concentration camps, found that starvation did not seem to provoke infectious disease other than tuberculosis.

3 Chandra and Newberne, 1977:1–6, 41–2; Gordon, 1978:2,339–45; Kark, 1974:249; Morley, 1980:115–28; and for additional discussion, see Bellagio Conference 1983.

4 For a discussion of the methodological problem, see Carmichael, 1983:252, 257; Kark, 1974:249; Murray and Murray, 1977:471; Taylor, 1983:484.

5 For a detailed examination of the epidemics of the early 1740s region by region, and of the use of the medical term "fever" in pre-industrial Europe, see Post, 1985:ch. 8.

6 The primary and secondary sources that document the excessively wet weather, grain harvest shortfalls, and widespread epidemic diseases of the early 1770s are too numerous to cite in total. The list of references that follows represents a variety of sources and also covers the entire geographical region under study, in the same sequence as the names of the countries found in tables 9.1–9.4: *Annual Register*, "Chronicle," 1770:97, 167, 172; 1771:65–6, 83–4, 99, 103, 120, 129, 134, 147; 1772:70, 109, 135, 145, 151–2, 243; 1773:43, 49, 75, 83; 1774:173–4; *The Scots Magazine*, February, 1772:97, 100–1, 215; June, 1772:327, 379; August, 1772:448; November, 1772:96; March, 1773:158; *London Evening Post*, May 28–30, 1771; June 18–20, 1771; June 22–5, 1771; July 16–18, 1771; August 24–7, 1771; September 10–12, 1771; September 24–6, 1771; November 9–11, 1771; December 10–12, 1771; January 18–21, 1772; February 11–13, 1772; February 15–18, 1772; March 17–19, 1772; April 11–14, 1772; April 16–18, 1772; July 25–8, 1772; September 10– 12, 1772; November 17–19, 1772; December 3–5, 1772; January 21–23, 1773; August 17–19, 1773; October 7–9, 1773; Lebrun, 1971:373–6; Kaplan, 1977a: chs. 10–13; Bruneel, 1980:199–221; Hélin 1963:173; *Acta Borussica*, 1931:IV, 129–137; Abel, 1974:200–57; Kisskalt, 1953:39–40; Kisskalt, 1914:535–9; Virchow, 1985:I, 399–401; Hecker 1839:I, 150–200; Bucholz 1773:v–vi, 1–2; Pelzel, 1817:930–4; Weinzierl-Fischer, 1954:478–514; *Wienerisches Diarium*, June 29, 1771; March 21, 1772; Bräker, 1970:162–8; Olivier, 1939:II, 1, 172–80; Corradi, 1865–94:VIII, 173–6; Bengtsson et

al., 1984:299—328; Utterström, 1954:132, 159—61; Imhof and Lindskog, 1974:915—33; Lassen, 1965:282; Drake 1969:65—7; Johnsen, 1939:425; Hirsch, 1883—6:I, 86—99, 545—81, 617—18; II, 204—22; Haeser, 1875—82: III,505—17.

7 Table 9.2 sources: Wrigley and Schofield, 1981; Flinn et al., 1977; Blayo, 1975; *Annual Register*, 1764—76; Bruneel, 1977; Dalle, 1963; De Brouwer, 1963; De Vos, 1963; Mentink and van der Woude, 1965; van der Woude, 1972; Süssmilch, 1775—6; Kisskalt, 1921; Baümler, Berlin, 1915—19:34 (67, 101); Blaschke, 1967; Ehrhart, 1936; François, 1975; Gehrmann, 1984; Glonner, 1896; Jungkunz, 1951; Oldenburg, 1870; Schmölz and Schmölz, 1952; Schreiber, 1939—40; Lehners, 1973; Schimmer, 1875; *Wienerisches Diarium*, 1764—1776; Burckhardt, 1908; Perrenoud, 1979; Pfister, 1985; Schürmann, 1974; Belletini and Tassinari, 1977; Beltrami, 1954; Donazzolo and Saibante, 1926; Ferrario, 1838—50; Romani, 1955; Sweden 1969; Drake, 1969; Dyrvik et al., 1976; Gille, 1949.

8 Mitchell and Deane, 1962; Flinn et al., 1977; Labrousse, 1932; Labrousse et al., 1970; Posthumus, 1946—64; Verlinden et al., 1959—73; *Acta Borussica*, 1931; Elsas, 1936—49; Pribram, 1938; Pfister, 1975; De Maddalena, 1974; Mauri et al., 1970; Romano, 1965; Friis and Glamann, 1958; Jörberg, 1972.

9 Notice and discussion of the British epidemics during the early 1770s are found in *Annual Register*, "Chronicle," 1772:135; 1773:86; Creighton, 1891— 4:II, 130—8, 143—51, 359—61, 535—41; Flinn et al., 1977:229—33; *London Evening Post*, November 14—17, 1772; Oswald, 1977:105—6; Pennant 1776:I, 312, 352; *The Scots Magazine*, 1770:729; 1771:706; 1772:728; 1773:706; 1774:721; Sinclair, 1791—8:III, 502—3.

10 For accounts of epidemic diseases in France during the early 1770s, see Adams, 1972:279; Jean-Pierre Goubert, 1974:35—7, 282—4, 337—40, 348— 51; Haeser, 1875—82:III, 514—15; Haustesierck, 1772:228—31, 259—72, 272—85; Hirsch, 1883—86:I, 88—90, 553; Kaplan, 1977a:II, 564; Lebrun, 1971:373—6; *London Evening Post*, November 17—19, 1772; Ozanam 1817— 23:IV, 25—6; Poitrineau, 1965:I, 97; Rousset, 1963:82—5.

11 See Bruneel, 1977:291—4; Bruneel, 1980: 202—9; Haeser, 1875—82:III, 513; Hirsch, 1883—6:I, 552; Ozanam, 1817—23:IV, 28—32; Slicher van Bath, 1965:192—3.

12 Bräker, 1970:162—8; Burckhardt, 1908:31; Haeser, 1875—82:III, 513; Mattmüller 1982:281—2; Olivier, 1939:II, 667—8, Perrenoud, 1979:469, 478; Trümpi, 1774:675—7.

13 Corradi, 1865—94:175—6; Del Panta, 1977:326—9; Del Panta and Livi Bacci, 1977:402—23; Knoefel, 1979:7—35.

14 Systematic mortality data are not available for Bavaria, the Rhineland region, and the western German states, except for some Prussian locations and a few imperial city-states. The index numbers found in table 9.2 are based substantially but not entirely on the number of deaths recorded in the kingdom of Prussia and the duchies of Saxony and Oldenburg. The sources listed for table 9.2 disclose the smaller German states and cities included in the index values.

15 The evidence documenting this generalization is extensive. For comprehensive

accounts of epidemics in Germany during the early 1770s, see Bucholz, 1773; Haeser, 1875–82:III, 506–17; Hecker, 1839:150–200; Kisskalt, 1914:535– 9, Kisskalt, 1921:545–59; Kisskalt, 1953:39–40, Virchow, 1985:I, 226–59, 399–401, 418–37, 451–2; and for contemporary press accounts of severe epidemic diseases and starvation in Germany, see *Annual Register*, 1771:83–5, 99, 103–4, 117–18, 120, 129–31; *London Evening Post*, May 28–30, 1771; June 18–20, 1771; June 22–5, 1771; July 16–18, 1771; August 1–3, 1771; December 10–12, 1771; February 11–13, 1772; February 15–18, 1772; *The Scots Magazine*, June, 1772:327; *Wienerisches Diarium*, March 21, 1772.

16 Wright (1966:44–5) states that approximately 10 percent of the population, "or somewhat less than 250,000 people, died in Bohemia." According to the official census carried out for the purpose of conscription, the population of Bohemia (excluding Moravia and Silesia) declined from 2,493,878 in 1771 to 2,265,867 in 1772, or a decrease of 228,011, thus somewhat less than 10 percent. The total decrease of the population of the kingdom of Bohemia including Moravia and Silesia from 1771 to 1772 amounted to 266,640 (see Weinzierl-Fischer, 1954:504). A contemporary press report datelined Prague, December 18, 1772, stated that as a result of the "epidemical distempers which prevail in Bohemia, there have died in that kingdom" from January 1, 1772, to September 1, 1772, a total of 168,331 persons. The account, which claimed to be based on "information received by the government," added that "the ravages of the preceding year were greater still," and also expressed the fear that "we apprehend that the four following months will present us with an account still more terrible" (*Annual Register*, 1772: 152).

17 For grain prices and famine conditions in Bohemia, 1770–2, see Blaich, 1969:299–331; Pelzel, 1817:932–4; Weinzierl-Fischer, 1954:487, 510; *Wienerisches Diarium*, June 22, 1771; for grain prices in Austria, see Pribram, 1938:372, 392, 523, 525.

18 For discussion of famine conditions in Bohemia and the extensive epidemics in Bohemia, Moravia, and Austria, see Pelzel, 1817:932–4; *Annual Register*, 1771:83–4; 1772: 70–1, 145, 152; 1773:43–4, 75; Haeser, 1875–82:III, 510–11; *London Evening Post*, November 9–11, 1771;January 18–21, 1772; March 26–8, 1772; January 21–3, 1773; Ozanam, 1817–23:IV, 230–2; Pelzel, 1817:932–4; Weinzierl-Fischer, 1954:497–504.

19 For accounts and descriptions of food shortage and epidemic mortality in Scandinavia, but especially Sweden, during the early 1770s, see *Annual Register*, 1772:243–5; 1773:10, 49, 84, 92; Drake, 1969:66–7; Fridlizius and Ohlsson, 1984:313–15; Haeser, 1875–82:III, 509, Hirsch, 1883–6:III, 317; Imhof and Lindskog, 1974:920–33; Johnsen, 1939:415, Lassen, 1965:282, *London Evening Post*, September 10–12, 1772; August 17–19, 1773; October 7–9, 1773, Prinzing, 1931:641–2; *The Scots Magazine*, August, 1772:448; December, 1772:676; October, 1774:546; Sogner, 1976:126–7, Utterström 1954:137–8, 144, 160–1.

20 For the etiology of typhus and relapsing fevers, see Benenson, 1975:259–60, 354; MacArthur, 1957:267–8, 275–6.

21 For the etiology and epidemiology of typhoid fever and bacillary dysentery, see

Benenson, 1975:285–8, 349–53; MacArthur, 1957:268–86; Murchison, 1862:409–19.

22 For a summary of current medical views on the influence of nutritional status on common human infections, see Bellagio Conference, 1983: 505–6.

23 For this medical view, see Chandra and Newberne, 1977:1–6; Dixon, 1962.

24 For a detailed account of the widespread increase in vagrancy and begging for all states during the early 1740s, see Post, 1985:chs 3, 6, 7, and 8. For the accounts of the early 1770s, see the references cited in notes 15–19.

25 For accounts of the mortal waves of dysentery that overspread Ireland and Scandinavia during the early 1740s, see Berkeley, 1956:VIII, 248–9; Creighton, 1891–4:II, 241–2, Imhof, 1976:623–36; Imhof and Lindskog, 1974:916; Jutikkala, 1945:28–39; Rutty, 1770: 77–81; Utterström, 1954:121–31.

26 For the pronounced increase in the incidence of vagrancy and begging in the southern Netherlands during 1741, see Bruneel, 1977:276–8, 638–41, 649–62, 663–70; Hélin, 1959:443–61; van Houtte, 1964:112–46, 246–7.

27 Evidence to support the conclusions stated in the foregoing paragraph is found in Post, 1985:142–201, 269–79. The primary and secondary sources that document the statements are also found on the pages cited.

28 Limitations of space prohibit not only a more detailed discussion of the mortality crises in each of the European states under study but also full documentation for the generalizations applicable to the northwestern European states. The generalizations are based on the reading of newspapers and other news journals for the years 1764–76 and on contemporary journals and accounts covering the same years, and also derive from the studies and monographs devoted to these subjects for this period in European history.

29 For employment, subsistence, living standards, and welfare services in Copenhagen during the years 1764–76, see Thestrup, 1971:27–57, 62–98, 258–61, 275, 283; for the social structure, living standards, and mortality trends in Denmark, see Anderson, 1984:115–20.

30 For harvests, famine, and epidemic disease in Norway, see Johnsen, 1939:415; for grain shipments from Denmark to Norway in 1772, see *The Scots Magazine*, 1772: 448; for a press account of the Norwegian epidemics, see *London Evening Post*, October 7–9, 1773; for the mortality crisis in Akershus, see Sogner, 1976:126–7.

31 The Swedish famine and mortality crisis received extensive coverage in the European press during the early 1770s; in addition, the Swedish mortality crisis has been more fully investigated than the parallel events in Norway. For a discussion of the political crisis and its adverse effects on relief efforts, see Hovde, 1943:I, 188–204; Roberts, 1986:189–205; for discussion of the harvest shortfalls, food shortage, epidemics, and mortality, see Fridlizius, 1984:72–95; Fridlizius and Ohlsson, 1984:299–318; Utterström, 1954:137–8, 144, 160–1; for press accounts, see *Annual Register*, 1772:243–5; 1773:49, 84, 92, 144; 1774:5; *London Evening Post*, August 17–19, 1773; *The Scots Magazine*, April, 1772:210; December, 1772:676; March, 1773:158; October 1774:546; November, 1774:607.

32 A comprehensive account of the destitution, social disarray, hunger, vagrancy,

and mass begging that predominated in the German states of Eichsfeld and Saxony is found in Abel, 1974:252−6. For similar accounts, see *Annual Register*, 1771:83−4, 120; Blaschke, 1967:126−9; *London Evening Post*, December 10−12, 1771; *The Scots Magazine*, February, 1772:100−1; June, 1772:327; Virchow, 1985:I, 422.

33 For such an account, see *Wienerisches Diarium*, March 21, 1772.

34 For accounts of mortality from epidemic disease in Prussia during the 1770s, see Haeser, 1875−82:III, 510−11; Hecker, 1839:183−4; Kisskalt, 1914:537− 9; Kisskalt, 1953:39−40; Virchow, 1985:399, 418−27.

35 For Prussia's population and resource losses as a consequence of the Seven Years War and the continuing difficulties and costs of reconstruction into the 1770s, see Hubatsch, 1975:96−7, 106, 148, 169−79.

36 For a full account of the Prussian subsistence crisis and the welfare and relief programs and policies of Frederick the Great, see *Acta Borussica*, 1931:IV, 49− 83, 105−26, 129−38; for the welfare and relief programs of the majority of the German states, see Abel, 1974: 210−50.

37 For a comprehensive account of the special commissar's findings, the famine in Bohemia, the relief measures adopted, the response of the provincial government, and the escalating scale of unemployment, hunger, epidemic disease, work migrations, and social disorder in general, see Weinzierl-Fischer, 1954:484−98; for the relief measures pursued by the Vienna government, see Blaich, 1969:299−331; for contemporary press notice of the famine and social disarray in Bohemia during 1771, see *Annual Register*, 1771:83−4, 120; *London Evening Post*, November 9−12, 1771.

38 *Annual Register*, 1772:70, 145; Beales, 1987:342−43; Blaich, 1969:318−29; Weinzierl-Fischer, 1954:504−12.

39 For medical discussion of the Austrian epidemics of 1771−2, see Hecker, 1839:182−3; for press accounts of the epidemics in Austria and Vienna, see *Annual Register*, 1772:70; *London Evening Post*, January 18−21, 1772.

REFERENCES

Abel, Wilhelm 1974: *Massenarmut und Hungerkrisen im vorindustriellen Europa*. Hamburg: Paul Parey.

Acta Borussica 1931: *Denkmäler der preussischen Staatsverwaltung im 18. Jahrhundert. Getreidehandelspolitik; Vol. 4: Skalweit, August, Die Getreidehandelspolitik und Kriegsmagazinverwaltung Preussens 1756−1806.* Berlin: Paul Parey.

Adams, Thomas M. 1972: An approach to the problem of beggary in eighteenth-century France: The *dépôts de mendicité*. University of Wisconsin: unpublished dissertation.

Anderson, Otto 1984: The decline in Danish mortality before 1850 and its economic and social background. In Bengtsson et al., (1984), 115−26.

Annual Register, 1764−76.

Baltus, Jacques 1904: *Annales de Baltus (1724−1756)*. Ed. abbé E. Paulus. Metz: Imprimerie Lorraine.

Bang, Frederick B. 1981: The role of disease in the ecology of famine. In John R. K. Robson (ed.), *Famine: Its Causes, Effects, and Management*. New York: Gordon & Breach Science Publishers, Inc.

Barker, John 1742: *An Inquiry into the Nature, Cause, and Cure of the Present Epidemic Fever*. London, Salisbury, and Bath: n.p.

Baümler, D.G. 1938: Medizinalstatistische untersuchungen über Weiden (Oberpfalz) von 1551 bis 1800. *Archiv für Hygiene*, 120:195–243.

Beales, Derek 1987: *Joseph II. Vol. 1: In the Shadow of Maria Theresa 1741–1780*. Cambridge: Cambridge University Press.

Bekmann, Johann Christoph 1751–3: *Historische Beschreibung der Chur und Mark Brandenburg*. Ed. B. L. Bekmann. Berlin: n.p., 2 vols.

Bellagio Conference 1983: The relationship of nutrition, disease and social conditions: A graphical presentation. *Journal of Interdisciplinary History*, 14, 503–6.

Bellettini, Athos and Tassinari, Franco 1977: *Fonti per lo Studio della Popolazione del Suburbio di Bologna dal Secolo XVI alla Fine dell' Ottocento*. Bologna: Instituto per la Storia di Bologna.

Beltrami, Daniele 1954: *Storia della popolazione di Venezia dalla Fine del Secolo XVI alla Caduta della Repubblica*. Padova: CEDAM.

Benenson, Abram (ed.) 1975: *Control of Communicable Diseases in Man*. Washington, DC: The American Public Health Association, twelfth edition.

Bengtsson, Tommy, Fridlizius, Gunnar, and Ohlsson, Rolf (eds) 1984: *Preindustrial Population Change: The mortality decline and short-term population movements*. Stockholm: Almqvist & Wiksell International.

Berkeley, George 1956: *The Works of George Berkeley, Bishop of Cloyne*. Ed. A.A. Luce and T.E. Jessop. London: Nelson, 9 vols.

Berlin, 1915–19: *Statistisches Jahrbuch der Stadt Berlin*, 34.

Bernier, T. 1887: Notice sur l'origine et la tenue des anciens registres d'état civil dans la province de Hainaut. *Mémoires de la Société des Sciences, des Arts et des Lettres du Hainaut*, 9, 523–92.

Blaich, Fritz 1969: Die wirtschaftspolitische Tätigkeit der Kommission zur Bekämpfung der Hungersnot in Böhmen und Mähren (1771–1772). *Vierjahrschift für Sozial-und Wirtschaftsgeschichte*, 56, 299–331.

Blaschke, Karlheinz 1967: *Bevölkerungsgeschichte von Sachsen bis zum Industriellen Revolution*. Weimar: Hermann Böhlaus Nachfolger.

Blayo, Yves 1975: Mouvement naturel de la population française de 1740 à 1829. *Population*, special number 30, 15–64.

Bräker, Ulrich 1970: *The Poor Man of Toggenburg*. Trans. Derek Bowman. Edinburgh: University of Edinburgh Press. Original Swiss edition 1789.

Bruneel, Claude 1977: *La mortalité dans les Campagnes: Le duché de Brabant aux XVIIe et XVIIIe siècles*. Louvain: Editions Nauwelaerts.

Bruneel, Claude 1980: Un problème de gouvernement: Le pouvoir face a l'épidémie de fièvre putride à Bruxelles en 1772–1773. In Arthur Imhof (ed.), *Mensch und Gesundheit in der Geschichte*, Husum: Matthiesen, 199–221.

Bucher, Silvio 1974: *Bevölkerung und Wirtschaft des Amtes Entlebuch im 18. Jahrhundert*. Luzern: Rex-Verlag.

Bucholz, Wilhelm 1773: *Nachricht von dem jetzt herrschenden Fleck-und Friesel-Fieber.* Weimar: Hoffmann.

Burckhardt, Albrecht 1908: *Demographie und Epidemiologie der Stadt Basel, 1601–1900.* Basel: Reinhardt.

Burri, Hans-Rudolf 1975: *Die Bevölkerung Luzerns im 18. und frühen 19. Jahrhundert.* Luzern: Rex-Verlag.

Carmichael, Ann 1983: Infection, hidden hunger, and history. *Journal of Interdisciplinary History*, 14, 249–64.

Chandra, R. K. and Newberne, P. M. 1977: *Nutrition, Immunity and Infection: Mechanisms of Infection.* New York: Plenum.

Cinq Études de Démographie Locale (XVIIe–XIXe Siècles) 1963. Brussels: Pro Civitate.

Corradi, Alfonso 1865–94: *Annali delle epidemie Occorse in Italia dalle Prime Memorie fino al 1850.* Bologna: Gamberini & Parmeggiani, 8 vols.

Creighton, Charles 1891–4: *A History of Epidemics in Britain.* Cambridge: Cambridge University Press, 2 vols.

Dalle, D. 1963: *De Bevolking van Veurne-Ambacht in de 17e en 18e eeuw.* Brussels: Paleis der Academien.

De Brouwer, J. 1963: De demografische evolutie in de meierij Erembodegem en de heerlijkheid Oordegem gedurende de XVIIe en XVIIIe eeuw. In *Cinq Etudes* (1963), 71–120.

Del Panta, Lorenzo 1977: Cronologia e diffusione delle crisi di mortalita in Toscana dalla fine del XIV agli initi del XIX secolo. *Ricerche storiche*, 7, 293–343.

Del Panta, L. and Livi Bacci, M. 1977: Chronologie, intensité et diffusion des crises de mortalité en Italie: 1600–1850. *Population*, special number 32, 401–46.

Delumeau, J. 1970: Démographie d'un port français sous l'ancien régime: Saint-Malo, 1651–1750. *XVIIIe Siècle*, 86–7, 3–21.

De Maddalena, Aldo 1974: *Prezzi e Mercedi a Milano dal 1701 al 1860.* Milan: Banca Commerciale Italiana, 2 vols.

De Vos, J. 1963: De omvang en de evolutie van het Eeklose bevolkingscjifer tijdens de XVIIe en de XVIIIe eeuw. In *Cinq Etudes* (1963).

Dixon, C. W., 1962: *Smallpox.* London: Churchill.

Donazzolo, P. and Saibante, M. 1926: Lo sviluppo demografico di Verona e della sua provincia dalla fine del sec. XV ai nostri giorni. *Metron*, 6, 56–180.

Drake, Michael 1968: The Irish demographic crisis of 1740–41. *Historical Studies*, 6, 101–24.

Drake, Michael 1969: *Population and Society in Norway, 1735–1865.* Cambridge: Cambridge University Press.

Dreyfus, François G. 1956: Prix et population à Trèves et à Mayence au XVIIIe siècle. *Revue d'Histoire Économique et Sociale*, 34, 241–61.

Dunsford, M. 1790: Historical Memoirs of Tiverton. Exeter: T. Brice.

Dyrvik, Ståle, Mykland, Knut, and Oldervoll, Jan 1976: *The Demographic Crises in Norway in the 17th and 18th Centuries.* Bergen and Oslo: Universitetsforlaget.

Ehrhart, Wilhelm 1936: Die Sterblichkeit in der Reichstadt Kempten (Allgaü) in den Jahren 1606–1624 und 1686–1870. *Archiv für Hygiene und Bakteriologie*, 116, 115–30.

Elsas, Moritz J. 1936—49: *Umriss einer Geschichte der Preise und Löhne in Deutschland vom ausgehenden Mittelalter bis zum Beginn des 19. Jahrhunderts. Vols 1 and 2.* Leiden: A. W. Sijthoff.

Faulkner's Dublin Journal, 1740—2.

Ferrario, Giuseppe 1838—50: *Statistica Medica di Milano dal Secolo XV fino ai Nostri Giorni.* Milan: Bernardoni, 2 vols.

Flinn, Michael (ed.) 1977: *Scottish Population History from the Seventeenth Century to the 1930s.* London: Cambridge University Press.

François, E. 1975: La population de Coblence au XVIIIe siècle. *Annales de Démographie Historique*, 291—341.

Fridlizius, Gunnar 1984: The mortality decline in the first phase of the demographic transition: Swedish experiences. In Bengtsson et al. (1984), 71—114.

Fridlizius, Gunnar and Ohlsson, Rolf 1984: Mortality patterns in Sweden 1751—1802 — a regional analysis. In Bengtsson et al. (1984), 299—328.

Friis, Astrid and Glamann, Kristof 1958: *A History of Prices and Wages in Denmark 1660—1800. Vol. 1: Copenhagen.* London: Longman, Green and Co.

Gehrmann, Rolf 1984: *Leezen 1720—1870.* Neumunster: Karl Wachholz Verlag.

Gentleman's Magazine, 1735—44, 1764—76.

Gilchrist, Ebenezer 1733—44: Of nervous fever. In *Medical Essays and Observations*, Edinburgh: Published by a Society in Edinburgh, V, 505—73.

Gille, H. 1949: The demographic history of the northern European countries in the eighteenth century. *Population Studies*, 3, 1—65.

Glonner, Stephan 1986: Bevölkerungsbewegung von sieben Pfarreien im kgl. bayerischen Bezirksamt Tölz seit Ende des 16. Jahrhunderts. *Allgemeines Statistisches Archiv*, 4, 263—79.

Gordon, John 1978: Epidemiological insights on malnutrition: Some resurrected, others restructured, a few retired. *American Journal of Clinical Nutrition*, 31, 2,339—51.

Goubert, Jean-Pierre 1974: *Malades et Médecins en Bretagne 1770—1790.* Paris: Klincksieck.

Goubert, Pierre 1960: *Beauvais et le Beauvaisis de 1600 à 1730.* Paris: SEVPEN, 2 vols.

Gutmann, Myron P. 1980: *War and Rural Life in the Early Modern Low Countries.* Princeton: Princeton University Press.

Haeser, Heinrich 1875—82: *Lehrbuch der Geschichte der Medicin und der epidemischen Krankheiten.* Jena: Gustav Fischer, third edition, 3 vols.

Haustesierck, M. Richard (ed.) 1772: *Recueil d'Observations de Médecine des Hôpitaux militaires.* Paris: L'Imprimerie royale, 2 vols.

Hecker, Justin Friedrich 1839: *Geschichte der neueren Heilkunde. Erstes Buch: Die Volkskrankheiten von 1770.* Berlin: Enslin, 2 vols.

Hélin, Étienne 1959: La disette et le recensement de 1740. *Annuaire d'Histoire Liégeoise*, 6, 443—77.

Hélin, Etienne 1963: *La Démographie de Liège aux XVII et XVIIIe Siècles.* Brussels: Académic Royale de Belgique, Mémoires.

Helweg-Larsen, Per, et al. 1952: *Famine Disease in German Concentration Camps: Complications and sequels.* Copenhagen: Acta Medica Scandinavica.

Hirsch, August 1883–6: *Handbook of Geographical and Historical Pathology*. Trans. Charles Creighton. London: The New Sydenham Society, 3 vols.

Houtte, G. van 1964: *Leuven in 1740, ein Krisisjaar*. Brussels: Pro Civitate, Verzameling Geschiedenis.

Hovde, B.J. 1943: *The Scandinavian Countries, 1720–1865*. Boston: Chapman & Grimes, 2 vols.

Hubatsch, Walter 1975: *Frederick the Great of Prussia: Absolutism and administration*. Trans. Patrick Doren. London: Thames and Hudson.

Hufton, Olwen 1974: *The Poor of Eighteenth-Century France 1750–1789*. Oxford: Clarendon Press.

Huxham, John 1759–67: *Observations on the Air, and Epidemic Diseases from the Beginning of the Year 1738, to the End of the Year 1748*. Trans. from the Latin by John Corham Huxham. London: J. Hinton, 2 vols.

Imhof, Arthur E. 1976: *Aspekte der Bevölkerungsentwicklung in den nordischen Ländern 1720–1750*. Bern: Francke.

Imhof, Arthur E. and Lindskog, B.I. 1974: Les causes de mortalité en Suède et en Finlande entre 1749 et 1773. *Annales ESC*, 29, 915–33.

Johnsen, Oscar Albert 1939: *Norwegische Wirtschaftsgeschichte*. Jena: Gustav Fischer.

Jörberg, Lennart 1972: *A History of Prices in Sweden 1732–1914. Vol. 1*. Lund: C.W.K. Glearup.

Jungkunz, W. 1951: Die Sterblichkeit in Nürnberg, 1714–1850. *Mitteilungen des Vereins für Geschichte der Stadt Nürnberg*, 42, 289–352.

Jutikkala, Eino 1945: *Die Bevölkerung Finnlands in den Jahren 1721–1749*. Helsinki: Annales Academiae Scientiarium Fennicae.

Kaplan, Steven L. 1977a: *Bread, Politics and Political Economy in the Reign of Louis XV*. The Hague: Nijhoff, 2 vols.

Kaplan, Steven L. 1977b: Lean years, fat years: The "community" granary system and the search for abundance in 18th-century Paris. *French Historical Studies*, 10, 197–230.

Kaplan, Steven, L. 1982: The famine plot persuasion in eighteenth-century France. *Transactions of the American Philosophical Society*, 72, 1–75.

Kark, Sidney L. 1974: *Epidemiology and Community Medicine*. New York: Appleton-Century-Crofts.

Keys, Ancel, et al. 1950: *The Biology of Human Starvation*. Minneapolis: University of Minnesota Press, 2 vols.

King, Lester S. 1958: *The Medical World of the Eighteenth Century*. Chicago: University of Chicago Press.

Kisskalt, Karl 1914: Hungersnöte und Seuchen. *Zeitschrift für Hygiene und Infektionskrankheiten*, 78, 524–40.

Kisskalt, Karl 1921: Die Sterblichkeit im 18. Jahrhundert. *Zeitschrift für Hygiene und Infektionskrankheiten*, 93, 438–511.

Kisskalt, Karl 1953: Epidemiologisch-statistische Untersuchungen über die Sterblichkeit von 1600–1800. *Archiv für Hygiene und Bakteriologie*, 137, 26–42.

Knoefel, P.K. 1979: Famine and fever in Tuscany. *Physis*, 21, 7–35.

Kundmann, Johann Christian 1742: *Die Heimsuchungen Gottes in Zorn und Gnade über das Herzogthum Schlesien in Müntzen.* Leipzig: David Siegerts.

Labrousse, E. 1932: *Esquisse du Mouvement des Prix et des Revenues en France au XVIIIe Siècle.* Paris: Dalloz, 2 vols.

Labrousse, E. et al. 1970: *Le prix du Froment en France au Temps de la Monnaie Stable 1726–1913.* Paris: SEVPEN.

La Mettrie, Julian Offray de 1755: *Oeuvres de Médecine.* Berlin: Fromery et Fils.

Lassen, Aksel 1965: *Fald og Fremgang; Traek af befolkningsudviklingen i Danmark 1645–1960.* Arhus, n.p.

Lebrun, François 1971: *Les Hommes et la Mort en Anjou aux 17e et 18e siècles.* Paris: Mouton.

Lehners, Jean-Paul 1973: Die pfarrei Stockerau im 17. und 18. Jahrhundert. In Heimold Helczmanovazki (ed.), *Beiträge zur Bevölkerungs-und Sozialgeschichte Österreichs.* Vienna: Verlag fur Geschichte und Politik, 373–401.

London Daily Post, 1739–42.

London Evening Post, 1770–3.

MacArthur, Sir William P. 1957: Medical history of the famine. In R. Dudley Edwards and T. Desmond Williams (eds), *The Great Famine,* New York: New York University Press, 263–315.

Mackay, M. M. 1935: A highland minister's diary. *Cornhill Magazine,* 152, 570–80.

Mattmüller, Markus 1982: Die Hungersnot der Jahre 1770–71 in der Basler Landschaft. In Nicolai Bernhard and Quirinus Reichen (eds), *Festschrift zum 65. Geburtstag von Professor Dr. Ulrich Im Hof,* Bern: Gesellschaft und Gesellschaften.

Mauri, L., Alfonsi, R., et al. 1970: Il movimento dei prezzi in Toscana dal 1748 al 1805. *Giornali degli Economisti e Annali di Economia,* 29, 636–53.

Mentink, G. T. and van der Woude, A. M. 1965: *De demografische ontwikkeling te Rotterdam en Cool in de 17e en 18e eeuw.* Rotterdam: Gemeentearchief.

Messance, M. 1766: *Recherches sur la Population des Généralités d'Auvergne, de Lyon, de Rouen, et de quelques Provinces et Villes du Royaume.* Paris: Durand.

Meuvret, Jean 1946: Les crises de subsistances et la démographie de la France d'ancien régime. *Population,* 1, 643–50.

Meuvret, Jean 1965: Demographic crisis in France from the sixteenth to the eighteenth century. In D. C. Glass and D. E. C. Eversley (eds), *Population in History,* London: Edward Arnold, 507–22.

Mitchell, B. R. and Deane, Phyllis 1962: *Abstract of British Historical Statistics.* Cambridge: Cambridge University Press.

Morley, David 1980: Severe measles. In Neville F. Stanley and R. A. Joske (eds), *Changing Disease Patterns and Human Behavior,* London: Academic Press, 115–28.

Murchison, C. A. 1862: *A Treatise on the Continued Fevers of Great Britain.* London: Parker, Son, & Brown.

Murray, John and Murray, Anne 1977: Suppression of infection by famine and its activation by refeeding – a paradox? *Perspectives in Biology and Medicine,* 20, 471–83.

Observations on the Present epidemic Fever 1741. London: n.p.

Oldenburg 1870: *Statistische Nachrichten über das Grossherzogt Oldenburg*, 11, 93.

Olivier, Eugène 1939: *Médecine et Santé dans le Pays de Vaud au XVIIIe Siècle, 1675–1798*. Lausanne: Editions la Concorde, 2 vols.

Oswald, Neville 1977: Epidemics in Devon, 1538–1837. *Transactions of the Devonshire Association*, 109, 73–116.

Ozanam, J. A. F. 1817–23: *Histoire Médicale Générale et Particulière des Maladies Épidémiques, Contagieuses et Épizootiques*. Paris: Méquignon-Marvis, 5 vols.

Pelzel, Franz Martin 1817: *Geschichte der Böhmen*. Prague: Zeitings-und Intelligens, fourth edition.

Pennant, T. 1776: *A Tour in Scotland and Voyage to the Hebrides*. London: Benj. White, second edition, 2 vols.

Perrenoud, Alfred 1979: *La Population de Genève du Seizième au Début du Dix-neuvième Siècle: Étude Démographique. Vol. 1: Structures et Mouvements*. Geneva: A Jullien.

Pfister, Christian 1975: *Agrarkonjunktur und Witterungsverlauf im westlichen Schweizer Mittelland zur Zeit der Ökonomischen Patrioten, 1755–1797*. Bern: Lang.

Pfister, Christian 1984: *Das Klima der Schweiz von 1525–1860 und seine Bedeutung in der Geschichte von Bevölkerung und Landwirtschaft*. Bern and Stuttgart: Verlag Paul Haupt, 2 vols.

Pfister, Christian 1985: Historisch-Statistischer Atlas des Kantons Bern. Personal communication.

Pickard, Ransom 1947: *The Population and Epidemics of Exeter in Pre-Census Times*. Exeter: Townsend.

Piuz, Anne-Marie 1974: Climat, récoltes et vie des hommes à Genève XVIe–XVIIIe siècle. *Annales ESC*, 29, 599–618.

Poitrineau, A. 1965: *La Vie Rurale en Basse Auvergne au XVIIIe Siècle (1726–1789)*. Paris: PUF, 2 vols.

Post, John D. 1984: Climatic variability and the European mortality wave of the early 1740s. *Journal of Interdisciplinary History*, 15, 1–30.

Post, John D. 1985: *Food Shortage, Climatic Variability, and Epidemic Disease in Preindustrial Europe*. Ithaca, NY: Cornell University Press.

Post, John D. 1987: Food shortage, nutrition, and epidemic disease in the subsistence crises of preindustrial Europe. *Food and Foodways*, 1, 389–423.

Posthumus, Nicolaas 1946–64: *Inquiry into the History of Prices in Holland. Vol. 2*. Leiden: E. J. Brill.

Pribram, Alfred Francis 1938: *Materialien zur Geschichte der Preise und Löhne in Österreich*. Vienna: Carl Ueberreuters Verlag.

Prinzing, Friedrich 1916: *Epidemics Resulting from Wars*. Oxford: Clarendon Press.

Prinzing, Friedrich 1931: *Handbuch der medizinischen Statistik*. Jena: Gustav Fischer, second edition.

Risse, Guenter B. 1979: Epidemics and medicine: The influence of disease on medical thought and practice. *Bulletin of the History of Medicine*, 53, 505–19.

Roberts, Michael 1986: *The Age of Liberty: Sweden 1719–1772*. London: Cambridge University Press.

Romani, M. 1955: Il movimento demografico in Lombardia del 1750 al 1850. *Economica e Storia*, 2, 412–52.

Romano, Ruggiero 1965: *Prezzi, Salari e Servizi a Napoli nel Secole XVIII (1734–1806)*. Milan: Banca Commerciale Italiana.

Rousset, J. 1963: Essai de pathologie urbaine. Les causes de morbidité et de mortalité à Lyon aux XVIIe et XVIIIe siècles. *Cahiers d'Histoire*, 8, 71–105.

Rutty, John 1770: *A Chronological History of the Weather and Seasons and of the Prevailing Diseases in Dublin*. London: Robinson & Roberts.

Scheppere, J. B. B. de 1741: *Détail Historique et Curatif de la Fièvre Maligne qui Régne Actuellement en toute la Flandre et Ailleurs depuis l'an 1737*. Ghent: Pierre de Goesin.

Schimmer, G. A. 1875: Die Bewegung der Bevölkerung in Wien seit dem Jahre 1770. *Statistische Monatschrift*, 1, 119–33.

Schmölz, Franz and Schmölz, Therese 1952: Die Sterblichkeit in Landsberg am Lech von 1585–1875. *Archiv für Hygiene und Bakteriologie*, 136, 504–40.

Schreiber, A. 1939–40: Die Entwicklung der Augsburger Bevölkerung vom Ende des 14. Jahrhunderts bis zum Beginn des 19. Jahrhunderts. *Archiv für Hygiene*, 123, 90–177.

Schürmann, M. 1974: *Bevölkerung, Wirtschaft und Gesellschaft in Appenzell-Innerrhoden im 18. und frühen 19. Jahrhundert*. Appenzell: Innerrhoder Geschichtsfreund.

The Scots Magazine, 1740–2, 1764–76.

Scrimshaw, N. S., Taylor, C. E., and Gordon, J. E. 1968: *Interactions of Nutrition and Infection*. Geneva: World Health Organization.

Short, Thomas 1749: *A General Chronological History of the Air, Weather, Seasons, Meteors, etc.* London: T. Longman.

Sinclair, Sir John 1791–8: *The Statistical Account of Scotland*. Edinburgh: William Creech, 21 vols.

Slicher van Bath, B. H. 1965: Study of historical demography in the Netherlands. In Paul Harsin and Étienne Hélin (eds), *Problèmes de Mortalité*, Liège: Actes du Colloque International de Démographie historique, 185–98.

Smith, Dale C. 1980: Gerhard's distinction between typhoid and typhus and its reception in America, 1833–1860. *Bulletin of the History of Medicine*, 54, 368–85.

Smith, Dale C. 1982: The rise and fall of typhomalarial fever: Origins. *Journal of the History of Medicine and Allied Sciences*, 37, 182–220.

Sogner, Sølvi 1976: A demographic crisis averted? *Scandinavian Economic History Review*, 24, 114–28.

Sundbärg, Gustav 1905: Döde efter kön, ålder och civilstånd i Sverige åren 1751–1900 samt medelfolkmängden efter kön och ålder under femårsperioderna för samma tid. *Statistik Tidskrift*, 2, 109–40.

Süssmilch, Johann Peter, 1775–6: *Die göttliche Ordnung in den Veränderungen des menschlichen Geschlechts*. Berlin: Buchhandlung der Realschule, fourth edition, 3 vols.

Sweden 1969: *Historisk Statistik för Sverige. Vol. 1: Befolkning, 1720–1967*. Stockholm: Statistika Centralbyrán.

Taylor, Carl E. 1983: Synergy among mass infections, famines, and poverty. *Journal of Interdisciplinary History*, 14, 483—501.

Thestrup, Paul 1971: *The Standard of Living in Copenhagen, 1730—1800.* Copenhagen: Gads Forlag.

Trümpi, Christoph 1774: *Neuere Glarner Chronik.* Winterthur: Steiners.

Utterström, Gustaf 1954: Some population problems in pre-industrial Sweden. *Scandinavian Economic History Review*, 2, 103—65.

van der Woude, A. M. see under Woude.

Verlinden, Charles, et al. 1959—73: *Dokumenten voor de geschiedenis van prijzen en lonen en Vlaanderen en Brabant. Vol. 1.* Bruges: Rijksuniversiteit te Gent.

Virchow, Rudolf 1985: *Collected Essays on Public Health and Epidemiology.* Ed. L. J. Rather. Canton, Mass.: Science History Publications, 2 vols.

Wall, John 1780: Account of the epidemic fever of 1740, 1741, 1742. In Martin Wall (ed.), *Medical Tracts*, Oxford: Prince and Cook, 337—55.

Walser, G. 1830: *Appenzeller-Chronik., Teil 3: 1732—1772.* Ed. G. Nuesch. Trogen: n.p.

Watkins, Susan Cotts and van de Walle, Etienne 1983: Nutrition, mortality, and population size: Malthus' court of last resort. *Journal of Interdisciplinary History*, 14, 205—26.

Weinzierl-Fischer, Erika 1954: Die Bekämpfung der Hungersnot in Böhmen 1770—72. *Mitteilungen des Österreichischen Staatsarchiv*, 7, 478—514.

Wienerisches Diarium, 1764—76.

Wolff, Johann Phillip 1743: *Consilium Medicum, welches über die dermahlen hier und dar anfangend und epidemicé grassirende Ruhr-Krankheit gestellet und mit getheilet hat.* Schweinfurth: Wittib.

Woude, A. M. van der 1972: *Het Noorderkwartier.* Wageningen: Veenman & Zonen, 3 vols.

Wright, William 1966: *Serf, Seigneur and Sovereign — Agrarian reform in eighteenth-century Bohemia.* Minneapolis: University of Minnesota Press.

Wrigley, E. A. and Schofield, R. S. 1981: *The Population History of England.* Cambridge, Mass.: Harvard University Press.

Yeomans, Andrew 1948: The symptomatology, clinical course, and management of louse-borne typhus fever. In F. R. Moulton (ed.), *Rickettsial Diseases of Man*, Washington, DC: American Public Health Association.

10

Food Supply in the Swiss Canton of Bern, 1850*

CHRISTIAN PFISTER

Hunger History and Food Availability

The approach discussed in this paper attempts to improve our understanding of the ways in which hunger in pre-industrial societies was linked to environmental, agroeconomic, demographic, and social parameters. The systems of food security, which were also important, will not be considered in this context. The focus is on quantitative evidence, on estimating the composition and the caloric value of food resources, their vulnerability to climatic hazards, and their social distribution at the level of the household. The nineteenth century marks the end of famine in continental Europe except in wartime, but food poverty has persisted. A remarkable data set allows us to examine this relationship in detail. The information is collected and interpreted in the context of a large historical databank called BERNHIST which is being created for the Swiss canton of Bern (6,000 sq. km, population 400,000 in 1850). This canton comprises roughly one-seventh of the population and the surface of Switzerland.

A systematic search (which included the local archives in the canton) has brought to light an unexpected wealth of quantitative evidence. As early as the mid-eighteenth century the Bernese administration was able and eager to set up statistical surveys. In the nineteenth century Bern was the first canton to set up a statistical office (Hildebrand, 1860). In the decades following the creation of this office in 1856, a series of very detailed demographic and economic data series was published (*Statistisches Jahrbuch*, 1868–76; *Mitteilungen des kantonalen statistischen Bureaus*, 1883ff). Bern is therefore an ideal place for quantitative studies.

* This research is supported by the Swiss National Science Foundation.

The BERNHIST databank is directed towards the following main objectives (Pfister and Schüle, 1989):

1 Examining the spatial distribution of population, resources, and infrastructure at different points in time to assess the magnitude of regional imbalances in economic development and carrying capacity, and to measure the flows of energy, money, and labor along the gradients of poverty.
2 Investigating the changes in distribution between the points of reference and relating this to environmental, economic, demographic, cognitive, and behavioral parameters.
3 Modeling some interactions between people, the economy, and the environment.

Using this data set, food production and distribution can be studied in space, across time, and in the social dimension, and is viewed in the context of a large body of thought which encompasses the flows of energy and nutrient materials in food-chains, and their relationship to social modes of production and reproduction on the one hand, and to flows of money on the other. This paper provides some basic results about food and its distribution in the mid-nineteenth century.

Our data enable us to estimate food shortage in Canton Bern around the mid-nineteenth century just before the coming of the railway.

The 1847 Food Survey

The availability and the quality of the data is crucial for assessing food production. In the canton of Bern the optimum data density for a hunger study is in the late 1840s. In 1845 the potato in Europe was being attacked for the first time by potato blight, caused by the fungus *Phytophtora infestans*, which had been raging in the United States since 1843. The ravages of disease on the 1845 potato crop combined with a poor grain harvest caused great distress in western and central Europe. A mild winter allowed disease-infected tubers which had been discarded in the fields during the 1845 harvest to survive and to carry over the infection on a large scale to the following year's crop (Bourke, 1984). The main consequences of the Irish potato famine are well known (Mokyr, 1985).

The effect on the lives of the poor in the canton of Bern is vividly described in Jeremias Gotthelf's novel, *Käthi die Grossmutter*, published in

1847. In October 1846 a food riot erupted in the capital which pointed to the discontent that was inherent and to the danger of social upheaval. Johann Rudolf Schneider, a physician and a member of the cantonal government, was in charge of famine relief. He was very busy collecting information on harvests and grain prices throughout Europe. On his advice, the government of the canton acquired wheat, oats, maize, and beans abroad in timely fashion. This measure perhaps prevented a widespread famine such as had occurred in 1816–17 (Fischer, 1963). In February 1847 Schneider decreed that between March 3 and 6, two officers should set up an inventory of selected items of stored food in every community. The list included different kinds of grain, potatoes (dried and fresh), maize, rice, legumes, dried fruit, cheese, smoked bacon and meat, stock for slaughtering, and even pickled cabbage. Dairy products, lard, and manufactured products such as sugar and macaroni were not considered. The name of the head of every household was noted, sometimes also his profession, followed by a detailed inventory of his food resources. More than 60,000 households are contained in the lists which are bound together in three giant volumes of ten kilograms each.

In order to assess the volume of the next crop, Schneider needed additional information. Forms sent to the 410 communities of the canton asked for data on the acreage sown in grain and planted in potatoes, on the amount of seeds needed, and on average yields. In addition, information had to be provided for the acreage planted in beans, cabbage, carrots, and turnips. In April a cattle census was set up which included data on the amount of cheese produced.

This body of evidence was the basis for getting reliable estimates on per capita food production at the community level. It had to be complemented with several other sources of data: two censuses taken in 1846 and 1850, statistics on fruit trees (1888), an analysis of yearly fruit yields per tree (1885–1927), data on the area of vineyards, information on milk yields per cow and per goat (according to size and race), and estimates of meat production derived from data on the cattle population.

Only a part of the biomass which is harvested in the fields is directed to human consumption. A realistic estimate of food production has to discount the amounts used for seeds and for feeding animals as well as for losses in storage, in the mill, and in food preparation. A part of the waste was recycled to pigs. This kind of variable is not adequately documented for the past. Often the analysis has to rely on estimates from contemporary sources, sometimes even from present-day manuals. In some cases we have to draw on assumptions. But it can be demonstrated from the model that the biases are rather small.

Food Shortage

Food shortage is viewed as insufficient availability of food within a bounded region (as defined in chapter 1). The area under investigation extends from altitudes of 400 m above sea-level to areas beyond the upper limit of vegetation at more than 2,000 m above sea-level. Natural parameters such as altitude, slope, and soil quality on the one hand, and cultural elements such as value systems, institutions, traditions, beliefs, and social organization on the other, determine essentially the pattern of agricultural activities. In this context we may distinguish three broad ecozones: the Kornland, where grain was the dominant crop; an intermediate hilly zone of mixed farming; and the alpine region, where dairy products accounted for the lion's share of food. To take the first step towards answering the broad question of food shortage, the average per capita production of food and its composition is estimated. In the next step the vulnerability of food resources to climatic hazards is examined.

Using this screening, the net food per capita in the Canton of Bern has been calculated for three zones. From table 10.1 we may conclude that the canton was self-sufficient on a per capita basis. Agricultural production in 1847 would even have met the 1973 FAO/WHO recommendations (von Blanckenburg, 1986). In the mid-nineteenth century, food requirements may have been lower than today considering the large proportion of children under 15 and the smaller statures of adults. On the other hand, the active population had to provide more physical work, in particular during the harvest peak. On balance, however, there is no doubt that food production was adequate. This finding contradicts the argument of contemporaries and historians who have interpreted the large imports of food in 1847 in terms of deficient domestic production. It may be concluded from figure 10.1 that in ordinary years imports and exports of food alternated according to the outcome of the harvests.

Within the canton considerable contrasts emerge between ecozones. Food resources per capita were diminishing according to altitude; production

Table 10.1 Net food production per capita in the canton of Bern, 1847

Ecozone	Kcal (total)	Grain (%)	Tubers (%)	Dairy (%)	Fruit (%)	Meat (%)	Other (%)
Kornland	3,150	42	20	21	10	4	3
Intermediate	2,500	34	20	26	14	5	1
Alpenland	2,080	6	26	49	8	9	2
Canton	2,750	36	21	26	11	5	1

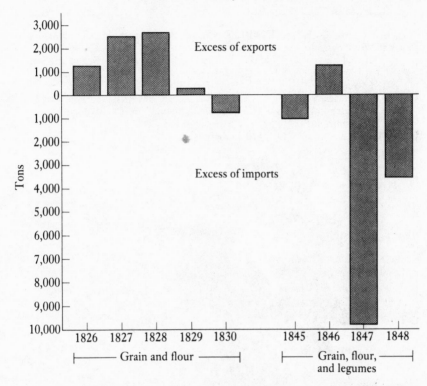

Figure 10.1   Balance of trade for selected commodities, 1826–1830 and 1845–1848

in the Kornland was abundant, while the Alpenland was on the verge of undernutrition. Outside the alpine region the central pillar of production was grain. Tubers (primarily potatoes) accounted for only one-fifth of the calories. Even in the Alpenland their contribution to the diet was not so paramount as is often believed. This finding must be borne in mind when investigating vulnerability to pests and climatic fluctuations. With increasing altitude the proportion of dairy products and meat increased at the expense of grain. In interpreting meat production in the Alpenland, we have to consider that animals often were sold for cash instead of being slaughtered. Therefore the figure of 9 percent in table 10.1 may be misleading in terms of meat consumption.

At the district level contrasts were still more pronounced (see figure 10.2). In the districts of Courtelary, Biel, and Bern industry had already taken root. The capital, Bern, was also a center for services. Thus production

AARB Aarberg   INTRL Interlaken   O-SIM Obersimmental
AARW Aarwangen   KONO Konolfingen   SAAN Saanen
  BI Biel   LAUF Laufen   SCHW Schwarzenburg
BUER Büren   LAUP Laupen   SEFT Seftigen
BURG Burgdorf   NEV La Neuveville   SIGN Signau
COURT Courtelary   NID Nidau   TRACH Trachselwald
ERLA Erlach   N-SIMM Niedersimmental WANG Wangen
 FRB Fraubrunnen   MOUT Moutier
FRUT Frutigen   O-HASLI Oberhasli

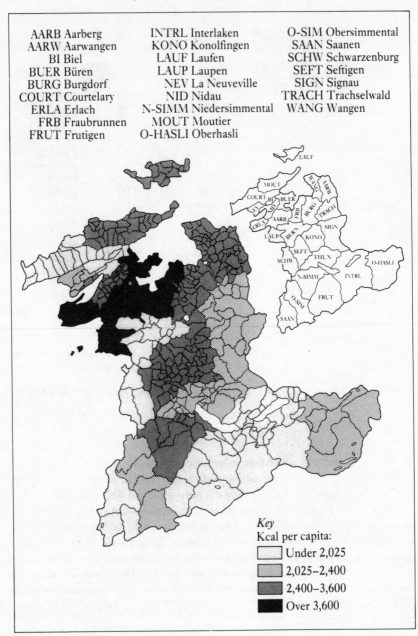

Key
Kcal per capita:

- Under 2,025
- 2,025–2,400
- 2,400–3,600
- Over 3,600

Figure 10.2   Net food production, 1847

figures in those districts do not mirror food standards. In the remaining districts, however, where agriculture was by far the dominant activity, food production may be interpreted as a fair proxy for gross national product. In the rich districts in the lowlands (Aarberg, Büren, Fraubrunnen, Erlach, Laupen), agricultural output per capita was almost double compared to the alpine districts of Saanen, Frutigen and Interlaken. The low figure of less than 1,800 calories for the prealpine district of Schwarzenburg points to widespread undernutrition. Gradients were steep even within the rich districts. This is illustrated from the production figure of 14,000 kcal for the tiny community of Ballmoos which consisted of five large farms only.

The spatial distribution of stored food is represented in figure 10.3. For computing the numerical basis of this map, the energy content of the food items in the list was aggregated at the community level after deducting seeds for the spring crops. The sums obtained were then converted to food-days on the basis of 2,500 kcal per capita. Finally, averages for each district, for the ecozones, and for the canton were obtained from community data. The map displays how long the population of each district could have survived on the basis of the food stored in private households if the total amount had been equally distributed.

The food which was hoarded in larders and storehouses would have been sufficient to sustain the entire population of the canton for 117 days – until the next harvest. This corroborates the finding that the population was far from exceeding the limits of carrying capacity. The gradient between the belt of rich districts north of the capital and the Oberland is larger than the production figures would suggest. To some extent this is connected to the fact that dairy products except cheese were not included in the list. In the Oberland fresh milk accounted for a considerable proportion of the diet. Outside the Oberland the amount of food stored in the richest district (Fraubrunnen) compared to the poorest district (Schwarzenburg) was still twice as large as would be expected from production figures. This suggests that hoarding food was widespread for several years.

Grain accounted for the bulk of the stored food (76 percent). Smoked bacon and meat amounted to 12 percent, and cheese to 5 percent, whereas the share of potatoes was as low as 1.8 percent. Supposedly this crop had been eaten by the poor or fed to the pigs of the rich by that time of the year. Fruit, vegetables, and cattle to be slaughtered accounted for the remaining 5 percent. The other items were negligible. In the Alpenland cheese and meat were more important than grain. Based on long-term prices, the money equivalent of all food items listed in the inventory has been evaluated at almost ten million francs, whereas it was twice as much at the height of the dearth.

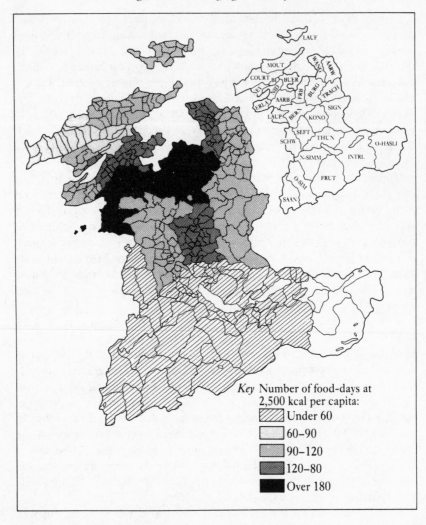

Figure 10.3   Food stored by private households, March 1847

Regional Gradients of Food Production

The regional gradients of food production and provisions in the mid-nineteenth century may be interpreted in terms of disparities in economic growth.

Net food production per capita in the 1760s (with seeds and duties deducted) has been estimated for a district in the Kornland (Büren) and

another one situated in the intermediate zone (Konolfingen). Grain production has been obtained from tithe records in combination with maplike
representations of land-use patterns (Frey and Stampfli, 1987). In both
districts agricultural output was already far from being inadequate. However,
the share of grain in the diet was considerably larger than around 1850.
Population more than doubled in both districts from 1760 to 1850 without
lowering per capita food production. On the contrary, food resources were
less vulnerable to climatic hazard, because they were more diversified. Also
the variety of food available to the average household was better balanced
in nutritional value. The share of milk in the diet had increased in particular.

   This increase in the quality and quantity of agricultural output is connected
to a more efficient use of existing resources, to the tapping of new sources
of solar energy, and to their combination in cascades, chains, and couplings
(Vester, 1976). Previously, yields within the three-field system had been
low on both the fields and the meadows because productivity was trapped
in a vicious circle. An appropriate starting point is to ask about limiting
factors.

   The low productivity is most frequently explained in the sources as
resulting from insufficient manuring. It is well known that nitrogen inputs
are the limiting factor for output in the vast majority of agricultural systems
(Postgate, 1980:165). Contemporary observers noted that manure was in
short supply because the number of cattle was too low. This was seen as
resulting from a shortage of hay which was a consequence of the small
acreage of meadows. This line of argument was highly political. In order to
secure the revenue from tithes paid in grain, land-use was laid down in
government records for every lot. Fields could not be converted into
meadows without the consent of the central authorities, the owners of the
title, and the village community affected by a decrease in temporary pasture.
Decisions to abolish this system were taken little by little by the communal
assemblies after the institutional barriers had been removed at the cantonal
level (Pfister, 1984).

   In order to fully use the dung potential of the livestock, covered basins
were built below the stables in which the dung-water was collected. It was
carried to the meadows, at first on people's backs, later on special horsedrawn
containers (Hauser, 1974). Progress in manure farming was accomplished
by keeping the livestock stabled all year round. As a consequence, more
manure could be recycled to the fields, and it was carried out more
frequently, which reduced nitrogen losses. In addition, new sources of solar
energy were tapped. Varieties of legumes such as clover were sown into the
fields and fallows: these plants are known for having a higher rate of
photosynthesis than grain (Kleiber, 1967:278) and for obtaining nitrogen
from the air by biological fixation − the fixation rate of clover amounts to

300 kg per hectare a year (Postgate, 1980:167). This additional supply of nitrogen allowed more land to be brought into cultivation: the fallow was abolished and the commons were converted into potato fields for the poor burghers. The energy efficiency of milk production also increased markedly because more fodder of a higher nutritive value was obtained per animal. In order to preserve the milk in a form which could be marketed, large-scale cheese manufacturing was introduced from the 1830s on. Soon it became the dominant rural industry in the canton.

We may conclude that food production was substantially enlarged by improving the efficiency of the existing flows of energy and matter. Because the more intensive production required additional inputs of labor, food production and population growth were positively related in a self-reinforcing process for some decades.

In the Alpenland, population growth was accompanied by pauperization and food shortage from the late eighteenth century. The number of cows per capita fell by one-third and the number of goats by one-quarter from 1790 to 1847. This decline suggests that the carrying capacity for cattle was at its limits. Population grew on the basis of the potato. In 1847 the net yield of potatoes was 77 percent higher than that of grain. It was estimated from the acreage planted in 1847 that the switch from grain to potatoes may have provided food for 11,000–12,000 more people. This is equivalent to 26–8 percent of total population growth registered between 1764 and 1850. Whether food for the remaining 72–4 percent was obtained at the expense of overall food standards deserves further analysis.

In the district of Schwarzenburg also the economy was deteriorating during the first half of the nineteenth century. The number of cattle per household declined from the 1830s; mortality was rising in the same period. Up to 1847 a Malthusian situation had developed, challenging the carrying capacity of the land.

The Vulnerability to Climate

The history of hunger is in the main linked to production losses brought about by natural hazards exceeding the capability of the society to buffer such losses. We have therefore to consider the severity of meteorological impacts and the vulnerability of the societies concerned. For each of those two major components the approach is different. Climate hazards may be assessed by comparing meteorological variables and agricultural ones across time. Vulnerability to climate hazard is analyzed by comparing the buffering capacity and the resilience of agrosystems and societies in different regions – that is, in the spatial dimension.

A proper assessment of meteorological impacts would require separate crop–weather models for the most important food resources. However, the data are not sufficient for this kind of approach. Instead the analysis is restricted to the meteorological vulnerability of grain and milk production, which were the two most important food resources in the canton.

Regarding grain harvests, it is crucial to disentangle losses related to quantity and quality. In the German-speaking part of Switzerland, the most deficient winter grain harvests are connected to extreme cold spells and a prolonged snow-cover in the months of March and April. Qualitative losses are connected to long wet spells during harvest time. In wet midsummers the ears sprout, the flour content of the crop is deficient, and the moisture content is high. During the following winter the grain will be affected by mold and insects. Losses in storage could be as large as one-third of a harvest (Pfister, 1984).

Likewise the meteorological vulnerability of dairy production depends very much on the quality and quantity of hay produced. During the winter months daily hay rations fluctuated according to the end and the beginning of the growing season, which is a function of temperatures in late autumn and spring. The energy value of hay depends to a great extent on weather conditions during the harvest period. Losses are rather small in a dry spell. However, if the hay is exposed to rain for several consecutive days, this reduces the raw protein and energy content of the hay to one-third or less of what would be expected. Milk production and grain production are therefore both sensitive to cold springs and wet midsummers (Pfister, 1984).

In order to compare meteorological impacts to grain price fluctuations from the sixteenth century on, a model was built which included the most important meteorological hazards. It can be demonstrated from this model that most of the well-known famines from the sixteenth century to the coming of the railway were connected to hazard constellations that included cold springs and wet mid-summers (Pfister, 1988). In the nineteenth century this pattern underlies the well-known European famine of 1816–17 (Post, 1977) and the less severe subsistence crisis in the early 1850s.

Vulnerability of food production in the long term is related to the frequency of crop failures. In areas which, from their natural environment, are marginal for a crop, the probability of a poor harvest is high. Moreover, in the case of an overall harvest failure, losses in those regions tend to be highest. The probability of grain harvest failures in Switzerland from excess rainfall has been assessed for the twentieth century (Jeanneret and Vauthier, 1977). Based on this data, the vulnerability of food production is demonstrated for those parishes where the percentage of grain from the total amount of gross calories produced (including the grain fed to animals, but without the amount required for seed) exceeded 45 percent in 1847 (see figure 10.4).

In most parts of the Kornland grain harvests were likely to fail every ten years on average. The zones of high risk (above 25 percent) are located in the uplands on the eastern and western fringes of the grain-producing area.

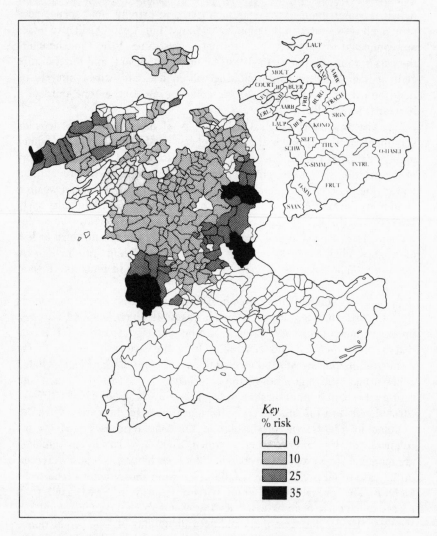

Figure 10.4   The risk of harvest failure in the grain-growing regions computed from meteorological data for 1901–1960

A figure of 25 percent represents a harvest failure in every fourth year. Nevertheless, grain was still the dominant staple food in some of these regions. This suggests that the crop mix was not adapted to environmental conditions. Given the great population pressure and the high wetness risk we would expect a larger share of potatoes in those areas, because this crop was known to be far more productive and less vulnerable to wet spells during the harvest than grain. The reasons for this paradox are far from being clear. It seems that the high risk of harvest failure is directly related to demographic crises.

The Demographic Impact

Taylor points out that "synergism between common infections and malnutrition probably accounts for more mortality, morbidity, and reduced growth and development than any other combination of factors" (1983:486). On the other hand it must be admitted that several infectious diseases are hardly or not clearly related to nutritional variables (Bellagio Conference, 1983). Also in the case of the European mortality crisis of the 1740s, which has been very carefully analyzed by Post (1985), the links between the shortage of food and epidemic disease proved more social than nutritional, owing more to social disarray and welfare crises than to sharply lowered human resistance to epidemic disease. This must be kept in mind in interpreting the results.

The data which underlie figure 10.5 have been created in the following way. As the first step, average mortality was computed for clusters comprising five years each over the nineteenth century. In the second step positive or negative deviations from the preceding cluster were calculated. Figure 10.5 displays deviations for the period 1851−5 in which the classical impact constellation of cold springs and wet midsummers occurred (Pfister, 1984).

To some extent the zones of high excess mortality coincide with those in which a high percentage of food was at risk in very wet midsummers. The figure for the poorhouse of Schwarzenburg (+38) is by far the highest in the canton. There, at least, excess mortality was directly related to famine conditions, as can be concluded from the sources (Leuenberger, 1987). On the other hand the zone of high mortality (more than 18 percent above the preceding period) includes rich districts such as Fraubrunnen and Büren and also the district of Bern. Conditions in the Oberland, however, were near normal though per capita food standards are known to have been low.

The analysis of fertility patterns is more conclusive. Le Roy Ladurie (1975) has demonstrated how food shortage might lower effective fertility by increasing the incidence of spontaneous abortion or by inducing temporary amenorrhea and sterility. In the canton of Bern, where data are available

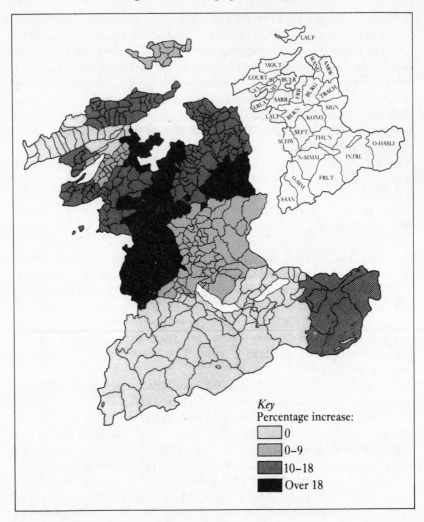

Figure 10.5   Excess mortality (deaths per thousand) in the districts for 1851–1855 compared to 1846–1850.

from 1700, slumps in the birth rate are good indicators of dearth at the district level. In this respect the severe famine of 1816–17 yields a clear-cut pattern (see figure 10.6).

This time too, the uplands at the western and the eastern fringe of the canton were hit hardest. Also the vulnerability of the Oberland was lower than would be expected from the production figures. On the other hand the impact was slight in the wealthy districts north of the capital.

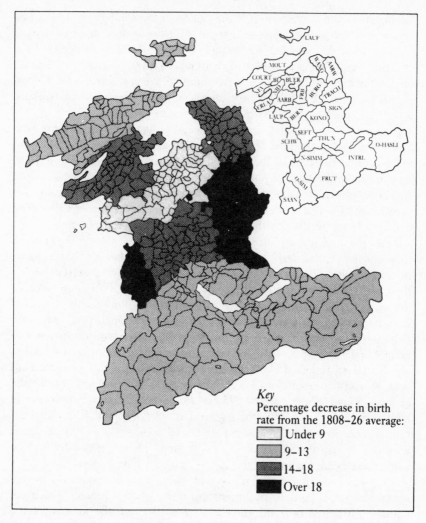

Figure 10.6   Deficits in the birth rate during the crisis of 1817

Food Poverty

Basically an inventory of stored food at the household level should allow
one to assess the importance of food poverty. This term has been defined
as a situation in which a particular household cannot obtain supplies of
food that are adequate to meet the needs of all its members (see chapter 1).
However, households without food provisions are only occasionally listed in

the inventory which was set up in the canton of Bern in March, 1847. The reason is obvious: the officers charged with the collection of data were likely to know the poor families in their community. Thus they spared the effort of walking long distances to visit empty larders. Fortunately data on the total number of households per community are contained in the federal census of 1850. A reliable proxy for the number of households without provisions could be obtained by merging the two statistics.

Figure 10.7 displays the size of the social group made up of those who had never had stored food at all, those who had run out of it earlier, and those who, at the time of the inquiry, had provisions left for five days or less, mostly in the form of potatoes. The number of people per household has been obtained from the federal census of 1850. The figures for percentage of overall population are adjusted to reflect the fact that poor households are smaller on the average than the cantonal norm.

More than one-third of the population in the canton was on the verge of subsistence in spring 1847 (the city of Biel is not conclusive in this respect, because most of its population relied on the market, and stored food is therefore not a meaningful indicator of poverty there). This figure exceeds the official poor statistics because it also includes households that lived from hand to mouth without getting poor relief. The high percentages for Schwarzenburg and Frutigen are not surprising given the insufficiency of agricultural production. The poor nutritional standards in those two districts are also clearly reflected in the military records: at the end of the nineteenth century recruits from those two districts were still the smallest in the canton (*Schweizerische Statistik, 1892*). But a considerable proportion of have-nots is also revealed in the region north of the capital, where agricultural production and the amount of stored food on a per capita basis exceeded by far the needs of the population. These results demand an assessment of inequalities in the food standard within communities.

The social distribution of the stored food has been estimated from a sample of 5,752 households originating from 20 communities which are equally distributed over the three ecozones. Because the figures for the Kornland and for the intermediate zone are very similar the graphical presentation is restricted to the Kornland (figure 10.8) and the Alpenland (figure 10.9). On the right side of each graph households are classified according to the size of their food provisions: the have-nots are contained in group 0; the have-littles (with food for 60 days or less) in group 1; the "middle class" (owning stored food for 60 to 120 days) in group 2; the well-off (with resources for more than 120 days) in group 3. The left side of the two graphs displays which percentage each class owned from the total amount (100 percent) of stored food in the community.

The amount of provisions is a good yardstick for the size of holdings in

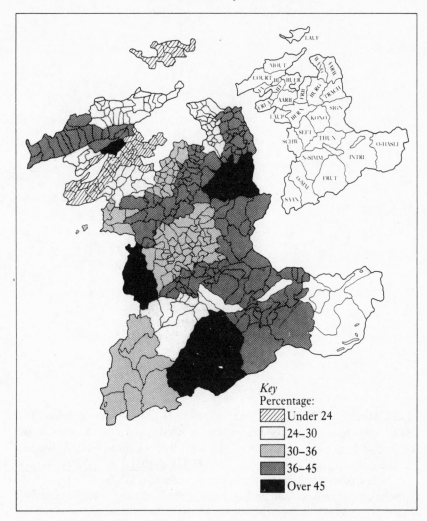

Figure 10.7   Percentage of population with stored food for five days or less, March 1847

an agrarian society in which entitlement for food is rooted in the ownership of land. For one large community for which the acreage of land sown and the amount of grain stored are both known for 1757 a coefficient of correlation of 0.84 has been obtained from the two variables (Pfister, forthcoming).

Much like many regions of France, the Swiss Kornland was a country of

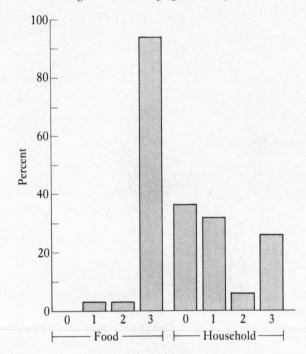

Figure 10.8   Social distribution of stored food in the Kornland zone, March 1847

small farmers and cottagers. Pierre Goubert (1960) has demonstrated that there was a fundamental dichotomy in the rural population of *ancien régime* France. A minority was "independent," that is, resilient to climatic hazards or even able to sell a surplus on the market during a dearth. As may be concluded from the sample, this class amounted to a quarter of the rural population in the Kornland and in the intermediate zone. Jeremias Gotthelf has expressively described the wealth of these farmers in his novels. To a considerable extent it consisted in food items, textiles, and commodities which were habitually hoarded in storehouses and shown to visitors as a status symbol. Storehouses were set apart from the main buildings so they would not be destroyed in a fire. The figures in figure 10.8 suggest that on average this class of prosperous farmers hoarded an astonishing 94 percent of the food resources in a community. Grain was by far the dominant item (80 percent). Meat, probably pork, accounted for a quarter of the stored food in the two intermediate groups.

The "middle class" of self-sufficient farmers was very small. Their

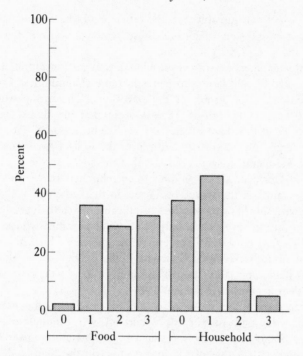

Figure 10.9   Social distribution of stored food in the Alpenland zone, March 1847

degree of self-sufficiency fluctuated according to the size of the harvest. In good years they could sell food on the market whereas they had to buy part of it in a dearth.

Two-thirds of the population were economically "dependent." They had to rely on wage labor in order to support their families. Within this class two groups may be distinguished: the so-called "Tauner" (Mattmüller, 1980) on the one hand, small peasants, day laborers, and craftsmen, who owned some source of food production, a plot of land, a cow, or a couple of goats. The landless, on the other hand, whose access to food was barely adequate in normal times, would entirely depend on poor relief and soup kitchens during a dearth. Without a minimum of social security, chronic undernutrition would then turn into acute famine.

The share of this lowest class increased from the late eighteenth century, as may be concluded from table 10.2. In two of the three communities listed, the percentage of the have-littles or have-nots grew by almost 50 percent from the late eighteenth century, while their share of the arable land diminished considerably. On the other hand, the number of wealthy families decreased somewhat, but those who survived in this struggle increased the size of their holdings.

In the Alpenland, ownership of stored food was less concentrated. Welfare institutions had bought large provisions in some communities. Their share was accounted to the group of the have-nots. The group who owned provisions for 1 to 60 (group 1) days accounted for almost half of the households. Also the share of the "self-sufficient peasants" (group 2) was somewhat larger. By contrast, the group of the well-off was only one-fifth that of the Kornland. It seems obvious that the social gradient was smaller than in the Kornland. This finding is corroborated by Netting's (1981) remarkable study on the village of Törbel in the canton of Wallis. In this place the ownership of cattle was the key indicator of wealth. It encompassed a range from one to seven cows only. The small peasants, who had one to three cows each, owned 75 percent of all animals. Households without cows seem not to have existed. Likewise in the lower Engadin almost every household had some land, though differences in wealth were more pronounced than in Törbel (Mathieu, 1987).

To what degree are these case studies conclusive for the Bernese Alpenland? Many people in the Oberland were undoubtedly undernourished. But obviously their resilience to subsistence crises was considerably higher than that of the lowest strata in the Kornland. Was this related to a kind of shared poverty, to a more efficient system of poor relief, or to a better adaptation of their agrosystem to climatic hazards? No conclusive answer can be given at the moment.

Table 10.2 Changes in landownership in three communities of the canton of Bern from the late eighteenth to the mid-nineteenth century

Community[a]	A: % of households below 1 ha and landless	A: % of arable	B: % of households above 5 ha	B: % of arable
Wo 1801	39	2.5	15	60
Wo 1847	63	1.8	10	55
Wi 1763	36	4.0	14	40
Wi 1866	52	3.1	10	50
Gh 1796	40	5.8	18	37
Gh 1847	57	1.1	11	29

[a] Communities: Wo = Worb Wi = Niederwichtrach Gh = Grosshöchstetten.
Source: Frey and Stampfli, 1987.

Food Deprivation

Food deprivation on the individual level can hardly be measured in the past. In this respect the historian has to rely on descriptive evidence. For the canton of Bern the novels of Jeremias Gotthelf are the best source. Riedhauser (1985) has compiled the passages in Gotthelf's work which refer to food and drink. Some of them point to disguised malnutrition in the lower strata.

In poor households, potatoes and turnips (*Rüben*) were the staple food: bread was liked as a dessert on Sundays. Coffee was a common drink. Often milk had to be bought from farmers in the neighborhood. The diet of the poor seems to have been low in fat: butter was a scarce resource, lard an object of aspiration, a symbol for something unattainable.

Gotthelf's descriptions leave no doubt that a gradient in food standards existed even within the household of wealthy farmers. Special dishes such as roasted meat or eggs were a privilege of the farmer and his wife in many houses, while lard was used sparingly and even then not by the servants. This explains why the qualities of a master's wife were often judged from the fat content of her roast potatoes.

Conclusions

Famines are known to be triggered by exogenous natural factors such as climatic fluctuations and human factors such as war, either isolated or in combination. In interpreting the data we should compare the severity within the area under investigation. In the case of the canton of Bern cold springs and wet midsummers were the most important elements of meteorological hazard. Within the canton those regions were hit hardest in which the crop mix was not sufficiently adapted to this kind of environmental stress and where the social buffers were inadequate.

Within the canton the coexistence of hunger and plenty has been demonstrated on three levels of analysis:

A regional gradient existed between the lowlands and the highlands; it was still more pronounced between districts within the Kornland region.

A social dichotomy was shown to exist at the level of the household. It was inversely related to food production. The gap was widest between wealthy farmers and the landless in the Kornland. In the Alpenland, where average nutritional standards were poorer, the social stratification was more balanced.

Variations in food standards at the level of the individual within a given household are mentioned by Gotthelf in his novels, showing a difference between masters and servants.

A limited leveling between areas of plenty and areas of scarcity and between social classes was attempted by the political elites, through the importation of food and the creation of soup kitchens. These measures aimed to prevent disorder, mass starvation, and mass migration. It may be misleading to relate such measures solely to a general insufficiency of food production. The unique BERNHIST databank provides an opportunity to compare these particular areas in population and environment as well as in production.

REFERENCES

Bellagio Conference 1983: The relationship of nutrition, disease, and social conditions: A graphical presentation. *Journal of Interdisciplinary History*, 14, 503–6.

Bourke, A. 1984: Impact of climatic fluctuations on European agriculture. In Hermann Flohn and Roberto Fantechi (eds), *The Climate of Europe: Past, Present and Future*, Dordrecht, 269–312.

Fischer, Hans 1963: *Dr. med Rudolf Schneider, Retter des westschweizerischen Seelandes.* Bern.

Frey, Walter, and Stampfli, Marc 1987: "Lieber schmale Bissen essen, als bei strenger Arbeit wohl zu sein." Die demographische, ökonomische und soziale Entwicklung in den bernischen Aemtern Büren und Konolfingen zwischen den 1760er und den 1880er Jahren. Lizenziatsarbeit, Historisches Institut der Universität Bern.

Goubert, Pierre 1960: *Beauvais et le Beauvaisis de 1600 à 1730.* Paris, 2 vols.

Hauser, Albert 1974: Güllewirtschaft und Stallmist—zwei grosse Erfindungen der Landwirtschaft. *Schweizerische landwirtschaftliche Forschung*, 13, 15–26.

Hildebrand, Bruno 1860: *Beiträge zur Statistik des Kantons Bern, im Auftrage der Berner Staatsregierung herausgegeben.* Vol. 1. Bern.

Jeanneret, F. and Vauthier, P. 1977: Kartierung der Klimaeignung für die Landwirtschaft. *Jahrbuch der Geographischen Gesellschaft Bern*, Beiheft 4.

Jonsson, U. 1981: The basic causes of hunger. In *United Nations University Supplement to the Newsletter*, 5, 1.

Kaplan, Steven L. 1977: *Bread, Politics and Political Economy in the Reign of Louis XV.* The Hague, 2 vols.

Kleiber, M. 1967: Der Energiehaushalt von Mensch und Tier. Ein Lehrbuch der Tierenergetik. Hamburg.

Le Roy Ladurie, Emmanuel 1975: Famine amenorrhea (seventeenth– twentieth centuries). In Robert Forster and Orest Ranum (eds), *Biology of Man in History*, Baltimore, 163–78.

Leuenberger, Peter 1987: Armennot und Armenverwaltung im Amt Schwarzenburg, 1830–1860. Lizenziatsarbeit, Historisches Institut der Universität Bern.

Mathieu, Jon 1987: *Bauern und Bären, Eine Geschichte des Unterengadins von 1650 bis 1800*. Chur.

Mattmüller, Markus 1980: Bauern und Tauner im schweizerischen Kornland. *Schweizer Volkskunde*, 70, 49–64.

Mitteilungen des kantonalen statistischen Bureaus 1883ff. Bern.

Mokyr, Joel 1985: *Why Ireland Starved: A quantitative and analytical history of the Irish economy, 1800–1850*. London.

Netting, Robert 1981: *Balancing on an Alp: Ecological change and continuity in a Swiss mountain community*. Cambridge.

Parry, Martin L. 1978: *Climatic Change, Agriculture and Settlement*. Dawson.

Pfister, Christian 1984: *Das Klima der Schweiz von 1525–1860 und seine Bedeutung in der Geschichte von Bevölkerung und Landwirtschaft*, 2 vols. Bern.

Pfister, Christian 1988: Fluctuations du climat et prix céréaliers en Europe, XVIe–XXe siècle. *Annales ESC*, 43, 25–54.

Pfister, Christian and Kellerhals, Andreas forthcoming: Bevölkerung, Verwaltung und Versorgung in Landgericht Sternenberg. In *Berner Zeitschrift für Geschichte und Heimatkunde*.

Pfister, Christian and Schüle, Hannes 1989: BERNHIST – a laboratory for regional history. Building up a dynamic data-basis for the spatial analysis of population, economy and the environment in the canton of Bern (Switzerland) 1700–1980. In Denley, Peter et al. (eds), *History and Computing II*, Manchester, 280–5.

Post, John D. 1977: *The Last Great Subsistence Crisis in the Western World*. Baltimore.

Post, John D. 1985: *Food Shortage, Climatic Variability, and Epidemic Disease in Preindustrial Europe, the mortality peak in the early 1740s*. Ithaca, NY.

Postgate, J.R. 1980: The nitrogen economy of marine and land environments. In K. Blaxter (ed.), *Food-chains and Human Nutrition*, London, 161–86.

Riedhauser, Hans 1985: *Essen und Trinken bei Jeremias Gotthelf: Darstellung und Motivation des Rekreativen in Alltag und Fest*. Bern.

Schweizerische Statistik, 1892: Ergebnisse der Aerztlichen Recrutenpruefungen im Herbst, 1890. Schweiz. Statistik, Lieferung, Bern.

Statistisches Jahrbuch für den Kanton Bern, herausgegeben vom kantonalen statistischen Bureau, 1868–1876. Bern, 9 vols.

Taylor, Carl E. 1983: Synergy among mass infections, famines, and poverty. *Journal of Interdisciplinary History*, 14, 483–501.

Vester, Frederic 1976: *Urban Systems in Crisis. Understanding and Planning of Human Living Space: The Biokybernetic Approach*. Stuttgart.

von Blanckenburg, Peter 1986: *Welternährung, Gegenwartsprobleme und Strategien für die Zukunft*. Munich.

Part V
Hunger in the Recent Past

A global economy and worldwide communication have become a reality, and world hunger has become part of common knowledge, as the faces of famine have looked challengingly from the nightly news, and citizens of many countries have reached out to help with food aid. The Working Group focuses, in chapter 11, on themes of organization, entitlement, and information in the global food system. Carl Riskin documents poverty in modern China, and the little-known famine in China during the Great Leap Forward. Nevin Scrimshaw notes changes in the world's nutritional problems from the deprivation diseases such as scurvy and beri-beri in earlier eras to the present deficiency diseases resulting from lack of iron, vitamin A, and iodine, deficiencies pinpointed well enough to suggest ameliorative actions. And, finally, Amartya Sen restates his concept of entitlement: the view that hunger and famine must be seen as economic phenomena with economic solutions. Taken together, these chapters document the complexity of assuming national responsibility for self-sufficiency in a world of international interdependence, while the incongruity of hunger persists in a world of plenty.

11

Organization, Information, and Entitlement in the Emerging Global Food System

SARA MILLMAN, STANLEY M. ARONSON,
LINA M. FRUZZETTI, MARIDA HOLLOS,
ROSE OKELLO, AND VAN WHITING, JR

Since the Second World War, the scale on which humans organize to produce and distribute food, and to identify and fight hunger, has increased. Food-flows, whether as trade or aid, link populations on opposite sides of the globe. Such transfers are not new: witness the discussions in chapters 2, 4, 5, and 8 of the present volume. The current scale and pervasiveness of these transfers, however, are unprecedented. New features of the food system in the recent past include changes in the organization of production globally which increase both total production and interdependency, the proliferation of information about hunger, and shifts in the basis of entitlement in many settings. In this essay, we start by developing the concept of a global food system and argue that changes over the last several decades have made this concept an increasingly realistic one. We then explore its implications, both beneficial and detrimental, for hunger.

The Emerging Global Food System

In referring to a global food system, we mean simply that both inputs to the food system (such as seed, fertilizer, know-how) and food itself regularly cross national boundaries. Food production, processing, and distribution connect the world more and more. Previous chapters have reviewed the long history of food transfers from the countryside to centers of urban growth and from colonies to imperial powers. In more recent periods, the network connecting consumers with distant producers, and producers with each other, has continued to grow in scale and complexity.

The context in which this global system is emerging is one of broader social, political, and economic change and contrast. Only since the Second World War have we lived in a world consisting almost entirely of formally independent nation-states. With the creation of many new states and the consolidation of others, a new set of problems and opportunities arose. Within countries, the problems included both the physical and the cultural challenges of uniting diverse peoples in a single polity under central control. Initial failures to create a true national unit abounded, as did regional and ethnic conflicts. On the other hand, independent nations with their own governments and institutions took on a series of governmental functions, among them the control of hunger, and began to experiment with institutions to increase production of food and to manage, if not to eliminate, hunger. Between countries, relations of power and dependency are still affected by past histories of exploitation and domination. Countries are now often classified as developed or developing. The former, which include all the powers that had colonies within the last century or so, are the wealthier and more industrialized. The latter, also sometimes referred to collectively as the Third World, include most of the new states.

The general increase in interdependency is reflected in an increase in dependency on food imports. Thus, for the world as a whole, internationally traded food as a share of total output rose from 8 percent in 1961−3 to 12 percent in 1983−5 (FAO, 1987a:39). During the same period, imports as a share of total food supplies doubled from 5 to 10 percent for a set of 93 developing countries (excluding China) and from 4 to 8 percent for the European centrally planned economies, and increased from 12 to 16 percent in the developed market economies.

The expansion of food transfers over distance might also be inferred from the rapid increase over the last few decades, in almost every country in the world, in the proportion of the population living in urban areas. For the world as a whole, the percent urban rose from 29.2 in 1950 to 41.0 in 1985 (World Resources Institute, 1987:27); absolute numbers of people living in urban areas grew still more rapidly, since this shift in distribution was combined with rapid growth of world population. The flows of food from rural areas required to feed these urban multitudes are unprecedented in scale, and imply far greater increases in transfer of food over distance than are apparent when we merely consider imports and exports at the national level. The continuing world-wide trend of urbanization implies a decline in the proportion of the total population that can take part in agricultural production, and thus an increase in the proportion whose entitlement to food must be based on some factor other than their own production of it. In fact, declining proportions of the labor force in agriculture are common throughout the world. Not only large-scale transfers of food over distance but also reliance on forms of entitlement involving exchange are inevitable attributes of an urbanizing world in which decreasing proportions of people are directly involved in agriculture.

Exchanges of food have increased far beyond those required to simply move it from a farm to a distant kitchen. Multiple steps of processing as well as distribution may separate the food products we buy in a supermarket from the farms on which their ingredients were grown. Some processing of food has been necessary as long as people have wanted to eat perishable foods out of season, or to turn inedible raw materials into palatable foods (for example, detoxification of cassava or production of margarine from oilseeds). Additional processing is now dictated by the great distances separating producers and consumers: these distances take time to traverse, and foods that are highly perishable must somehow be preserved if they are to reach their destination in usable form. Modern food processing reflects a further elaboration of the division of labor: much of the preparation of food, as well as its production, is carried out commercially by specialists rather than within each consuming household. As such, it is intimately linked to the movement of women into formal employment and their declining availability for production within the household.

The interdependency of a global food system is evident in many ways. It is reflected in the fluctuations of grain prices in the US in conjunction with forecasts of harvests in the USSR, in shipments of food aid around the world in response to reports of famine, and in the concerns about the possible global environmental impact of the destruction of tropical forests in Latin America to increase pastureland for raising beef for US consumption (Myers, 1981). The global diffusion of technological innovations and consumption patterns demonstrates this increased interdependency. Televised images of starving children in Ethiopia, of flood victims in Bangladesh, and of the homeless in the cities of the United States communicate vividly the shared humanity of the hungry and the viewer. In each of these instances, information plays a central role. Forecasts of harvests are essential if shortfalls are to be made up by imports before they affect local food supplies, and if grain traders are to adjust prices in accord with this expected increase in demand. Media coverage of hunger events has done much to generate a popular sense of global interconnectedness and to increase the salience to individuals of developments and conditions far away.

Implications of this increasing interdependency for hunger are numerous. They include increases in total production for the world as a whole and in the ability to remedy local production shortfalls and provide kinds of food that cannot be produced locally. These gains, obtained through an increasingly complex system of exchanges, imply increased vulnerability to exchange problems, while the changes in diet and in production within localities associated with integration into the global food system are not uniformly beneficial.

Thus the underlying causes to which hunger must be attributed have shifted over time. Both production failures rooted in the natural environment and the effects of social structures and relations continue, as always, to play a role. However, our increasing ability to avoid or compensate for the impacts of variation in the natural environment, blocking their translation into hunger, implies both a reduced role for such environmental factors and a more dominant one for our social arrangements.

Increased Global Food Production

Several lines of argument suggest that increasing integration of the world food system should tend to favor production increases. The specialization in production permitted by trade may allow increases in quantity and perhaps also quality of food (and other goods) produced. For at least some kinds of goods, production can be organized more efficiently if it is done on a relatively large scale; the specialization of production permitted by international trade makes it possible to take advantage of such economies of scale. Expanded markets and the possibility of exchanging what one produces for other valued goods provide incentives for increased production. Further, well-developed international exchange and communication networks should facilitate the diffusion of any advances in productive technology.

According to the theory of comparative advantage, trade may improve the welfare of all regions, if each specializes in the product for which it is best suited. A variety of factors, including characteristics of the environment such as soil quality or rainfall patterns, and characteristics of the available labor force, determine which places can best produce which goods. In agriculture, for instance, this would imply a closer match of crops with ecological niches (and thus potentially increases in both quantity and quality of food produced) as compared to a strategy of local self-sufficiency that would require growing a range of crops in each location. For the pursuit of comparative advantage to be an optimal strategy for all countries, each must have a comparative advantage in the production of some good for which there is external demand. Furthermore, if constraints of land, climate, labor, or capital limit the advantage to small sectors, an export-oriented strategy may not support necessary imports. Similarly, if the comparative advantage is duplicated in many countries (as in those specializing in such major cash crops as cotton, tea, or coffee), a policy of pursuit of comparative advantage within each country may generate so much of the product that world prices plummet and import earnings for each country remain low. A final qualification is that net benefits to be gained from specialization in production and international trade are partly a function of the costs of international transfers. Sharp increases in shipping costs, for instance, would tend to make a strategy of local self-reliance more advantageous.

Increases in total world food production are apparent, not only in the rapidly expanding global population, but also in rising per capita food supplies. Thus, over the period 1961–3 to 1983–5, per capita food available for direct human consumption increased in both developing countries (from 2,320 to 2,660 calories per day) and developed countries (from 3,160 to 3,410 calories per day). Increases were smallest in the lowest-income countries (except China), and between 1979–81 and 1983–5 per capita food availability actually fell in 37 developing countries, mostly in sub-Saharan Africa (FAO, 1987a:27). This deterioration appears to have been a function of slow improvements (and in some cases even absolute decreases) in food production in this region, continuing rapid population growth, and weak demand abroad for exports these countries needed to sell to finance food imports. Nonetheless, for the world as a whole, food production since the Second World War has more than kept pace with population growth. Contrary to the expectations of Thomas Malthus (see chapter 1), exponential population growth has continued for the two centuries since he wrote without triggering the grim checks he saw as implicit in the assumed lesser growth potential of the means of subsistence. Some such limits may still lie ahead. Nonetheless, the trend over the last several decades has been one of modest progress rather than deterioration in overall food availability per capita for the world as a whole. If food were distributed equitably, current supplies would be more than adequate to provide an ample diet to all, although it would be one in which animal products are considerably less abundant than they now are in the diets of the developed countries (Kates et al., 1988:51). Of course, increases in per capita food availability do not guarantee any reduction in proportions of the population with inadequate access to food, although they would tend to favor such reductions.

The generally favorable trend in per capita food availability may be traced in part to expansion of the area of land under cultivation, and in part to sharp increases in production per unit of land. The latter may be attributable in part to specialization, although it is not clear how this component can be separated from the use of more productive technology. The application of Green Revolution technology has contributed to massive improvements in yields of many basic food crops in Asia and Latin America, as well as in the more industrialized regions. "Green Revolution" refers here to the cultivation of improved and more productive strains, generally bred in large part for their strong response to inputs of fertilizer, pesticides, and water, in combination with provision of these inputs. Development of improved strains reflects international cooperation in agricultural research, while the inputs of seeds, fertilizer, and pesticides are traded internationally on a large scale. While international impetus was necessary for the development and spread of these technologies, the major advances in their applications were accomplished by national bureaucracies charged with agricultural production rather than alleviating hunger per se.

Local Vulnerability Lessened

When food crop harvests fail in an isolated area, shortage is likely to result. The same consequence need not follow when linkages between areas permit large-scale transfers of food. The growth in international trade of food, combined with international food aid, has weakened the link between local food production failures and hunger, at least that based on food shortage. In sub-Saharan Africa, for example, the decline in per capita grain production of some 22 percent between 1965 and 1984 was associated with only about a 14 percent decline in per capita consumption (World Resources Institute, 1987: Figure 4.2) − still a distinct deterioration, but less than if sharp increases in imports, especially of wheat and flour, had not made up much of the deficit. As a crude indicator of trend in numbers at risk of famine, the populations of countries in which famine is reported may be summed by year and compared over time (Kates et al., 1988). The resulting "Famindex," displayed in figure 11.1, shows a downward trend. While food shortage is not the only cause of famine, improvements in capacity to avert potential food shortage surely deserve some credit for this pattern of progress.

Transfers of food over time, as well as transfers over distance, serve to blunt the impact of poor harvests. Storing up grain in good times is nothing new, of course; the seven fat years and seven lean years of the Biblical account refer to a pattern of alternate abundance and scarcity, and a strategy for maintaining consumption, repeated throughout human history. However, the global scale on which this now occurs is a departure from past experience. In 1988−9, largely due to severe drought in the US, world food consumption is expected to exceed production for the second consecutive year (USDA, 1988). In the absence of large stockpiles, consumption would inevitably have to fall along with production in such difficult years.

Food transfers take the form either of trade or of aid. In the former case, the recipient must pay for them; in the latter, the sender must find it worthwhile to donate them. In either case, the food must be transported

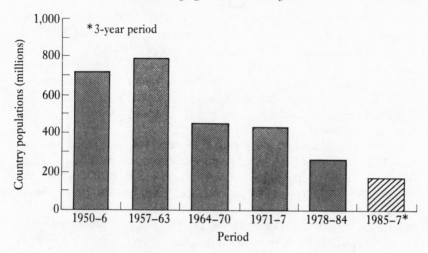

Figure 11.1 The "Famindex," 1950–1987: average annual population in countries with famine as reported in *The New York Times*

from the place where it was produced to the place where it is to be consumed. When food shortage does occur, in a world in which massive flows of trade and aid routinely respond to food deficit situations, we must seek the explanation at least in part in the imperfections of these response mechanisms. Thus, the uncertainties of trade, and the competing agendas and logistical difficulties complicating international aid, are among the causes to be considered when a food shortage occurs.

Increased Vulnerability to International Exchange Problems

The argument that specialization and trade contribute to increase in production for the world as a whole does not necessarily imply increased food production within every country taken separately. In fact, decreasing food production within some countries as global integration proceeds is to be expected in this scenario. Some countries, pursuing their comparative advantage, specialize in the production of non-food products to the extent that most of their food must be imported. Others focus efforts on producing foods particularly well suited to the local environment and exchange these in international trade for different foods (and other goods) produced more efficiently elsewhere.

The pursuit of comparative advantage (and thus increasing reliance on exchanging goods across national boundaries) has been advocated as an essential component of development efforts. An opposing view, however, argues that such specialization creates greater vulnerability to the vicissitudes of international trade. From this latter perspective, countries may do better to seek self-sufficiency in food production even if this strategy appears to pay less in the short term. For example, if exchange rates alter for the worse, if external demand declines, or if other countries establish protectionist barriers, a country that has chosen to specialize heavily in producing a narrow range of goods for export may find itself unable to finance essential food imports.

The increase in world trade of food over recent decades, which occurred in both developing and developed countries, was concentrated in the 1970s (FAO, 1987a:40). Much of the increase has been to further enrich the diets of the richer countries (for example, grain imports to the Soviet Union as an input to meat production). In the recent past, weak growth in demand in the developed countries for exports of the developing countries has limited the ability of the latter to finance imports. The rising costs of other essential imports have combined with the scarcity of foreign exchange to hold food imports down in the poorer developing countries.

For example, Zambia, whose exports of copper have generated most of its foreign exchange, borrowed to maintain social services and imports of food and capital goods when the price of copper started down in 1975; by now, export earnings are not even sufficient to service foreign debt (George, 1988) and no further credit is available. Shortages of fuel and spare parts (previously imported) have brought the nation's transportation system to a near standstill, impeding internal exchange and reducing productivity. Rising food prices, declining food sales, and increasing malnutrition indicate the relevance of these developments to hunger. Similar scenarios can be sketched in relation to declining world prices for major cash crops such as cotton, coffee, and tea, on which many developing countries rely heavily for foreign exchange.

Policies to promote "structural adjustment" of developing countries to the world-wide recession of the 1980s, largely involving still more emphasis on export production and sharp cutbacks in government spending to control inflation and external debt, have been blamed for increasing inequality in much of Latin America (George, 1988). Declines in the purchasing power of wages and increasing unemployment push more people into absolute poverty, while social services on which the poor depend are weakened. In some instances these austerity policies have withdrawn or limited those entitlement programs designed to insure that the poor could at least get enough to eat, such as subsidies of staple foods (tortillas, beans, bread, rehydrated milk) in Mexico. At the same time, the numbers needing such safety nets have increased.

When internal food production is insufficient to meet consumption requirements, and the country's trade position does not permit enough purchase of food on the international market to make up this deficit, international aid is the only recourse if food shortage is to be avoided. For such aid to be made available, need must be recognized and a donor must choose to respond to that need. Delays in both diagnosis and decision, compounded by the time required to actually implement a decision to help, may allow a period of deepening hunger even in instances in which aid mechanisms do operate. Logistical difficulties may impede timely delivery of supplies; transportation networks within many developing countries leave some areas inaccessible at least seasonally, even if delivery into the country from abroad goes relatively smoothly.

Both individual countries and international organizations act as donors of food aid. In the latter case, the international donors themselves are dependent on contributions from individual nations. The decision of a potential donor to give help is a function of a set of factors, including but clearly not limited to a diagnosis of need. The US "Food for Peace" Program, for example, also serves as a means to dispose of farm surplus. Furthermore, aid is often used as a diplomatic international weapon. Use of food as a weapon is not limited to situations of open violence; friends may be rewarded by access to surplus foods at concessionary rates, while enemies may be penalized by denial of food, despite their willingness to pay full market price. Official spokespersons for both the United States and the Soviet Union have acknowledged the role of foreign policy in their decisions about food aid and trade. These multiple agendas are not always consistent in their implications for policy, and sometimes keep aid from being provided despite clear need. Aid may be unavailable, or at least slow in coming, if potential donors are not friendly toward the needy country.

The largest remaining problems in avoiding severe food shortage, however, are related to more open human conflict. We continue to see food shortage employed as a military weapon. Famine is most persistent in war zones, such as Ethiopia in the 1980s (Clay and Holcomb, 1986), where attempts to deliver aid are often met with hostility from both sides, and where ongoing struggle disrupts production and distribution, and thus perpetuates shortage. In 1987, 17 countries with a combined population of 425 million experienced significant disruption of their food systems in war, either as an intentional act of aggression or incidental to the conflict (Kates et al., 1988:5).

Internal Change Associated with Integration into the Global Food System

Integration of previously isolated populations into the global food system has affected them in complex and variable ways. In addition to the increased reliance on international transfers discussed above, the local organization of production changes to take advantage of new opportunities in international trade and to apply imported technology. These changes in production in turn affect both supplies of food and arrangements on which access to food rest; in some settings, they may also alter the allocation of food within the household. Furthermore, the introduction of unfamiliar foods from abroad often alters dietary preferences. This set of effects adds up to changes in actual food consumption.

Food Poverty and the Organization of Production

Early applications of Green Revolution technology in some settings tended to marginalize small landholders. Because production with the new technologies is maximized by the simultaneous use of a package of costly inputs, the new opportunities favored those already well off. Although smaller farmers often did adopt the new varieties, they did so later. Rewards they won were often less than for earlier adopters, if only because the increased production had lowered prices (Lipton, 1985). In parts of Asia, small farmers have joined together in cooperatives to improve their ability to take advantage of the new opportunities; such initiatives seem to have led to wider sharing of the benefits of production increases. However, where the potential advantage-reinforcing effect of the new technology operated strongly, it may have been among the factors causing increasing landlessness among the formerly marginal farmers (Lappé and Collins, 1977). This in turn is among the factors encouraging the rapid urbanization viewed as so problematic by many Third World governments.

Where the inputs for Green Revolution production are provided by governmental allocation rather than market forces, a similar concentration of productivity increases may occur as investment is focused on geographic areas with the greatest agricultural potential and on crops for export.

Labor requirements per acre are higher with the modern varieties, so that employment opportunities on larger farms might be expected to increase with their adoption (Lipton, 1985). However, this need is often met by a shift to more mechanized productive technology, imported from settings where labor is expensive and other inputs relatively cheap, designed to minimize labor requirements. Thus, application of agricultural technology from the developed countries sometimes means that employment opportunities on the newly consolidated large farms are limited. As a result, the newly landless in rural areas may have little chance to replace subsistence agriculture with exchange of labor for the wages needed to purchase food. The shifting structure of production associated with integration into this system may generate food poverty for some by depriving them of a secure entitlement to food even as production is increased.

Internal Change: Intra-household Food Allocation

In addition to loss of entitlements for some households, the shift from subsistence agriculture to wage labor in large-scale commercial agriculture may affect hunger by altering the control over resources within the household. In much of Africa, women have traditionally played a central role in subsistence agriculture and have borne primary responsibility for seeing that their families are fed (FAO, 1987b; George, 1988). With the reorganization of production associated with new technology and export crops, women have tended to lose customary land access rights, yet wage opportunities and tenancy on rural development and irrigation projects have been less available to women than men. Reports from several countries suggest that malnutrition has increased as norms about how men should use the resources they control have failed to adjust for the fact that women no longer have resources permitting them to provide adequate food.

Evidence on the allocation of food within households is scant; the per-household data requirements to explore this issue are so great that researchers are generally restricted to small samples which are not necessarily representative of any larger population. Comparison of the results of the few existing studies suggests that no generalization applies across all settings (see useful reviews by Haaga and Mason, 1987; Harriss, 1986; Van Esterik, 1984). Thus, in one study parents somehow manage to feed their children adequately even while they go hungry themselves; in others, children are likeliest to be deprived when there is not enough to go around. Even within parts of South Asia where females are thought to be the targets of discrimination on many dimensions, some studies find no gender bias in food allocation and others find as expected that males are better fed than females. Comparisons of nutritional status measures or even mortality rates of males vs females, in the absence of any direct evidence on intra-household food allocation, sometimes do and sometimes do not show a female disadvantage where one is expected on cultural grounds; in this type of study differential access to medical care is a contending explanation, given the synergy between disease and malnutrition.

One observation that does seem to be consistent with a relatively high proportion of the intra-household food allocation studies, however, is that earners are favored. Paradoxically, in a household that cannot provide an adequate diet to all its members, a pattern of allocation favoring earners may actually be to the benefit even of those against whom it discriminates.

If earning power and thus household income is protected by this allocation, the total amount of food that income can buy will be greater than if distribution were entirely equitable, and a smaller share of a larger household supply may mean more food than an equal share of a smaller supply.

Internal Change: Dietary Preferences

The globalization of the food industry has also begun to change food preferences significantly. Traditional diets in many cultures incorporate food combinations and preparation methods that increase their nutritive value (Messer, 1984), such as the customary combinations of grain and legume that jointly provide more complete protein than if the two foods are eaten separately. These traditions, however they arose, do not generally rest on a scientific understanding of nutritional requirements and the composition of particular foods. Thus, the displacement of elements of the traditional diet by the introduction of new foods may lead to nutritional deterioration if the new foods do not provide the same nutrients. Shifts to more refined grain products, for instance, imply declines in intake of protein and B vitamins from grain which must be balanced by increases from other sources if dietary quality overall is to be maintained.

When new foods introduced are more expensive as well as less nutritious than those they displace, their impact may be especially damaging. The promotion of commercial infant formula in the Third World has been a source of particular concern, based on the recognized superiority of breast milk under even the most favorable conditions and on the increased difficulty of using alternative foods safely under conditions of poverty and poor sanitation.

Even if the new foods are good substitutes nutritionally for those they replace, their acceptance may entrain growing reliance on international trade, especially if they cannot be produced locally; reduced demand as a result for locally produced foods may lead to production declines, further reinforcing dependence on food imports. The acquired taste for wheat products, for instance, has been implicated in the ongoing economic crisis of Nigeria (Andrae and Beckman, 1985). During the oil boom of the 1970s, wheat imports to this major oil producer increased rapidly, while labor and other resources were withdrawn from agriculture and internal production of major food crops fell sharply. When oil revenues collapsed in the 1980s, dependency on continuing wheat imports made adjustment difficult.

Food processing raises a number of difficult issues in poor countries, which can be summarized as problems of appropriate technology and appropriate products. The requirements of food processing firms mean that they often work to upgrade the technological capabilities of their farmer suppliers, but just as with Green Revolution grains, the result is that big farmers are successful, while small farmers and laborers get left behind.

While the technology of food processing helps to preserve and enrich foods, it also tends to increase their cost and so to aim at a wealthier clientele: those able to convert their food needs into "effective demand." Advertising is a pervasive characteristic of the food processing industry, and this highlights the problem of appropriate products. Most would probably agree that Coca-Cola and Nestlé infant formula are well-made, acceptable products for those who can afford them. But when such products are massively promoted in poor countries, they are purchased by the poor as well as the rich. When this occurs, more nutritious (and often cheaper) foods may be displaced from the food budget. The technology of food processing holds promise for food preservation, but its marketing poses risks to those at the margin of subsistence.

Some shifts in diet introduced from abroad have clearly been beneficial. For instance, the introduction of iodized salt has reduced the incidence of iodine deficiency, responsible in its extreme form for goiter and cretinism and even in milder instances for some degree of mental impairment (see chapter 13). The new foods have been a mixed blessing to their recipients, with potential to improve diet and potential to disrupt it as well.

Managing a Complex Food System: The Role of Information

Both trade and aid depend on information as to where food is required and where it is to be found. Failure to diagnose a situation of incipient shortage, or reluctance to admit that help is needed, can prevent the mobilization of available resources.

A pair of sub-global examples serve to show the crucial role of information in a very large food system. These refer to famine in the world's two largest countries, China and India. China experienced what was probably the largest famine ever, generating famine-related deaths estimated at 17 to 30 million and a deficit of births of comparable magnitude, between 1958 and 1961. This is in contrast to the country's impressive progress against chronic malnutrition since the Revolution, evidenced in increases of an inch per decade in height of eighteen-year-old males between 1951–8 and 1979 (Jamison and Piazza, 1987:479). During the same period, India seems to have eliminated the crises of severe local shortage and elevated mortality so common in earlier times, although it continues to experience high levels of chronic malnutrition. The failures and successes of information systems are central to these two stories. We shall explore the problems that led to the Chinese famine, and the famine-prevention system which seems to have brought at least the crisis form of hunger under control in India.

The Case of China

In the great Chinese famine, the major causes appear to have been shifts in the organization of production which both reduced incentives for production and created misinformation on an enormous scale (Ashton et al., 1984; Peng, 1987). During the 1950s, agriculture was reorganized into progressively larger-scale collectives, while private plots and free markets in grain were abolished, effectively divorcing individual work effort and reward. A corresponding collectivization of consumption, as workers took their meals in large mess halls where they were encouraged to eat as much as they wanted, may have also led to overconsumption and consequently greater scarcity later, as traditional strategies of thrifty food management at the household level ceased to operate. As the Great Leap Forward progressed, collectives were encouraged to divert effort from agriculture to build up rural industry and services.

Underlying this policy of de-emphasizing agricultural production was a flawed information system, which generated vast overestimates of grain production for the nation as a whole, thus making it appear that cutbacks need not cause hardship. Production targets, set from above and influenced by political pressure as much as by any realistic assessment of what could be accomplished, were progressively inflated as they were applied to smaller and smaller production units. In turn, those responsible for submitting production statistics for aggregation were subject to strong incentives to report fulfillment or over-fulfillment of these targets. These inflated production reports led in the next round to still more unrealistic targets. Over time the statistics thus tended to depart further and further from reality; at one point provincial estimates of grain production summed to some 2.5 times the amount now considered to have been the actual national total. In response to this apparent abundance, cultivated acreage was reduced and workers were shifted from agriculture to other pursuits, while amounts of grain appropriated by the state to provision rapidly growing urban populations were increased. Total actual production of grain fell by some 30 percent between 1958 and 1960. Time series both of demographic indicators and of per capita grain availability estimates show that the severity and timing of the crisis varied widely across the country, but there is a general pattern of earlier and sharper crisis in rural areas as excess urban appropriation maintained tolerable conditions in the cities longer.

A range of natural catastrophes (drought, flooding, typhoons, plant disease, and insect pests) in 1959 and 1960 compounded the declines in production that would have been expected from this shift in effort. The total amount of land affected by these natural environmental problems in 1959, however, was no greater than that similarly affected in 1956 and 1957, before the crisis set in (Peng, 1987).

Further evidence for the official misapprehension of the situation lies in the continuation of large-scale grain exports — enough to provide 2,000 calories per day for 16 million people for two years — during fiscal year 1959–60. The situation remained largely unrecognized outside of China until early 1961, when offers of aid from the International Red Cross were made and rejected. Political issues in the acceptance as well as the provision of aid are apparent here: Ashton (Ashton et al., 1984) quotes China's foreign minister, Chen Yi, as "telling Japanese visitors to Peking that China would never 'stoop to beg for food from the US,'" and President Kennedy as rejecting the possibility of US aid on grounds that the Chinese "belligerent attitude" made a favorable response from them unlikely.

The Case of India

Mortality crises of famine have been conspicuous by their absence from India in recent decades, despite the continuing occurrence of climatic events comparable to those causing major dislocations in other settings, and in India itself in the past. McAlpin (1987), focusing on the situation in Maharashtra Province, identifies the essential features of drought policy there as early intervention based on local knowledge, relief in the form of employment that sustains incomes and contributes to development, rebuilding of agricultural/pastoral capital depleted by drought, organization of response by the government of the affected area, and gradual policy development incorporating the lessons of experience. It is noteworthy that this policy seeks to maintain entitlement, rather than assuming that simply shipping in food is a solution. The lesson may have been learned from earlier experience; Sen's analysis (1981) of the Bengal Famine of 1943, which caused an estimated three million deaths, suggests that entitlement failure may cause severe crises of hunger even in the presence of ample supplies of food.

The first task for an information system, in this view, is identification of potential crisis situations far enough in advance to permit action which will avert damage rather than merely responding to it. Local officials in India are responsible for monitoring early warning signs such as late or scanty rains, unplanted fields, rising grain prices, and unusual population movement.

To mobilize resources from higher levels of government, current developments must be contrasted with the usual situation; thus, time series of the same indicators are necessary.

The "watchdog" role played by a free press may also be central to India's good record of averting potential hunger crises in the recent past (Ram, 1986). Governmental bodies are often reluctant to recognize a problem, but aggressive reporting of even a single hunger death generates a public outcry which pushes the government to respond.

Once a problem situation has been identified, the next role for the information system is in exploring possible responses. Local officials are also responsible for developing lists of potential public works projects and for identifying persons who will need relief other than employment. Quick diagnosis and response keeps the situation from developing into a famine. With income maintenance, families avoid the need to sell assets which may push people into lasting food poverty when drought occurs in other settings. Public works programs which build up such infrastructure as irrigation systems or roads can leave localities well positioned to increase production once the drought is over, rather than in a state of disarray. Hunger and malnutrition persist on a wide scale in India, but severe, debilitating hunger and massive, widespread famine have been effectively controlled. Local implementation of this policy no doubt varies and may often fall short of protecting all those in drought situations from loss of any productive assets, but at least the famine crises of elevated mortality so common in India's history seem to be a thing of the past.

International Information Infrastructure

If information systems are central to the functioning of a food system as large and complex as those of the world's two largest countries, they are even more so for management of the emerging global food system. Information can help to lessen regional and national vulnerability to food shortage. Major actors in this system are prolific producers and voracious users of information.

Data on projected harvests around the world, for instance, are essential inputs both to trade and aid, allowing forecasts of the need for large-scale food transfers. The US Department of Agriculture assembles such information continuously and issues updates on a weekly basis. Information on factors in addition to those affecting expected harvests (such as refugee flows) which might contribute to food shortage is sometimes incorporated in the monthly bulletins of the Famine Early Warning System of the US Agency for International Development, tracking the situation in a limited number of famine-prone countries in Africa. Kinds of evidence on which these efforts draw range from accounts of individuals in the field, to weather reports, to satellite imaging which provides clues as to the growth of vegetation.

A number of organizations collect related information with respect to current food supplies. The Food and Agriculture Organization (FAO) of the UN maintains "food balance sheets," calculating amounts of specific foods available for each of almost all the world's countries. Required inputs include information on production, wastage, imports, exports, and stocks; results are often presented in summary form as per capita caloric availability within countries or regions. Based on FAO data, it has been estimated (Kates et al., 1988:3) that in 1985 30 percent of the world's population, or 1,485 million people, lived in countries in which per capita caloric availability was less than that required for health, growth, and productive work. Of the 46 countries included in this total, 29 are located in sub-Saharan Africa, eight in south and southeast Asia, and six in the western hemisphere.

Per capita caloric availability in turn is used by both the FAO and the World Bank to generate estimates of numbers of people in each country who cannot afford an adequate diet. These estimates draw also on definitions of caloric requirements (varying widely between the FAO and the World Bank) and on any available evidence on income distribution and income—food purchase relationships; the latter are extrapolated from other settings when direct measures for a particular country are not available. The World Bank calculated (1986) that in 1980 some 730 million people in 87 developing countries (excluding China) lived in households that were too poor to obtain the food energy they needed to work. The FAO food poverty estimate for 1983—5 of 348 million in 93 developing countries, again excluding China (ACC/SCN, 1987), is based on the lower caloric requirements to sustain growth in children and minimal activity in adults as opposed to work. Using either standard, the food poor live mainly in South Asia and Africa.

Nutrition surveys incorporating anthropometric measures of wasting and stunting of small children have been carried out in many developing countries, in some cases with international assistance. The World Health Organization compiles results of these studies, which provide clear evidence of the prevalence of child malnutrition and of variations in its prevalence within and between countries. Results are then extrapolated to countries for which direct measures of child malnutrition are not available. Estimated proportions of children underweight vary widely by region within the Third World, ranging from 6.4 percent for South America to 66.7 percent for South Asia (ACC/SCN, 1987).

In addition to these extremely large-scale efforts to generate information in comparable form for much or all of the world, a vast and rapidly growing literature addresses virtually every aspect of hunger. Ranging from investigations of the prevalence of specific deficiency diseases in some local population, to anthropological work on food habits, to discussions of the etiology of anorexia nervosa and bulimia in the developed countries, to agro-economic studies of the impact of technological change in particular settings, to theoretical discussions of food policy, the diversity and quantity of this work challenge any attempt at synthesis. Notable additions to the literature during this period include several vivid first-hand descriptions of starvation. Sorokin's discussion of the Russian famine of 1919–20, *Hunger as a Factor in Human Affairs*, although originally written in 1922, was suppressed at the time and first appeared in print in 1975 in the United States. Reports by a group of doctors of the starvation experience they were undergoing in the Warsaw Ghetto during the Second World War (Winick, 1980) and an experimental study at the University of Minnesota of starvation (Guetzkow and Bowman, 1946), for which conscientious objectors volunteered as alternative service, added to our understanding of the meaning of starvation to those experiencing it. Although some questions about hunger still cannot be addressed with existing data, the researcher faces the opposite problem with respect to some other issues: the amount of information is too great to process.

International Institutions in the Global Food System

A historically new development in this era is the emergence of international bodies dealing with issues of food production and distribution, and responding to situations of famine or chronic malnutrition, at a global level. These include, at the governmental level, a range of units of the United Nations system as well as regional organizations. In addition, the national governments of many countries maintain offices dealing with hunger abroad via trade and/or aid. In the private sector, transnational corporations dealing with various aspects of food production, processing, and distribution act to shape people's consumption aspirations through advertising. They are major actors in the global food system, often with resources in excess of those commanded by some of the nations with which they deal. Private voluntary organizations are a relatively recent entrant to the scene; individuals now have the option of attempting to deal with hunger in parts of the world they may never see through affiliation with internationally organized activist groups. Scientists work together in institutions such as the Consultative Group on International Agricultural Research (CGIAR) or the International Food Policy Research Institute (IFPRI) on collaborative studies of aspects ofthe global food system.

Public Organizations: Research and Development

Most of the intergovernmental system has grown up since the Second World War, although it began earlier with the League of Nations. Many units of the United Nations are involved in issues of food, distribution, and consumption. For some, such as the Food and Agriculture Organization (FAO), hunger is a central concern; for others, it is a focus because of its linkage to a somewhat different topic. The World Health Organization (WHO) and the United Nations Children's Fund, for instance, deal with hunger-related diseases and with mothers and children as especially vulnerable to hunger. In discussing the four international food organizations headquartered in Rome − FAO, the World Food Council (WFC), the World Food Programme (WFP), and the International Fund for Agricultural Development (IFAD) − Talbot and Moyer (1987) trace the multiplicity of units and overlap of functions to varied and changing coalitions and interests of the constituent countries. They argue that the structure, by providing channels through which the different blocs of countries may pursue their interests, facilitates the balancing of these interests. It may also broaden the set of countries participating, since a nation which objects to the activities of one body has several others from which to choose. Similar functions may be served by the multiplicity of other UN bodies addressing hunger, despite the apparent difficulty this multiplicity presents for the formulation and implementation of coherent policy.

In another major development, research has been stimulated and centralized by the creation of a series of autonomous agricultural research centers, under the general coordination of CGIAR. Beginning with the International Rice Research Institute in 1960, nine such centers had come into existence by 1976. Combined budgets grew from $6 million in 1968 to $85 million a decade later (Wortman and Cummings, 1978:129−31).

Research currently under way to develop new strains precisely tailored to particular ecological or commercial requirements through genetic engineering also involves much international cooperation. One strand of research seeks to develop varieties that will maintain yields under adverse environmental conditions without the dependency on expensive inputs of fertilizer, pesticides, and irrigation that has characterized much of the Green Revolution. If these efforts succeed, they may help to reduce the vulnerability to exchange difficulties that has resulted from dependence on imported inputs.

Internationalization of Normative Concerns

Freedom from hunger has gradually come to be more and more widely perceived as a basic human right. The notion that people should not have to go hungry has a long record in history, but over time both its application and the set of people considering themselves responsible for its implementation have broadened. Thus, in the Roman Empire, the powerful were expected to provide subsidized grain to citizens in times of scarcity, but non-citizens were not entitled to draw on this resource (see chapters 4 and 5). As famine came under control in Europe, national governments came to be seen as responsible for preventing famine within their borders (see chapter 8). It seems that people have always felt that humans should not starve, but not all were viewed as fully human. Over time, interpersonal boundaries defining that set with whom one can identify have become less restrictive. "Nationalization" in this sense has already occurred, but internationalization of normative concern has only just begun. As the list of intergovernmental organizations and the many private voluntary organizations discussed below demonstrates, much has been done along organizational lines. But little has followed in terms of funding: development assistance as a share of donor country economies has been shrinking rather than growing as needed (Sewell et al., 1985:16–17). With the development of the UN system after the Second World War, the idea of freedom from hunger as a basic human right was formally extended to all. The Universal Declaration of Human Rights of 1948 provides that "everyone has the right to a standard of living adequate for the health and well-being of himself and his family, including food" (quoted in Eide et al., 1984:164), and many subsequent UN statements have supported this principle.

Not only governmental and supragovernmental organizations are active in the fight against hunger. Increasingly individuals are seeking to intervene, sometimes at a local level but often in response to hunger far away. Much of this activism emerges around highly visible crises, and is quite episodic. For example, the various aid concerts of the last several years, triggered by famine which could be seen on the news in the United States and other wealthy countries every evening, brought forth an outpouring of support for relief efforts in sub-Saharan Africa from millions of people. This sort of disaster response does not solve any underlying problems, although it surely saves some lives; its significance lies partly in the simple fact that large numbers of people are accepting at least some limited responsibility as individuals to support the basic human right to freedom from hunger around the world.

Some activist efforts based on individual voluntary participation have been more sustained. For example, the consumer movement to control the promotion of infant formula in the developing countries eventually involved a coalition of over 100 groups working in 65 countries. Activities over more than a decade peaked with the Nestlé Boycott from 1977 to 1984. The campaign and the surge of public opinion it generated surely deserve much of the credit for the 1981 adoption by the World Health Assembly of the World Health Organization's suggested "Code of Marketing for Breast-milk Substitutes," subsequent regulatory legislation within many countries, and eventual voluntary agreement to comply by most of the major companies selling infant formula in the Third World. The Code, a nonbinding recommendation to member governments, restricts promotional practices thought to be misleading but does not limit the sales of infant formula.

The Hunger Project, started in 1977, has sought to engage individuals in action to end hunger, providing information about issues and initiatives "in a way to empower them to participate effectively in its solution" (The Hunger Project, 1987). A decade later, the organization claimed a worldwide enrollment of 5,200,000 individuals in 152 countries who had taken "personal responsibility for hunger and the end of hunger," and had sponsored educational and development activities related to hunger around the world.

Taken together, we find much to celebrate, as well as much to lament, on the normative front. Famine and hunger continue. But most national communities have accepted the moral imperative of eliminating hunger, at least of the life-threatening variety. And increasingly, both intergovernmental and private groups are organizing to develop and spread knowledge about hunger, and to begin to combat it.

Conclusions

The emerging global food system is a fact of life. Its implications for hunger are both positive and negative.

On the benefit side, we can count overall increases in productivity and in the variety of foods available to consumers throughout the world, and improvements in the ability to avoid shortage when local production shortfalls occur.

These benefits are gained through an increasingly extensive and complex array of exchange mechanisms, which are associated with their own problems and difficulties. Reliance on market mechanisms leaves nations and groups within nations vulnerable to loss of access to purchased food if demand for their own goods and services declines. A growing sense that enough to eat is a basic human right, reflected in welfare policies within countries and in programs of international food aid, is only partially translated into actual reductions in hunger. The practical difficulties of identifying situations in which aid is needed, and of actually delivering aid in a timely fashion, are compounded by conflicting economic, political, and humanitarian agendas.

Transfers of large amounts of food over long distances take time, so the ability of the system to deliver food to consumers when they need it is contingent on the availability of accurate advance information. The triumphs and failures of information systems play a central role in the recent history of famine, and the construction of an international information-gathering infrastructure is a noteworthy element of the attempt to manage the global food system.

The increasing scale and complexity of transfers of food and technology are continuations of a trend we have seen in earlier times as well. Unique to the recent past, however, is the emergence of international organizations to manage this complexity. These organizations represent public, private, and grass-roots interest in world-wide development. On balance, the process of globalization that has taken place in recent decades points towards the possibility of a global society in which hunger has been vanquished.

REFERENCES

ACC/SCN 1987: First Report on the World Nutrition Situation. United Nations Administrative Committee on Coordination, Subcommittee on Nutrition, November.

Andrae, Gunilla and Beckman, Bjorn 1985: *The Wheat Trap: Bread and underdevelopment in Nigeria*. London: Zed Books Ltd.

Ashton, Basil, Hill, Kenneth, Piazza, Alan, and Zeitz, Robin 1984: Famine in China, 1958−1961. *Population and Development Review*, 10, 613−45.

Baer, Edward 1983: An update on the infant formula controversy. *Studies in Family Planning*, 14, 119−22.

Clay, Jason W. and Holcomb, Bonnie K. 1986: *Politics and the Ethiopian Famine 1984−1985*. Cambridge, Mass.: Cultural Survival, Inc.

Eidie, Asbjorn, Eide, Wenche Barth, Goonatilake, Susantha, Gussow, Joan, and Omawale 1984: *Food as a Human Right*. Tokyo: United Nations University.

FAO 1987a: Agriculture: Toward 2000. Food and Agriculture Organization of the United Nations, Rome.

FAO 1987b: Women in African food production and food security. In J. Price Gittinger, Joanne Leslie, and Caroline Hoisington (eds), *Food Policy: Integrating Supply, Distribution, and Consumption*, Baltimore and London: Johns Hopkins University Press, ch. 7.

George, Susan 1988: *A Fate Worse Than Debt*. New York: Grove Press.

Grigg, David 1985: *The World Food Problem 1950−1980*. Oxford: Basil Blackwell Ltd.

Guetzkow, Harold Steere and Bowman, Paul Hoover 1946: *Men and Hunger*. Elgin, Illinois: Brethren Publishing House.

Haaga, John G. and Mason, John B. 1987: Food distribution within the family. *Food Policy*, May, 146−60.

Harriss, Barbara 1986: The intrafamily distribution of hunger in south Asia. Unpublished paper for WIDER Project on Hunger and Poverty; Seminar on Food Strategies, Helsinki.

Hopkins, Raymond F. 1987: Interests and regimes: The subjective dimension of international politics. Paper presented at the Annual Meeting of the American Political Science Association, November.

The Hunger Project 1987: A Shift in the Wind, 23.

Jamison, Dean K. and Piazza, Alan 1987: China's food and nutrition planning. In J. Price Gittinger, Joanne Leslie, and Caroline Hoisington (eds), *Food Policy: Integrating Supply, Distribution, and Consumption*, Baltimore: Johns Hopkins University Press, 467–84.

Kates, Robert W., Chen, Robert S., Downing, Thomas E., Kasperson, Jeanne X., Messer, Ellen, and Millman, Sara 1988: *The Hunger Report: 1988*. Brown University, Providence, R. I.: The Alan Shawn Feinstein World Hunger Program.

Kutzner, Patricia L. and Lagoudakis, Nickola 1985: *Who's Involved with Hunger: An organization guide for education and advocacy*. Washington, DC: World Hunger Education Service, fourth edition.

Lappé, Frances Moore and Collins, Joseph 1977: *Food First*. New York: Ballantine Books.

Lipton, Michael 1985: *Modern Varieties, International Agricultural Research, and the Poor*. Washington, DC: Consultative Group on International Agricultural Research, The World Bank.

McAlpin, Michelle 1987: Famine relief policy in India: Six lessons for Africa. Occasional Paper OP-87–2, The Alan Shawn Feinstein World Hunger Program, Brown University, Providence R. I.

McComas, Maggie, Fookes, Geoffrey and Taucher, George 1983: *The Dilemma of Third World Nutrition: Nestlé and the Role of Infant Formula*. Nestlé SA.

Messer, Ellen 1984: Anthropological perspectives on diet. *Annual Review of Anthropology*, 13, 205–49.

Myers, N. 1981: The hamburger connection: How Central America's forests become North America's hamburgers. *Ambio*, 10, 3–8.

Peng, Xizhe 1987: Demographic consequences of the Great Leap Forward. *Population and Development Review*, 13, 639–70.

Piazza, Alan 1986: *Food Consumption and Nutritional Status in the PRC*. Boulder, Colo.: Westview Press.

Ram, N. 1986: An independent press and anti-hunger strategies. Paper presented at the United Nations University/World Institute for Development Economics Research conference, "Hunger and Poverty: The Poorest Billion", 21–5 July.

Sen, Amartya 1981: *Poverty and Famines*. Oxford: Oxford University Press.

Sewell, John W., Feinberg, Richard E., and Kallab, Valeriana (eds) 1985: *US Foreign Policy and the Third World: Agenda 1985–6*. New Brunswick: Transaction Books.

Sorokin, Pitirim Alexandrovitch 1975: *Hunger as a Factor in Human Affairs*. Gainesville: University Presses of Florida.

Talbot, Ross B. and Moyer, H. Wayne 1987: Who governs the Rome food agencies? *Food Policy*, November, 349–64.

USDA 1988: *World Food Needs and Availabilities, 1988/89: Summer*. (August.) Washington, DC: Economic Research Service, United States Department of Agriculture.

Van Esterik, Penny 1984: Intra-family food distribution: Its relevance for maternal and child nutrition. Cornell Nutritional Surveillance Program Working Paper Series, No. 31.

Whiting, Van R., Jr 1985: Transnational enterprise in the food processing industry. In Richard S. Newfarmer (ed.), *Profits, Progress and Poverty: Case studies of international industries in Latin America*, Notre Dame, Ind.: University of Notre Dame Press.

Winick, Myron 1980: The Warsaw Ghetto starvation studies. *Centerpoint*, 4, 70–3.

World Bank 1986: *Poverty and Hunger: Issues and Options for Food Security in Developing Countries*. Washington, DC: The World Bank.

World Resources Institute 1987: *World Resources 1987*. New York: Basic Books.

Wortman, Sterling and Cummings, Ralph W., Jr 1978: *To Feed This World: The Challenge and the Strategy*. Baltimore: Johns Hopkins University Press.

12

Food, Poverty, and Development Strategy in the People's Republic of China

CARL RISKIN

In recent years China's leaders have laid much stress on the goal of raising living standards. "Socialism means eliminating poverty. Pauperism is not socialism, still less communism," according to Deng Xiaoping.[1] Part of the reason for this emphasis is the slowness with which living standards rose during the two decades before the beginning of the economic reform movement in the late 1970s. With continued poverty went chronic hunger, although the exact scope, location, and temporal ebb and flow of it are unknown. Nor do we know the whole story of the great famine that afflicted China in the period 1959–61, and about which some concrete information became available only 20 years later.

This paper offers an overview of China's development experience since the founding of the People's Republic in 1949, with emphasis on the influence of changing development strategy upon the food situation. Because so little precise information is available about the distribution of poverty, food, and hunger, even today when the Chinese government is collecting and releasing far more statistics than ever before, parts of the discussion of this particular subject are unavoidably impressionistic or deductive.[2]

Aggregate Food Supply and Nutrition

Food grains (which in Chinese statistics include soybeans, tubers at 5-to-1 weight ratio, and pulses) have consistently supplied some 86–9 percent of available energy and 80–5 percent of available protein (Piazza, 1983:17–18). Aggregate grain production grew by an average of 2.8 percent per year from 1952 to 1987 (table 12.1). On a per capita basis, food production averaged 0.9 percent growth per year over this period: the two decades

Table 12.1   Aggregate and per capita food grain production, 1952–87

Year	Aggregate output MMT^a	Per capita output (kg)	Year	Aggregate output MMT^a	Per capita output (kg)
1952	163.92	288.00	1970	239.96	293.00
1953	166.83	287.00	1971	250.14	297.00
1954	169.52	285.00	1972	240.48	279.00
1955	183.94	302.00	1973	264.94	300.50
1956	192.75	310.00	1974	275.27	305.50
1957	195.05	306.00	1975	284.52	310.50
1958	200.00	306.00	1976	286.31	307.50
1959	170.00	255.00	1977	282.73	299.50
1960	143.50	215.00	1978	304.77	318.50
1961	147.50	223.00	1979	332.12	342.50
1962	160.00	240.50	1980	320.56	326.50
1963	170.00	249.00	1981	325.02	327.00
1964	187.50	269.00	1982	354.50	351.50
1965	194.53	272.00	1983	387.28	379.50
1966	214.00	291.00	1984	407.31	395.50
1967	217.82	289.00	1985	379.11	362.67
1968	209.06	270.00	1986	391.09	368.92
1969	210.97	265.00	1987	400.00	372.08

^a MMT = million metric tons.
Sources: Beijing Review, 1988: January 11–17, 2; State Statistical Bureau, 1983, 1985; ZTZ, 1987: 16, 28.

1956–77 saw only a 0.2 percent per year growth rate, but for 1978–85 it averaged 2.6 percent per year.

Energy, protein and fat availabilities between 1952 and 1982 are given in table 12.2. The World Bank has estimated that energy availability fell short of estimated requirements in 1953 (put at 2,023 kcal) by 5 percent. In 1979 availability exceeded the higher requirements of that year (2,185 kcal) by 18 percent.[3].

Overall protein availability appears to have been sufficient throughout the entire period, but consideration of protein quality (which determines the degree of absorption and utilization of amino acids) changes the picture. In several lean years actual protein utilized may have fallen significantly short of requirements (Piazza, 1983:23–7). Lardy (1983:156) believes that there was a serious protein deficiency problem in rural areas in the mid-1970s, as evidenced by "widespread anemia among children."

Table 12.2 Daily per capita availability of energy, protein, and fat, 1952−82

Year	Total energy (kcal)	Annual change in energy (%)	Total protein (g)	Total fat (g)
1952	1,861	−	51	24
1953	1,879	1.0	50	23
1954	1,895	0.9	50	24
1955	2,005	5.8	53	25
1956	2,051	2.3	53	24
1957	2,045	−0.3	55	24
1958	2,053	0.4	54	26
1959	1,722	−16.1	46	22
1960	1,453 (1,875)	−15.6	39	16
1961	1,558	7.2	43	16
1962	1,660	6.5	45	17
1963	1,776	7.0	46	19
1964	1,934	8.9	50	22
1965	1,967	1.7	53	22
1966	2,078	5.6	53	23
1967	2,042	−1.7	52	23
1968	1,931	−5.4	49	22
1969	1,881	−2.6	48	22
1970	2,076 (2,131)	10.4	52	23
1971	2,082	0.3	51	23
1972	2,006	−3.7	49	24
1973	2,160	7.7	53	25
1974	2,194	1.6	54	24
1975	2,210	0.7	55	24
1976	2,220	0.5	56	24
1977	2,236	0.7	56	25
1978	2,360	5.5	58	25
1979	2,562	8.6	65	31
1980	2,487 (2,611)	−2.9	64	2
1981	2,517 (2,650)	1.2	65	33
1982	2,729	8.4	68	38

Sources: World Bank, 1984:164, based on methodology of Piazza, 1983. The source notes that figures in parentheses show estimates of energy availability based only upon a 20 percent wastage rate for grain, as assumed by the Chinese government. The World Bank estimates are based on commodity specific deductions for seed, feed, waste, and manufacturing use.

Table 12.3 Per capita consumption of various foods in selected years, 1952–86

Year	Grain (kg)[a]	Edible oil (kg)[b]	Pork (kg)	Beef, mutton (kg)	Poultry (kg)	Fresh eggs (kg)	Aquatic products (kg)
1952	197.67	2.05	5.92	0.92	0.43	1.02	2.67
1957	203.06	2.42	5.08	1.11	0.50	1.25	2.34
1962	164.63	1.09	2.22	0.79	0.38	0.76	2.96
1965	182.84	1.72	6.29	1.02	0.36	1.42	3.33
1970	187.22	1.61	6.02	0.82	0.32	1.32	2.94
1975	190.52	1.73	7.63	0.72	0.35	1.63	3.26
1976	190.28	1.60	7.38	0.66	0.35	1.76	3.52
1977	192.07	1.56	7.25	0.71	0.36	1.85	3.23
1978	195.46	1.60	7.67	0.75	0.44	1.97	3.50
1979	207.03	1.96	9.66	0.82	0.57	2.08	3.22
1980	213.81	2.30	11.16	0.83	0.80	2.27	3.41
1981	219.18	2.94	11.08	0.85	0.83	2.44	3.57
1982	225.46	3.54	11.76	1.03	1.02	2.53	3.85
1983	232.23	4.03	12.35	1.11	1.18	2.96	4.02
1984	251.34	4.70	13.02	1.25	1.35	3.90	4.36
1985	254.35	5.13	13.99	1.32	1.56	4.98	4.89
1986	255.94	5.24	14.41	1.34	1.72	5.27	5.40
Average annual growth rate (%)							
1952–7	0.5	3.4	-3.0	3.8	0.03	19.7	26.6
1965–77	0.4	-0.8	1.2	-3.0	0.0	2.2	0.0
1977–86	3.2	14.4	7.9	7.3	19.0	12.3	5.9

[a] Grain is measured as "trade grain", which counts some grains after being husked and others unhusked.
[b] "Edible oil" refers to vegetable oil and includes the oil equivalent of oil-bearing crops.
Source: ZTN, 1987:711.

It is difficult to document improvements in nutrition over the history of the People's Republic of China (PRC) up to the early 1980s (table 12.3). The rise in estimated life expectancy at birth from 34 years in 1952 to 69 years in 1982 (World Bank, 1984:113), a proud achievement by international comparative standards, was the product of many factors other than nutrition. Anthropometric surveys showed gains between 1957 and 1977 in height for age of school-age children in some urban and prosperous suburban areas, notably suburban Shanghai, Beijing, and Guangzhou (Canton), but areas more representative of the conditions of most Chinese have not been examined over time (Jamison and Trowbridge, 1984; World Bank, 1984:19–20). Such surveys in 1975 and 1979 suggested there was little malnutrition in urban areas but that it was a continuing problem in rural ones. There is also considerable regional variation in the incidence of malnutrition, with provincial rural rates of stunting ranging up to 37.1 percent in Sichuan.[4] Both a higher incidence of diarrheal diseases and a poorer average diet are thought to explain the greater prevalence of malnutrition in rural areas (World Bank, 1984:31).

Development Strategies and Food

There seems little doubt that in the early years of the PRC, the fulfillment of basic needs improved markedly as a result of the end of the long period of war, including civil war, and the accession to power of a regime able to assert control over the entire nation and willing and able to effect radical institutional change. In the course of the first half of the 1950s, farm output increased rapidly and wealth was substantially redistributed, virtually eliminating directly private-property-based inequalities.[5] At the same time, campaigns to educate the population about sanitation, health, and birth control, to reduce or eliminate mass communicable diseases, and to provide some basic medical care to the millions who had previously had access to none, quickly raised life expectancy and began to cut population growth, especially in the cities.

China's essay in Soviet-type central planning of development, of which the only relatively good example is the First Five Year Plan period (1953–7),[6] had complex effects on mass welfare. On one hand, the adoption and strengthening of central planning and control over resources facilitated the redirection of the latter into high-priority uses; this ensured that those resources that the state permitted to be allocated to consumption, both private and social, and to health, education, sanitation, and other welfare-related sectors were used effectively to meet the most pressing basic needs.

On the other hand, other aspects of the First Plan approach limited its positive effects on living standards. Deliberately high investment rates constrained the growth of real consumption and, furthermore, precipitated the extraordinarily fast collectivization of agriculture in 1955−6.[7] Collectivization and its successor, the rural communes, also had complex effects on production and living standards. They contributed to technical change, including the adoption of new high-yield varieties of various grains and of farm chemicals, to a major extension of the irrigated area, and to extensive terracing and other improvement of land. But collectivization also facilitated de facto state control of agriculture, which both weakened work incentives and permitted arbitrary and irrational state decisions about land use and income distribution to override the peasants' own desires. As a result, the growth of food production lagged well behind its potential, as became evident when reforms beginning in the late 1970s stimulated the rapid closing of this gap.

The First Plan also featured the installation of capital intensive technologies from the USSR. This limited the rate at which new non-agricultural employment could be created, which in turn constrained the growth of the total wage bill and of personal income.[8]

Per capita consumption increased during the First Plan years by an overall 34 percent: 27 percent for the rural population, 38 percent for the urban, according to official statistics (ZTN, 1986: 646). Yet the increase was unevenly distributed; for instance, the rural population of Ningxia Hui Autonomous Region, one of the poorest regions of China, saw an increase in net per capita income of less than 3 percent over the five years (Ningxia huizu, 1985:33).

In 1958 a dramatic change in development strategy took place, and with it came the beginnings of an era of political conflict within the Chinese leadership and population that was to last for two decades. Mao Zedong, looking for a road to socialism and economic development quite different from that taken by the Soviet Union, introduced a set of policies whose logic was most apparent in their extreme implementation during the years of the Great Leap Forward (1958−60) and the Cultural Revolution (1966−9).

Mao was striving for an approach that would not only eliminate the rigid bureaucratism of central administrative planning, as developed in the Soviet Union during the Stalin years, but also severely limit the role of the market, seen by Mao as a breeding ground of capitalist attitudes and behavior. He attacked and decimated both the functional bureaucracy that ran central planning and the vestiges of market relations, but he had in mind no third alternative institutional arrangement to suggest as a means of coordinating economic activity. The result was a chaotic and inefficient attempt by individual localities and productive units to be "self-reliant" −

which, indeed, was their only option given the collapse of central planning during these periods.[9]

The Famine of 1959–1961: Extent and Measurement

The first vigorous attempt to implement these ideas was the ill-fated Great Leap Forward (GLF), which saw the reorganization of the farm collectives into giant communes, the undertaking of huge water conservancy and other projects using armies of labor, and the establishment of hundreds of thousands of small industrial shops throughout the countryside. The damage that GLF policies inflicted on the land, on labor incentives, and on food production contributed to producing one of the great famines of history. Food-grain output, after peaking in 1958, fell sharply in 1959 and 1960 to reach a 1960 nadir some 29 percent below the 1958 peak (table 12.1). The average per capita level of grain consumption in the countryside fell from 204 kg in 1957 to only 154 kg in 1960, and one estimate of the national average for per capita, daily caloric intake in the latter year put it at only 1,453 calories (table 12.2).[10]

According to official statistics, the increase in mortality rates during the three years 1959–61 implies that over 15 million excess deaths occurred above the "normal" level implied by the 1957 mortality rate. Some western demographers, by estimating unreported mortality, have reached a figure almost twice this number (Ashton et al., 1984).[11] There remain many questions about the sources and quality of the statistics for the famine years, and no exact estimate of famine mortality can be accepted with confidence. But there seems little doubt that what occurred was of catastrophic dimensions.

Contributing to the situation were serious natural disasters, especially in 1960, and the counterfactual question of what degree conditions would have deteriorated to had the government policy environment been optimal is unanswerable. Hence the relative responsibility of failures in that environment cannot be assessed with precision. But what we know about the events of that period strengthens the general belief that the lion's share of responsibility lies with state policy.

For instance, the widespread construction of dams and reservoirs with masses of human labor proceeded without any assessment of their impact on the water table, with the result that the fertility of much land, especially in the crucial North China Plain, was adversely affected (Walker, 1977:558). Innovations, such as deep ploughing and close planting, promoted by the Party as shortcuts to increased yields, were pushed irrationally, to the point of reducing yields. Farm labor was thrown into small-scale industry and transport even during the heavy seasons when it could not be spared. The military organization of farm production under the early commune setup, and the "socialization" of peasants' personal property in the earlier part of the Leap, harmed morale and work motivation. The elimination in many places of farmers' private plots, where they had been able freely to raise things for their own consumption or for sale on local markets; the over-centralized and highly redistributive character of the early communes; and the initial adoption of a public dining-hall system featuring free food, all weakened peasant incentives and encouraged wasteful consumption.

In addition, the politically motivated exaggeration of harvest size and destruction of reporting systems, in line with the belief of the time that harping on objective constraints dampened the enthusiasm of the masses, kept the leadership in the dark about real supply conditions: "Leaders believed in 1959–60 that they had 100 MMT [million metric tons] more grain than they actually did" (Bernstein, 1984:13). When famine conditions developed, some local cadres, afraid of the political implications of revealing them, failed to seek relief or even sealed their localities.

Excessive procurement of grain by the state was a major contributor to rural shortages (Bernstein, 1984; Lardy, 1983) and thus probably to rural mortality. The government, for a while believing in miracle harvests and then anxious to protect urban consumption, took 10 percent more grain out of the countryside in 1959 than in 1957. Even in 1960, when mortality was at its highest, 4 percent more was taken from the countryside than in 1957.[12] The result was that the cities were cushioned against disaster at the expense of the countryside. Thus commenced a period, lasting until the 1980s, in which rural per capita grain supplies stayed below urban.[13] The government finally began to import grain in 1961 − two years late − in order to supply the coastal cities and take some pressure off the countryside.

The famine of 1959–61 illustrates how shortfalls in food supply can go hand in hand with a particular pattern of deprivation of food entitlements. Economic policy was itself partly responsible for the sharp fall in supply that occurred, but it also allocated the resulting burden so as to protect urban interests against rural. Finally, the disorganization in the information system, which was in retrospect an inevitable outcome of the application of Maoist ideas, greatly increased the toll by retarding the central government's awareness of, and reaction to, the crisis.

Although recovery proceeded rapidly from 1962 on, the per capita grain production levels of the best pre-Great Leap Forward year (1956) were not reached again until 1975 (table 12.1). World Bank estimates of calorie consumption per capita find the 1958 level being matched only in 1970 (table 12.2). Clearly China's record in improving the food situation of its population over this period left much to be desired.

Causes of the Food Problem in Late Maoist China

The failure of consumption to grow during the late Maoist period is somewhat mysterious: despite later accusations that the Maoist leadership worshipped poverty as a prime virtue, Mao's own writings always favored rising incomes and living standards. But several of the policies that were pressed during the last two decades of Mao's life, as well as various structural aspects of his approach, worked against this happening. For instance, a principal farm policy was that of local food-grain self-sufficiency (represented by the slogan, "take grain as the key link"). This policy, in keeping with a general encouragement of local self-reliance, was in part designed with an eye to possible war with the Soviet Union and the need to ensure that local people could support themselves if internal trade and communications were disrupted. It also epitomized Mao's attempt to avoid local dependence on distant coordinative bureaucracies. For a while, moreover, it became a necessity when the chaotic struggles of the Cultural Revolution period decimated the bureaucracy whose job it was to redistribute food.

The state, which monopolized trade in food grains, was in a position to enforce its wishes by withholding grain from areas that tried to follow their comparative advantage in other products. The result was that grain basket areas were deprived of their markets, while non-grain regions produced grain inefficiently. This policy ended by stunting the incentive and ability to grow more grain in both types of areas, while forcing many non-grain areas into an artificial poverty by depriving them of their best income-earning opportunities. Self-reliance more generally catered to the entrepreneurial instincts and acquisitive interests of local cadres, who drove up investment rates in an attempt to develop the local economy and increase their resource base.

Another policy that hurt agriculture was the maintenance of a large "scissors gap" or price differential between farm and industrial prices. Since the early days of the PRC this gap has functioned as a virtual tax on agriculture, a means for the state to remove surplus to support its industrialization program. In particular, the relative prices of modern producer goods, such as farm chemicals and machinery (Yang and Li, 1980:207), were extremely high in China relative to their international levels. A kilogram of rice exchanged in China for less than half the amount of fertilizer it could command on the world market, and it took five or six times as much rice to purchase a tractor of given horsepower in China as in Japan (ibid.). These prices imposed heavy burdens on farmers who were increasingly dependent on modern inputs to overcome diminishing returns from scarce land. Between 1962 and 1976 the increase in production costs

Table 12.4 Food-grain (unprocessed grain) procurement for selected years, 1952–84

Grain year[a]	(1) Output MMT	Marketing[b]		(4) Gross marketing ratio (2)/(1)	(5) Net marketing ratio (3)/(1)	(6) Proportion of output resold to countryside (4)−(5)
		(2) Total MMT	(3) Net[c] MMT			
1952	163.92	33.3	28.19	0.20	0.17	0.03
1957	195.05	48.0	33.87	0.25	0.17	0.07
1958	200.00	58.8	41.73	0.29	0.21	0.09
1959	170.00	67.4	47.57	0.40	0.28	0.12
1961	147.50	40.5	25.81	0.27	0.17	0.10
1964	187.50	47.4	31.85	0.25	0.17	0.08
1968	209.06	48.7	37.87	0.23	0.18	0.05
1970	239.96	54.4	42.02	0.23	0.18	0.05
1975	284.52	60.9	43.98	0.21	0.15	0.06
1978	304.77	61.7	42.71	0.20	0.14	0.06
1979	332.12	72.0	51.70	0.22	0.16	0.06
1980	320.56	73.0	47.97	0.23	0.15	0.08
1981	325.02	78.5	48.77	0.24	0.15	0.09
1982	354.50	91.9	52.02	0.26	0.15	0.11
1983	387.28	119.9	85.27	0.31	0.22	0.09
1984	407.31	141.7	94.61	0.35	0.23	0.12

[a] The grain year runs from April 1 to the following March 31.
[b] "Marketing" includes tax procurements, state quota procurements, above-quota purchases, and free-market sales.
[c] "Net" refers to total marketing less state resales to the countryside.
Source: Riskin, forthcoming: table 11.

per hectare for six surveyed grain crops exceeded the gain in output value per hectare, causing net income per hectare to fall (Yang and Li, 1980:207−8).

Farm prices also fared poorly against those of industrial consumer goods. Such items as sewing machines, alarm clocks, portable radios, and cameras exchanged in Hong Kong, for instance, for between two and ten times as much rice as in the PRC (Liu, 1980:5−6). Low farm prices not only hurt production incentives; they also contributed to the urban−rural gap in income and entitlement to food over much of the period.

Nor was the state practice of dictating to the communes as if they had been state farms propitious to agricultural advance. Nominally, the communes and production teams were collectives, and policy should have been made by their members. However, the commune had a dual role: politically it was the lowest level of state administration while economically it was a producers' collective. The ambiguity in its status facilitated state interference in cropping patterns, technological choices, and income distribution.

Food Distribution

Maoist policies were highly egalitarian with respect to local income distribution; that is, they produced very equal distributions of necessities *within* localities and units. Health care, sanitation, and maintenance of minimum food consumption levels led to unusually high life expectancy. At the same time, however, the strong local egalitarian bias in the approach put rigid caps on the consumption of successful units, resulting in a leveling down of consumption. On the other hand, the policy of self-reliance, which left localities largely dependent upon their own resources, meant that disparities among localities and units were bound to increase. And the overall gap between city and countryside widened considerably as well.[14] Official statistics have it rising from 2.3-to-1 in 1964 to 3.2-to-1 in 1978. If urban subsidies were included in the calculation, the gap would widen still further.

It was widely reported in the late 1970s and early 1980s that in 1978 100 million peasants had yearly per capita grain rations of less than 150 kg (Jiang et al., 1980:53), which converts to a daily intake of only 1,500 calories (Lardy, 1982:161, n. 9). Even though "ration" refers to a base figure probably somewhat lower than actual consumption,[15] such a figure implies a widespread want of food not known to have existed in the 1950s.

Per capita food availability (that is, output plus imports) was no lower in the 1970s than in the 1950s, but the state's capacity to redistribute grain, especially between surplus and deficit provinces, seems to have declined (see Table 12.4). Total tax plus purchases fell as a fraction of grain output from 25–30 percent in the 1950s to only 20–1 percent in the 1970s (column 4). Of this, the amount kept to feed the cities and build up stocks is shown in column 5. The last column shows grain resold to deficit areas of the countryside. During the First Five Year Plan period this averaged 8.6 percent of output but it fell to an average of only 5.7 percent during the years 1966–76 (Riskin, forthcoming: table 11). If indeed 100 million or more people found themselves short of food, the small fractions of the harvest available for state relief would not seem to have been enough to meet the need.

Despite proportionally smaller interprovincial transfers of food grain, the provincial distribution of grain consumption did not in fact become more unequal.[16] This is because the grain self-sufficiency policy leveled the differences between provincial per capita outputs by forcing non-grain regions to grow grain while discouraging surpluses on the part of grain basket regions. The fact that greater equality, of a sort, seems to have gone hand in hand with the growth of underfed regional populations helps to make the post-Mao leadership's case against the particular kind of egalitarianism that marked the late Mao period.

In 1979, to provide an adequate caloric intake for the ten provinces which fell short of sufficiency and also ensure that the residents of Beijing, Shanghai, and Tianjin got the national average of 2,600 kcal, a total of 10 million metric tons of unprocessed wheat would have been required (Piazza, 1983:43) – approximately what China imported net of grain exports in 1979. Universal adequacy of food energy was thus feasible, from the viewpoint of total supplies. However, imports went to raise urban standards above the national average, while poor provinces such as Guizhou, Gansu, Yunnan, and Qinghai were left short. The problem thus lay in the impact of state policy on provincial entitlements, rather than in inadequate total supplies.

The picture was very different in 1984. The average provincial output per capita was substantially above that of the 1950s, while interprovincial inequality rose only slightly. The reforms beginning in 1978 produced growth in per capita output for every province but one (Guangxi) between 1979 and 1984 (Riskin, forthcoming, table 13) and per capita consumption of food indeed began to increase at rates well above the previous ones, as is shown in table 12.5. On a broad regional level, then, the trade-off of some greater inequality for general improvement in food availability seems to have been a good bargain.

Grain consumption per capita grew by almost 4 percent per year between 1977 and 1984 compared with prior long-term rates of well under 1 percent. Although absolute consumption levels of meat, fish, eggs, and other non-cereals are still very low, their differentially high growth rates

Table 12.5 Per capita food consumption (kg), 1978 and 1984

Consumption per capita of:	1978	1984
Food grain	196.0	251.3
Edible oil	1.6	4.7
Pork	7.7	13.0
Eggs	2.0	3.9

Source: ZTN, 1988: 801.

until very recently held out the hope that the Chinese diet would finally begin to escape from its overwhelming dependence on cereals. Unfortunately, most of these gains were made by 1984, after which agricultural progress began to slow. And late in 1987 pork and sugar were once again subjected to rationing in major cities.[17]

Whereas we have discussed available information about interprovincial distribution of food availability, little is known about the distribution of food at lower levels. Hunger is of course closely tied to poverty and the information about this is rather sparse. Poverty is discussed almost exclusively as a *regional* matter, since the mountainous western provinces of Gansu, Guizhou, Ningxia, Qinghai, Shaanxi, Sichuan, and Tibet contain a large share of the approximately 70 million peasants said to live below the official poverty line (Delfs, 1987b:84). Nationally, this line corresponds to an annual income of Rmb 200 ($53) as a rule of thumb. But it varies by region, and in Hebei one must get less than Rmb 120 ($32) *and* less than 180 kg of grain to be eligible for tax relief (Hebei Statistical Office, 1986:81–2).[18]

Some idea of the variation that exists *within* even a poor province such as Ningxia is provided by table 12.6, which presents 1985 data on the differentials in food consumption between mountainous and flat areas of the province. The advantage of plains residents over hill residents in consumption per capita ranges from 60 percent for edible oil to over 5-fold for sugar. The difference in grain consumption was smaller, as would be expected, but still pronounced: mountain residents had 215 kg per capita of grain in 1983, whereas the rural average was 249 kg.[19]

The effort to develop poverty regions has been spotty. On the one hand, large amounts of money have been devoted to a few high priority projects, such as in Dingxi district of Gansu Province (Chen Junsheng, 1987; Delfs, 1987b). On the other, numerous poor regions facing intractable physical conditions have found themselves both ill-equipped to take advantage of opportunities opened up by the reforms and facing a political climate less

Table 12.6   Per capita consumption of various non-grain foods in Ningxia Hui
Autonomous Region: plains vs mountain regions

Food item (kg/cap.)	Province total	Plains	Mountain	Ratio
Vegetables	204.00	313.00	87.00	3.6
Edible oil	6.10	7.50	4.60	1.6
Poultry	0.55	0.78	0.30	2.6
Sugar	1.86	3.05	0.59	5.2

Source: Ningxia huizu, 1985:93.

conducive to redistributive measures. As the deputy party secretary of Shandong Province pointed out in August 1987, referring to his province, "two-thirds of the poverty-stricken villages still do not have adequate food and clothing to date" and "more than 5.8 mill. people throughout the province still have difficulty in securing potable water."[20]

The central government began to address the problem systematically in 1980 with a state budget grant to aid impoverished rural areas. The amount of this grant rose from Rmb 500 million during the years 1980–3 to Rmb 800 million in 1986 (Delfs, 1987b). Various ministries and banks "have started to provide special funds or cheap loans totaling 2 billion yuan each year to the old liberated areas, ethnic minority areas, border areas, poor areas, and economically underdeveloped areas" (Chen Junsheng, 1987: 27). Probably additional to this is Rmb 1 billion per year in special loans at subsidized interest rates that the State Council authorized to "help solve the problem of feeding and clothing the people in the poor areas during the Seventh 5-Year Plan [1986–90]." This program is concentrating on 273 poor counties in 21 provinces (Cheng Junsheng, 1987:27). The state also instituted a "work relief" program in which Rmb 2.7 billion's worth of grain, cotton, and cloth between 1985 and 1987 was allocated as wages in kind to workers on development projects in selected poor areas. In 1988 low-grade industrial products were to be added to this payment-in-kind program, which is also to be expanded gradually to encompass the whole country. A Leading Group for Poor Region Economic Development was established under the State Council in 1986, to coordinate the proliferating programs (ibid.).

Poverty within areas not designated as poor is a topic about which we know very little. It is treated summarily in Chinese statistics. In 1986, for instance, 34,000 state social welfare units aided 426,000 people. Urban and rural collectives took care of 2.4 million childless elderly, injured, and weak. Impoverished households (*pinkun hu*), a separate category from the above, are the responsibility of their regions or localities (*Renmin Ribao*, February 22, 1987).

In one particular region – Hebei Province – households below the poverty line in villages not in designated poor areas can obtain tax relief "according to local financial conditions," after discussion by the village and approval at the township and county levels. Where tax relief does not fully address the problem, local finances are the first source of further aid; if these are insufficient, help can be sought from the provincial government (Hebei Statistical Office, 1986:81–2). Guidelines for help are thus vague and data about those who avail themselves of it are scanty.

Chinese scholars and officials have begun to understand that the change from collective organization to family farming and individual enterprise, and the consequent weakening of control by the government and local authorities over income distribution, have left something of a vacuum in the area of social welfare. They are realizing the necessity both of getting accurate information about the extent and depth of hunger and poverty, and of setting up new social welfare institutions (such as health insurance and unemployment insurance) to deal with them.

Reform

There were three principal kinds of reform in the countryside. First, beginning in 1978, farm prices were raised sharply, by an average of 22 percent for all agricultural purchases. Smaller price hikes followed in subsequent years, and the proportion of state purchases at higher above-quota and negotiated prices also rose from negligible levels in 1977 to reach 60 percent in 1981 (Travers, 1984:242).[21]

However, industrial prices also rose during the first half of the 1980s and without comprehensive price indexes we cannot know with certainty in what direction the *commodity* terms of trade moved after 1980. But, with farmers using their new freedom and incentives to select more profitable output mixes and to work with greater effort and efficiency, the *single factoral* and *income* terms of trade must both have risen,[22] giving farmers greater access to industrial goods.

Second, the policy of local food-grain self-sufficiency was abandoned and farmers were encouraged to grow what was suitable to their conditions. This change stimulated the reallocation of many resources from grain to other crops and – especially in the case of labor – from farming generally to non-farm occupations (see below). This was a major contributor to the rise in rural income in the several years following 1978.

Third came the most well known of the reforms and the one to which their gains are most often attributed: the breakup of the commune and adoption of household farming on the basis of long-term contracting of land from the village. This lessened (if not entirely eliminated) the ability of state organs to dictate to the farmers and finally got rid of the problematic work-point system of income distribution that had been in place for two decades.[23]

Linked to de-communization and encouragement of diversification was a state commitment to increasing the autonomy of peasants. The abandonment of the commune institution was justified because it removed the state from direct political control of farm production activities. The substitute *xiang* or township government is a purely political body. The death of the commune also meant the weakening of the structures of egalitarian distribution in the countryside. Individual household farming, under the encouragement of state policy favoring "letting some get rich first," has encouraged those with superior skills, labour power, or political access to forge ahead of their less well-endowed neighbors.

The post-reform gains in agriculture were thus based on a series of institutional changes. These allowed the exploitation of the potential that had grown up during the era of collectivism but had been unrealized due to policy impediments to effective incentives as well as to the rational allocation of resources. For instance, irrigated acreage grew from 27 million ha in 1957 to 45 million ha in 1979 (and by not a hectare since; see ZTZ, 1987:36). Similarly, much terracing and other "farmland capital construction" had taken place under the collectives, which paid off only after the reforms provided incentives for the peasants to exploit the enhanced potential of the land.

There was also an enormous labor surplus in agriculture in the collective period. Claude Aubert has made rough estimates of its size, as shown in table 12.7. While the information on recorded labor days per hectare was collected for income payment purposes and probably does not accurately reflect actual work-time expended, the scale of the nominal surplus – equal to several times estimated requirements – has to reflect a serious redundancy of labor in agriculture.

What kept this surplus on the farms? Peasants were not banned from taking non-agricultural jobs and, in fact, rural industrialization was one of the hallmarks of the late Maoist strategy. However, three factors conspired to limit off-farm employment opportunities: (a) individual entrepreneurship was essentially eliminated, so that local development depended mostly on the initiative, talent, and political connections of the local cadres; (b) population movement to towns and cities was largely banned; and (c) there was a strong ideological bias against trade and services as wasteful "non-productive" activities. (See chapter 6 for a historical perspective.)

Table 12.7   Labor days per hectare, estimated and recorded

	Required	Recorded		Surplus	
		1976	*1984*	*1976*	*1984*
Wheat	80	450	236	370	156
Corn	90	450	253	360	163
Rice	200	600	340	400	140

Source: Aubert, 1987:12. 1984 figures from ZNTN, 1986:161.
Note: Aubert's estimates of requirements are based on interviews with peasants, and deliberately made high (often double Taiwan's). "Recorded" refers to labor days paid for under the collective distribution system. These are nominal and exaggerated, but the gap is still significant.

The reforms effectively removed these constraints, and since 1980 there has been a shift of some 50 million people out of farming and into rural industry, trade, construction, transport, and services. Family private enterprises alone absorbed 12.5 million people between 1981 and 1985, mostly in trade (6 million), industry (2.4 million), and transport (1.4 million) (ZNTN, 1986:12).

Official projections to the year 2000 call for a farm labor force of only 225 million (in 1986 it was 305 million) out of a total rural labor force of 405 million (in 1986, 380 million), assuming that 10 percent (45 million) migrate to the cities. The realization of such a goal would require the creation of 100 million new, non-agricultural, rural jobs.[24] As Aubert points out, such a massive shift in the occupational structure of the labor force would finally bring the labor–land ratio into line with requirements. But it is hard to see where the 100 million new off-farm jobs could be created by the end of the century (Aubert, 1987).

The reforms also tended to raise the birth rate. Having lost control of this during the chaotic years of the 1960s, the government began strongly emphasizing population control again in the 1970s. The crude birth rate fell dramatically, from 37.9 per thousand in 1965 to 17.8 in 1979. But the household contracting system, by reducing social control of individual behavior, weakening the collective social welfare institutions, and creating more income-earning opportunities for children, put a premium on having larger families. The national crude birth rate rose from a low of 17.5 per thousand in 1984 to 20.8 in 1986 (ZTZ, 1987:16).

In sum, the dramatic increases in farm output and peasant incomes initially stimulated by the reforms were due largely to three factors: (a) reallocation of resources from low to high value crops and products made possible by the abandonment of the "grain first" policy; (b) initial improvement in agriculture's terms of trade with industry; and (c) rapid expansion of off-farm employment opportunities. These factors were short-term in nature. The terms of trade probably stopped improving for agriculture sometime in the early 1980s. Diversification within agriculture has noticeably slowed, with animal husbandry and forestry actually declining as a fraction of total agricultural product. Sideline production other than village industry grew hardly at all after 1981. Only village industry has remained buoyant (ZTZ, 1987:25), and it is questionable how long it can continue to be so.

When the sources of the post-reform spurt in agriculture had played themselves out, the rate of growth in rural output and incomes slowed again, even as the population growth rate began to rise. And the investment in agriculture needed for long-run growth was not forthcoming, either from the state or from the farmers themselves. The farmers have put their resources into assets that are either more secure than farming (such as housing) or more profitable (such as trade or industry). The state, in the meantime, has had to worry about large budget deficits, disturbing inflation, and chaotic urban reforms; lulled by the early success of the rural reform on the basis of institutional change alone, it has given insufficient attention to the long-term needs of agriculture. In 1986, capital investment in agriculture, as a fraction of total investment, was the lowest (3.3 percent) it had ever been.

Conclusion

Over the forty years of its existence, the PRC has tried out some very different approaches to feeding its people. From collective organization of labor and distribution of income it has moved to family farming. Both systems have strengths and weaknesses. The particular strength of the new system, on which some impressive gains have depended, is its encouragement of individual initiative. Perhaps its most serious potential problem lies in the many people whose conditions of life and work make individual advance under the new conditions difficult or impossible. Therefore the delicate search continues for a set of policies that incorporate an appropriate blend of values for China — individualism, acquisitiveness, and a willingness to take risks, with cooperation, solidarity, and compassion.

NOTES

1   Quoted from Deng's *Build Socialism with Chinese Characteristics* (in Chinese, enlarged edition: 53) by Chen Junhong (1987:3).

2 For a more detailed discussion of aspects of this paper, see Riskin (forthcoming).

3 See World Bank (1984:169–72). The estimates use WHO/FAO standards and data on age-specific average body weights, age distribution, and assumptions about activity levels.

4 However, the rural figure is biased downward because it includes suburban areas of major cities.

5 Inequalities *indirectly* produced by prior property inequality – such as inequalities in educational attainments and social connections – of course continued to affect incomes.

6 While subsequent Five Year Plans continue to be cited by the statistical authorities as a convenience in periodizing recent history, they were merely nominal. The Second Plan (1958–62) was made defunct by the Great Leap Forward (1958–60) and the famine it precipitated; and the Third and later plans were deprived of any real significance by the Cultural Revolution (1966–9) and its after effects. See Riskin, 1987.

7 The failure of China's farms to produce growing surpluses to support rapid industrialization was a crucial factor in leading Mao Zedong to abandon his previous commitment to gradual and voluntary cooperativization of agriculture and push through the collectivization in record time. See Selden, 1981.

8 However, this effect should be seen as complementary – and subordinate – to the physical planning decision to limit directly the flow of resources into consumer goods industries and agriculture. Given the latter decision, a faster growth of employment and income could only have contributed to inflationary pressures.

9 For a detailed discussion of the rationale and implications of Mao's ideas about economic structure and development, see Riskin, 1987.

10 The method of estimation used by the Chinese government yields a higher calorie intake of 1,875 kcal for 1960 (see note to table 12.2). Ashton et al. (1984:622) put it at 1,535 kcal for that year.

11 This estimate, of 29.5 million premature deaths, also has problems associated with it. It results in part from an unrealistically low estimate of "normal" deaths obtained by applying normal infant mortality rates to the abnormally small number of births that took place during the crisis. Furthermore, the ratio of child to adult mortality fluctuates in ways that are hard to explain. Unreported deaths are also assumed to fluctuate sharply – from 28 to 47 percent of actual deaths during the famine years.

12 These figures are net of resales to deficit rural areas. Table 12.4 gives figures on state extractions in 1959 and 1961.

13 ZMWTZ (1984:27). ZTN (1983:509) indicates that urban residents enjoyed an edge in consumption of between 380 and 490 kcal per day for each year from 1978 to 1982. Other statistics indicate that rural inhabitants overtook their urban counterparts in grain consumption around 1980; but the latter probably maintained their advantage in non-grain food consumption.

14 The idea of an urban–rural gap is of course an artificial construct, since conditions differ greatly *within* each of those sectors, and especially among rural localities. The gap between prosperous suburban farming communities and remote villages was as great as that between cities and the rural average.

15 The term "rations" (*kouliang*) is used in the source. Rations are usually lower than total grain consumption (see Walker, 1982:578–82).

16 The coefficient of variation in fact declined by almost a half between the 1950s and 1979, suggesting that provincial equality increased. See Riskin, forthcoming, tables 12, 13. The leveling was mostly downward, with high producers, such as Heilongjiang, Jilin, and Inner Mongolia, declining and no provinces rising to take their place.

17 Rationing in the case of pork was reimposed because of the appearance of a market-created hog cycle reminiscent of those encountered in market economies. It was applied only to state supplies; free-market supplies continued to be available at higher prices. In the case of sugar, rationing was imposed because of rapidly accelerating demand from China's growing soft drink industry. See Delfs (1987b:100–1).

18 Average rural consumption in 1985 was 257 kg unprocessed. The poorest province, Tibet, had 199.6 kg, followed by Hebei, 214, Xinjiang, 216.6, Guizhou, 219.1. See ZTN, 1986.

19 *Ningxia Huizu* (1985:64,71). The figures are in unprocessed grain. No figure is given for plains residents, nor is there a breakdown of the population by residence that would permit its calculation. If the plains residents came to 75 percent of the total population, their average per capita consumption would be 260 kg.

20 Joint Publications Research Service, CPS 87–052 (1987:52). The deputy secretary criticized the aid-the-poor work as having "developed in a very uneven manner. In particular, in the areas near reservoirs, remote mountainous areas, beach areas along Huang He [river], and villages having rather big problems in potable water supplies, the difficult conditions in livelihood and production have yet to be radically changed .... in the Yimeng mountainous area, 2,180 villages are not accessible to cars, and more than 3,500 villages do not have electricity" (ibid).

21 There were three classes of farm sales to the state. Mandatory sales quotas bore the lowest price. Then came above-quota sales. If the state needed more grain, it offered still higher "negotiated" prices.

22 The commodity terms of trade index, N, is here simply P_a/P_i (where P_a and P_i are price indexes for agricultural and industrial goods). The single factoral terms of trade, here $N \times Z_a$ (where Z_a is an index of farm labour productivity), measures changes in the command over industrial goods of a unit of agricultural labour. The income terms of trade, here $N \times Q_a$ (where Q_a is an index of agricultural output), measures changes in agriculture's overall access to industrial goods.

23 For a discussion of the work-point system, see Riskin (1987:92–5).

24 Actually, even more jobs would be required, since the rural population is growing faster than had been hoped.

REFERENCES

Ashton, Basil, Hill, Kenneth, Piazza, Alan, and Zeitz, Robin 1984: Famine in China, 1958–61. *Population and Development Review*, 10(4).

Aubert, Claude 1987: Rural capitalism vs socialist economics? Unpublished ms.
Bernstein, Thomas P. 1984: Stalinism, famine, and Chinese peasants. *Theory and Society*, 13.
Chen Junhong 1987: Only by accelerating the development of the productive forces .... *Guangming Ribao*, October 25, tr. FBIS-CHI-87−224, November 20.
Chen Junsheng 1987: Sum up new experiences, reform the work of helping poor areas − two questions concerning the economic development of poor areas in nine southern provinces and regions. *Renmin Ribao*, November 14; FBIS-CHI-87−224, November 20.
Delfs, Robert 1987a: A model of poverty. *Far Eastern Economic Review*, September 10.
Delfs, Robert 1987b: Hands for the handouts: *Far Eastern Economic Review*, September 10.
Delfs, Robert 1987c: Piggy in the muddle. *Far Eastern Economic Review*, December 17.
He Tang (ed.) 1986: *Zhongguo Nongye Nianjian 1986*. Beijing: Agricultural Publishing House.
Hebei sheng renmin zhengfu 1986: Guanyu jianmian pinkun diqu nongye shui de tongzhi. (Hebei Provincial People's Government: Notice regarding reduction or cancellation of the agricultural tax in poor localities.) In Hebei Statistical Office (1986), 81−2.
Hebei Statistical Office 1986: *Hebei Sheng Jingji Tongji Nianjian, 1986*. China Statistical Publishers.
Jamison, Dean T. and Trowbridge, F. L. 1984: The nutritional status of children in China: A review of the anthropometric evidence. (PHN Technical Note GEN 17.) Supplementary Paper No. 8 of World Bank.
Jiang Junchen, Zhou Zhaoyang and Shen Jun 1980: Lun shengchan he shenghuode guanxi wenti. (On the relations between production and livelihood.) *Jingji Yanjiu*, 9.
Lardy, Nicholas R. 1983: *Agriculture in China's Modern Economic Development*. New York and Cambridge: Cambridge University Press.
Lardy, Nicholas R. 1982: Food consumption in the People's Republic of China. In Randolph Barker, Radha Sinha, and Beth Rose (eds), *The Chinese Agricultural Economy*, Boulder, Colo.: Westview.
Liu, Jung-chao 1980: A note on China's pricing policies. Paper presented to Workshop of the Department of Economics, SUNY Binghampton, March 19.
Ningxia huizu zizhiqu noncun chouxiang diaocha dui bian (ed.) 1985: *Qianjinzhongde Ningxia nongcun*. (Rural Sample Survey Group of Ningxia Hui Autonomous Region, (ed.): *Ningxia's Advancing Countryside*.) Beijing: Chinese Statistical Publishing House.
Piazza, Alan 1983: *Trends in Food and Nutrient Availability in China, 1950−81*. World Bank Staff Working Papers Number 607. Washington, DC: World Bank.
Riskin, Carl 1987: *China's Political Economy: The Quest for Development since 1949*. Oxford: Oxford University Press.
Riskin, Carl forthcoming: Feeding China: The Experience since 1949. In Jean

Dreze and Amartya Sen (eds), *Hunger: Economics and policy*, Oxford: Oxford University Press.

Selden, Mark 1981: Cooperation and socialist transition in China's countryside. In Mark Selden and Victor Lippit (eds), *The Transition to Socialism in China*, Armonk, NY: M. E. Sharpe.

State Statistical Bureau 1983, 1985: *Statistical Yearbook of China*. Beijing: Economic Information and Agency, Hong Kong.

Travers, Lee 1984: Post-1978 rural economic policy and peasant income in China. *China Quarterly*, 98.

Walker, Kenneth R. 1977: Grain self-sufficiency in north China. *China Quarterly*, 71.

Walker, Kenneth R. 1982: Interpreting Chinese grain consumption statistics. *China Quarterly*, 92.

World Bank 1984: *China The Health Sector*. Washington, DC: World Bank.

Yang Jianbai and Li Xuezeng 1980: The relations between agriculture, light industry and heavy industry in China. *Social Sciences in China*, 2.

ZMWTZ (*Zhongguo Maoyi Wujia Tongji Ziliao 1952–1983*) 1984: (Statistics on China's commerce and prices, 1952–1983.) Office of Commerce and Price Statistics, State Statistical Bureau, Beijing: China Statistical Publishing House.

ZNTN (*Zhongguo Nongcun Tongji Nianjian*) 1986: (Rural Statistical Yearbook of China.) Beijing: China Statistical Publishing House.

ZTN (*Zhongguo Tongji Nianjian*) 1983, 1986, 1987, 1988: Volumes for 1983, 1986, 1987, and 1988. Beijing. China Statistical Publishing House.

ZTZ (*Zhongguo Tongji Zhaiyao*) 1987: Beijing: China Statistical Publishing House.

13

World Nutritional Problems

NEVIN SCRIMSHAW

In both Europe and North America, mountainous surpluses of food are produced with costly subsidies and are stored at almost prohibitive costs. Moreover, Australia and Argentina have large quantities of grain and meat to export, and Brazil now competes for world soy markets. Thailand is a strong rice exporter, and a number of other developing countries have reduced or eliminated their need to import food and are potential food exporters.

Nevertheless, in the world today, more people suffer from malnutrition than ever before. The Fifth FAO World Food survey estimates over 490 million persons in 1979–81 to be undernourished each year by the criterion of a dietary energy intake less than an estimated "minimum requirement" of $1.4 \times$ basal metabolic rate. However, this is not sufficient for more than sedentary survival without physical work or the maintenance of long-term cardiovascular fitness (Food and Agriculture Organization, 1987). By the more appropriate criterion of an intake adequate for productive physical activity, the number is close to one billion persons (Reutlinger and Alderman, 1980). For hundreds of millions of individuals the hidden hungers of iron deficiency, avitaminosis A, and iodine deficiency disorders are more common and significant than simple lack of food. Iron and iodine deficiencies affect at least 500 million persons.

When globally there is plenty of food for all and when agricultural technologies are available to increase it still further, the existence of so much malnutrition is difficult to believe. It is true that global food production in countries and regions fluctuates from year to year with climatic and other conditions. Yet this is not the cause of chronic hunger or even of the frequent famines that still occur in some parts of the world. They are due to the inability of large segments of the population of developing countries to produce or purchase sufficient food (Scrimshaw, 1987). This chapter will examine the tragic consequences for individuals and societies of global malnutrition.

Significance of Malnutrition for Developing Countries

For some populations, dietary energy intakes average 10 percent to 20 percent lower than "requirement" estimates suggest. These persons are undernourished because they cannot afford enough food for a desirable level of physical activity. However, they are not wasting away and dying of starvation. Therefore, some compensatory mechanism must be involved that enables them to survive on apparently inadequate caloric intakes. The critical question is whether or not this adaptation has serious biological, social, and economic costs.

Sukhatme and Margen (1982) have suggested that the adaptation may be one of increased efficiency of metabolism, but careful research studies indicate that, at most, no more than 15 percent of the adaptation could be accounted for by this mechanism and probably much less (Beaton, 1985). Recent studies in the Gambia suggest that BMR may be seasonally reduced 8–10 percent with severe deficiency (Lawrence et al., 1989). There is good direct evidence that most of the adaptation comes about through reduced physical activity (Beaton, 1985; G. Beaton and Taylor, 1981).

Because survival requires that work activity be sustained as much as possible, most of the reduction occurs in discretionary activities. These are essential for household improvements, supplementary economic activities, community organization, and those activities on which development plans depend. When the adaptation required is too great or the individual is forced to maintain activity despite reduced food intake, weight loss must occur.

If the caloric deficiency is sufficiently severe, work activity will be affected as well (Spurr, 1983). An example of this can be seen in much of Central America: plantation workers are paid by the task rather than by the hour because there is so much variation in the amount of work that a poorly nourished laborer can complete in an hour. Torun and Viteri (1981; and see United Nations University, 1979) observed that male workers on a plantation in Guatemala worked hard for the hours necessary to complete their tasks and then remained sedentary for the rest of the day and slept long hours in the afternoon and at night. When they were given food ad libitum for lunch, caloric intake and discretionary activity markedly increased (Viteri and Torun, 1975).

A study of road-workers in Kenya reported an increase of 12.5 percent in daily productivity after an average of 53 days of caloric supplementation (Wolegemuth et al., 1982). Such observations are not confined to developing countries. The productivity of one group of calorie-restricted industrial workers in Germany during the Second World War increased 47 percent when caloric intake was increased by 500 calories per day (Kraut, 1946).

The activity of children is similarly affected by caloric restriction. Viteri and Torun (1981) observed in detail for one month the activity patterns and growth of children in a home for the recuperation of malnourished children in Guatemala. They then carried out the same observations when the caloric intake was reduced 10 percent and later 20 percent for similar one-month periods with protein and other nutrient intakes unchanged. With the first food intake reduction there was a notable decrease in play activity, but growth was not affected, and zero energy balance was soon achieved. With a 20 percent decrease in dietary energy a further reduction in physical activity was not enough to compensate, and growth was also affected.

Since, in peasant societies, women keep working from early morning until night, their adaptation must lie in the rate and efficiency of their work. Moreover, in some societies they are observed to lose weight during the hungry season (Spalding et al., 1977). While physiological adaptation to calorie deficits may be complete in the sense that energy balance is achieved, the behavioral consequences are clearly of social significance.

For women, the consequences extend not only to their household activities and child care but also to the birth weight of their infants. This is particularly significant because low birth weight due to undernutrition during pregnancy is associated with higher infant morbidity and mortality and with poorer growth. In a recent study sponsored by the United Nations University (UNU) in the Philippines, supplementary food for undernourished families resulted in significantly less sedentary time and even more energy expenditure per unit time in some activities.

Adaptation to low food intakes beyond reduced physical activity requires stabilization of weight at a lower level than that associated with good ad libitum nutrition. Adults in the low income groups in developing countries are typically thin and obviously undernourished. If higher energy intake is required and caloric intake is not sufficient for energy balance, weight loss occurs and semistarvation results.

For young children, such a reduction in physical activity decreases the interaction with their environment that is essential for normal cognitive development and results in long-term consequences for learning and behavior. When the energy deficit is more severe, their growth will be permanently stunted and future work capacity reduced.

Effects of Severe Calorie Restriction

The discussion thus far has considered degrees of enforced caloric restriction to which populations can adapt by reduced physical activity, sustained or seasonal weight loss, or, in the case of children, impaired child growth.

However, the degree of undernutrition may be so severe that progressive weight loss ensues with marked loss of strength and endurance in adults, and in children the condition known as marasmus.

When individuals who are not obese lose only 10 to 15 percent of their body weight due to inadequate food, changes such as slowed heart rate, reduced ability to concentrate, and increased tiredness are apparent. The individual literally consumes muscle tissue to protect the essential visceral organs, including the liver, pancreas, and intestines. Heart muscle shares in the loss with a reduction in cardiac capacity (Keys et al., 1950). With weight losses of 15 to 20 percent individuals become depressed, apathetic, and weak and reduce their activity to a minimum (Taylor and Keys, 1950; Winnick, 1979; Young and Scrimshaw, 1971).

When infants receive little or no breast milk and no adequate replacement for it, marasmus develops as body weight is lost. At first subcutaneous fat serves as a major energy source, and the breakdown of lean body mass furnishes amino acids for both gluconeogenesis and new protein synthesis. When the subcutaneous fat is gone and loss of lean body mass becomes more rapid, death is near. Symptoms and signs of kwashiorkor do not develop, because amino acids are released by the breakdown of skeletal muscle and are available for protein synthesis.

When a diet is deficient in protein relative to calories, the result is kwashiorkor, even if calories are fully adequate (Scrimshaw and Behar, 1961). Infection is usually a precipitating factor. This disease occurs most commonly at the time of weaning when breast milk is no longer sufficient as a sole source of food and the complementary food fails to provide needed protein. The clinical signs are edema, skin and hair changes, apathy, and diarrhea. Because amino acids are not available for normal protein synthesis, intestinal enzyme activity, total serum protein, and albumen and many serum enzymes are reduced, and the liver becomes filled with fat due to lack of transport protein. If the condition is acute and untreated it usually ends in death from superimposed infection, to which the child with kwashiorkor has little resistance.

Long-term Consequences of Malnutrition in Children

There are two serious long-term consequences of even mild to moderate protein-energy malnutrition in preschool children. One of these is that the slower growth is never made up, so the child becomes a stunted adult. While it is apparent that people who have been stunted in childhood and survive to adulthood can work very hard and develop endurance, they are still at a disadvantage in the performance of manual labor. Many studies confirm this observation. In Guatemala the physical capacity of plantation workers has been found to be less for stunted individuals as judged by treadmill measurements and field observations of capacity to cut sugar cane (Flores et al., 1985; Immink et al., 1984; Viteri, 1976). Similar findings have been reported from Colombia (Spurr, 1984; Spurr et al., 1977), the Sudan (Davies et al., 1976), and India (Satyanarayana et al., 1978). The same relationship has been described for school-age boys from Colombia (Spurr et al., 1984), Brazil (Desai et al, 1984; Dutra et al., 1985), and India (Satyanarayana et al., 1977a). Desai et al. (1984) showed that stunted adolescent males had their physical capacity reduced by one-third when measured by work at a near maximal heart rate. The same significant relationship has been reported for Ethiopian (Areskog et al., 1969) and Indian (Satyanarayana et al., 1977b) adult males. Gopalan has warned of the fallacy of considering that "small is beautiful" when referring to the stunting that occurs with chronic malnutrition in childhood (Gopalan, 1982).

It is quite true that the capacity to do hard physical work may be decreasing in importance in developing countries and that size, if it is genetically determined, is of no significance for learning and behavior. But if growth is retarded because of malnutrition, there is a significant effect on cognitive performance (Craviotto et al., 1966) that is due to a synergistic combination of the malnutrition and the social circumstances associated with it. School performance is adversely affected and the loss is not likely to be made up.

Relationship of Hunger and Malnutrition to Infection

Reference has already been made to the synergistic interaction of malnutrition and infection. Any infection, no matter how mild, worsens nutritional status and most nutritional deficiencies increase susceptibility to infection. The result is more serious than could be predicted from the effects of either alone. Infections, even those as mild as immunizations with attenuated virus strains, cause measurable anorexia and increased metabolic losses of nitrogen, vitamin A, ascorbic acid and other vitamins, minerals, and other nutrients (Chandra and Newberne, 1977; Scrimshaw et al., 1968a). These catabolic effects are compounded by the diversion of amino acids and other nutrients essential for the synthesis of immunoglobulins and a variety of other metabolites associated with the response to infection. If the gastro-intestinal tract is affected by the infection, absorption of nutrients may also be impaired.

These biological effects of infection on nutritional status are often compounded by behavioral ones. In many societies individuals with fever and other symptoms of infectious disease receive starchy gruels instead of solid food. This practice is particularly hazardous for young children. The combined result of all of these effects is that the infection may precipitate acute clinical manifestations of nutritional deficiency disease if the individual is already marginally deficient in a specific nutrient.

There is also extensive evidence for the role of malnutrition in reducing resistance to infection so that both morbidity and mortality from infectious diseases are increased, even in marginally malnourished populations (Chandra and Newberne, 1977; Scrimshaw et al., 1968a). The mechanisms include interference with cellular immunity, including T-cell function; impaired phagocytic capacity; reduced, delayed cutaneous hypersensitivity; and defects in complement formation. With more severe malnutrition, the results are reduced antibody formation and alterations in epithelial integrity (Chandra and Newberne, 1977).

In populations living under adverse environmental circumstances in which diarrheal and other infections are frequent, new infectious episodes occur before nutritional recovery from the effects of the previous one. This explains the appearance of nutritional disease after an infection that seems to be no more serious than many previous ones. Death rates per 1,000 preschool children in developing countries may be 20–40 times higher than in Europe and North America. Most of these deaths are due to the synergism of malnutrition and infection, regardless of the reported terminal cause (Puffer and Serrano, 1975).

Effects of Specific Nutrient Deficiencies

At the beginning of the twentieth century two classical deficiency diseases, beri-beri and pellagra, were leading causes of death and disability in many countries. Beri-beri due to thiamine deficiency was the major cause of death and disability in the predominately rice-eating populations of Asia. Increasing variety in the diet with rising standards of living has made this condition disappear as a public health problem. As recently as the 1930s in the US and the 1940s in southern Europe, Egypt, and parts of Africa, pellagra due to niacin deficiency was a major health problem. This disease was confined almost exclusively to populations consuming a predominately corn or sorghum diet, low in both niacin and the amino acid tryptophan, which to a limited extent can serve as a precursor of niacin. With the exception of a small, predominately sorghum-eating population in central India, pellagra has disappeared as a public health problem, due also to greater variety in the diets of populations in which the predominant food was once maize. Although also dependent on maize, the populations of Mexico and Central America largely escaped this problem because their method of alkaline treatment to prepare their maize increased the availability of niacin and tryptophan, and the beans and coffee in their diet contributed additional niacin.

Two additional classical deficiency diseases, scurvy and rickets, have also almost entirely disappeared. Scurvy was first recognized as a disease of sailors on long voyages. It was prevented in the British navy by the use of limes. This was long before it was recognized that lack of Vitamin C, found in high concentration in limes and other citrus fruits, was responsible. Although it has long ceased to be a public health problem even in developing countries, it has recently reappeared among refugee populations in Africa. Until the early decades of the present century, rickets was common in the young children of northern Europe because of the lack of sufficient winter exposure to sunlight to convert enough ergosterol in the skin to an active form of vitamin D, and the lack of vitamin A in the diet. The giving of fish-liver oil and, later, synthetic vitamin A drops to infants eliminated the problem. It is still occasionally seen among children raised in north Africa without exposure to the sun.

Despite the disappearance of these classical vitamin deficiency diseases, there are still three widespread specific nutritional deficiencies with major adverse functional consequences both for individuals and for societies as a whole. These are deficiencies of iron, vitamin A, and iodine. While there are other potential nutritional disorders they are not of major public health and social significance.

Iron Deficiency

Iron deficiency is the most common single-nutrient deficiency in the world today. Iron deficiency anemia is found in about one-third of the population of many developing countries and another third can be identified bio-chemically as iron deficient even though they do not manifest anemia. The significance of iron deficiency lies in the increasing evidence that both cognitive performance and resistance to infection are reduced even when the disorder is only mild to moderate in degree and not accompanied by anemia (Scrimshaw, 1984). As would be expected, these functions are still more affected when the iron status is poor enough to cause anemia. This pattern of iron deficiency effects also appears to hold true for work capacity and productivity.

The evidence for the effect on cognitive performance comes mainly from observations in the United States, Guatemala, Egypt, and Indonesia. These studies show that infants, preschool children, and schoolchildren who are iron deficient have impaired performance on a series of appropriate behavioral tests. When they are then given either an iron supplement or a placebo on a double-blind basis, test performance becomes normal in those receiving the iron, if the deficiency is mild to moderate, and it is unchanged in those receiving the placebo.

This was the finding in studies of preschool children in Cambridge, Massachusetts (Pollitt et al., 1982), Guatemala (Pollitt et al., 1981), and Egypt (Pollitt et al., 1985). If the iron depletion is severe, however, as in some preschool children in the studies in Guatemala and Egypt, full recovery of test performance is not seen within the supplementation period of two months. In research in Indonesia (Soemantri et al., 1985) complete recovery of the hemoglobin concentration of anemic schoolchildren, after three months of supplementation with 10 mg per kg per day of ferrous sulfate, was accompanied by improvement but not complete recovery. No changes were seen in the placebo group. Similar studies have not yet been conducted with adults, but there is no reason to believe that the results would be different.

To study the effects of iron deficiency on physical fitness, Viteri and co-workers measured Harvard Step-Test performances on a Guatemalan plantation (Viteri, 1976). Scores were linearly related to hemoglobin level, and the performance of most of the anemic workers improved strikingly with iron supplementation, while for most a placebo had no effect. The take-home pay of Indonesian rubber tappers, who were paid by the amount they collect, was linearly related to their hemoglobin level (Basta et al., 1979). When they were given an iron supplement for 60 days, their collections and pay increased by 36 percent. Similar relationships between hemoglobin and both treadmill performance and productivity have been described for tea plantation workers in Sri Lanka (Edgerton et al., 1982) and Indonesia (Hussaini et al., 1985).

Equally significant is the relationship between iron deficiency and an increased frequency and severity of diarrheal and respiratory infections observed in studies in Alaska (Brown et al., 1967), Indonesia (Hussein et al., 1988), and a number of other countries. Iron deficiency lowers the activity of the iron-dependent enzymes that are needed in phagocytic cells to kill ingested bacteria, with a decrease in T-cells that are important for effective phagocyte function. It also affects the kind of delayed cutaneous hypersensitivity that is exemplified by the tuberculin reaction and that is an indicator of resistance (Chandra and Newberne, 1977).

Iodine Deficiency Disorders

Endemic goiter is global in distribution wherever populations depend on local food supplies grown on iodine-poor soil. The latter includes regions that have been glaciated, mountainous areas, and ones with heavy rainfall. Except where iodized salt has been introduced, goiter is still prevalent along the Andean chain of mountains, across Central Africa and the Asian subcontinent, and along the entire length of the Himalayan chain, with large pockets of severe disease in China as well as in Burma, Vietnam, and New Guinea (Ma Tai et al., 1982; Stanbury, 1985).

Until recently, iodine deficiency was identified only with a compensatory swelling of the thyroid gland known as endemic goiter and with cretinism, a manifestation in the child of severe iodine deficiency during pregnancy. The typical cretin has profound mental deficiency, a characteristic appearance, a shuffling gait, shortened stature, and a spastic dysplegia. The subject is typically deaf and mute, and commonly dies unless given good care.

It is now recognized that even when cases of cretinism are small in number in a population, their presence indicates a much larger number of persons who do not have any of the classic features of cretinism, but whose linear growth, intellectual capacity, and neurological functions are compromised to varying degrees (Stanbury, 1985). Thus the burden to the community due to iodine deficiency lies in the widespread functional impairment in the population. The tragedy is that these conditions are all readily preventable through the iodation of salt or the administration of iodinated oil to women of childbearing age.

Vitamin A Deficiency

Severe vitamin A deficiency results in xerophthalmia or dry cornea, and in a softening of the cornea, keratomalacia. The deficiency can progress to eventual prolapse of the iris, loss of the lens, and a scarred, blind eye. This kind of lesion is most often seen in children with severe protein-calorie malnutrition or as an aftermath of diarrhea, measles, or other communicable diseases of childhood in children already in borderline nutritional status with respect to the vitamin. Vitamin A deficiency also exacerbates iron deficiency (Mejia and Arroyave, 1982) and is associated with increased susceptibility to infections (Sommer et al., 1983, 1984).

The trials of vitamin A fortification in Guatemala (Mejia and Arroyave, 1982) and of periodic massive doses in Indonesia (Tarwotjo et al., 1986) also indicated a reduction in morbidity and mortality from infectious disease. There are also indications from studies in Indonesia (Hussaini, 1982) and Guatemala (Mejia and Arroyave, 1982) that vitamin A supplementation improves iron status.

Relationship of Food Production to Undernutrition

Widespread chronic hunger has not been eliminated in the developing countries that have benefited most from the Green Revolution, even when they have achieved agricultural surpluses. Therefore the answer to the world food crisis cannot lie in food production alone. It must also be recognized that the agricultural techniques involved in the spectacular increases in crop yields of recent decades have been associated with serious environmental costs, some of which cannot be sustained indefinitely. The costs include, variously, loss of topsoil, fertilizer and pesticide runoffs, reduced habitats for plant and animal species, diminishing genetic diversity of major food plants, accelerated use of petroleum and other non-renewable resources, and the need for government subsidies due to the high cost of inputs.

India in the 1950s required millions of tons of North American grain to feed its people and obtained this readily from the United States at concessionary prices. This enabled it to concentrate on the urban and industrial sectors to the neglect of policies that would assist local food production. In the 1960s, largely for political reasons, India initiated price incentives and other policy changes to lessen its dependence on such imports. Aided by Green Revolution technologies, agricultural production increased rapidly and, by 1970, India acquired a 22-million-ton grain reserve. This enabled it to feed over 12 million refugees from Bangladesh in 1971 and ever since to avert the frequent local famines that have long plagued it. Unfortunately, this has not led to abolition of hunger in that country. In China, the introduction of market incentives in 1982 resulted in a 15 percent increase in rice production and a 40 percent increase in wheat production in four years.

Diet and Disease in Industrialized Countries

Cardiovascular Disease

Mention should be made of the growing evidence of the relationship between diet and hypertension (Iacono and Dougherty, 1987), and that of the amount and kind of dietary fat with atherosclerosis and coronary heart disease (Hegsted et al., 1965; Keys et al., 1957, 1965). There is a close linear association between cholesterol levels and heart disease (Keys, 1970, 1980; McGee and Gordon, 1976). The saturated fatty acids predominating in animal fats and coconut oil tend to elevate serum cholesterol. The unsaturated fat characteristic of most vegetable oils consists mainly of monounsaturated fat, which is neutral in its effect on cholesterol, and polyunsaturated fat, which lowers cholesterol level.

Both the omega-6 fatty acid, linoleic, that predominates in vegetable oils, and smaller amounts of the omega-3 fatty acid, alpha-linolenic, found in soybean oil and some fruits and vegetables, are essential in the diet and contribute to the cholesterol-lowering effect. The need for the omega-3 fatty acid can also be advantageously met by fish oils. The amount of cholesterol in the diet over a fairly broad range has less influence than does fat intake, because healthy persons alter endogenous cholesterol synthesis in response to dietary intake.

It has also become clear that about 15–20 percent of the population will have increased blood pressure with sodium intakes that are the equivalent of more than 3 to 5 g of salt per day. A comparison of mean population blood pressures and mean salt intakes in 27 populations has shown convincing linear relationships for both systolic and diastolic blood pressures (MacGregor, 1985). In Asia, the sodium intakes are increased by the use of soy sauce containing 30–50 percent salt and by monosodium glutamate, which is also a significant source of sodium in the diet. The relatively large amount of salt added to processed food is a serious concern. There is also evidence that reducing saturated fat in the diet tends to lower blood pressure (Iacono and Dougherty, 1987). Overweight and obesity also play a significant role in the development of a number of diseases including coronary heart disease, hypertension, some cancers, and type-2 diabetes (National Institutes of Health, 1985).

Cancer

As other causes of death are eliminated or reduced, cancer continues to increase as a cause of morbidity and mortality of the elderly. There is increasing evidence that dietary factors influence the occurrence of some forms of cancer. For example, societies with a high intake of smoked and salted foods have a higher prevalence of cancers of the esophagus and stomach (Committee on Diet, Nutrition and Cancer, 1982). The incidence of breast and colon cancer is low in Japanese in Japan consuming a traditional diet, but much higher in ethnic Japanese living in California.

The principal differences seem to be the amount of animal fat and dairy products consumed (Buell, 1973). This is supported by a close correlation between the levels of dietary fat of different ethnic groups and rates of breast cancer in Hawaii (Kolonel et al., 1981). The evidence for the role of fiber in reducing cancer of the gastrointestinal tracts is less convincing, but diets low in fiber are also likely to be low in vitamins such as A, E, and C which are thought to reduce cancer risk (Greenwald and Lanza, 1986).

The Future

Scientific and Technological Potential

There are good reasons for confidence in the technical ability of the world to produce enough food. Much land is presently farmed inefficiently. Changing to more appropriate crops and technologies could make large differences in total production. Moreover, the demonstrated potential of new or newly appreciated technologies, such as multiple cropping and intercropping, are now exploited to only a limited degree. In addition, for all of the principle crops there are large discrepancies between the crop yields of the most advanced countries and of less developed ones, and between the most advanced farmers in the developing countries and the great majority.

There are enormous quantities of organic residues, from fruit and vegetable processing, cellulosic and starchy residues, and animal and human wastes that are now barely exploited but can be converted into microbial biomass for fertilizer, feed, and in some cases for human consumption. Although the economics are currently not attractive, a tiny fraction of the world's annual petroleum use would suffice to produce almost unlimited amounts of yeast or bacterial or fungal biomass suitable for animal feeding, which in most cases could also be processed for food use. Yeasts grown on petroleum hydrocarbons are an important source of animal feed in the Soviet Union and a filamentous microfungal protein produced on starchy waste is being successfully marketed in food products in the UK.

The knowledge is at hand, and more is likely to be forthcoming, to avoid most adverse environmental impact of the new technologies. Developments such as trickle-irrigation to avert salination, biological pest control measures, multiple cropping that reduces vulnerability both to pests and to erosion, and a variety of measures to reduce overuse of fertilizers are already available. There is no doubt that the technological boundaries of world food production will expand enormously as the new techniques of genetic engineering and biotechnology begin to bear fruit.

Social, Economic, and Political Factors

The practical results lie largely in the future, but the potential is far greater than is generally recognized. These and other successes or potential successes of science and technology only highlight the problems that cannot be solved by agricultural research and biotechnology. These are the political and institutional constraints on both food production and the purchasing power of those who need the food. They include inequitable land-tenure systems, exploitive land tenancy relationships, disincentive pricing for agricultural commodities, neglect of rural infrastructures and human services to rural areas, and vigorous pursuit of new privileges by elites with little concern for the plight of the poor.

It is true that external global factors such as fluctuations in oil prices, falling prices for many Third World exports, subsidized agricultural sales by the US and the EEC, and adjustment pressures from lending agencies have seriously complicated national options and decisions. Moreover, the world food problem is global in its dimensions, but it must be solved at the national level first and foremost, for this is where the problem lies. The great differences in the success of countries in preventing hunger cannot be explained primarily on the basis of natural resources.

To consider alleviation of hunger without taking into account the social, economic, and political factors involved would be a serious mistake. We must face the fact that food production is only indirectly at the root of the world food crises. With few exceptions food continues to be produced everywhere in response to effective demand − that is, the amount that someone can pay for, barter for, or acquire the land to produce for subsistence.

Agricultural and food science and technology can do much to improve the efficiency of production, to reduce post-harvest losses, to facilitate more efficient distribution, and to overcome environmental obstacles to production. By attention to the needs of the small farmer and the stimulation of small rural industries, they can also contribute to effective demand, but food science and technology cannot by themselves solve the basic problem of lack of entitlement, the inability of the poor to acquire the food they need.

The clearest examples of hunger due to inadequate food production would be expected in the frequent famines that have plagued humankind throughout history and are still continuing. Yet careful analysis reveals that most famines are due not to an absolute shortage or unavailability of food but to a lack of entitlement in a population (Sen, 1981). The same is true of most protein-energy malnutrition.

Increasing entitlement of the poor is the necessary factor for the elimination of protein-energy malnutrition. However, this usually requires political actions that are extremely difficult to bring about in most societies. The social and economic changes that may be required may be fiercely resisted or the need for them simply ignored. The prevention of the remaining major deficiencies, those of iron, vitamin A, and iodine, can be achieved by technological means that are feasible and relatively economical. However, since they too require political will and political action, they may be difficult to bring about where governments are not sensitive to the health needs of the population.

The addition of iodine to salt has been demonstrated to be capable of

eliminating endemic iodine deficiency disorders wherever it has been im-
plemented. Usually, this does not even require an increase in the cost of
salt to the public. It does require legislation or decrees requiring it and a
system of monitoring compliance. In Colombia the prevalence of endemic
goiter fell from 83.1 percent in 1945 to 1.8 percent in 1965 where iodized
salt was introduced (Rueda-Williamson et al., 1966). In Guatemala in 1954
endemic goiter prevalence was 38 percent, with some highland village
populations having prevalence rates as high as 90 percent (Munoz et al.,
1955). Within three years after the addition of potassium iodate to all salt
for human consumption was required and enforced, prevalence rates dropped
to 12 percent; they later fell to 5 percent (Scrimshaw et al., 1968) and
remained low for two decades. However, with the political turmoil of the
last few years, enforcement of iodization was neglected, and goiter rates
rose again until controls were reintroduced.

In the case of vitamin A, the cheapest and most obvious solution has
proved difficult. Most societies with a serious problem of avitaminosis A
have ready access to green leaves in the wild or the capability of growing
them in home gardens. But efforts to encourage the consumption of local
leaves as a source of vitamin A activity have been relatively unsuccessful.
However, massive oral doses of Vitamin A tested in India (Pereira and
Begum, 1973; Reddy, 1986), Thailand (Thanangkul et al., 1986), Brazil
(Araujo et al., 1969), and the Philippines (Latham and Solon, 1986) have
provided UNICEF with a practical means of preventing xerophthalmia in
many countries. Moreover, Arroyave's (Mejia and Arroyave, 1982) successful
fortification of sugar on a national scale in Guatemala and Costa Rica is
now being extended to other countries.

The National Institute of Nutrition in Hyderabad, India, has demonstrated
a practical means of double fortification of salt with both iodine and iron.
Viteri et al. (1981) in Central America and Layrisse et al. (1976) in
Colombia have demonstrated that the addition of EDTA-iron to refined
sugar is practicable. It is also feasible to fortify cereal products and infant
foods with iron, and this has long been the practice in North America and
most European countries.

*Measures to Reduce Nutrition-related Disease in Industrialized
Countries*

The first step in national efforts to improving diets in industrialized countries
and among the more affluent in developing countries is nutrition and
health education of the public. An important step is the formulation of
nutrition guidelines. Those established for Australia are shown in table
13.1. Like those from Norway (Blythe, 1978), the United States (Staff of

Table 13.1   Dietary guidelines for Australians

Increase breastfeeding
Provide nutritional education on a balanced diet
Reduce the prevalence of obesity
Decrease total fat consumption
Decrease refined sugar consumption
Increase consumption of complex carbohydrates and dietary fiber
Decrease consumption of alcohol
Decrease consumption of salt

Source: Nutrition Task Force, 1987

the Select Committee on Nutrition and Human Needs, 1977), the UK (UK Department of Health and Social Security, 1978), Sweden (Bruce, 1986), and Japan (Hosoya, 1985), they emphasize a balanced diet characterized by a decrease in the percent of fat calories, particularly from saturated fat, less dietary cholesterol, lower salt intake, less refined carbohydrate, more green and yellow vegetables, and an energy intake to maintain an appropriate body weight.

The most recent recommendations are those developed for nutrition and health in Latin America (Bengoa et al., 1988), which follow the same pattern. However, the recommendations note the need for essential fatty acids, both those in the linoleic (omega-6) series and alpha-linolenic acid (omega 3). It is recommended that these fatty acids make up 10–20 percent of the polyunsaturated fat in the diet. Alpha-linolenic acid can come from soy oil or from its derivatives, eicosapentanoic and decosahexanoic acids, found in fish oil and the fat of wild animals. The report reviewed the evidence for a relationship between dietary fat and cardiovascular disease and came to the conclusion that a range of 20–25 percent of calories from fat was appropriate and that a ratio of saturated, monounsaturated, and polyunsaturated of 1:1:1 is a desirable target. However, a greater amount of monounsaturated fat such as predominates in olive oil is acceptable as long as the percent of total fat in the diet does not exceed the guidelines. A higher amount or proportion of saturated fat, it is concluded, would lead not only to an increase in serum cholesterol with increased risk of coronary disease, but also in essential hypertension and an increased risk of some forms of cancer.

Whether or not governments have had official education campaigns or even national dietary guidelines, information emphasizing the relationship between diet and health, and particularly between diet and both heart disease and cancer, has been widely disseminated through magazines, newspapers, radio, and television. Despite considerable misinformation as well, this has started a trend with clearly documented effects on food practices in a number of countries and a concurrent decrease in deaths from heart disease. It remains to be seen whether breast cancer will also decline.

The willingness of populations to respond to health advice should not be overestimated. The use of tobacco is a far greater risk factor for both heart disease and cancer than any known dietary factor and yet cigarette smoking has until recently continued to increase, particularly among women. However, in the United States at least, the peak has been reached and there is a distinct downward trend in cigarette smoking that is more marked in men than in women. No discussion of world food problems should omit reference to the adverse effects of rapid population growth; in the present volume this topic is discussed in chapter 1.

Summary

Hunger and malnutrition, exacerbated by infectious disease and high rates of population growth, remain major problems of most developing countries in today's world, with profoundly adverse individual, social, and economic consequences on these countries. A combination of improved agricultural policies and the application of new technologies can ensure adequate food production in almost all countries. Similarly immunization, environmental sanitation, and other health measures can reduce the burden of infectious disease.

While adequate food production and measures to control infectious diseases are essential prerequisites, they clearly do not assure the end of chronic hunger. It is essential for these countries to address factors responsible for the equitable distribution of food and not just its production. The true solution must be sought in a comprehensive process of social, economic, and political development that is ecologically sound and that directly attacks both rural and urban poverty. Science and technology have an essential role to play in this comprehensive process, but the final determinants of success will be political and social progress that leads to adequate food entitlements for all.

REFERENCES

Araujo, R. L., Araujo, M. B. D. G., Rosangela, D. P., et al. 1969: Evaluation of a program to overcome vitamin A and iron deficiency in areas of poverty in Minas Gerais, Brazil. *Archivos Latinoamericanos*, 636, 642–54.
Areskog, N., Selinus, R., and Vahlquist, B. 1969: Physical work capacity and

nutritional status in Ethiopian male children and young adults. *American Journal of Clinical Nutrition*, 22, 471–9.

Basta, S., Soekirman, Karyadi, D., and Scrimshaw, N. S. 1979: Iron deficiency anemia and the productivity of adult males in Indonesia. *American Journal of Clinical Nutrition*, 32, 916–25.

Bauernfeind, J. C. (ed.) 1986: *Vitamin A deficiency and its control*. New York, San Francisco: Academic Press.

Beaton, G. and Taylor, L. E. 1981: The uses of energy and protein requirement estimates. Report of a workshop. *Food and Nutrition Bulletin*, 3, 45–53.

Beaton, G. H. 1985: The significance of adaptation in the definition of nutrient requirements and for nutrition policy. In K. Blaxter and J. C. Waterlow (eds), *Nutritional Adaptation in Man*. London: John Libbey, 219–32.

Bengoa, J. M., Torun, B., Behar, M., and Scrimshaw, N. S. 1988: *Guias de Alimentacion; Bases para su desarrollo en America Latina*. Caracas: Fundacion Cavendes.

Blythe, C. 1978: Norwegian nutrition and food policy. In *Food Policy*. Sussex, UK.

Brown, C. V., Brown, G. W., and Bonehill, B. 1967: Relationship of anemia to infectious illness on Kodiak Island. *Alaska Med*, 9, 93.

Bruce, A. P. E. 1986: The implementation of dietary guidelines. In *Proceedings of the ILSI Meeting*. Algarve, Portugal: ILSI.

Buell, P. J. 1973: Changing incidence of breast cancer in Japanese-American women. *Journal of the National Cancer Institute*, 51, 1479–83.

Chandra, R. K. and Newberne, P. M. 1977: *Nutrition, Immunity, and Infection: Mechanisms of interactions*. New York: Plenum Press.

Committee on Diet, Nutrition and Cancer 1982: *Diet, Nutrition and Cancer*. Washington, DC: National Academy Press.

Craviotto, J., De Licarche, E., and Birch, C. 1966: Nutrition, growth and neuro-integrative development: An experimental and ecologic study. *Pediatrics*, 38, 319.

Davies, C. T. M., Brotherhood, J. R., Collins K. J., et al. 1976: Energy expenditure and physiological performance of Sudanese cane cutters. *British Journal of Industrial Medicine*, 33, 181–6.

Desai, I., Waddell, D. S., Dutra de Oliveira, J., et al. 1984: Marginal malnutrition and reduced physical work capacity of migrant adolescent boys in southern Brazil. *American Journal of Clinical Nutrition*, 40, 135–45.

Dutra de Oliveira, J., Dos Santos, J., and Desai, I. 1985: Commentary. In O. Brunser et al. (eds), *Clinical Nutrition of the Young Child*, New York: Raven Press, 92–4.

Edgerton, V. R., Ohira, Y., Gardner, G. W., and Seniratne, B. 1982: Effects of iron deficiency anemia on voluntary activities in rats and humans. In E. Pollitt and R. L. Leibel (eds), *Iron Deficiency: Brain biochemistry and behavior*, New York: Raven Press, 141–60.

Flores, R., Immink, M. D. C., Torun, B., Diaz, E., and Viteri, F. E. 1985: Functional consequences of marginal malnutrition among agricultural workers in Guatemala. Part I. Physical work capacity. *Food and Nutrition Bulletin*, 6, 5–11.

Food and Agriculture Organization 1987: *Fifth World Food Survey*. Rome: FAO.

Gopalan, C. 1982: The nutrition policy of brinkmanship. *Bulletin of the Nutrition Foundation of India*, October, 1–2.

Greenwald, P. and Lanza, E. 1986: Role of dietary fiber in the prevention of cancer. In V. T. De Vita, S. Hellman, and S. A. Rosenberg (eds), *Important Advances in Oncology*, Philadelphia: J. B. Lippincott, 37–54.

Hegsted, D. M., McGandy, R. B., Myers, M. L., and Stare, F. J. 1965: Quantitative effects of dietary fat on serum cholesterol in man. *American Journal of Clinical Nutrition*, 17, 281.

Hosoya, N. 1985: Diet for health promotion. *Ji-ryo*, 67, 413–17.

Hussaini, M. A. 1982: The use of fortified salt to control vitamin A deficiency. Bogor Agricultural University, Bogor, Indonesia: unpublished Ph.D. thesis.

Hussaini, M. A., Djojosoebagio, S., and Karyadi, D. 1985: Socioeconomic and dietary correlates of iron deficiency on an Indonesian tea plantation. In: *Proceedings of the Eighth Annual INACG Meeting, Bali, Indonesia*, 14–17 November 1984, New York: Nutrition Foundation.

Hussein, M. A., Hassan, H., Abdel-Ghaffar, A., and Salem, S. 1988: Effect of iron supplements on the occurrence of diarrhea among children in rural Egypt. *Food and Nutrition Bulletin* 10(2), 35–9.

Iacono, J. M. and Dougherty, R. M. 1987: Dietary polyunsaturated fat and blood pressure regulations. In *AIN Symposium Proceedings. Nutrition '87*, Bethesda, Md.: AIN, 105–9.

Immink, M. D. C., Viteri, F. E., Flores, R., and Torun, B. 1984: Microeconomic consequences of energy deficiency in rural populations in developing countries. In E. Pollitt and P. Amante (eds), *Current Topics in Nutrition and Disease*, New York: Alan R. Liss, 355–76.

Keys, A. (ed.) 1970: Coronary heart disease in seven countries. *Circulation*, 41(Suppl. I), I–1.

Keys, A. 1980: *Seven Countries: A multivariate analysis of death and coronary heart disease*. Cambridge, Mass.: Harvard University Press.

Keys, A., Anderson, J. T., and Grande, F. 1957: Prediction of serum cholesterol responses of man to changes in fats in the diet. *Lancet*, 2, 959.

Keys, A., Anderson, J. T., and Grande, F., 1965: Serum cholesterol response to changes of diet: II. The effect of cholesterol in the diet. *Metabolism*, 14, 759–65.

Keys, A., Brozek, J., Henschel, A., Mickelsen, O., and Taylor, H. L. 1950: *The Biology of Human Starvation*. Minneapolis: University of Minnesota.

Kolonel, L. N., Hankin, J. H., Lee, J., Chu, S. Y., Nomura, A. M. Y., and Hinds, M. W. 1981: Nutrient intakes in relation to cancer incidence in Hawaii. *British Journal of Cancer*, 332–9.

Kraut, H. A. and Muller, E. A. 1946: Calorie intake and industrial output. *Science*, 104, 495–7.

Latham, M. C. and Solon, F. S. 1986: Vitamin A deficiency control in the Philippines. In Thanangkul et al. (1986), 389–404.

Lawrence, M., Lawrence, F. I., Cole, T. J., Coward, W. A., Singh, S., Whitehead, R. G. 1989: Seasonal pattern of activity and nutritional consequences in the

Gambia. In D. Sahn (ed.), *Causes and Implications of Seasonal Variability in Household Food Security* (forthcoming).

Layrisse, M., Martinez-Torres, C., Renzi, M., Velez, F., and Gonzales, M. 1976: Sugar as a vehicle for iron fortification. *American Journal of Clinical Nutrition*, 29, 8–18.

McGee, D. and Gordon, T. 1976: The results of the Framingham study applied to four other US-based epidemiologic studies of cardiovascular disease. In: W. B. Kannel and T. Gordon (eds), *The Framingham Study: An epidemiological investigation of cardiovascular disease*, Washington, DC: US Government Printing Office.

MacGregor, G. A. 1985: Sodium is more important than calcium in essential hypertension. *Hypertension*, 7, 628–40.

Ma Tai, Lu Tizhang, Tan Yubin, Chen Bingzhong, and Zhu Xianyi 1982: The present status of endemic goitre and endemic cretinism in China. *Food and Nutrition Bulletin*, 4, 13–19.

Mejia, L. A. and Arroyave, G. 1982: The effect of vitamin A fortification of sugar on iron metabolism in preschool children in Guatemala. *American Journal of Clinical Nutrition*, 36, 87–93.

Munoz, J. A., Perez C., and Scrimshaw, N. S. 1955: Endemic goiter in Guatemala. *American Journal of Tropical Medicine and Hygiene*, 4, 963–9.

National Institutes of Health 1985: Consensus development panel on the health implications of obesity statement. *Annals of Internal Medicine*, 103, 1073–7.

Nutrition Task Force of the Australian Commonwealth Department of Health 1987: *Toward Better Nutrition for Australians*. Canberra: Australian Government Publishing Service.

Pereira, S. M. and Begum, A. 1973: Retention of single oral massive dose of vitamin A. *Clinical Science and Molecular Medicine*.

Pollitt, E., Lewis, N., Leibel, R. L., and Greenfield, D. B. 1981: Iron deficiency and play behavior in preschool children. In P. J. Garry (ed.), *Human Nutrition*, Washington, DC: American Association for Clinical Chemistry, 290–301.

Pollitt, E., Soemantri, A. G., Yunis, F., and Scrimshaw, N. S. 1985: Cognitive effects of iron-deficiency anemia (letters to the editor). *Lancet*, 1 (8421), 158.

Pollitt, E., Viteri, F. E., Saco-Pollitt, C., and Leibel, R. L. 1982: Behavioral effects of iron deficiency anemia in children. In *Iron Deficiency: Brain biochemistry and behavior*, New York: Raven Press, 195–208.

Puffer, R. and Serrano, P. 1975: *Patterns of Mortality in Latin American Children*. Washington, DC: Pan American Health Organization.

Reddy, V. 1986: Vitamin A deficiency control in India. In Bauernfeind (1986), 389–404.

Reutlinger, S. and Alderman, H. 1980: The prevalence of calorie deficient diets in developing countries. *World Development*, 8, 239–411.

Rueda-Williamson, R., Tellez, F. P., Hoyos, F. P. M. J. A., and Naranjo, L. U. 1966: La efectividad de la yodacion de la sal en la prevencion del bocio endemico en Colombia. *Archivos Latinoamericanos de Nutricion*, 16, 65.

Satyanarayana, K., Naidu, A., and Narasinga Rao, B. 1978: Nutrition, physical work capacity and work output. *Indian Journal of Medical Research*, 68(suppl.): 88–93.

Satyanarayana, K., Naidu, A., and Narasinga Rao, B. 1979: Nutritional deprivation in boyhood and the size, activity and physical work capacity of young boys. *American Journal of Clinical Nutrition*, 32, 1769–75.

Satyanarayana, K., Naidu, A., Chatterjee, B., and Narasinga Rao, B. 1977: Body size and work output. *American Journal of Clinical Nutrition*, 30, 322–5.

Scrimshaw, N. S. 1984: Functional consequences of iron deficiency in human populations. *Journal of Nutritional Science and Vitaminology*, 30, 47–63.

Scrimshaw, N. S. 1987: The phenomenon of famine. *Annual Review of Nutrition*, 7, 1–21.

Scrimshaw, N. S. and Behar, M. 1961: Protein malnutrition in young children. *Science*, 133, 2039–47.

Scrimshaw, N. S., Taylor, C. E., and Gordon, J. E. 1968a: *Interactions of Nutrition and Infection*. WHO Monograph Series no. 57. Geneva: World Health Organization.

Scrimshaw, N. S., Guzman, M. A., Flores, M., and Gordon, J. E. 1968b: Nutrition and infection field study in Guatemalan villages, 1959–1964. V: Disease incidence among preschool children under natural village conditions, with improved diet and with medical and public health services. *Archives of Environmental Health*, 16, 223–4.

Scrimshaw, N. S., Franco, L. V., Arellano, R., Sagastume, C., Mendez, J. I., and de Leon, R. 1968c: Efecto de la Yodacion de la Sal sobre la Prevalencia de Bocio Endemico en Ninos Escolares de Guatemala. *Boletin de Oficina de la Sante Panamericana*, 60, 222–8.

Sen, A. 1981: *Poverty and Famines: An essay on entitlement and deprivation*. Oxford: Clarendon.

Soemantri, A. G., Pollitt, E., and Kim, I. 1985: Iron deficiency anemia and educational achievement. *American Journal of Clinical Nutrition*, 42, 1221–8.

Sommer, A., Katz, J., and Tarwotjo, I. 1984: Increased risk of respiratory disease and diarrhea in children with pre-existing mild vitamin A deficiency. *American Journal of Clinical Nutrition*, 40, 1090–5.

Sommer, A., Tarwotjo, I., Hussaini, G., and Susanto, D. 1983: Increased mortality in children with mild vitamin A deficiency. *Lancet*, ii, 585.

Spalding, E., McCrae, J., Rutishauser, I. H. E., and Parkin, J. M. 1977. A study of severely malnourished children in the Gambia. *Journal of Tropical Pediatrics and Environmental Health* 23(5):215–219.

Spurr, G. B. 1983. Nutritional status and physical work capacity. *Yearbook of Physical Anthropology*, 26, 1–35.

Spurr, G. B. 1984: Physical activity, nutritional status and physical work capacity in relation to agricultural productivity. In E. Pollitt and P. Amante (eds), *Energy Intake and Activity*, New York: Liss, 207–61.

Spurr, G. B., Barac-Nieto, M., Reina, J., and Ramirez, R., 1984: Marginal malnutrition in school-aged Colombian boys: Efficiency of treadmill walking in submaximal exercise. *American Journal of Clinical Nutrition* 39, 452–9.

Spurr, G. B., Maksud, M. G., and Barac-Nieto, M. 1977: Energy expenditure, production, and physical work capacity of sugar cane loaders. *American Journal of Clinical Nutrition*, 30, 1740–6.

Staff of the Select Committee on Nutrition and Human Needs, United States Senate 1977: *Dietary Goals for the United States*. Washington, DC: US Government Printing Office, second edition.

Stanbury, J. B. 1985: Iodine deficiency disorders: Clinical presentations and continuing problems. *Food and Nutrition Bulletin*, 7, 64–72.

Sukhatme, P. V. and Margen, S. 1982: Autoregulatory homeostatic nature of energy balance. *American Journal of Clinical Nutrition*, 35, 355–65.

Tarwotjo, I., Tilden, R., Satibi, I., and Nendrawati, H. 1986: Vitamin A deficiency control in Indonesia. In Bauerfeind (1986), 445–60.

Taylor, L. and Keys, A. 1950: Adaptation to caloric restriction. *Science*, 112, 215–19.

Thanangkul, O., Promkutkaew, C., Waniyapong, T., and Damrongsak, D. 1980: Comparison of the effects of a single high dose of vitamin A given to mother and infant upon plasma levels of vitamin A in the infant. Meeting on vitamin A deficiency and xerophthalmia. NUT/WP/74.14. Jakarta. World Health Organization.

Torun, B. and Viteri, F. E. 1981: Energy requirements of pre-school children and effects of varying energy intakes on protein metabolism. In "Protein-energy requirements of developing countries: evaluation of new data," *Food and Nutrition Bulletin*, Suppl. 5, 229–41.

UK Department of Health and Social Security 1978: *Prevention and Health: eating for health*. London: HMSO.

United Nations University 1979: Protein-energy requirements under conditions prevailing in developing countries: Current knowledge and research needs. *Food and Nutrition Bulletin*, Suppl. 1, 79, 73.

Upton, A. C. 1979: Statement on diet, nutrition and cancer. In *Hearings of the Subcommittee on Agriculture, Nutrition, and Forests*.

Viteri, F. E. 1976: Definition of the nutrition problems in the labor force. In N. S. Scrimshaw and M. Behar (eds), *Nutrition and Agricultural Development. Significance and potential for the tropics*. New York: Plenum Press, 87–98.

Viteri, F. E. and Torun, B. 1975: Ingestion calorica y trabajo fisico de obreros agricolas en Guatemala. *Boletin de Oficina de la Sante Panamericana*, 75, 58–74.

Viteri, F. E. and Torun, B. 1981: Nutrition, physical activity and growth. In M. Ritzen, A. Aperia, and K. Hall (eds), *The Biology of Normal Human Growth*, New York: Raven Press, 265–73.

Viteri, F. E., Alvarez, E., Bulux, J., et al. 1981: Iron fortification in developing countries. In *Nutrition, Health and Disease in International Development*, New York: Liss, 345–54.

Winnick, M. (ed.) 1979: *Hunger Disease, Studies by the Jewish Physicians in the Warsaw Ghetto*. New York: Wiley-Interscience.

Wolgemuth, J. C., Latham, M. C., Hall, A., Chester, A., and Cromtom, D. W. T. 1982: Worker productivity and the nutritional status of Kenyan road construction laborers. *American Journal of Clinical Nutrition*, 36, 68–78.

Young, V. R. and Scrimshaw, N. S. 1971: The physiology of starvation. *Scientific American*, 225, 14–21.

14

Food Entitlements and Economic Chains

AMARTYA SEN

Hunger, Entitlements, and Linkages

It is not a new question, "Why hunger?" remains as relevant a query today as it has been for thousands of years. But the answer cannot be quite the same as in the past. The enormous expansion of productive power, especially in agriculture, that has taken place over the last few centuries has certainly made it possible to guarantee adequate food for all. The persistence of chronic hunger and severe famine despite more than adequate productive opportunities poses a range of questions that would not have been immediately relevant in the past, when production possibilities were much more limited. This is not to say that issues of technological transformation and expansion of production have ceased to be important. Much more can certainly be achieved, and the rewards from productive expansion can indeed be very substantial. But even with existing technologies and the current state of knowledge, a better marshalling of our resources and a better system of distribution can eliminate much of the nutritional shortfall that is observed across the world today. Hunger and famine have to be seen as *economic* phenomena in the broadest sense − including production, distribution, and utilization of food − and not just as reflections of problems of food *production* as such.

Production, distribution, and consumption of food are linked together in the form of chain relationships − connecting producers to markets, markets to purchasers, and purchasers to consumers. Food deprivation, hunger, and starvation can result from dysfunctioning of any of these links. A person suffers from food deprivation and consequently undernourishment, morbidity, and possibly mortality if he or she is unable to establish command over an adequate quantity of food. For example, if a person does not have the means of buying enough food, he or she is not in a position to demand that food in the market. Insofar as the supply of food and ultimately the production of food commodities depend on market demand, this absence of demand will have a corresponding reflection in a lower supply and production of food. Superficially, while it may look as if there is not food enough for this person's needs, the cause of the problem may well rest on the shortfall of demand, and thus on the inadequacy of means to purchase, rather than on the limitations of productive opportunities. In fact, in most economies in the world, the response of production and supply to prices and demands bear out the importance of the demand factor in the determination of output and supply.

In order to understand the nature of hunger, we have to examine the person's "entitlements" to food and related commodities.[1] The starving person who does not have the means to command food is suffering from an entitlement failure, and the causal antecedents of this may lie in factors far away from food production as such. In each social and economic system there are rules governing the rights that people respectively have to exercise command over food and other necessities. In a private ownership economy, these rights are closely related to the ability to establish ownership over food and related goods. In order to understand the determination of entitlements we have to examine the person's *endowment* position (for example, what goods and services can he or she exchange for food) as well as *exchange opportunities* (for example, at what rate can the person exchange what he or she owns for food). In the entitlement analysis of food deprivation and hunger which I have tried to present elsewhere, especially in my book *Poverty and Famines* (Sen, 1981), the crucial roles of both endowments and exchange entitlement relationships have been correspondingly investigated.

In going *beyond* market systems, other types of rights have to be considered in understanding entitlements over food that a person can enjoy. This can include claims against the state, such as the right to work (if such a right is acknowledged), the right to unemployment benefits (if there is such a social security arrangement), and so on. A person can establish command over food by making use of these different rights, and the entitlement analysis of hunger in general and famine in particular must take note of the institutional structure − covering legal and political as well as economic factors − that determine a person's entitlements and, through that, his or her ability to avoid starvation, undernourishment, and deprivation.

Two different aspects of the prevalence of hunger have to be clearly distinguished. There is, first, the problem of periodic famines, acute starvation, and mass mortality. Despite the enormous increase in productive abilities and national income in the world, there have persistently been severe famines across the globe. Famines in Ethiopia, Somalia, Sudan, Mozambique, the Sahel countries, Biafra, Bangladesh, and Kampuchea are just a few examples − many more can be given.

This problem of the persistence of famines has to be distinguished from that of the unrelieved continuation of food deprivation, hunger, and undernourishment in a large part of the world. Most often, in fact, hunger does not take its toll in a dramatic manner at all, with millions dying in a visible way (as happens with famines). Instead, endemic hunger kills in a more concealed manner. People suffer from nutritional deficiency and from greater susceptibility to illness and disease. The insufficiency of food, along with the inadequacy of related commodities (such as health services, medical attention, clean water, etc.), enhances both morbidity and mortality. It all happens rather quietly without any clearly visible deaths from hunger. Indeed so quiet can this process be that it is easy to overlook that such a terrible sequence of deprivation, debilitation, and decimation is taking place, covering − in different degrees − much of the population of the poorer countries in the world.

In understanding the causation of regular hunger and chronic undernourishment on the one hand, and severe famines on the other, the failures of entitlement have to be correspondingly examined. While regular hunger is largely a result of inadequate entitlements on a continuing basis, famines are the result of disastrous declines of entitlements, which typically occur rather suddenly. The landless laborer in a poor agricultural economy may be in a state of chronic shortage of command over food, and this will be reflected in persistent undernourishment of families in such occupation groups. This need not lead to dramatic starvation and immediate mortality, but the food deprivation makes the families more prone to disease, leading to a higher probability of death at a premature age. Seasonal unemployment, low wages, and other economic deprivations become, thus, reflected in health conditions and demographic facts. But all this may happen quite gently. In contrast, members of the same occupation group of landless laborers may die in large numbers suddenly if there is a dramatic decline in employment or if there is a sharp rise in food prices, ushering in a famine. In this case the entitlement failure takes a much sharper and more severe form. Of course, both these processes may be observed in the same country at different periods of time. For example, in Bangladesh, the regular shortage of entitlements is causally associated with systematic undernourishment of the poorer rural population, without there being a famine all the time, but that population itself provided the bulk of the victims when famine struck in 1974.[2] The economic processes involved in regular hunger and transient famine may well be quite distinct, but they both involve failure of entitlement over food and related commodities, in different forms.

Production and Entitlements

In understanding hunger, including famine, the focus of attention has to be on the dysfunctioning of the various links in the food-chain covering production, distribution, and utilization, which are different aspects of entitlement relations. For example, famines may be caused by production failure, leading (a) to a direct decline of entitlements of those, such as peasants, whose means of survival depend on food that they grow themselves, or (b) to a sharp rise in prices, thereby affecting the ability to command food on the part of those who have to buy food in the market. But a famine can also occur without a decline in production, and indeed sometimes may take place in situations of peak food availability. There have indeed been, in recent years, many major famines without any decline in food output or availability per head.[3] The Bengal famine of 1943, the Ethiopian famines of 1973 and 1982, and the Bangladesh famine of 1974 are good examples. Indeed, during the Bangladesh famine of 1974, food output and availability per head in Bangladesh were higher than in any other period in the three preceding years and the two following ones. If one were to look only at output and availability for predicting famine, one would most certainly not have picked 1974 as the year of the famine, but that was indeed the year in which famine struck. In order to understand that famine – and indeed other famines – we have to look at the entitlements of the different occupation groups, and how they moved over time. In the case of the Bangladesh famine of 1974, the victim groups were affected by (a) loss of agricultural employment as a result of floods during the planting and transplanting seasons, (b) general inflationary pressure in the economy leading to a decline in real wages, and (c) sharply rising food prices in the months following the flood, involving a good deal of speculative activities.[4]

The dissonance between the causal analysis of famines in terms of declines of food output and availability, on the one hand, and entitlement failures, on the other, does not lie in the fact that availability and entitlements are unrelated to each other. They are, of course, linked in many different ways. First, the output of food grown by themselves provides the basic entitlement to food of some people, such as the peasants. Second, one of the major influences on the ability of anyone to purchase food is the price of food, and that price is influenced by the production and availability of food in the economy. Third, food production can also be a major source of employment, and any reduction in the production of food (due to, say, a drought or a flood) would reduce employment and wage income through the same process that leads to a decline, later on, of the output and availability of food. Fourth, if and when a famine develops, having a stock of food available in the public distribution system is clearly a major instrument in the hands of authorities to combat starvation. Public intervention can take the form of either direct distribution of food (in cooked or uncooked forms), or adding to the supply of food in the market, thereby exerting a downward pull on the possibly rocketing prices.

It would indeed be amazing if food entitlements were entirely uninfluenced by food output, since the physical presence of food cannot but be an influence on the possibility of acquiring food through direct ownership or exchange. The dissonance does not arise from a denial of these important links. Indeed, the interconnection between the entitlement view and the availability view of food deprivation has to be seen, along with noting their conflicts. The dissonance arises from the fact that the links do not establish a connection between availability and entitlement in such a way that the food commands of different sections of the population move up and down in proportion to the total availability of food in the economy. If food were to be distributed over the population on some egalitarian principles operated by some central authority, that assumption of proportional movements might well have been sensible. However, the actual command over food that different sections of the population can exercise depends on a set of legal and economic factors including those governing ownership, production, and exchange, involving different parts of the food-chain. It is, thus, quite possible for some groups (for example, a particular occupation group such as landless rural laborers, pastoralists, fishermen) to have a sharply reduced food entitlement, even when the overall availability of food in the economy is unaffected or increasing. For example, a decline in the price of animal products vis-à-vis cheaper calories in the form of food grains, or a reduction in the price of fish vis-à-vis the price of staple food, may adversely affect the pastoralists and fishermen, respectively, and there have indeed been famines in which these changes in exchange rates have played a crucial part in the decimation of the respective occupation groups (for instance, in the Bengal famine of 1943, the Ethiopian famine of 1973, the Sahelian famines of the early 1970s). Changes in employment, wages, prices, etc., can all take a major and decisive part in the initiation and intensification of famines.

The dissonance between the availability view and the entitlement view is particularly important to note in the context of economic policy. An undue reliance – often implicit – on the availability view has frequently been a contributory factor in the development of a famine, by making the relevant authorities smug about the food situation. Policy-making requires a concern with each of the important links in the food-chain, affecting command over food of vulnerable occupation groups.

Famine Relief, Food, and Cash

There are many policy implications related to the shift in the focus of analysis from production (and availability) to entitlements in general, including the various links in the economic chains. One important question concerns the form of the relief that may be provided in helping famine victims. In African famines, relief has typically taken the form of distribution of free food in relief camps and distribution centers. While such relief has saved some lives, it has often been ineffective and inefficient, and the scope and appropriateness of this form of relief require careful scrutiny.

It is necessary to distinguish between two things that are achieved by food relief to famine victims, to wit: (a) giving the destitute the *ability* to command food, and (b) providing this relief in the actual form of *food itself*. Though these two aspects are integrated together in direct food relief for famine victims, they need not in general be thus combined. For example, *cash relief* can provide the ability to command food without directly giving any food to the victim. Indeed, cash relief can stimulate other parts of the food-chain in terms of the response to increased demand as a result of the greater purchasing power of the famine victims.

A person's ability to command food can be seen as having two distinct elements, namely, his or her "pull" and the supplier's "response." If a person starves because of loss of employment and the absence of means of buying food, then that is a failure originating on the "pull" side. On the other hand, if the person's ability to command food collapses because of an absence of supply, or due to the "cornering" of the market by some manipulative traders, then this is a failure arising on the "response" side. In most famines – whether in Africa or Asia – the element of "pull failure" has tended to be the dominant one in the genesis of the collapse of entitlements of the famine victims. In this situation, creating purchasing power for the famine victim may be an obvious and immediate way of recovering some of the lost ground.

One of the big differences between the famine relief practiced in India and that typically used in Africa is the much greater reliance on cash distribution in India. While direct distribution of food is also used in India, a lot of the relief efforts in India in fact typically take the form of paying cash wages for work. If the dispossessed find temporary employment and a cash wage, their ability to command food in the market is radically enhanced. Even if no food is brought to the famished by vehicles owned or requisitioned by the government, food does tend to move in response to the enhanced demands. The crucial issue, then, is to recreate the entitlement of those who have lost their means of support (for example, as a result of loss of employment due, say, to a flood or a drought).

The famine relief efforts in India have been, on the whole, quite successful, and there has occurred no famine in India since independence in 1947. In fact, the roots of this type of famine relief policy go well back into earlier periods, to the Famine Codes formulated in the 1880s, but often these reliefs were used only minimally or not at all in the pre-independence period. In fact, sometimes the Famine Codes were not even invoked (for instance, in the Bengal famine of 1943). While the relief policies pursued in India in the post-independence period can be seen as extensions and refinements of policies that were worked out earlier, it is only in the post-independence period that famines have been effectively eliminated by the unvarying use of these policies, including the use of employment programs and wage disbursement (often in the form of cash payments).[5] Many threatened famines have been averted in different parts of India in different years using such relief schemes; for example, in Bihar in 1967, in Maharashtra in 1973, in West Bengal in1979, and in Gujerat in 1987.

The use of cash disbursement has the advantage of quickness, which is particularly important in the light of much-discussed delays in the relief system in the case of some African famines, such as those in Sudan, Somalia, and Ethiopia. The provision of cash income leads to giving aid to the potential famine victims immediately. It also has the effect of pulling food into the famine-affected regions in response to the enhanced market demand as a result of cash disbursements.

The cash disbursement system also helps to prevent the widely observed phenomenon of what has been called a "food counter-movement," by which food moves *out* of the famine-stricken regions to more prosperous lands. This has occurred in many famines, such as the Irish famines of the 1840s, the Ethiopian famine in Wollo in 1973, and the Bangladesh famine of 1974. There is nothing terribly puzzling about this, since non-famine regions (England in the case of the Irish famines, Addis Ababa and Asmara in the case of the Wollo famine, India in the case of the Bangladesh famine) often have greater purchasing power and greater pull in comparison with the famine-stricken regions, and as a result food can easily be attracted away through the market mechanism from the famine regions to non-famine areas.[6] When additional cash income is provided in the famine region – for instance, through employment schemes – such "food counter-movements" can be reduced or eliminated, and this itself may be very important.

There are, of course, problems also with providing relief in the form of cash income and employment schemes. Much will undoubtedly depend on the efficiency of the market structure in the economy in question. If the markets are so distorted that the expansion of demand will not lead to "response," there may be no alternative to the government itself moving the food to the victims and directly arranging food distribution. On the other hand, the administrative resources of the government are also restricted, and the record of famine relief based on large-scale movement of food grains by the government has not been particularly encouraging in many African countries. When the administrative structure is limited or inefficient, the case for using cash relief to regenerate entitlements and to create the "pull" for food movement may be a sensible policy. Indeed, in those African countries in which cash relief has been tried, such as Botswana, the record of achievement seems to be very creditable.[7]

The system of cash relief also has some additional advantages. It regenerates the infrastructure of trade and transport in the economy, through increased demand and more economic activities, and this can be of lasting benefit, especially since famines tend to disrupt these links in the economic chain. Further, since the distribution to destitutes usually requires the setting up of "relief camps," the system of direct feeding or direct distribution of food can be very disruptive to normal family life as well as to pursuing normal economic activities, in particular the continued cultivation of land. In contrast, providing relief in the form of subsidiary employment without making people move from their homes has the advantage of being less disruptive for work and living. While the decision on the balance between cash relief and food relief must depend on a careful and pragmatic assessment of the exact conditions in the country or region in question, it is worthwhile to consider the possibility of providing food to famine victims via the means of cash. When hunger and famines are seen not just in terms of availability of food, but primarily in terms of entitlement failures, it becomes natural to consider these other means of changing the operation of the dysfunctioning food-chains. It is this broadening of the economic perspective related to this more general approach that may be seen as being the most important aspect of the proposed change of famine analysis.

Indeed, the form of famine relief is only one policy problem which is affected by the entitlement approach, and there are many other policy issues thoroughly dependent on the nature of the approach adopted.[8] Even in the context of assessing the form of famine relief (for instance, whether food or cash), there are many different policy instruments that can be considered, including the importation of food from abroad, the introduction of rationing and control, or of speculation, the taxing of incomes of non-victims to give the famine-affected population a better competitive edge in the market, etc. These policy issues have to be examined severally and jointly in the formulation of public policy to deal with famine relief.

Famine Prevention and Productive Diversification

There are comparable policy implications for other aspects of anti-famine policy, such as the *prevention* of famines (as opposed to giving *relief* to the famine victims). As was mentioned earlier, even in achieving this prevention an alert system of distribution of cash wages and employment schemes may be important.

We have to distinguish clearly between (a) food production as a source of income and entitlement, and (b) food production as a source of supply of the commodity food. The seriousness of the decline in African food production per head has often been seen as the main source of Africa's food problem. There is some truth in this diagnosis, but this is not only because food production is important as a source of supply of the vital commodity food; it is also because food production provides employment, income, and entitlement to a vast section of the African rural population. The decline in food output has also led to an entitlement deterioration, and this deterioration has been brought about by several distinct influences acting together, including the loss of employment opportunities, reduction in incomes earned, and a general collapse of vital links in the food chain.

In enhancing the entitlements of the deprived and vulnerable groups of the population, expansion of food production can indeed, in many circumstances, have an important role. In fact, policy decisions regarding the relative balance of economic expansion in different sectors must depend on a careful calculation of relative benefits that can be obtained (taking into account the risks that have to be faced) from expansion in different fields.

A reasonable calculation of these relative benefits cannot be achieved simply on the basis of plans to undo prevailing production trends − even if these trends are correctly seen as responsible for the present state of affairs. For example, there are good grounds for giving priority to the expansion of food production in some parts of Africa, but that ground is not provided just by observing the historical fact that in these countries food output per head has declined, or that food imports have increased, or even that the decline of entitlements is directly linked to the production crisis. Policy decisions have to be based on assessing the present circumstances and the anticipated future ones, rather than taking the simple form of trying to reverse the decline from past achievements.

In fact, insofar as the crisis of food production in Africa relates, at least partly, to climatic deterioration, that itself may be a good ground for considering other avenues of entitlement guarantee. The climatic deterioration must, of course, be encountered and halted. There is, in fact, a good chance that in the long run a more favorable economic and climatic environment for agricultural expansion in general and increased food production in particular may materialize, through programs of afforestation, irrigation, and so on. But economic policies should not be determined on the basis of imagining that such a change has already taken place. If it turns out that, given the climatic uncertainties and the ecological problems, food production will remain very vulnerable to fluctuations in some parts of Africa for a long time to come, then it will be a mistake to rely too much on that one uncertain source of income and entitlements. This is an argument for putting greater relative emphasis on other types of production, including industrial expansion, from which more benefits with greater certainty may be derivable in the present circumstances.

Entitlement analysis, focusing on different parts of the chain relations, points directly to the necessity of considering seriously the case for greater diversification of the productive structure in Africa. Alleged magic solutions of the problem of African hunger, typified by such commonly invoked slogans as "put all the resources in agriculture!" (a favorite theme of "naturalists") or "raise agricultural and food prices to boost production incentives!" (a favorite theme of many international institutions, including the World Bank), may deliver substantially less than they promise. There is, in fact, no escape from basing policy on a careful calculation of relative benefits – including the respective uncertainties – in choosing between different intersectoral balances.

Indeed, it is arguable that anti-hunger policies in Africa must give a very solid place to the expansion of non-food production and the diversification of the economy. There is often a noticeable reluctance to consider the promise of industrialization for the future of Africa. Sometimes the reluctance arises from being unduly impressed by the favorable land–population ratio of most African countries compared with, say, Asia. But the choice between industry and agriculture has to be influenced by many considerations of costs and benefits, in addition to the availability of land. Climatic consideration itself is a factor. The opportunity for economic growth that is provided by branching out into industries has been well demonstrated by the historical experience of many different countries in different parts of the world, and Africa cannot ignore these opportunities. Also, the contribution that industrialization makes to skill formation and to the modernization of the economy and of the society may be an important factor. The indirect influence of that technological transformation on agricultural productivity itself (including productivity in the food sector) cannot, by any means, be ignored.

As it happens, most of the successful agricultural economies in the world also happen to be industrialized, and this fact may not be a mere accident. Skill is as important an input for agricultural production as land, and the diversification of production seems to help the formation of skill. The favorable nature of the land–population ratio has, rightly, not been seen as a good ground for eschewing industrial production in Australia, Canada, or the United States. Dismissing that economic alternative for Africa on the ground of its high land–population ratio reflects, at the very least, some economic short-sightedness. While successful industrialization tends to be a long-run process, that process has to be started at some stage for it to yield fruits in the future. Also, the experiences of many developing countries have shown that in some branches of industry rapid progress can be made by new entrants, yielding benefits without much delay.

All this is not to deny the importance of expanding food production in sub-Saharan Africa. Agricultural expansion in general, and that of food production in particular, will undoubtedly be one major instrument − but not the only one − in combating hunger in Africa. Various strategic aspects of enhancing production in sub-Saharan Africa have received expert attention and scrutiny in recent years,[9] and there are many lessons to be learned from economic reasoning as well as from empirical observation of actual economic experiences. Given the number of people who derive their entitlements from food production in Africa, and given the limited speed at which this dependence can be reduced (though reduced it must be in the long run), the importance of expanding food production in Africa, *among* the strategies to combat hunger in that continent, cannot be denied. It is really more a question of the *balance* between the different elements in anti-hunger policy for Africa, and it is in this context that the tendency to over-concentrate only on food production as a solution to the food problem in Africa has to be firmly resisted. The chain relations influencing food entitlements call for attention being paid to many other parts of the economic process. A narrowly focused concentration only on food production may well be wasteful and dangerous. The challenge of continuing hunger in Africa demands an approach that is adequately broad and balanced.

Concluding Remarks

In this paper I have tried to present briefly the entitlement approach to the problem of hunger relating to both regular undernourishment and transient famines, and also have tried to examine the policy issues raised by the use of the entitlement approach. While only a few policy questions were explicitly discussed, similar analyses can be presented in other areas of public policy, related to the general problem of hunger and the particular problem of famine.

Some of the areas of policy and action may take us well beyond purely economic reasoning. One of the particular fields of interest in the context of the problem of hunger is the division of food within the family, particularly between men and women, and especially that between boys and girls.[10] There is some evidence from different parts of the world of systematic biases related to gender (for instance, greater undernourishment of women and particularly of female children). The sequence of chain relations does not end only with the purchase of food, since there is the further problem of division of food *within* the family, based on purchases made on behalf of the family as a whole. These problems of intra-household distributions linking the purchase of food in the market with the consumption of food by individuals in the family have to be investigated to get a better understanding of an important aspect of food deprivation found in some societies. Here again the notion of entitlement, related to the sense of perceived legitimacy, can be a major issue. Often, the greater share of men vis-à-vis women, or of boys vis-à-vis girls, reflects a traditional sense of what is legitimate and what is right. While these notions of legitimacy do not have the sanction of law enforced by the state, their grip on the actual distributions within the family may well be very strong indeed, enforced by convention and social pressure. There is considerable evidence of such traditional biases in the intra-household divisions of food.

There are many other issues in which the entitlement perspective is relevant. The economic, political, and social factors involved in the chain relations and their consequences call for careful scrutiny. What is needed is an adequately broad approach, instead of concentrating narrowly on only production and availability.

There is no one magic solution to the problem of food deprivation in the world in which we live. But there is one unifying focus – related to entitlement problems in food-chains – that provides the basis for analyzing the diverse dysfunctionings that are present and for seeking appropriate remedies. The overwhelming need is for relating policy and action to theory and understanding. This is an exacting task and its demands are large. But the rewards may be large too. The survival and well-being of a substantial section of humankind may depend on it.

NOTES

This is the text of a lecture at the Smithsonian Institution International Colloquium on "Science, Ethics, and Food," October 6–7, 1987. It draws on an earlier presentation by the author to a Brown University colloquium on "perspectives on the history of hunger."
1 See Sen, 1981.
2 Alamgir, 1980; Ravallion, 1987; Sen, 1981, ch. 9.
3 See Sen, 1981, chs 6–10.
4 See particularly Ravallion, 1987.

5 Drèze, forthcoming; Sen 1986.
6 See Sen, 1981, chs 7 and 10.
7 See Drèze and Sen, 1990.
8 See Drèze and Sen, 1990; 1986.
9 See Swaminathan, 1986. See also Eicher, 1986; Glantz 1987; Idachaba, forthcoming; Mellor et al., 1987.
10 See Sen, 1984.

REFERENCES

Alamgir, M., 1980: *Famine in South Asia*. Boston: Oelgeschlager.
Drèze, Jean, forthcoming: Famine prevention in India. WIDER Conference Paper. In Drèze and Sen, forthcoming.
Drèze, Jean and Sen, Amartya 1990: *Hunger and Public Action*. Oxford: Clarendon Press.
Drèze, Jean and Sen, Amartya (eds), forthcoming: *The Political Economy of Hunger*. Oxford, Clarendon Press.
Eicher, C. K. 1986: *Transforming African Agriculture*. San Francisco: The Hunger Project.
Glantz, M. H. (ed.) 1987: *Drought and Hunger in Africa*. Cambridge: Cambridge University Press.
Idachaba, F. forthcoming: Policy options for African agriculture. WIDER Conference Paper. In Dreze and Sen. forthcoming.
Mellor, M. W., Delgado C., and Blackie, M. J. (eds) 1987: *Accelerating Food Production in Sub-Saharan Africa*. Baltimore: Johns Hopkins University Press.
Ravallion, Martin 1987: *Markets and Famines*. Oxford: Clarendon Press.
Sen, Amartya 1981: *Poverty and Famines: An essay on entitlement and deprivation*. Oxford, New York, Delhi: Oxford University Press.
Sen, Amartya 1984: *Resources, Values and Development*. Cambridge, Mass.: Harvard University Press.
Sen, Amartya 1986: Food, economics and entitlements. Elmhurst Lecture at Triennial Meeting of International Association of Agricultural Economists, at Malaga. Published in *Proceedings*, and in *Lloyd's Bank Review*, 1986, 160.
Swaminathan, M. S. 1986: *Sustainable Nutritional Security for Africa*. San Francisco: The Hunger Project.

Part VI
Conclusion

Part VI
Conclusions

15

On Ending Hunger:
The Lessons of History

ROBERT W. KATES AND SARA MILLMAN

The persistence of hunger in a world of plenty is a deeply troubling paradox of our time. To understand that paradox and how to resolve it, we have adopted a long view, studying hunger in its historical context. Our view consists of four time scales: ages, millennia, centuries, and decades. Within each we provide a discussion of some central themes and from one to three more closely focused studies of what is known or might be inferred about the hunger of the times. The basis for continuity and a common viewpoint throughout the volume is a causal analysis of three linked conditions that lead to hunger: food shortage, where there is not enough food in a bounded region; food poverty, where there may be sufficient food but some households do not have sufficient means to obtain it; and food deprivation, where the household may have sufficient food, but food may be withheld from individuals, special nutritional needs may not be met, or illness may prevent proper absorption. In this final chapter, we summarize and then bring together insights from the four periods to characterize the continuities and changes in hunger prevalence, the scale and complexity of food entitlement, and the structure of causation. We conclude by considering the implications of what we have learned for the future – the lessons of history for overcoming hunger.

The Long View

From the long view of ages, some 20,000 years, the examined themes focus on the great natural variations of climate and biota within which human beings increased their numbers and spread their occupance as their food supply grew and diminished, and the millennia-long transition from foraging for food to the domestication of animals and plants known as the Neolithic Revolution (chapter 2). Cohen reports on the insights of paleopathology into the prevalence of hunger before and after the transition, and the role of scarcity in facilitating these great changes in the ways of human life (chapter 3). In sum, the history of hunger from the view of ages is a history that emphasizes the causes of hunger in major natural and technosocial changes, knows little of the actual experience of hunger but infers a broad range of consequences from skeletal remains, and marks the greatest of long-term adaptations, the invention of agriculture.

The millennial view examines the last 6,000 years, identifying as central themes (chapter 4) what is known of hunger following the intensification of agriculture, the development of new urban centers (Mesopotamia), the emergence of a hierarchical division of labor by class and territory (Greece and Rome), and its transition into the early medieval period in Europe. Garnsey reports on the successful coping with famine that marked the high periods of Athens and Rome (chapter 5) and Yates on the more turbulent and somewhat less successful experience in early dynastic China (chapter 6). Turner skillfully employs a new set of reconstructed population data to document the remarkable decline of Mayan civilization, in which hunger surely must have played a part, but whether as cause, effect, or both, can only be speculated upon (chapter 7). In sum, the history of hunger over the range of the millennia is a history that marks the accumulation of an agricultural surplus in temple, palace, city, and state and the emergence of an elaborate social organization to produce, gather, and distribute such surplus. At its height, such organization was able to provide food security for large numbers of people; in its dissolution, it placed large numbers at risk of hunger.

Over the last six centuries, the story of how the European world coped with and overcame famine, and the impact on hunger of the emergence of the modern nation-state, colonialism, and international trade, are the selected themes addressed in chapter 8. Two detailed case studies, Post's study of the great eighteenth-century European food crises and epidemics (chapter 9) and Pfister's study of nineteenth-century food availability in the Swiss canton of Bern (chapter 10) illuminate the successful European struggle against famine and the social and ecological basis for the variable distribution of hunger and hunger-related mortality. In sum, the history of hunger in recent centuries is most detailed for Europe, where food shortage, but not food poverty, was overcome by increased productivity, new foods, and national efforts to move food, curtail prices, and offer relief in food crises. As with the successes of the classical empires, much less is known about the impacts on the peripheries whose wealth, crops, labor, and foodstuffs made much of European progress possible.

In this century, particularly in the decades since the end of the Second World War, the international food system beginning to emerge in Europe in the century perspective becomes global, reducing the vulnerability to local production failures but increasing dependence on exchange mechanisms. This trend and the complex effects of integration into the global food system on local populations are the themes of chapter 11. The potential of large integrated food systems to reduce hunger or to increase it when they fail is recounted by Riskin for the Chinese experience (chapter 12). Scrimshaw summarizes what is known about the health and activity outcomes of nutritional deprivation (chapter 13) and Sen discusses the entitlement failures that underlie both episodic and persistent hunger (chapter 14). In sum, the recent history of hunger is a story of rising expectations, partially met and partially still unfulfilled. More is known about the world-wide prevalence of hunger than ever before, yet such knowledge remains incomplete and exceedingly approximate. For the world as a whole, the estimated proportions with inadequate access to food have declined over the last four decades, yet population growth has balanced this progress so that absolute numbers have remained almost constant. Governments, international organizations, and private voluntary organizations focus their efforts on fighting hunger around the world; yet these efforts are plagued by logistical difficulties, conflicting approaches and priorities, sometimes deliberate obstruction, and in many places an unwillingness to address fundamental social inequities.

Continuities and Change

From this long view of hunger in history emerge both continuities and change in the prevalence of hunger, the forms of food entitlement, and the predominant causes for hunger's persistence. In all, we draw twelve conclusions as to the dynamics of hunger, and then use these to consider the future.[1]

The Prevalence of Hunger

As far as can be discerned, there has always been some hunger. Paleolithic bone remains provide evidence both of cumulative indicators of stress in terms of growth and age-of-death, and episodic indicators of teeth and bone that indicate growth arrest and anemia (Goodman et al., 1984). Indications of the causes of stress are available in the evidence of natural fluctuations in the availability of plants, animals, and fish, suggesting, at the very least, periods of seasonal hunger; and in simulated weather patterns of past climates and direct evidence of shifting vegetation patterns suggesting periods of climate-induced stress (chapter 2).

But while some hunger has always been with us, the prevalence of hunger has varied greatly. The history of hunger is marked by occasional plenty, diminishing food shortage, and continuing if not growing food poverty. In recent times, there is evidence for smaller proportions but constant or even increasing numbers of hungry people.

Fluctuating Feasts and Famines   The history of hunger for most groups and places abounds with alternating periods of sustained deprivation and relative plenty, interspersed with long periods of almost or barely enough food, or what has been called "Malthusian deadlock" (chapter 4). The balance between productive innovation, population growth, surplus appropriation, and natural variation has fluctuated over time leaving a record, albeit spotty, of fluctuating feast, famine, and marginal subsistence. This is true at all of the four time scales that we have examined.

We illustrate these fluctuations employing an anthropometric measure closely linked to nutrition – human height – and more specifically, for most of the period, the height of adult males. At the scale of ages and millennia, the data represent reconstructions of height based on bones recovered from burial sites. At the scales of centuries and decades we have actual records of measured heights, mainly from institutionalized populations. To our knowledge, these are the only data that are available in comparable form for all the time scales employed in our historical analysis. Thus

Figure 15.1   Fluctuations in human height over ages, millennia, centuries, and decades

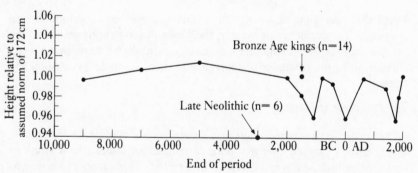

(a)   Ages: Eastern Mediterranean adult males *Source:*   Angel, 1984

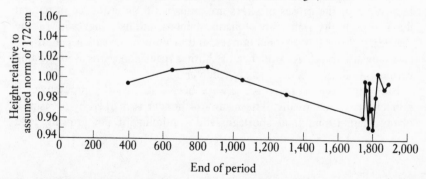

(b)   Millennia: English males *Source:*   Kunitz, 1987

we draw on four separate compilations of height data to illustrate these fluctuations.

These are shown in figures 15.1 (a)–(d) and represent burial remains from 11,000 years of human occupation in the Eastern Mediterranean (Angel, 1984), 1,500 years of English burials (Kunitz, 1987), measured heights from 220 years of US native-born males (Fogel, 1984), and 50 years of Shanghai schoolchildren in China (Piazza, 1986). To make the data comparable, the burial remains are plotted on the graphs by the date of the end of the time period in which they were grouped in the original sources; the institutional data by the period in which the data were collected. The adult male height estimates (figures 15.1 a,b,c) are expressed relative to an assumed adult norm of 172 cm; the Shanghai schoolboys (figure 15.1d) relative to the mean value of the series.

It is only for the Shanghai schoolchildren's drop in height in 1942 that the cause appears clear – hunger and disease induced by the food shortages and living conditions of wartime occupation. For the others, various food shortage and disease episodes are suggested or speculated upon as the cause of the transition. Thus in the time series representing the perspective of ages, Cohen (chapter 3) hypothesizes that it was a Malthusian crisis that led to the development of agriculture from hunting and gathering and that is reflected in the diminished height of the times. Angel (1984), the

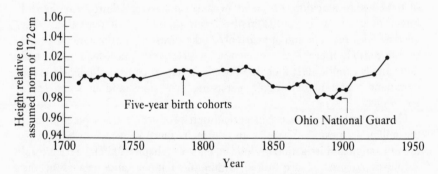

(*c*)   Centuries: US males *Source:*   Fogel, 1984

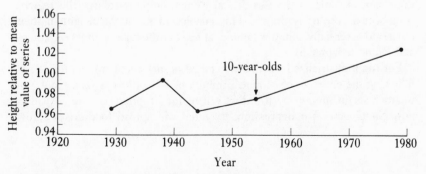

(*d*)   Decades: Shanghai male children *Source:*   Piazza, 1986 assembler of the time series used to illustrate the ages perspective, noted the coincidence of indicators of decreased nutritional status with increases in both population density and disease incidence, abetted by swampy lowland locations. Similarly, Kunitz (1987) attributed declining heights in the 1,500-year series in England to various periods of rising population, declining wages, and food crises. And Fogel (1984) speculated that the remarkable decline in the middle of the 220-year series of heights in the US was due to the increased inequality of income in the nineteenth century.

Whatever the complex of causes, the implication seems clear at all scales of analysis. The improvement in diet and the diminution of hunger has not been simply upwards and onwards from the cave. The more recent data – for example, the encouraging drop in the proportion of food-poor hungry – need to be considered in light of these long-term fluctuations. The recent progress in diminishing hunger is not guaranteed to continue.

Less Food Shortage, Continuing Food Poverty Over time, the predominant character of hunger shifts, from widespread and frequent food shortages to continuing and chronic food poverty. The recurrences of absolute food scarcity over a region diminish as the productivity of its agriculture increases and as its trade expands, making possible the provision of central food storage and the importation of food. Food shortages, the absolute scarcities of food within a region, do occur because of harvest failure, war, loss of hinterlands, or radical shifts in the terms of trade. But over time, they become less frequent and appear only in the direst of circumstances. In the recent period, there is evidence that food poverty, in which individual households cannot meet their food needs despite regional sufficiency, is the dominant condition of hunger, persisting over time, and in some cases increasing.

One remarkable increase in agricultural production takes place during the millennial period. There is an enormous increase in productivity with the utilization and irrigation of flood-plain soils (chapter 2). The agricultural surpluses so created are stored within the temples and palaces of the emerging city-states. The development of food-producing colonies and the expansion of trade in the Greek and Roman empires enlarge the regions from which surplus is drawn. This enables them, at the height of their power, to essentially conquer famine, at least in the main centers of Athens and Rome (chapter 5).

For the industrialized world a watershed occurs about two centuries ago following the eruption of Mount Tambora in 1816 (Post, 1977). Cool, wet weather set in motion by the dust veil of the eruption, combined with a post-Napoleonic-War depression, triggered widespread food crises across

Europe and North America. But for the first time, European states and cities organized to prevent widespread famine, raising funds and importing food from Russia and the Baltic States.

This effort was to mark the beginning of the end of famine in Europe except in the regions considered the periphery of the empires, such as Ireland and Transylvania in the nineteenth century, and except for its reappearance in the Ukraine in the 1930s and in occupied Europe in the 1940s. But the end of famine was not to be the end of hunger, and it took 160 years, interrupted by the First and Second World Wars, before the remnants of food poverty were virtually eliminated in Europe.

In the Third World, the end of famine due to harvest failure, but not war, is in sight everywhere but in Africa. For example, with the exception of the Bengal famine (caused by an entitlement failure and not a harvest failure), India has managed its recurrent food shortages without widespread famine for over 40 years, and perhaps for 100 years (Sen, 1988). Yet the highest proportion of hungry people in the world can be found in India, victims of an endemic and continuing food poverty (chapter 11).

Rates Down, Numbers High and Constant   Over the last three and a half decades, as shown in figure 15.2, the proportion of hungry people in the world had diminished by almost half − from 23 percent to 10 percent using the FAO data set and estimation method (Grigg, 1985; Kates et al., 1988). Nonetheless there are probably as many hungry people today in the world as ever before. Depending on the viewer's perspective, this may reasonably be seen as either progress or stagnation.

This latest round of declining proportions and rising numbers is surely tied to the rapid expansion in population beginning in Europe in the eighteenth century and in Asia, Africa, and Latin America in this century. As this rapid growth slows, the number of hungry will begin to diminish if progress in reducing the proportion of people hungry continues. The scale of this recent explosion of population growth is probably unique in human history, but bursts of rapid population growth occurred in the past within many regions. At such times, in specific regions, there may well have been periods of population growth and increased productive capacity creating a similar paradox.

The Scale and Complexity of Entitlement

Over time the scale and complexity of entitlement changes. The availability of food extends to the entire globe from the earlier limits of a day's walk, a hunting trip, or a seasonal migration. The nature of entitlement changes from access to natural resources and the dependencies of kinship to a

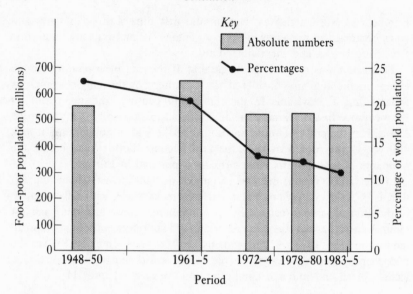

Figure 15.2 Numbers and proportions of world population in households with dietary energy less than that required for minimal activity, 1948–1985
Source: Kates et al., 1988.

complex set of resources, gifts, and exchanges. And responsibility for kin extends to strangers and unknowns a world away.

Food Availability: From Local to Global   From single sites, people who forage for food traverse the area of a day's walk, and in their seasonal rounds they cover areas of hundreds of square kilometers. Early farming communities drew the bulk of their food supplies from smaller areas. One of the earliest city states, Uruk, for example, probably grew most of its sustenance within 20 kilometers of the city walls, except for its animal production (Adams, 1972). Two millennia later, Greece and Rome derived much of their sustenance from overseas colonies across the Aegean and Mediterranean seas. At its height, Rome required 200,000 tons of grain for its 1 million inhabitants, most of it shipped by sea from Africa, Sardinia, and Sicily (Garnsey, 1988; Rickman, 1980).

   With the collapse of these great empires, food hinterlands shrank, only to enlarge again in most industrialized countries. More than one grain in ten crosses an international boundary. Reliance on external food sources has increased as diets have diversified to include products produced only in some distant climatic zone. Today we can speak of the global food supply and calculate its sufficiency – enough to feed 120 percent of the world's population on a near-vegetarian diet distributed by need, but only enough to feed half of the world's people on a developed-country diet (Kates et al., 1988). This historic enlargement of scale in food availability has led to diminished episodes of food scarcity, but it may also have undermined local food security and made very large numbers of people vulnerable to rare, but extremely serious, failures of entitlement.

Entitlement: From Resources to Exchange   Food entitlement takes three basic forms: (a) access to resources to collect or to produce food, (b) the exchange of resources (property, money, labor power) for food, and (c) the receipt of gifts or grants of food or of the resources to procure food (Sen, 1982).

The simplest form of food entitlement for human beings was natural entitlement – their own labor employed to extract edible plants and animals from nature and the distribution of the collected food to dependent members. Archeological research tells us something about the nature of natural entitlement and the kinds of resources available to prehistoric peoples. These insights are based on ethnographic analogy, using remnant groups of foragers studied with modern observational techniques. For example, from the extensive database on the San peoples of the Kalahari desert, an area one would conventionally consider as resource-poor, we learn that their natural entitlement drawn from up to 50 animal and 100 vegetable sources provides a healthful annual diet of about 70 percent plant and 30 percent animal origin (Lee, 1984).

Recent studies suggest that domestication took place slowly over several thousand years (Lewin, 1988). With the development of domesticated plants and animals, there is the beginning of surplus production and storage rooted in what Allan (1965) has called for Africa the normal surplus (chapter 1). In addition, methods of food storage were developed, and in highly variable environments large stores of food were preserved for use in poor seasons. Simultaneous with the extensive production of a surplus were improvements in plants and animals and in productive technologies that increased the land's productivity.

As population increased, became sedentary, and engaged in agriculture, natural resources, including the most productive lands, water, and grazing, became less available and more valued. Thus they became objects of appropriation and investment. Territorial claims to land and water became identified with extended family clans, clan alliances, and early urban states. Human labor from slaves, captives, and various dependent and subservient persons was appropriated or purchased with surplus grain or its monetary equivalent, and was invested in agricultural infrastructure and production as well as in non-agricultural production. The hierarchical division of

Conclusion

society expanded – and with it the types of food entitlement: access to productive resources, the sale of labor power, exchanges, and gifts. By 4,000 years ago, the city-states of Mesopotamia began to leave us thousands of clay tablets that record these increasingly complex transactions and relationships.

The basic triumvirate of entitlement has not changed over time. What changes is the mix: from a primary emphasis on household self-provision, to slave, servant, or serf status where labor is appropriated in return for minimal entitlement, to market exchange of labor and production, and most recently to the development of extensive safety nets of food security. But the current form of welfare – one that attempts to place a minimal subsistence threshold beneath all households – has been in place for clan members for ages, was available to citizens in Greece and Rome millennia ago, and was extended to most inhabitants of European states two centuries ago. And as the mix of entitlement changes, so does the moral prerequisite for an enlarged entitlement, the sense of responsibility for others.

Moral Responsibility: From Kin to Kind   The expansion of the scale and complexity of entitlement is paralleled by the extension of relationships and moral responsibilities. These expand from the immediate extended family to the clan; to members and economic dependents of the tribe; to the emergent ethnic sharers of common language and culture; to religious brethren; to citizens of nations and their domains of political and military conquest; and, increasingly in recent times, to humankind itself (and beyond to species of mammalian and avian origin).

The beginning of this moral evolution may rest on the biological dependency of child upon parent. Sociobiology has made a case for evolutionary pressure towards altruism in kin relations generally, not simply between parents and children (Hamilton, 1964). Some then argue that this is extended to groups in the expectation of reciprocity or in the need to undertake collective action to provide the sustenance required for reproductive success (Trivers, 1971). In any event, culture soon blends with biology.

Altruism shifts from reproductive necessity to moral imperative. Over time there is a steady expansion of responsibility, marked, however, by many fits, starts, and retreats. From the biological responsibility of the family, the right to entitlement expands to loosely linked families, to common language speakers, to fellow religionists, to citizens, to servants, and now slowly beyond the nation-state to all the world's peoples. Thus, for example, Americans in a recent poll supported by large majorities giving aid to less fortunate people overseas (Contee, 1987). But this recent poll represented a decrease from previous levels of support for such aid. And in the midst of this gradual extension of responsibility, it is fascinating to contemplate the unlikely forms it may take, as in the combination of popular music, satellite video transmission, and world-wide caring expressed in the temporary outpourings of concert largesse in response to the African drought of 1983–4.

Changing Causal Structure

The prevention of hunger requires the addressing of its underlying causes, but the structure of causation changes over time. Hunger appears when environmental change or deterioration limits what can be produced, when agricultural productivity declines or slows, when population numbers grow too quickly relative to food production, and when those in power appropriate too great a share of agricultural production or maintain large numbers at the margin of existence (chapter 1). These underlying causes endure, but the mix of proximate causes appears to change in important ways. Over time, natural variability as a cause of hunger diminishes, and other forms of entitlement failure come to predominate. Hunger created in the course of warfare persists, even as the scale and technology of warfare change. And while absolute scarcity diminishes, the enlargement of scale, so important to the reduction of scarcity, continues to make places marginal and makes possible catastrophes of enormous size, when errors in food-system management occur.

Less Nature, More Exchange Entitlement Failure For foragers, dependent solely on natural resources, the dominant causes of hunger were natural variability in the flow of such resources and, to a lesser degree, human-induced change in resource availability and in control over access to such resources. Within the span of human lifetimes, extreme climate events, plant and animal diseases, and fluctuations in natural predator–prey relationships among desirable species might make foraging for food more difficult. Over longer periods of time, even slowly increasing human populations could have put pressure on favored resource sites or species, as in the case of the reputed extinction of the so-called megafauna of the Pleistocene era. Such pressure has been put forth as an explanation for the effort required to create the Neolithic Revolution in agriculture (chapter 2).

When surpluses developed, societies became more complex and stratified, entitlement relationships increased in type and number, and the opportunities for hunger through more complex exchange-based forms of entitlement failure increased as well. As the direct linkage of people to their subsistence disappeared and they lost control over adequate productive resources, then the variability in entitlement – shifting commodity prices, wages, employment opportunities, and terms of trade – replaced the variability of nature. Today, for the food poor, it is the daily inadequacy of food entitlement and the threat of its further decline that make them so vulnerable to hunger.

Continuing Warfare: Sieges, Long Marches, and Guerilla War   Hunger as a weapon is at least as old as the first siege of a city. Laying waste the fields of adversaries, diverting the irrigation water they needed for production, and raiding their livestock were also common. Armies have long "lived off the land," actually seizing what they need from the workers of the land and leaving hunger and desolation in their path. With advances in the technology of warmaking and the enlargement of scale of the hinterland from which food supplies were drawn, sieges were expanded into blockades with interdiction of the movement of supplies, including food, from both sea and air. The destructive power of naval blockades, bombs, and shell-fire were further increased with the development of incendiaries, napalm, chemical defoliants, and biological agents. Older techniques of battle mesh with the new in places like Afghanistan, Ethiopia, Mozambique, Nicaragua, and the Sudan, where the destruction of food supplies or their interdiction become weapons of guerillas and counterinsurgents alike, creating hungry civilian populations. Indeed, at this point in time, the single most important obstacle to ending famine is the continued use of hunger as a weapon of war.

Marginal Peoples, Marginal Places   A major constant in the history of hunger is the maintenance of marginal peoples and marginal places, keeping large numbers of people at continuous risk of hunger. Indeed, it is probably the generic characteristic of hunger vulnerability. Over time the nature of marginality changes and the places of marginal livelihood shift, but the principles remain the same. Large numbers of people live near the minimum levels of survival and reproduction, and any downward fluctuation in their sustenance leads to widespread hunger. Why is this so?

Human labor has always been a major resource and source of entitlement. The minimal requirements for subsistence seem to have been well known even long ago, as recorded, for example, in ration lists from Mesopotamia and Egypt. The economies of empires or corporations seem well served by trying to obtain labor at the lowest cost of minimal subsistence. Also, in expanding political and economic systems, there are surely large fluctuations in the need for labor to staff armed forces, provide corvees for public works, or meet seasonal labor demands in agriculture. Reserves of such labor can be maintained at lowest cost by slavery or captivity, or tied by serfdom or indenture, or purchased in a buyer's market of agricultural dispossession, reserve unemployment, poor-house welfare, or international disparities in levels of living. The reserve army of the industrial unemployed or underemployed, that Marx thought was distinctive of the European capital ism that he studied, has its generic counterparts across time and culture (chapter 1).

These modes of economizing on labor are supported by cultural and ethnic classifications of human devaluation. Non-economic distinctions as to human worth that permit or encourage enslavement, captivity, serfdom, or impoverishment are well ensconced in human social history. Complex distinctions of citizenship, belief, caste, kinship, and race emerge to justify and reinforce the separation of the well-fed from the poorly-fed.

Places too become reservoirs for such minimum maintenance, as seen in areas that export large numbers of laborers as migrants (or to use the current euphemism, "guest workers"), while providing for needed domestic reproduction at low levels of subsistence and high inputs of family labor. But places seem to suffer in a way different from people. Lacking the mobility of people, places become marginalized by the shifts in centers and peripheries, by changes in transport technologies, or by environmental deterioration. The dry areas of Sahelian-Saharan Africa, once prosperous crossroads of the caravan trade; the rustbelts of modern industrial societies; the busts following the boom exploitations of crops, lumber, or minerals – all are witness to the creation of marginal places. Ironically, the very enlargement of scale that permits the reduction of food scarcity is one of the factors reducing the viability of some places.

Big Systems, Big Mistakes The enlargement of scale can also place extraordinarily large numbers of people at peril of hunger at the same time. Such a phenomenon is evident in the creation of famine when elaborate food distribution systems break down by reason of market disruption, administrative failure, or wartime conditions. The last 50 years provide ample examples of each. Mass starvation returned to western Europe after a hiatus of a hundred years during the Second World War. Three million or more Bengalis died in 1943 from the failure of the grain market to adequately distribute rice, compounded by a localized natural disaster and wartime decisions to favor urban Calcutta (Greenough, 1982). And the greatest famine of this century, and perhaps of all times in terms of numbers, led to the deaths of an estimated 15 million or more people in China during the years 1959–61. These were the years marked by the Great Leap Forward, when the Chinese command economy de-emphasized agricultural production in an attempt to achieve rapid industrialization (chapters 11 and 12).

Hunger as Cause

As the causal structure of hunger changes over time, hunger itself emerges as a cause of social and demographic change. In particular, the preceding

402   *Conclusion*

chapters report on hunger as the cause for conflict within and between societies and for hunger as impetus to population growth and decline.

Cause for Conflict   Hunger, or anticipated hunger, as a cause for conflict, a threat to authority within states, and a source of competition between states, appears often in the historical record. Dynasties fell in ancient China when especially severe famine occurred (chapter 6). Rulers were viewed as responsible for such disasters, not in the sense that they should have distributed grain, but because the floods or droughts causing widespread harvest failure were considered divine retribution for the ruler's impious behavior. In the Roman era, government efforts to insure a supply of grain in times of scarcity may be read as a strategy to avoid political upheaval (chapter 5). Bread riots were among the events leading up to the French Revolution, and as we write food riots in Algeria threaten to topple a government which reduced food subsidies. And much of the guerilla warfare in recent decades uses hunger and rural poverty as a justification for armed struggle.

Despite these many examples, what is also striking in history are the examples of people starving amidst plenty. Greenough (1982) cites the Bengal famine of 1943 as a classic case of people starving on the streets in front of warehouses filled with grain. The apathy and lethargy associated with severe deprivation (chapter 1) make violent challenge to authority least likely when it might otherwise seem most appropriate. We more often see a violent reaction if future hunger is anticipated or if deterioration in diet occurs which leaves people dissatisfied but not so seriously undernourished as to make violent action impossible. The literature of violence talks more of relative deprivation than absolute deprivation.

The role that actual hunger plays in warfare between states is less clear. But hunger as anticipation, or as metaphor, is used to justify resource competition between groups in non-stratified societies, and territorial war and conquest between states. Indeed, such resource competition and the conflict it engenders is a major driving force in the evolution of human societies, according to a recent review (Johnson and Earle, 1987). Creating and ensuring a grain supply was an early impetus to colony formation in the empires of antiquity, with subsequent conquest or displacement of indigenous peoples, a practice continued for a variety of commodities in both the New and Old World by the European empires.

Cause for Population Change   In chapter 1, three major theoretical perspectives were set out linking population growth, hunger stress, and material production. Thus Malthus saw hunger and its consequences as a positive check to population growth. Boserup saw population growth and its stresses, including hunger, serving as motivation for the adoption and diffusion of technological innovation, which in turn allowed for increased population and/or rising living standards. Marx, whose own population theory is less well known than his vehement rejection of Malthus, saw the causes of population growth and decline in the organization of production and the living standards engendered.

To the extent that the hunger history reported on in this book addresses these issues, the cumulative direction is clearly Boserupian. Beginning with the impetus to shift from hunting and gathering to a more demanding agricultural system (chapters 2 and 3), proceeding through the intensification of agriculture through the major innovations of irrigation (chapters 2 and 4), to the development of European peasant agriculture (chapter 8), increasing population density is seen as motivation for the employment of a more productive technology and social organization, but one often requiring harder work and loss of individual independence.

Conversely, the signs of Malthusian collapse are not evident even in major food crises, or are observed only as brief slowdowns in population growth, as in the Bengal famine of 1943, the starvation in occupied Europe in the Second World War, and the Chinese famine of the Great Leap Forward. Rather than collapse, what is seen is Malthusian "deadlock": high populations were maintained in medieval Europe in the face of famine and pestilence (chapter 4).

In Malthusian thinking, applying the preventive checks of fertility limitation may prevent hunger from bringing the positive checks of mortality into operation. This is seen in delays in marriage and pervasive celibacy. Deliberate avoidance of childbearing within sexual unions may also act as a preventive check, although rejected by Malthus himself as morally abhorrent. In earlier days the exposure of infants served a similar function of deliberate limitation of family size, although in Malthusian terms this would be classified as one of the positive checks of mortality rather than the preventive checks of averted births (chapter 4). To a degree, Marx implied such behavior, but limited it to the population made surplus by capitalist accumulation in nineteenth-century Europe.

The Future of Hunger

Despite the long-term persistence of hunger, this is a remarkable time. As we contemplate the future of hunger, we can see that its diminution and perhaps even its demise may be *attainable*. Almost surely these are not unique thoughts in history. Early humans discovering new riches of nature to gather and hunt may have felt similarly. The organizer of the subsidized food system upon whose dole were upwards of 320,000 Romans might have contemplated hunger's end, at least for Roman citizens. Our perspective finds the demise of hunger attainable because for almost three decades now there may have been enough food in the world for all its people, the rudiments of an international food safety net for the end of famine and food shortage is well in place, the proportion of households in food poverty is on the decline, and renewed international efforts to end food deprivation for children are under way.

The demise of hunger may be attainable because we passed the first threshold of theoretical food sufficiency in the 1960s (enough to provide a near-vegetarian diet for all if distributed according to need) and we are approaching a second threshold of improved diet sufficiency (enough to provide 10 percent animal products). But we are still a long way from a third threshold of a full but healthy diet with the choices available in industrialized nations. Projecting world food demand, under alternative assumptions of both diet and population growth, indicates that nearly three times the present level of food production might be required for an improved diet and almost five times for a full, but healthy, diet, some 60 years from now (Kates et al., 1988).

The demise of hunger may be attainable because for the first time in human history it is possible to contemplate the end of food scarcity, famine, and mass starvation. With the exception of its intentional creation or perpetuation as a weapon of war or genocide, a combination of effective famine early-warning systems, national and global emergency food reserves, and improved experience with distribution and food-for-work programs has brought the end of famine well within sight. Despite the continuing African famine experience, famine is already rare and becoming even rarer. Our FAMINDEX, a continuing series using *New York Times* reports of famines since 1950, shows a decline in the population living in countries with reported famine since the peak period in 1957–63 (chapter 11).

The demise of hunger may be attainable because we know that the end of food poverty does not require the end of all poverty. The evidence is recorded in the increasing heights of the Chinese people – an inch taller per decade between 1951–8 and 1979 – in the falling infant mortality statistics of the state of Kerala in India, and in the rising life expectancies in Sri Lanka: all places where hunger has receded dramatically in recent times, even though their extremely low incomes have grown slowly at best.

The demise of hunger may be attainable because there has been a decreasing trend in measures of food poverty. The proportion of the world that is *food poor* has probably diminished by half over the last three decades, although progress has slowed dramatically in recent years.

And the demise of hunger may be attainable because we are marshalling major international efforts to intervene on behalf of the food deprived – through child-survival programs that reduce the likelihood of children's malnourishment, vitamin A interventions that identify and correct dietary deficiencies leading to xeropthalmia, and programs to control endemic goitre, cretinism, and other iodine-deficiency disorders (chapter 13).

But the demise of hunger is surely not guaranteed. The gains over the last three decades took place early in the period. Over the last decade progress in reducing hunger worldwide came to a halt or reversed itself. The recurrence of famine is still possible despite the extensive international safety net. War continues to create famine and to obstruct its relief. Large integrated food systems are still liable to the catastrophic failure reported on in Bengal and in China. And new potential catastrophes, low-probability but very high-consequence events, always threaten humankind: a nuclear winter following even a limited nuclear war (Harwell and Hutchinson, 1985); a massive entitlement failure following a worldwide economic depression; a rapid change in agroecology consequent to a global climate change; or a reversal or marked slowing of the world decline in population birth rates.

Even the diminution of hunger is much too slow. As the *proportion* of hungry in the world has decreased, the *numbers* have not – and they are in fact still rising. If the current rate of progress in diminishing the proportion of hungry in the world – about 1 percentage point every 5 years – is combined with the projected growth of population, the absolute number of hungry in the world will still rise until the year 2000, and only then begin to decline. It would take until the year 2050, 60 years hence, to reduce the proportion of hungry people in the world to 3 percent, assuming continuing progress at the current rate (Kates et al., 1988). In the meantime, half of the world's women who carry the seeds of our future may be anemic, a third of the world's children may be wasted or stunted in body and mind, and perhaps a fifth of the world's people can never be sure of their daily bread, chapati, rice, tortilla, or ugali.

The demise of hunger is much too slow because many have a stake in hunger, albeit often unwittingly. There is a *hunger industry* in an increasingly interdependent world. It is a diverse industry that includes warriors of all persuasions who use hunger as a weapon, rich people in poor countries whose comparative advantage is cheap labor, and farmers and agribusiness people who market grains to the hungry. It also includes a vast network of professional organizations that work to end hunger – the UN agencies, the relief organizations, the rock concert organizers, and even university people. From this welter of good and mean intentions, it is no wonder that the prescriptions for hunger's demise vary so widely while the desire to end hunger becomes more universal.

Hunger is one of the set of seemingly intractable issues in which those concerned with the issues diverge sharply in both their analyses and their policy prescriptions: one sector addressing the problem incrementally, activity by activity; one sector addressing the greater context, implying that fundamental social change is a prerequisite for problem solution. And within each approach, there is a diversity of views as to which activities are efficacious − or for which fundamental changes are required. These divergences are *not* simply manifestations of reformist or radical analysis or style, although these are surely evident, but arise from deeply held concern, which in one case is expressed by a desire to "light a candle rather than curse the darkness," and in the other by great frustration over the enormous human loss incurred by the slow pace of hunger's demise.

We suggest that it is possible to seek a common middle ground, to accept that a significant fraction of the world's hunger, as much as a half, can be readily attacked by using the better and the best of current capabilities and programs, if these are applied appropriately to the varied contexts of hunger in the world. But at the same time, it is clear that further progress will require fundamental change in structures, institutions, and values. Our recounting of hunger in history points to the needed directions of that change. The global production of food needs to expand threefold over the next sixty years, and particularly in regions bypassed by the green revolution. World population needs to stabilize by then, and in order to do so the rate of increase must begin to turn down in Africa in the next decade. Resilience to forthcoming changes in climate and environment needs to be enhanced. Food entitlement needs to be realized as a birthright. But most important, all these changes need to include the excluded, the marginal people and places constituting the bulk of the world's hungry.

NOTES

1 These major trends and future implications appear in a more abbreviated form in Kates et al., 1988.

REFERENCES

Adams, Robert McC. and Nissen, Hans 1972: *The Uruk Countryside: The Natural Setting of Urban Societies.* Chicago: The University of Chicago Press.

Allan, W. 1965: *The African Husbandman.* Edinburgh: Oliver and Boyd.

Angel, J. Lawrence 1984: Health as a crucial factor in the changes from hunting to developed farming in the Eastern Mediterranean. In M. N. Cohen and G. J. Armelagos (eds), *Paleopathology at the Origins of Agriculture,* New York: Academic Press, 51−73.

Contee, Christine 1987: *What Americans Think: Views on development and U.S. – Third World relations*. New York: Interaction.

Fogel, Robert W. 1984: Nutrition and the decline in mortality since 1700: Some preliminary findings. Working Paper No. 1402. Cambridge, Mass.: National Bureau of Economic Research, Inc.

Garnsey, Peter 1988: *Famine and Food Supply in the Graeco-Roman World: Response to risk and crisis*. Cambridge: Cambridge University Press.

Goodman, Alan H., Martin, Debra L., Armelagos, George J., and Clark, George 1984: Indications of stress from bone and teeth. In M. N. Cohen and G. J. Armelagos (eds), *Paleopathology at the Origin of Agriculture*, New York: Academic Press, 13–49.

Greenough, Paul R. 1982: *Prosperity and Misery in Modern Bengal: The famine of 1943–44*. New York: Oxford University Press.

Grigg, David 1985: *The World Food Problem 1950–1980*. Oxford: Basil Blackwell.

Hamilton, W. D. 1964: The genetical theory of social behavior. I and II. *Journal of Theoretical Biology*, 7, 1–32.

Harwell, M. A. and Hutchinson, T. C. 1985: *Environmental Consequences of Nuclear War. Volume 2: Ecological and Agricultural Effects*. SCOPE 28. Chichester: John Wiley and Sons.

Johnson, Allen W. and Earle, Timothy 1987: *The Evolution of Human Societies: From foraging group to agrarian state*. Stanford: Stanford University Press.

Kates, Robert W., Chen, Robert S., Downing, Thomas E., Kasperson, Jeanne X., Messer, Ellen, and Millman, Sara R. 1988: *The Hunger Report: 1988*. Brown University, Providence: The Alan Shawn Feinstein World Hunger Program.

Kunitz, Stephen J. 1987: Making a long story short: A note on men's height and mortality in England from the first through the nineteenth centuries. *Medical History*, 31, 269–80.

Lee, R. 1984: *The Dobe !Kung*. New York: Holt, Rinehart & Winston.

Lewin, Roger 1988: A revolution of ideas in agricultural origins. *Science*, 240, 984.

Piazza, Alan 1986: *Food Consumption and Nutritional Status in the PRC*. Boulder, Colo.: Westview Press.

Post, John D. 1977: *The Last Great Subsistence Crisis in the Western World*. Baltimore: Johns Hopkins.

Rickman, G. E. 1980: *The Corn Supply of Ancient Rome*. Oxford: Oxford University Press.

Sen, Amartya 1982: *Poverty and Famines: An essay on entitlement and deprivation*. Oxford: Clarendon.

Sen, Amartya 1988: Food entitlements and economic chains. In B. W. J. Le May (ed.), *Science, Ethics and Food*, Washington, DC: Smithsonian Institute Press, 58–70.

Trivers, R. L. 1971: The evolution of reciprocal altruism. *Quarterly Review of Biology*, 46, 35–57.

Contributors

Mark Nathan Cohen received his AB degree from Harvard in 1965 and Ph.D. in Anthropology from Columbia in 1971. He was a Fellow at the Center for Advanced Study at Stanford in 1978–9 and a John Simon Guggenheim Fellow in 1985–6. He is currently professor of Anthropology at SUNY, Plattsburgh and considers himself an archaeologist interested in patterns of economic change and their consequences for health and nutrition in prehistory. He is the author of *The Food Crisis in Prehistory* (1989), and an editor of *Biosocial Mechanisms of Population Regulation* (1981) and *Paleopathology at the Origins of Agriculture* (1984).

William Crossgrove received his AB degree from Ohio University and his Ph.D. in Germanic linguistics from the University of Texas at Austin. He is professor of German at Brown University, and most of his recent publications have dealt with aspects of medieval German herbals and other texts written for practical use.

Peter Garnsey was educated at Sydney University and Oxford University, and has taught at the University of California at Berkeley and the University of Cambridge, where he is currently University Lecturer in Ancient History. His most recent book is *Famine and Food Supply in the Graeco-Roman World: Responses to Risk and Crises* (1988).

Robert W. Kates is University Professor and Director of the Alan Shawn Feinstein World Hunger Program, Brown University, Providence, Rhode Island, USA. He received a Ph.D. degree in geography from the University of Chicago in 1962. His most recent books include (as co-editor) *Climate Impact Assessment: Studies of the Interaction of Climate and Society* (1985); *Perilous Progress: Managing the Hazards of Technology* (1985); *Geography, Resources, and Environment. Vol. I: Selected Writings of Gilbert F. White* (1986); and *Corporate Management of Health and Safety Hazards: A Comparison of Current Practice* (1988).

Robley Matthews received his BA degree from Rice Institute and his Ph.D. from the Department of Geology, Rice University, with specialization in Sedimentology and Stratigraphy. He is currently Professor of Geological Sciences, Brown University, and has published extensively regarding the Cenozoic stratigraphic record of climate dynamics. He teaches a freshman/

sophomore course which brings a deductive mode of problem-solving to questions of global interaction between humanity and the resource base. A book on this topic, *Beyond 2000: A Minimum Model for the Global Future*, was published in 1989.

Sara Millman's BA, MA, and Ph.D. are from the University of Oregon, University of Washington, and University of Michigan, respectively. She is Assistant Professor of Sociology at Brown. Much of her research focuses on issues of infant feeding and weaning practices and their relationship to children's health and development and their mothers' reproductive patterns.

Lucile F. Newman received a BA degree from Brown University, MA from Columbia University, and Ph.D. from the Department of Anthropology, University of California at Berkeley. She is currently Professor of Community Health and Anthropology in the Division of Biology and Medicine at Brown University. Her recent publications include *Women's Medicine: A Cross-Cultural Study of Indigenous Methods of Fertility Regulation* (1985), and "Premature infant behavior: An ethnological study in a special care nursery" (1986).

Christian Pfister is Professor of Social and Economic History at the University of Bern. He received his Ph.D. from the same university. He is the author of a book and numerous articles in German, French, and English on the reconstruction of weather and climate from historical records and the response of agrarian societies to climatic change in Central Europe, e.g., "Variations in the spring-summer climate in Central Europe from the High Middle Ages to 1850" (1988). More recent is his engagement with population and environmental history: "Population, energy and environment in the highlands and lowlands of Switzerland," in *The Earth as Changed by Human Action*, forthcoming.

John D. Post is Professor of History at Northeastern University. He received his Ph.D. from the Department of History, Boston University in 1969. His recent publications include "Food shortage, nutrition, and epidemic disease in the subsistence crises of preindustrial Europe," *Food and Foodways* I (1987), *Food Shortage, Climatic Variability, and Epidemic Disease in Preindustrial Europe* (Cornell University Press, 1985), and "Climatic variability and the European mortality wave of the early 1740s," *Journal of Interdisciplinary History* 15 (1984).

Carl Riskin received his BA from Harvard College and his Ph.D. from the University of California at Berkeley. He is Professor of Economics at Queens College, City University of New York, and Senior Research Scholar at the East Asian Institute, Columbia University. He is the author of *China's Political Economy: The Quest for Development since 1949* (1987) and of numerous articles on China's modern economy. He is currently collaborating with Chinese scholars on a project to study China's income distribution.

Nevin Scrimshaw received a Ph.D. and MPH from Harvard University and an MD from the University of Rochester. An Institute Professor Emeritus at MIT, where he was Head of Department of Nutrition and Food Science from 1961 to 1980, he was the founding Director of the Institute of Central America and Panama from 1949 to 1961. He initiated and directs the Food and Nutrition Program of the United Nations University. His extensive research publications are concerned with dietary protein, energy, iodine and iron deficiencies, interactions of nutrition and infection, and other aspects of clinical and public health nutrition.

Amartya Sen was educated at Calcutta and Cambridge. He is currently Lamont University Professor at Harvard University. Prior to joining Harvard, Sen was Drummond Professor of Political Economy at Oxford and a Fellow of All Souls College. He is President of the International Economic Association and is a past President of the Econometric Society. His publications have ranged over welfare economics, social choice theory, decision theory, ethics, social and political philosophy, economic methodology, development economics, project evaluation, and analysis of inequality, poverty, and famines. At Harvard he teaches in both the economics and philosophy departments.

B. L. Turner II received BA and MA degrees from the University of Texas at Austin and a Ph.D. from the Department of Geography, University of Wisconsin-Madison. He is currently a professor in the Graduate School of Geography and Coordinator of The Earth as Transformed by Human Action Program at Clark University. His recent publications include *Pulltrouser Swamp: Ancient Maya Habitat, Agriculture, and Settlement in Northern Belize* (1983), *Comparative Farming Systems* (1987), and "The specialist-synthesis approach to the revival of geography: The case of cultural ecology" (1989).

Robin D. S. Yates received his BA degree from Oxford University, his M.A. from the University of California at Berkeley, and his Ph.D. from the Department of East Asian Languages and Civilizations, Harvard University, where he specialized in early Chinese history, philosophy, and technology. He is currently the Burlington Northern Professor in Asian Studies at Dartmouth College, and his recent publications include *Washing Silk: The Life and Selected Poetry of Wei Chuang (834?–910)* (1988), and articles on early Chinese social, legal, and military history. *Science and Civilisation in China* vol. 5, part 6: "Military Technology," in collaboration with Dr Joseph Needham, will appear shortly.

Index